Beginning
Interrogating Ha

T&T Clark Enquiries in Theological Ethics

Series editors

Brian Brock
Susan F. Parsons

BEGINNINGS
INTERROGATING HAUERWAS

Brian Brock and Stanley Hauerwas

Edited by
Kevin Hargaden

LONDON • NEW YORK • OXFORD • NEW DELHI • SYDNEY

T&T CLARK
Bloomsbury Publishing Plc
50 Bedford Square, London, WC1B 3DP, UK
1385 Broadway, New York, NY 10018, USA

BLOOMSBURY, T&T CLARK and the T&T Clark logo
are trademarks of Bloomsbury Publishing Plc

First published in Great Britain 2017
Paperback edition first published 2018

Copyright © Brian Brock and Stanley Hauerwas, with Kevin Hargaden, 2017

Brian Brock and Stanley Hauerwas, with Kevin Hargaden have asserted
their right under the Copyright, Designs and Patents Act, 1988,
to be identified as Author of this work.

For legal purposes the Acknowledgements on p. xiii constitute
an extension of this copyright page.

All rights reserved. No part of this publication may be reproduced or
transmitted in any form or by any means, electronic or mechanical,
including photocopying, recording, or any information storage or
retrieval system, without prior permission in writing from the publishers.

Bloomsbury Publishing Plc does not have any control over, or responsibility for,
any third-party websites referred to or in this book. All internet addresses
given in this book were correct at the time of going to press. The author and
publisher regret any inconvenience caused if addresses have changed or sites
have ceased to exist, but can accept no responsibility for any such changes.

A catalogue record for this book is available from the British Library.

A catalog record for this book is available from the Library of Congress.

ISBN: HB: 978-0-5676-6995-7
PB: 978-0-5676-8383-0
ePDF: 978-0-5676-6996-4
ePub: 978-0-5676-6997-1

Series: T&T Clark Enquiries in Theological Ethics, 2

Typeset by Newgen Knowledge Works (P) Ltd., Chennai, India

To find out more about our authors and books visit
www.bloomsbury.com and sign up for our newsletters.

CONTENTS

Foreword   vii
  by Kevin Hargaden
Acknowledgments   xiii

Chapter 1
BIOGRAPHY, THEOLOGY, AND RACE   1
  Writing "Stanley Hauerwas"   1
  The ethics of writing the self   12
  The ethics of writing the other   25
  Hard work and good work   29
  Work, race, and the church   33

Chapter 2
CONTINGENCY, VIRTUE, AND HOLINESS   41
  Contingency and Aristotle's social conservatism   41
  Subversives and prophets in Israel and Greece   52
  On MacIntyre and becoming holy   57

Chapter 3
TEMPERAMENT, HABIT, AND THE ETHICS GUILD   63
  Temperament and habit   63
  Is provocation a virtue?   72
  Holmer, language, and ethics   80

Chapter 4
ECCLESIAL POLITICS, PEACEMAKING, AND THE ESCHATOLOGY
OF WORSHIP   95
  Practicing dying and the politics of the church   95
  Radically ordinary   102
  Saints, exemplarity, and advent   110
  The body's grammar and the Christian story   116
  Hexis and worship   123

Chapter 5
ARE CASUISTRY, NATURAL LAW, AND VIRTUE METHODS?   129
  On casuistry   129
  On natural law   144

Habits and repentance	147
Is virtue narcissistic?	155

Chapter 6
JUST WAR, PACIFISM, AND GENDER

JUST WAR, PACIFISM, AND GENDER	159
Nonviolence as interrupter of national narratives	159
Pacifist or just warrior?	170
Yoder and the self-deceptions of nonviolence	180
Gender troubles and structured violence	184
Peacemaking and worship	193

Chapter 7
MEDICAL ETHICS, DISABILITY, AND THE CROSS

MEDICAL ETHICS, DISABILITY, AND THE CROSS	195
Caring, curing, and cracks in the social order	195
Disability and the meaning of community	206
What we do in experimental medicine	214
Vanier, L'Arche, and Aristotle	222
The sight of the Holy Spirit	229

Chapter 8
PREACHING, PRAYING, AND PRIMARY CHRISTIAN LANGUAGE

PREACHING, PRAYING, AND PRIMARY CHRISTIAN LANGUAGE	239
Learning to write for Christians	239
Observations on method in preaching	249
Reading, memorizing, and commenting on scripture	256
Praying with God and in front of people	273
The fearful joy of being Christian	283

Afterword
THE END WAS THERE IN THE BEGINNING
Brian Brock and Kevin Hargaden — 291

Notes	305
Bibliography	333
Index of Names	341
Index of Bible References	344
Index of Subjects	345

FOREWORD

Kevin Hargaden

I did not intend to be a theologian. There was a summer when I realized I was no longer an atheist, then there was a job I took helping students deepen their faith, and in time I came to realize that I was a Christian. Later still, seeking some respite from the New Year blues that hit hard in January, my wife and I spent a weekend in west Cork. That part of the Irish coast from Kinsale to Bantry is among the most beautiful stretches of scenery in Europe, but what I most remember from that trip is the book Claire had just finished and greatly enjoyed. It had an intriguing title: *Living Gently in a Violent World*.[1] Is it a sign of a good holiday or a bad one that the most memorable aspect of it is devouring a book?

Living Gently was my gateway drug and soon, having burned through *A Peaceable Kingdom* and *Resident Aliens*,[2] I got on to the hard stuff and was hooked. Reading Stanley Hauerwas's books helped me learn to be a Christian. Reading them, I also found the resources to cope with the most difficult part of being a Christian, which was the demand that such lives be lived in community. I was exhausted by the idea of church but found in Hauerwas the exhortation to neither feel guilty for that nor to give up. Living into my baptism and learning to pray with the body of Christ made all the difference. It was only in church—and the Irish church is hardly the "adventuresome church" that is spoken of in *Resident Aliens*[3]—in the dysfunctional yet essential communities we call church that the truth of Christianity could be explored again and again. You don't find the gospel in ideas, but in the bread and wine shared with bullies and micro-managers, saints and exemplars. Hauerwas taught me this, and it was a deep comfort and profound encouragement. I wrote him a letter about the ideas I had been having about wealth and Jesus's parables and much to my surprise he wrote back. He told me I should seek out a fellow in Aberdeen named Brian Brock. He told me, "What you want to be is a theologian," which is certainly not what I started out wanting to be.

In his essay "How I Think I Learned to Think Theologically" from his recent *The Work of Theology*, Hauerwas clarifies that there he is "not trying to finally 'pull it all together.'"[4] It would be a mistake to read this collection of interviews as an attempt to set the record straight one last time. He has insisted for years that his prayers and his sermons are as significant to his work as his essays and his traditional academic books, just as he has consistently committed to coauthoring books with others. These interviews do not represent an unusual remix of Hauerwas's greatest hits then, but are another atypical (yet entirely appropriate) genre in which to do theology, fitting neatly alongside his sermon collections, his Willimon collaborations, or his collection of prayers. Friendship has been a central topic in his writing, and friendship has been the central context in which he was able to write. How appropriate it is then that these conversations between friends should be the very substance of this book.

That these conversations take place between friends is testified to by the regular occurrence of insight and illumination between Brock and Hauerwas. The hard questions being asked prompt surprising answers. It becomes clear that even on the work of Stanley Hauerwas, Stanley Hauerwas is still learning. He has claimed in the past that "a strong reason to have a friend is so one's own good can better be seen."[5] Here he is sometimes stumped under questioning from his friend, but more often he marvels at the creative ways his work could be read. Hauerwas has often insisted that we are never liberated from failing to mean what we say. Throughout this book he is forced to live that out, clarifying what he means, what he meant to mean, and what he wished he didn't mean. Theologians do not get to make up what they talk and think and write and pray about. They take orders from the church. When in Aberdeen, they go to church together. That he engages in this conversation with Brock in particular is not a coincidence or a question of convenience or circumstance. It enacts the theology he has written through the decades. This is not the first time interviews with him have been published. Four brief interviews intended for magazines were included in the 2004 book *Disrupting Time*. In the foreword to that book he wrote, "I do not think I am particularly good at being interviewed" and admits that, "like any academic who has been around for a long time, I have standard answers to standard questions."[6] In this book, Brock has attempted to intentionally refuse the standard questions in order to provoke some new answers. There are new answers and fresh formulations here, woven together with many classic "Hauerwasian" themes. If nothing else, this collection should put to an end forever the call from critics that Hauerwas has to give "practical" examples. Some might wait eagerly to see him put under pressure with some of the hard questions that his work seems to demand, but all readers will likely be interested by the unexpected directions that the answers take.

If it would be a mistake to read this book as a final bow before he slips properly behind the retirement curtain, it is also a mistake to read this book as being simply about Hauerwas. The real estate required to store Brock's writings is considerably smaller than for Hauerwas, but in his first two books, *Christian Ethics in a Technological Age*[7] and *Singing the Ethos of God*,[8] he displays a distinctly Hauerwas-esque ability to engage an orchestra of sources in exploration of the Christian life, which he describes as "nothing other than practical experimentation in attentiveness to God's love for concrete neighbours."[9] That he has inherited richly from Hauerwas's work is evident throughout his writing. He admits as much in *Captive to Christ, Open to the World* where he says, "I have been so deeply influenced by, and remain so reliant on work he's done."[10] That reliance does not hinder Brock from pursuing quite distinct theological concerns by quite different means; that much will be clear from the questions asked in this book.

In phrasing the questions that shape this book, Brock has not only pushed the conversation onward but has done so by offering an expansive, generous, but not uncritical interpretation of Hauerwas's corpus. This is an example of how theologians should read each other. Detailed and patient, it also interrogates when necessary, not just seeking to clarify but to expand on what has been said, to bring out connections that are not immediately evident, and to penetrate to criticisms of substance. As Don Wood, our colleague at Aberdeen, noted upon reading an early draft, this is neither an introduction to Hauerwas nor a survey of his work. Rather, it is a "sourcebook" for future readings. It is in this sense that we have entitled the book *Beginnings*. This is more than an ironic gesture for a book cowritten by an established scholar in his mid-seventies. There are those points in time when things start, even when it appears to be coming toward the end. There is a freshness about this book that constitutes a new thing. Under questioning, the answers open up perspectives on Hauerwas's work that have too often been missed.

When considering the sheer breadth of topics covered in his essays, Hauerwas has often vouched for himself as an amateur dabbling in areas that are outside his expertise. But a theologian who calls so centrally on Aristotle and Aquinas, Barth and Yoder, Trollope and Murdoch, Wittgenstein and Anscombe as his friends (this list could stretch on!) is obviously not amateurish when it comes to reading. His critical engagements with Niebuhr or Ramsey or Rorty or other repeated opponents are informed by the very same careful and appreciative reading that he dedicates to James or MacIntyre. So there is a fittingness to Brock's careful reading which reminds me of how Barth read Calvin. "Being taught by Calvin," he wrote, "means entering into dialogue with him, with Calvin as the teacher and ourselves as the students, he speaking, we doing our best to follow him and then—this is the crux of the matter—making our own response to what he says."[11] Brock has listened and followed Hauerwas, and it is a rare and wonderful set of interactions collected here, whereby we get to see Hauerwas react to the response Brock has made.

The chapters presented here are not chronologically ordered, but they are largely intact as they were recorded. They are composed of eight batches of conversation, which took place in Brock's office and home at different times from October 2014 to March 2016 during Hauerwas's visits to Aberdeen as professor of Christian ethics. I transcribed the interviews, which were lightly corrected by them both. The text was given its final form by excising a few dead-end discussions and a light reordering of chapters in order to increase its readability and minimize repetitions.

While there is a rich tradition in continental Europe of books in an interview format, the genre is unusual in the Anglophone world. Even within that interview genre, this book creates its own special niche. Very often such books are composed of interviews between journalists and public intellectuals or clearly demarcated senior, established scholars bestowing wisdom on a younger, junior figure. The conversations here, between friends, are not like that. That they are transcribed conversations does present a challenge, however. The text before you is quite like a script. Reading it requires active interpretation. Several early readers were clearly confused by a number of long passages where Brock is talking and Hauerwas is apparently silent or responds very briefly. In the room, or on tape, those are heated conversations where the two men are excited by the insights being forged. In order to aid comprehension at those sensitive points, I have inserted editorial footnotes indicating the tone of the conversation.

In my youth, there was a craze for "Choose Your Own Adventure" novels where the reader directed the plot by selecting different paths through the book. This interview format is very amenable to such an approach. There is a logic to how the book has been assembled, moving from discussions of method and sources and how to be a theologian through biography and the implications of theological work before arriving at the lived reality of worship and discipleship. Yet a reader can choose to dip in and out, charting their own course through the material. The "script" will be "performed" differently by each reader.

A coherent narrative arc holds this book together. Each chapter begins with an introductory paragraph that familiarizes the reader with the material therein and points toward critical issues addressed. Hauerwas often compares his work in theology to his work as a bricklayer, and our hope is that with each successive chapter another brick is added to the apocalyptic arch we discern in his work. The capstone comes in the Afterword where Brock and I elaborate more fully on how reading Hauerwas in an apocalyptic key unlocks many of the problems readers commonly find with him.

The first chapter examines the relationship between biography and theology, especially focusing on *Hannah's Child*. The conversation spirals from the ethics of writing to the ethic of work and on into the ethics of race. Many of the themes explored in the later chapters are flagged here, as the writing of memoir becomes a distinctive vantage point from which to consider virtue and contingency and how being a Christian invariably implicates a person in stories they do not get entirely to determine. The interviews took place in March 2015.

The second chapter turns to consider the role contingency plays in Hauerwas's work. We discover how his deployment of such language is rooted in a deep theological commitment about what it means to be creatures. It explores some of the conflicts that can be perceived between some of Hauerwas's major sources, specifically the different perspective that MacIntyre offers on Aristotle compared with Thomas's reading. Continuing from the conversations in Chapter 1, the reader will notice how Brock seeks always to get beyond Hauerwas's self-description to examine how the different pieces fit together and play out in his work. It is excerpted from one of the later interviews, conducted in October 2015.

The third chapter deals with what it means to be a Christian ethicist. As any reader of Hauerwas might predict, the conversation circles around habits, virtue, character as well as provocation, temperament, and the influence of those who form us. It is bracketed at the beginning by a discussion of a rarely considered 1980 speech Hauerwas delivered at the American Academy of Religion and at the end by a rarely acknowledged influence in the form of Paul L. Holmer. This opening discussion establishes Hauerwas's relationship to the guild as determined by an ironic sense of humor about the entire academic endeavor, and the second establishes the debt that Hauerwas owes to Holmer, whose writing exhibits the same humble funniness. Together these two strands of discussion demonstrate the ways in which, even from the beginning, Hauerwas's writing has been drawing deeply from the wells of Kierkegaard and Barth. These conversations were mostly conducted in October 2014.

The fourth chapter turns from questions of an individual's ethical significance to that of the community. The conversation targets questions about how it is that a peaceful church works. At this stage, the book's interviews have truly become dialogues within themselves and the themes of selfhood and the need for the examples of others, embodiment and the fundamental orientation of the Christian narrative rise to the surface in rich and vivid ways that echo what has come before and establish what comes next. These interviews were conducted in October 2015.

The fifth chapter addresses some of the core linguistic moves that have become associated with Hauerwas's writing. He has written much about casuistry and virtue and natural law but in ways that do not fit comfortably within the typical understanding of those phrases. Brock interrogates this tension and in so doing calls into question the utility of that trajectory for Christian ethics and discipleship more generally. This conversation took place in October 2015.

The sixth chapter brings the classic Hauerwasian emphasis on pacifism into the firing line. There we find why it matters, even if terms like "pacifism" or "non-violence" can be easily sidelined, that Christians peacefully battle against the warmongering of our age. The violence that can be embedded in a peace ethic is discussed as Hauerwas addresses the troubling legacy of John Howard Yoder and together they consider the structural violence and the sexism that is built into both the university and the church. These conversations took place in October 2015.

One of the underappreciated aspects of Hauerwas's work is how his sometimes-controversial stance on pacifism is the opposite side of the coin of his less often celebrated theology of disability. In the seventh chapter this connection is made explicit in a powerful way. The discussion of disability and medical ethics flows into questions about Jean Vanier and L'Arche before concluding with a profound reflection on the role of the Spirit in the Christian life. Hauerwas is often described as an essayist—for good or for ill—but here in this interview a harmony of the different strands in his work can be discerned. These conversations took place in March 2015.

In the final chapter this harmony is sustained as the sermons, prayers, and biblical commentary that Hauerwas has produced over the years are considered in detail. As one of the few academic theologians working today to have published a relatively large corpus of this sort of writing, it is clear that he has thought a lot about how these different forms of speech are best approached. Brock gets deep under the skin of the reasons he has approached these genres as he has, both as written and as spoken performances. Under sustained interrogation Hauerwas's common insistence that this material is the most important in his writing is revealed to be an expression of his sense that it will be most helpful to all Christians who wrestle, as he hopes we all will, with the fearful and joyous task of being Christian. This interview was recorded in March 2016.

The book closes with an afterword reflecting on the perspective that these interviews offer on Hauerwas's work. The secondary material on Hauerwas's writing is already extensive and continues to grow. Well-determined readings of Hauerwas are now firmly in place; he might be a sectarian, albeit one with an important prophetic voice, or he might be unintentionally reinventing Schleiermachean liberal Protestantism, or he might be the most articulate commentator on the work of Alasdair MacIntyre. This is not how Brock and I read him. In the Afterword, we present an account of Hauerwas's work that pulls away from the headline points that have informed how new readers engage with his many essays and books. The influence of both MacIntyre and Yoder is directly acknowledged in the interviews. But it is set within a broader frame that has been too-rarely recognized. In this short essay we propose that Hauerwas's indebtedness to Barth and his assumption of an apocalyptic horizon is the key for understanding how the diversity of his writings fits together. In *Unleashing the Scriptures*, Hauerwas wrote about how "we all have moments and times in our lives when we seem disposed to hear, see, and understand what at another time we would not have noticed."[12] We did not start these interviews with the intention of demonstrating how Hauerwas's emphasis on virtue and habit is an attempt to explore what it might mean to live in the world disrupted by God's time, but Hauerwas himself has provided the words that have come to make sense of all the contingent factors that were at play in such a breakthrough.

*

I took Hauerwas's advice. I got in touch with this fellow, Brian Brock. My wife and I decided that we would interrupt our lives for four years and move to northern Scotland. I did not intend to be a theologian but reading Stanley Hauerwas started me on that path.

Some months after we had moved, I was idly thumbing through *Living Gently in a Violent World* and I noticed for the first time a paragraph at the end of the introduction entitled "How This Book Came To Be." There, John Swinton explained that the book arose from a "unique conference"[13] held in Aberdeen, where Hauerwas and Vanier met in person for the first time and through "their gentle conversations began to tease out the implication of the church's situation."[14] The end of my theological apprenticeship was there in the beginning; in the making of friends comes the possibility of exploring the gospel. It is our hope that *Beginnings* would continue that work of gentle conversations between friends that seek to tease out what it means to be the people of God in this time.

ACKNOWLEDGMENTS

Readers will soon discover that this is Brian and Kevin's book. They did the work that makes this a book worth reading. I am the guy that from time to time says: "right," or "that is just right," or "I wish I had said what you said as clearly as you said it," and so on. The truth of the matter is my less than informative responses to Brian's questions are his fault. After all he is the one that read me so well that his characterizations of what I have said left me with little to say. That is not quite right either. Often his characterizations exposed limits about what I have said that made me think further about how I have said what I have said as well as what I now need to think given what I have thought.

I am not sure I understood quite what I was getting into when I first responded with enthusiasm to Brian's suggestion about this book and the conversational format. I thought, however, it was one way to fulfill some of the responsibilities I assumed by becoming the Chair in Ethics at the University of Aberdeen from 2014 to 2016. Because Brian knows how to ask the hard questions the book turned out to be more work than I imagined, but it has been good work. I hope, moreover, in some ways it honors the fine faculty that I discovered during my tenure at Aberdeen.

I confess I find it somewhat embarrassing to be the subject of this book. But I have had to learn to trust readers. Few read me better than Brian. I should like to think that this book will attract some new readers and give a fresh perspective for past readers because the subject is not me but rather how we all need one another if we are to be the theologians we were meant to be.

But this is not only Brian's book. It is Kevin Hargaden's book too. He has made this book happen. He has with good humor and great sensitivity turned our conversations into readable prose, edited the volume for publication, and constructed the bibliography and index. He is also to be credited for observing that an afterword would make the contribution of the book far more obvious.

The three of us would also like to thank Martin Wendte, Carole Baker, Diane Decker, Susan Parsons, Philip Ziegler, Michael Mawson, Don Wood, Amy Erickson, Sam Tranter, Andrew Errington, Claire Hargaden, Stephanie Brock, Godlieve Orye, Scott Prather, Allen Calhoun, Chrissy Weeks, Margaret Synnott, D. J. Konz, Joseph Lear, Keith Adams, Alison Chino, Declan Kelly, Emily Hill, Aisling Geraghty and Katja Schroeder, for their invaluable feedback on earlier drafts of the manuscript.

Finally dear reader we would like to thank you for being willing to enter into this conversation. May it never end.

Chapter 1

BIOGRAPHY, THEOLOGY, AND RACE

March 27, 2015

This extended opening discussion examines the theological decisions that oriented Hauerwas as he wrote his memoir, Hannah's Child. *Special attention is devoted to teasing out the ways in which telling our story is a theologically and ethically potent act. The emphasis on contingency in the memoir will become a subject in itself in a later chapter.* Hannah's Child *exhibits one of Hauerwas's fundamental contentions that the writing of theology is a specific type of generalization of an author's practical and local knowledge. The implications of such claims are pursued in more detail in discussions of some of the more complicated moments of Hauerwas's own story, including his marriage to his first wife Anne, as well as his understanding of work and race.*

Writing "Stanley Hauerwas"

BB: Today I want to explore three general regions of questions provoked by *Hannah's Child*. The first concerns how the theologian or ethicist should understand the relation of their writing to their living, the difficult and theologically far-reaching question of the relationship between telling our story and self-knowledge. We write and read while we continue living our lives, and at the same time our writing can be one of the ways we try to get a hold on our lives and make sense of how we should live. A memoir like *Hannah's Child* raises this question in an especially obvious way.

This first question opens directly into methodological questions about how you decided to handle these problematics as you wrote *Hannah's Child*. Toward the end of the conversation I want to concretize the discussion by looking at a range of sensitive issues you treat in the book. Being truthful about our lives raises some real challenges, and I suspect that we'll better understand you and what you've done in the book, if we pay special attention to how you approach narrating some of the ticklish moments in your life. So that's the general overview.

SH: That's wonderfully put.

BB: In our conversations in the past, you have compared your story to Wesley's. It's an evocative comparison because Wesley's life was surprising to him, not least in the way that his success as a public figure diverged so radically from his downward-spiraling private life, particularly in relation to his marriage to Molly Vazeille. This poignant theme is echoed in your memoir, which recounts in what I think is really grueling detail your suffering through your first wife Anne's slow descent into an extended mental health crisis.

Without revisiting the details of that story, I would like to explore the practical issue that it raises in a particular and perhaps even unique way for the academic theological ethicist: how do we deploy or harness or draw on our own biographical experiences in our work? In our roles as professional theologians, when is it appropriate directly to invoke our own experience? How do we negotiate the reality that in our day jobs we talk about how Christians should live in modernity, which seems to make all we write hostage to the example we live out?

Hans Reinders, for instance, has recently suggested that if you were more consistent with your own writings about disability, you'd be more involved in friendship with people with learning difficulties.[1] I will take a similar tack in our third conversation when I will ask you how your own academic performance at the 1980 AAR meeting[2] holds up to your theory of the virtues. So the problem of how to relate our theological writing to the life experiences out of which it has grown is one which continually haunts me and which I have never satisfactorily answered for myself. That's why, at this point, I can't really imagine writing a book like *Hannah's Child*. I can imagine some reasons *why* you did it, and as well see some hints about *how* you did it, but that doesn't give me enough to imagine myself doing it. Is the decision to write a book such as this a vocational decision, related to your time, place, and ecclesial role, or is it something we can talk about in more general terms?

SH: I have always assumed that as someone who occupies the vocation of being a theologian, I should never try to do theology in a way that justifies the limits of my own life. I've never appealed in the work I do to my own subjectivity with phrases like, "'I'm not prepared to believe . . .'" because I think that one of the lessons you learn from the gospel is to not let the gospel be judged by our own lives, because the lives we're given through the gospel are greater than what our subjectivities embody. So, I think of myself as about a half-Christian. And I'm not going to justify the half that isn't Christian by appealing to the authority of the limits of my own life. I assume that if we do our work well as theologians, it will be a judgment on our own experiences.

I suspect my reaction against taking our subjectivities seriously involves my worry about the kinds of theology that were in play when I began my training in the 1960s. In that context people would declare what modern people could or could not believe. I thought that was an extremely limiting way of thinking. I thought it's better to make the best you can of what it is you've been given as a way to avoid what I regard as a kind of narcissism that takes too seriously your role as a thinker. That's the reason why I often deny that the theologian is a thinker. We don't ask what we are prepared to believe; we ask, "What does the church believe?" And that turns out to be so much more interesting than we could imagine.

That's why I don't—at least I think I don't—appeal in the kind of writing I've done to "my own experience." The phrase that I think you use in Hans's characterization of my work—namely personal experience—philosophically I'm not even sure I can make sense of the notion of personal experience. Whatever is characteristic of our lives is so because of the language we share with others. I certainly recognize, however, that we each bring to our work insight gained from the particularity of our lives that may make some contribution to the illumination of what we're trying to say as theologians.

Think about my appeal to bricklaying in my work. Is the appeal to bricklaying an appeal to personal experience? Well, certainly bricklaying is very important to me, as you will raise later, about the importance of hard work. But I do not think how you display what it means to be taught to be a bricklayer, and the implications that may have for how you think about the work of theology—I don't think that is only accessible to those who have learned to lay brick. So you can articulate what it means to lay brick in a way that draws other people in. I take that to be crucial for avoiding a kind of subjectivism that I think is really quite limiting.

For example, this has to do with the grammar sometimes used by people who feel oppressed. "As a woman, I'm not prepared to agree with 'X' or 'Y.'" "As a Chicano, I'm not prepared to agree with 'X' or 'Y' because it's oppressive," etc. I value outrage, but I worry that those moves can result in a failure to see that what it is they are not prepared to believe may turn out to be, when appropriately appreciated, within the tradition, an alternative that is about God's salvation from oppression. "I'm not prepared to believe in the maleness of Christ because maleness is oppressive." Well then that doesn't get at what Christ's maleness does to maleness. That's the kind of thing I'm thinking about.

BB: That's very useful. Tell me if I have heard you right, then: To the accusation that the life that we know about, that you've lived, not living up to your own theory, your response would be, "Of course it doesn't."

SH: Of course it doesn't.

BB: And if it did, it could only do so in heaven.

SH: Right. Right. I think that's exactly what I think.

You've got to be very careful with it, because you don't want it to become an excuse that you use to justify the limits of your own life. You do want to try to live consistently with what you think. You just discover that what you think makes it important to acknowledge that you often are inconsistent.

Think about issues like: What do you do, if you are, as I have been, a chaired professor in a major research university, making a lot of money? How is that consistent with the Christian commitment not to let Mammon determine our lives? You can say, "Oh well, I don't pay any attention to what I make!" You may not pay any attention to it, but it's clearly there! And my answer is, "I don't have an answer, to know how to adjudicate the fact that I have made a lot of money." I can say, "Well I've given a lot away," but that's not sufficient, because money makes you secure, that you know what's coming in, giving some away is no big deal.

BB: And you can't take the CEO's line—that you're worth it.

SH: No. Of course not!

I mean, "You get paid $100,000 a year to read books? Wow! That's a great deal!" I bring that up because I don't know how to square that circle. It's just the way things are. And I'm not going to pretend that is not a problem, but I don't know how to deal with it.

BB: Let me pick up the comment about experience and your questions about personal experience. Would you want to say that all our writing is somehow from or toward things that have happened to us proximately, and so in some sense our writing is always biographical? I mean, to put that in terms of a question: What would it mean to write about things that were genuinely remote from our lived experience? But of course, at the same time, writing about what we've seen or touched gains power when it's digested and presented, and the power that it gains comes from the ways that people can read it as communicating more than our individual narrative would on its own.

What makes your bricklaying example powerful is the role it plays as a paradigm that can be generalized in a specific way. It is this generalizability that lets people think, "Oh wait, I am sitting in the library reading books and exhibiting the virtues that one might learn on a work-site." Having seen something in our own place, as authors our task is to do the work of trying to show how what we've seen in *our* own place is faced by other people in *their* places. It's becoming a pretty boring academic habit today, in my view, and it goes along with your complaint about subjectivization of the academic task, to rob academic writing of its power by insisting that it's merely a projection of biographical experiences. Here I'm thinking about biblical scholars suggesting that Paul's disability was the origin of his theology of the cross or reading Foucault's homosexuality as the mainspring of his theories about the power of social institutions to coerce human behavior.

So on the one hand, you had to tell your story in a way that didn't give undue fuel to the almost inevitable temptation to use it to undermine the authority of your previous writings by psychologizing. On the other, you've often stressed that good theological ethics is always context-sensitive. These twin trajectories were bound constantly to provoke the accusation that in the context of your own biography, your theological writings weren't making sense. And here, I have in mind the accusation that seems to constantly recur that your talk about the church is vacuous because you have a flexible denominational allegiance, or at least you used to.

You're obviously aware of all that, and I'd like to get you to help us think about how your choice to tell your story in the first place is a type of answer to those problems.

SH: *Hannah's Child* was the result of an idea that Greg Jones had, who was then my dean, that I should apply for a grant from the McDonald Foundation—it's called the Agape Foundation. Alonzo McDonald then gave me a grant—I had applied and I got money for a sabbatical to write what he characterized as some kind of "great book." I, of course, immediately didn't want to do that. But Alonzo said that he would like for me to bring together a number of people who would respond to what I'd done so far and help me discern what I should do with the time I had left. So I did. It was a terrific day of discussion. People like Gerald McKenny, Jim Wetzel, Kelly Johnson, Travis Kroeker, Tracy Lysaught, Eric Gregory, Rom Coles, David Ayers—I think there were ten or twelve people there. There was a discussion about how to understand whatever I had done and so on. And as the discussion developed, the idea of *Hannah's Child* began to take shape. I thought such a book would be a way to defeat the idea of a "great book" and also to display who had made me possible. *Hannah's Child* is fundamentally a book about how friendship constitutes life and my life in particular.

I don't know if I knew what I was doing when I wrote *Hannah's Child*, but I really loved writing it. I didn't think of it as an attempt to explain how my experiences had produced the kind of work that I have done as a theologian. Rather, the first line in the book is very important: "I did not intend to be Stanley Hauerwas." Chad Pecknold picked that up in a wonderful review in *Pro Ecclesia*.[3] What the book was meant to do, partly, was to remind people I'm a human being. I understand that there's a public persona out there called Stanley Hauerwas that has a prominence that I find hard to relate to. I wrote the book to honor my parents and to celebrate God's care of me through having people claim me, to make me more than I am, and more than I could ever do on my own.

I don't spend much time reflecting on what might be regarded as my own sufferings in the book. I don't, for example, dwell on my relationship with Anne [Stanley's first wife] and all the years of going through her suffering mental illness. People think, for example, that when I wrote an earlier book and titled it *Truthfulness and Tragedy*, I must have been thinking about being married to Anne and having to live with her mental illness. I didn't think of that as tragic at all. I didn't think that I was doing anything out of the ordinary. It was just what I did. And I didn't think that "experience" should be, or needed to be reflected in how I thought.

So, *Hannah's Child* was, and I hope is, an account of how God gave me a life that I could not have anticipated by making me, through other people, more than I could have imagined. I didn't think of it as an account of my experiences, I suppose, is a way to put it.

The other thing that I wanted *Hannah's Child* to be is a recognition of the fact that I am a writer and that I really thought hard about the style in which the book should be written. I love Trollope because of his extraordinary ability to draw a character in two or three paragraphs. I hoped by reading the book you could see John Score or you could see Stuart Henry as extraordinary people who made my life possible.

For example, a line that I can't remember exactly how I put it but: "Stuart was a Calvinist, for whom the world was very dark, condemned to live among Methodists, for whom there was no darkness at all."[4] Those kinds of sentences that displayed people are what I really like to do.

I've thought about this, Brian, since I wrote *Hannah's Child*. I've thought about how one of the things in ethics that we need is compelling characterizations of good people. We don't really know how to do it. Novels do it so much better. I've thought about how I would have liked to do characterizations, somehow or the other, but I probably won't because I don't know how.

Anyway, that's just rambling on.

BB: Great. Well, we'll definitely follow that last point up. Let me make two observations about the answer you've just given. The first is that it seems to me that good reading connects things in every direction. So I have to admit having read *Hannah's Child* makes it harder to resist seeing how certain moves in your work would have been attractive to you at certain points in your life, given the pressures you were facing in your lived experience. But you have very nicely shown how that impulse itself should be understood as a temptation, because it can't avoid being a projection of how we think we would have felt under those circumstances. So it sounds to me like your ethical and theological analysis is that reading your corpus through *Hannah's Child* should be understood theologically as a *temptation*.

SH: I am sure that there are connections that people are able to make better than I am able to make between *Hannah's Child* and my work. *Hannah's Child* is a narrative that is meant to work retrospectively. I've always maintained that we live prospectively but the most important moral decisions we make are retrospective. What destroys us is not what we do, but the justifications we give for what we do.

It could be *Hannah's Child* could be read as a kind of exemplification of how I have been taught to think about the nature of the moral life by people like Iris Murdoch and MacIntyre. I didn't want (and I thought a lot about it), I didn't want in writing the book to simply say, "And at this point I wrote and the argument was and these are ideas you should take seriously."

BB: Sure, that's not interesting.

SH: It's just not interesting. So I didn't want the book to be another vehicle for trying to say what I've thought in *Vision and Virtue*[5] or some other book. I did try to suggest certain influences that were working on me that gesture towards why I've said some of the things I've said, and not others. The more important question for me was, how to write a book like *Hannah's Child* and avoid clichés. Clichés such as: Working-class boy makes good! You have to recognize that the cliché is there and you can't try to explicitly defeat it. You have to show the story is much more complex.

BB: The other observation I was going to make, and hearing your explanation just now brought it home to me, has to do with the role you've given to honoring your friends in writing the book. I initially asked you if you could give any general advice about writing such a book, of the variety, "This is how one should approach writing such a book at the end of one's career." I contrasted any answer you might give to that question with an account of what you've done explained as a vocational act driven by the particular contingencies of your own life. The answers you have given, taken cumulatively, seem to suggest that you understood writing the book as springing from vocational considerations.

What's fascinating about that to me is that the way you put it stresses that you wanted to question the weight being placed on the public character "Stanley Hauerwas." You point to the friends who "made you" in order to push back against what you see as a widespread overvaluation of "famous" characters. And that's a local, particular type of response which is not necessarily generalizable to people in other times and contexts. What's interesting to me theologically is that's exactly the opposite of what we see Paul doing in 2 Corinthians 11–12, where he is forced to shore up the authority of his ministry and his message by talking about everything he has gone through in his life—his sufferings—but he feels forced to do this precisely because the self-absorbed Corinthians won't accept his teaching unless he points out that he has lived what he has taught. You and he are making very similar gestures but to opposite ends, it seems to me. He is being treated like rubbish, even though he's an apostle, and so he tells his story to counter that. You're being treated like the hero, so you talk about your friends to puncture that. Is that correct?

SH: That's right.

I didn't write my story to say, "Do this." It's the story I had to tell, and it had to be told that way because that's the way my life has been lived. Namely, I've always been saved by friends who by claiming me as a friend make me more than I am. It turns out by making me more than I am, I am not the same "I am" I was before the friendship. I say God isn't there for me the way God is there for Paula [Gilbert, Stanley's wife] or for Timothy Kimbrough. That's not a complaint, because I assume God knows what God is doing by not being there for some of us in the way that God is there for others. That means that some of us really have to think very hard about what it means when we say God, but we couldn't do that without having been known by people like Paula and Timothy Kimbrough. I try to express how their faith has made me a Christian, because otherwise I couldn't imagine it.

BB: Again, that's a pretty precise inversion of Paul's case, because the apostle's faith, in a very real sense, is necessary to make the churches the churches.

SH: Absolutely. And he says that throughout: "I want you to copy me!" I could never say that to anyone. I want you to copy me! Paul had to say that. That was right.

There are people that I have known and loved that should say that to me, but I found it very hard to say to anyone that they should copy me.

BB: Having talked a bit about the question of why you wrote the memoir, let's talk more seriously about how you went about doing it.

For instance, in every presentation of the self in writing, the writer has to locate herself within the conventions of the culture and the writing, identifying the canon which the writer wishes to join. You've already, as you do in the book, talked about Trollope being your model in a sense. To write is to opt into all the exclusions and elisions that positioning oneself within a canon demands. The ambiguity of all confessional, autobiographical, or memoir writing lies in the writer having to inhabit those conventions, the conventions of the day, and therefore to present themselves as inevitably artificial constructions. Writing in this way necessarily straddles the fuzzy boundary between literary convention and personal memory, and memory itself is organized by conventional tropes and frames of reference. I take this to be one of the core reasons that you've resisted the comparison of *Hannah's Child* to Augustine's *Confessions*, and you only very guardedly and partially embrace this connection in your responses to those reviewers who have suggested it. You proposed instead that you stand closer to the tradition of the English realist novelists. That's a positioning in relation to an established canon that I'd like to understand how to negotiate.

You've already said that you thought long and hard about how to write the book and the core question there had to be of what form would convey rather than threaten what you believe is most important about the particularity of your own life and theology. Is that right?

SH: I think that's right. It's lovely put.

It's always important to try to read an author for what they don't say, as well as what they say. There's much in *Hannah's Child* that isn't said. I tried to avoid the "personal," because I didn't want—and this has to do with the point I made at the outset today—I didn't want *Hannah's Child* to be a legitimation of "my experience." So I didn't talk very much about my experience.

I didn't notice a trope that is much used when I was writing the book, but folks kind enough to read the book have called my attention to it: the trope "I didn't understand." For example, I say I didn't understand what it meant to go to seminary, I didn't understand what it meant to marry Anne, and I didn't understand what it meant to move from Notre Dame to Duke. I didn't. I really didn't, because I'm the kind of person that tends to make decisions and be willing to live them out, without having thought them through! That has worked out OK for me.

I've talked with friends in the academy who have had a job offer, and they use phrases like, "I'm not sure this would be a good career move." I could never use a phrase like that. It's never occurred to me that I have a career that I needed to be one place rather than another for the advancement of a career. My life has happened to me. That's a wonderful thing.

For one to have a life that's happened to you has analogical similarities to Augustine, because his life happened to him. He was making career moves, and they turned out not to be happy ones. Monica happened to him! I don't think anyone could write a book like *The Confessions* today, and I wasn't trying to for sure. We're too self-conscious to write a book like *The Confessions*, which is a prayer from beginning to end. Somebody—Jean Vanier—might be able to do it, but most of us don't have those sorts of lives.

I do think one of the things *Hannah's Child* is a witness to is God showed up even in a life as weird as mine, in ways that my life is unintelligible if God is not God. And that has to do with what happened to me.

BB: If I am hearing you right, your response to Gerald McKenny's comment in his review of *Hannah's Child*,[6] that it was not his experience of friendship that your career "just happened to you," is that you don't see the efforts you admit you made to "advance your career" as the most salient reality of your story.

SH: I think that's right. Although I am obviously an ambitious sonofabitch!

I mean I want to make a difference. You want to make a difference Brian. We are very tiresome people who keep pushing and pushing and pushing.

BB: So how's that different from a career, from having a career?

SH: How could you have a career if you made the mistake of becoming a theologian, which presupposes there's no academic status that you could ever achieve? What a gift that is! I guess that's how I think that it differs from having a career. Namely, we want to win on our own terms.

You and I are Texans. There's always a kind of outlaw mentality that we entertain. I'd be interested what you think. Namely: We'll play the game, but our way.

BB: That's exactly how I would put it. I've never fallen very deeply into the fetish of our clan of being sports fans. I only recently realized why, reading some other material that the way children play is that they constantly make up games. They only play the game for a little while and then they change the game. We can say that making up the game is really the creative part, playing the game is the conventional part. I think I resonate strongly with your way of putting what a theologian is, because it's the creative parts, saying "OK, we're working in a university now, but that's not really what we're doing."

SH: Of course that's an invitation to deception, self-deception. Namely: "It's not really what we're doing." Oh yes, you really are doing it.

BB: That's true, but what we're constantly trying to teach people is how the game might be put together differently.

SH: When I say we're outlaws, I tend to think it works this way. Think about the old M*A*S*H program:[7] what was so attractive about Alan Alda's character is that he did it his way because he was so good at what he did. So if you are an outlaw, you have to be very good at what you do.

BB: I've caught you using the language of elites now and then, which tends to be located very much within conventional frames, but it sounds like you are looking for a quite different vision of an elite.

SH: Elites are necessary if you believe as I do that hierarchy is morally required for the discovery of the common good. I mean here to indicate why it is that Dorothy Day is a more important person to have within the Christian tradition than you and me. That's an elitist view. And it's hierarchical. That's what I mean.

BB: So the institutions that we know today, whether ecclesial or secular, follow in the wake of lives that you are referring to as elite.

SH: Right. I hope so. I mean, Paul's admonition that the church has to wait for the lesser member to speak is an elitist claim. The lesser member is the elite. Egalitarianism can destroy the lesser member.

BB: That's a good point so I will tempt you to expand.

SH: Egalitarianism, to the extent that it assumes that a person is a person without taking account of their history and particularity means that they will be treated equally in a way that they ought to be treated unequally in order to value their contribution to the community. So, I say egalitarianism is the opiate of the masses. It is what the elites use to say, "Oh well we'll all be treated equally," to make sure their own privileges are not in danger. Separated from an account of the hierarchy of the goods, I think egalitarianism is absolutely destructive.

My way of putting it is that if a community discovers, as it should, that it has a deep need for music and if a young woman has talent and desire to play the cello, and will undergo the training necessary to do that, then the demand for equality says that such a person should not be excluded from being able to do that. So, equality works as a test to ensure that people are not excluded from the diverse roles of the society.

BB: That's interesting. That's especially interesting to me because a few years ago I had a conversation with a senior administrator for the schools in Aberdeen as they were cancelling special education provision. She said to me, "Well do you want me to cancel the music programs at all the schools across the city?" And I said, "The kids that are going to be affected if you do are going to go on to college and have lots more education. You've decided instead to cancel these special kids's 'college education.'" Is that kind of what you had in mind?

SH: Yes.

BB: Let's wrap up this first leg of the discussion. You have, in several ways, explained how you understand the reciprocal relation between discursive and particular writing, but in *Hannah's Child* you resist saying that the life and stories recounted in the book are exemplifications of your theological claims. As you say in the introduction to the memoir, "I worry, therefore, that what I have written here might be just more of 'my work' disguised as memoir. Or, more accurately,

I worry that if readers take this memoir to be an explanation of 'my work,' then it may have the same effect on them as Anthony Trollope's autobiography had on his audience."[8]

In the 2012 afterword you respond to some of the reviews of the book, which nevertheless appear to read the book in exactly this way, including some highly sophisticated readers such as Gerald McKenny. And I'm hoping you can shed more light on this issue now that you've worked through it so concretely. Do we need this book in order to understand your essays? Does the memoir give your other writings more or less authority? What kind of authority does it have in comparison to the other writings?

SH: Who am I to say that the book doesn't help you understand what I've written elsewhere, when people tell me the book helps them to understand what they've read by me elsewhere? Who am I to deny what they tell me?

BB: So on one hand, a text is a text, and you can't control it.

SH: I can't control it. So I take it that it's got to be true. If someone tells me that it has helped them do that, then it must. So, good!

And then what kind of authority does *Hannah's Child* enact that may make what I've argued elsewhere more persuasive? Is it the authority of people discovering that I'm a nice guy? I mean, I am serious.

BB: So not to take your bombastic, public, shouting, having an argument with someone on stage as the final story.

SH: My father was an extraordinarily gentle man. I am not even close to his willingness to live without defending himself. But I'd like to think his life is embodied in at least some of my life. I am a gentle person. I hope that comes through. And I think that that lends a certain kind of authority to what I do. I think what is beginning to be understood is . . . for example, I wrote the Presidential Address for the Society, drawing on Cora Diamond's claim that reality is difficult.[9] I hope people are beginning to appreciate the fact that I've always assumed that to be a Christian doesn't mean that you have a way of overcoming difficulty. What you are given as a Christian is a way to go on.

God made me preternaturally a happy person. I've had some tough things happen in my life, but genetically I just have the energy to keep going. But it doesn't mean that I then say, "Oh well, I've overcome," or something like that. You just keep going. I hope that comes through and people see my account for what seems to be a very aggressive stance as a Christian is aggressive because it gives you a way to muddle through.

Which brings us back to the beginning—is the grammar of the language that I just used an appeal to personal experience that's embodied in my work? I don't have any idea.

BB: I think there's going to be many people out there who have run across "Stanley Hauerwas" and have taken away the message that he's combative all the way down. In so far as that's the case, telling your story—and I would even say having this conversation—is letting people see that that's not all there is. In this sense these sort of exposures "behind the curtain" are important for your corpus to continue to be taken seriously as the traces of a richly polyvalent life and theology.

SH: The resurrected Jesus is still the crucified Jesus. The crucifixion is a triumph, because in the crucifixion God takes into God's very life what we deserve but God refuses to use what we deserve against us—that is to be killed. God refuses because God is love all the way down and would have us be his friends. That's at the heart of what I hope is my "work" in a way that helps us go on with patience in a world that wants to solve those kinds of agonies in a manner that some people have to pay the price. I've tried to avoid that.

The ethics of writing the self

BB: That perfectly leads into the second circle of questions I wanted to talk about, which have to do with the problem, or the task, of telling our story and self-knowledge. Following straight on from what you've just said, it seems pretty obvious that one of the core theological themes of *Hannah's Child* is the insistence that Christians have to learn to live as if God is in control and they do not control their own lives. The assumption guiding my line of questioning thus far is that this affirmation must also shape the acts of reading and writing. Like you said, the theologian today is a writer. Reading is an act of trust in the text or an author. It's a willingness to allow oneself to be led sequentially through ideas or vistas in a manner that inevitably changes the reader. We have to trust ourselves to the author or text, who may well let us down by not giving us anything back after we have given them that trust.

You've commented to me that you know that you made a big demand on the reader's trust in the first chapter of *Naming the Silences*,[10] which begins with a very long retelling of a novel, and it certainly does ask for trust from the reader. The authors of novels and autobiographies are demanding this trust in especially pointed ways because they invite us to work through the often painful confines and details of particular locales we might wish we had never visited.

The remarkable thing is that even authors need to exercise this same trust towards themselves, since they can't know when they begin to write what they will discover at the end of the process. The South African novelist J.M. Coetzee puts his finger on this reality as he describes his own process of writing. "First you give yourself to (or throw yourself into) the writing, and go where it takes you. Then you step back and ask yourself where you are, whether you really want to be there."[11]

I take your repeated insistence that you "write to find friends" to display a luminous faith that your efforts are fruitful because they reach out to unknown readers and, at its face, this seems quite often to have been requited.[12] So my question concerns how, as a theologian, your trust in God is related to your trust that in writing, a self will emerge in the "hard work" of recollection. How does the *act* of writing play into the reshaping of the self who emerges from the process?

On the one hand you seem to suggest, and I like this very much, that writing is how you pray—despite you saying that we can't do what Augustine did a few minutes ago—and in writing you receive the self God sees in you. "My writing is exploratory because I have no idea what I believe until I force myself to say it. For me, writing turns out to be my way of believing."[13]

Granting your entirely welcome clarification here, that belief is too narrow a term, you also use language that strongly suggests that exploration has an end, namely, self-knowledge. "I've written this memoir in an attempt to understand myself, which requires the attempt to master one's life as stages en-route to a decisive self-recognition."[14]

This all fits fairly well with contemporary narratives of self-discovery, but then you end your introduction on a different note, saying that you have written "to invite friends old and new to take pleasure in the life God has given me."[15]

All this is bound to leave the reader unprepared for your change of tack in the afterword, "I can honestly say I didn't write *Hannah's Child* to better understand myself, nor did I try to write the book to be better understood by others."[16]

You often tell us that your friends changed you in specific ways; that teaching at Augustana taught you this, that teaching at Notre Dame taught you that. Why then this strong insistence that you are "unable to state what I learned by writing the book, [but] I can at least acknowledge that I must have been changed by having done so"?[17]

How does this fit with your final insistence that God alone tells us who we are, and therefore, "the task of theology is the integration of a narrative as a form of exploration, an exploration of how the self can be written truthfully."[18]

It's not clear to me how exactly this set of claims fit together.

SH: What a set of confusions you have exposed! I don't know if I can straighten them out. I don't believe, of course, that we're ever masters of our lives. Often people, after having read *Hannah's Child*, will observe, "That is really a courageous thing to have done, to have written *Hannah's Child*." And I say, "Really?" And they say, "Yeah. It just made you so vulnerable." And I thought, "Oh no. I didn't know that!"

So, I didn't feel peculiarly vulnerable for having written the book, but I suppose that there's something in that suggestion. And the vulnerability— when I say that I wrote it to try to understand myself—I mean first and foremost I would like to think I am the book's first reader.

It is interesting when people will often say, "It must have been very hard to have written about Anne." And I say, "Well, actually, it wasn't, while I was writing it," because I was working so hard to make sure that I wrote it artfully, in a manner that she did not become the bad guy, because I did not think that was truthful, although the pain she exacted on Adam [Stanley's son] and myself was real. But, when I've been asked to give readings of the book and they want me to read parts that I've written about Anne—that's really hard! I didn't cry when I was writing it, but I cry when I am reading it!

BB: Fascinating.

SH: It's like reading someone else's painful story to which we oftentimes have an emotional relation. I have that kind of reaction to my own prose. I'm surprised that it's there. So, probably my disavowal that I didn't learn anything from having written the book is probably too blunt a claim. I did learn things from having written the book. I'm not sure how to say what I learned from having written the book, other than I learned that having written the book, I am no longer the same person that wrote it. So, the writing itself produced someone that is now more articulate about who they are, because they wrote the book.

BB: If I am hearing you correctly, the force of your answer is to also take one step back from your comment right at the beginning of the introduction that I already mentioned. "I've written in an attempt to understand myself, which requires the attempt to master one's life."[19]

SH: I shouldn't have used "master."

BB: You may have attempted it, but given your tale about what happens when you read it, you didn't succeed. But the emphasis on the importance of incorporating one's own past in order for the self to develop moral integrity is the type of formulation that is regularly emphasized throughout your writings.

SH: That's right. Obviously memory—and you raised earlier the issue of memory—as a skill, is necessary for that. Memory is essential to our being able to live well, and memory remains one of the most fragile aspects of our lives that we have, because the temptation to mis-remember is so, so strong.

I hope the story I told about Anne is truthful. Jonathan Tran's lecture at the retirement event goes after the story of Anne in a very interesting way.[20] I try to tell the story about Anne and myself in a manner that did not make me the hero, because I wasn't. That was, I think absolutely crucial for the book, and my life. So, in that way, they go together.

Let me return to your point about conventional tropes, because there were certainly other tropes I tried to subvert, and Surviving A Troubled Marriage was one of them, as was Working Class Kid Makes Good as well as How Not To Be Spoiled By Success. Those conventions are all there in a way, in that I tried to subvert every one of them that I thought was not true. But you have to have conventions, and you also have to know how to stiff arm them.

BB: Is that why you recently observed that "'I did not intend to be "Stanley Hauerwas"' is an ironic signal that the whole of *Hannah's Child* is ironic"?[21]

SH: I think so. By that I mean that *Hannah's Child* is the attempt to remind people that I'm a human being who is just trying to get through the day. Therefore, I am subverting "the best theologian in America" by in particular showing how it is that my life depends so determinatively on friendship. It's funny, I was just talking to Don Wood and he asked me as a theologian of note, how do I handle that? And I said, "Through irony." He said that is interesting because Katherine Sonderegger recently told him that you must never forget that theology is fundamentally an erotic discipline. I think that irony is a way to show that the theologian is committed to thinking about matters that will always call the theologian into question.

BB: In that essay you say that all of your theology is ironic because all of it is inflected by the eschatological light of Christ's work, which suggests that the distance that allows you to critique your own discipline and your own society is, at the same time, distancing you from your own life. So, eschatology even breaks up our self-narration. We shouldn't take ourselves too seriously if we take Christ seriously.

SH: That's right, but you better take Christ seriously. Oftentimes, when you say that, it doesn't follow.

BB: Another convention that's there is "Conversion Narrative," which I think for many people was one of the most the striking things about the book. Not least because you open the story with "I couldn't get converted" and end with "Wow, hey, I got converted!" So it's a conversion narrative.

SH: It is.

BB: You've been to a tent revival, and you gave us one in the end.
    That's again right to the point of what I am worrying away at because you link your conversion, ultimately, to the activity of writing. And writing amidst the cloud of witnesses. Is that accurate?

SH: I think so.

BB: So you embrace that particular convention but you obviously put some thought into calling it a memoir.

SH: I did. I read a lot of secondary material on memoirs.

BB: I mean, memoirs can be just one damn thing after another.

SH: Right.

BB: But it's not that at all. It's not quite a confession, but it has confessional aspects. It's not really apology, but it makes some apologetic moves.

SH: Oh that's true.
    One: I don't believe in definitions. So, memoir, like any substantive description, is going to be a complex concept that depends on exemplification. But in general, an autobiography is characterized by this kind of grammar: "On Saturday I was in San Francisco giving this lecture and then on Monday of the following week I went to Singapore." If that's an autobiography, I knew I did not want to do that. The last thing in the world I wanted to turn it into is a travelogue or "this is the story of my success; look at all these things I did!"

BB: I think the German professors do those because they know the archivists are going to be constructing a corpus. Bethge's biography of Bonhoeffer[22] has that feel at many points, like, "Let's not leave anything out because posterity needs to know where he was on Thursday."

SH: And there's a little of that in Busch's biography of Barth.[23] Barth was doing a biography.

BB: Why do you think he ran aground on that?

SH: I don't know, but my hunch is that Barth just found God so much more interesting than Barth.

BB: I am sure that's true.

SH: He just didn't see why he needed to do it. That's why Barth is Barth, and I'm not.

BB: But it sounds like you could only stay interested in Stan long enough because you discovered it was about God the whole time.

SH: I hope that's right. I think memoir takes as its limit the presumption I'm writing about what I can remember, rather than what I can research. I didn't try to do any research. I gave all my papers to Duke, and there is quite a bit there. It's a lot. I didn't go through any of it to see what I did, when. I have a friend, Curtis Freeman, who has been in my papers in preparation for an article in a journal about "Baptists on Hauerwas."[24] It's a lovely journal, and I did a response to it. Curtis went into the archive to see what I did when I lectured to Baptists. He told me about occasions I could not remember at all. I remember some of it, but I could not remember much about when I spoke here or got in a fight there. But, Curtis dug it all up. It's all there.

I've thought it would be really interesting for someone in American religious history to get into my archive, because I am old, and I've known everyone. That is not quite true. But I've not only known many, but I've written back and forth with a number of them. I had conversations with the biographer of Neuhaus. He called me up and he said he so was taken with the correspondence between Richard and myself, because as people in deep and profound disagreement, we maintained a respect for one another that he admired. You know, that's nice. But I did not remember how Richard and I related.

BB: I find the gesture that you just made striking, which you also make in a similar way at the beginning of the *Matthew* commentary[25]—you think of your writing as authenticated, in part, just because you did it all in one fell swoop. Its authority doesn't lie anywhere other than the activity of writing. Rousseau makes exactly the same gesture at the beginning of his *Confessions*. He means it in a thick sense. "I'm just going to say what I have to say and not go back and revise it, because that would falsify it."[26] He sort of tries to outrun his self-reflexivity.

SH: That's exactly right. That's a lovely description.

BB: That's what you think you did?

SH: I had never thought of it. But that's a wonderful description, Brian. There's a terrific book by a philosopher named Ann Hartle that Alasdair and I published in that "Revisions" series that we edited. It was a study of Rousseau's *Confessions*.[27] She does it in comparison to Augustine and Plutarch, because she says whereas Augustine had God telling him who he was—I was thinking of Hartle when I wrote *Hannah's Child*—where Augustine has God to tell him who he is. Plutarch has Rome to tell him who he is. Rousseau didn't have anyone to tell him who he is, other than Rousseau. He is able to tell his life by being alienated from the life he is, by death. So, she argues strongly that that is the beginnings of the Western European necessity to die, in order to be alienated from who you are, so you might know who you are.

BB: Dostoevsky takes that straight on in his book *The Idiot*, which has a lot of confessions in it. And he has a farcical scene in which a young romantic keeps talking about how proximity to death makes truth shine out more clearly. He therefore presents suicide as capable of breaking him out of the prison of self-reflexivity. And it's farce, because when he goes to do it the gun jams! And then everybody laughs at him.[28] So that's Dostoevsky's way of saying there is no way of outrunning self-reflexivity. There is no mechanical way to force your utterance about your life to be true. And Dostoevsky's response to that problem is to indicate that the truth of our life can only be exposed by grace. More to the point, that there is no secular version of confession because it needs absolution and absolution can't be given by the narrator.

And that's kind of where I want to lead, and this is all going in the direction that I hoped it would. Let me find my way to my point with a long question. The basic spectrum that I'd like to lay out and get you to comment on starts on one side with Augustine, who speaks to God and leaves the judgment of the truth or falsity of his self-narration to God. At the other end of the spectrum secular thinkers like Rousseau or Coetzee judge themselves and leave the authority of that judgment to the audience. If the audience just thinks, "Well that doesn't make any sense" or, "They're self-deluded," then their narratives will just die the death of obscurity. And you're standing between those two, somehow. I think that's interesting. It sounds like an expression of an intuitive grasp of where we stand today as Christians, trying to tell our own stories. So what you said you were doing is trying to find a pattern that constitutes a unity to your life amid the welter of things that just happen.

SH: But what just happens becomes what you have gone through in taking retrospective ownership.

BB: Bringing us back to the problem of memory or mastery, most pressingly, the psychological tendency to forget or repress the bad things we've done.

SH: That's right. One of the worst things that can happen to someone is to allow themselves to be described as a victim, because as soon as you take on that description, your oppressor has won. You cannot ever describe your life without them, but they can describe their lives without you.

Of course, what they've done to you is what happens to you. But you're only able to be free when you provide a way of telling the story of your life in which the main plot line is, "I wasn't doing anything, but they did this."

So I think I did not choose my mother but she became and is part of my life by the very fact that I couldn't be who I am without having owned my mother.

BB: OK. That is analogous to Augustine in that he is owning his life, as well. But there seems to be one important difference between your approach and Augustine's, in that Augustine addresses himself to God as he owns his life, though he clearly hopes others will listen in and become interested in this God. As BeDuhn's *Augustine's Manichaean Dilemma*[29] has illustrated with great clarity, Augustine's narrative of his life is carefully constructed. He is telling his story well after his conversion, and he does so for all the reasons we've just talked about within the tropes available to him and his (largely Manichean) audience. Nevertheless, it's addressed to God. You, on the other hand, say, "I did not write *Hannah's Child* for God but first and foremost for myself"—which sounds a bit Rousseauian—"for my friends, and my readers, and in the hopes of making new friends and readers."[30] This aim brings you into good company, it seems to me, with the rest of the modern tradition, which must ask what it means to tell the truth of one's life if there is no God before whom one might confess.

And here Coetzee's stab at autobiographical writing is a useful comparison because it's a nonbeliever's ethically strenuous attempt to write his own story.[31] As we've said, "non-believer" might be too strong a term, but his core moral aim is to avoid falling into self-justification. And he solves the problem by defining confession as speaking the truth about oneself, against the more prosaic narration of just things that happened. I think you are resonating with that position. He develops this definition by way of an analysis of Augustine's *Confessions*, specifically the famous passage about having stolen pears. He suggests we can't understand the text as just reporting a sin, or a crime, that Augustine has committed in his past. But we have to see his writing of a confession as a search for the truth about himself that would make this historical act intelligible. The crafting of Augustine's *Confessions* is therefore not simply a description of something that happened, but produces a truth that didn't previously exist, through the activity of articulating the truth of the self. So he knows he did the thing, but he hasn't come to terms with why he did the thing. And again, that sounds analogous to your own approach.

Coetzee further observes that the true self that Augustine discovers is ashamed and shameful self that is implicitly in need of rescue. For Coetzee then, ethically responsible autobiographical writing is properly addressed to one's self and emerges from the processes of coming to own the life one has led. Whatever authority such confessions can have in a secular context emerges from the reader's admiration for the author's willingness to confront their own worst selves rather than evading or justifying what they've done.

This is the point of the spectrum on which I've asked you to locate yourself. Let me add another analogy to that spectrum. It seems to me that Augustine paints his own portrait like an icon. He writes to God and trusts that he will only be perceived truly by others if his life is transfigured by grace. His humanity must be genuinely clothed and transfigured in the eyes of the readers being bathed in grace. Probably there is a better word to be used there than "by grace"? By God's own presence?

You, in contrast, paint realistically. You write realistically. And therefore your aesthetic looks a lot like those churches in the Orthodox world who, influenced by Western modes of representation, started painting their icons of the saints not in the classic style, transfigured, but within Western realistic traditions of depiction. Orthodox theologians say that that's a decay of their tradition which sees "realism" as the *transfigured* self, not just the "natural" body that can be realistically depicted according to what believer and unbeliever can both see. Like a good Westerner, you ask us to imagine the saints in their contexts, realistically portrayed with historical density. I take this to be the point of your saying that the canon that orients your memoir is the English realist novelists.

Coetzee's approach is more hyper-modern—like Rothko's images such as those in the chapel in Houston[32]—of which you are so fond. His writing is both beautiful and an expression of an aniconic and ascetic impulse which is designed to press his *readers* to become more responsible, as *they* judge him. So Rothko isn't saying "this is about God" or "there is a God." He's saying, "Stand before this piece of art and come to terms with yourself and this whole field of 'God' that is confronting you."

Have I done justice to where you would locate what you did in *Hannah's Child*?

SH: All that is just almost too smart for me, Brian. I'm not sure how to locate myself within those descriptions, which I find very powerful. As you know, grace is not a word I use. I don't use grace because in Protestantism, oftentimes grace is identified with a reality that is somehow not God, and that just seems to be a problem.

I love Rothko's chapel. You're right. But I don't want my prose to mimic those paintings. But I am just not sure what to say. What do you think I ought to say?

Coetzee, you say, expresses an aniconic and ascetic impulse which is designed to press his readers to become more responsible. From what I know about Coetzee, that seems exactly right and it just seems to me stupid. You're going to press your readers to be more responsible? What does that mean? I have received a number of letters in response to *Hannah's Child* that say, "This book has helped me return to Christianity." Many people can read *Hannah's Child* that can't read *Truthfulness and Tragedy*. That pleases me, that they are taking it seriously again.

But I didn't let you answer how you would answer.

BB: I think maybe the most succinct way to position the question has to do with the fact that in their own ways, Augustine and Coetzee share something. Coetzee's an interesting character because he's a genuine secularist or agnostic, but he just as clearly thinks that our salvation depends on another time breaking in on us. Like Kafka he has that New Testament sense that there is *chronos* and *kairos* and that no action on our behalf in *chronos* can create truth. So there really is something like a divine horizon in his work. And that means that like Kafka and Augustine, the telling of the tale is designed to open a truth not so far from Jesus's parables, and that is "Be awake!" One of my burning questions, to which I'm sure we'll return, is how central apocalyptic horizon has been in your thought, and I'm pointing to that question by asking about how you approached the writing of *Hannah's Child*.

SH: I'm sure you're right.

I just remember something that you raised earlier and I don't think I responded to it adequately, and that's the formative character of this writing as establishing authority. That's putting it exactly right. It's what I want. I want the writing to be so compelling that you find it impossible to say, "Well, I just think it's all bullshit." Just to the extent that the writing does that, it establishes authority in that way and you can begin to see how legitimacy works.

When I started working in Christian ethics I had some sense that I was going to be an outlier. I thought the way you changed the world is by changing the world. You just have to provide an alternative, within the frame that's been there; Rauschenbusch through Gustafson. So, I thought, "I just have to write," because if you don't write, you don't have any authority.

BB: I wanted to ask about that precise point as well, because I've said before that the narrative grabbed me with an almost irresistible force. It took me several readings to appreciate the technical prowess on display and see the artifice more clearly. One of the most obvious literary features of the text is its composition in the first-person voice. It's a rhetorical form which almost irresistibly captures the reader, and you've now said that that's what you were looking for. But this rhetoric isn't ethically neutral. It almost forces us to take the side of the author in all the events narrated. What you don't do, thank the Lord, is fall into the trap of bad autobiographies, which are clearly settling scores or justifying morally questionable acts which the author knows are morally questionable.

SH: Now people did think that I settled academic scores with McBrien and Campbell.

BB: Do you accept that?

SH: There's some of that.

BB: Would you call that a failure then?

SH: Probably. But I didn't know of an alternative. The bottom line is Hauerwas has trouble working for people who he doesn't respect. He doesn't respect ambitious people who want to be more than their talent would allow them to be. I thought that had to be said.

BB: Managers.

SH: Exactly. So it wasn't exactly personal, but it had a kind of one-up, I gotchya, because they sure as hell got me!

BB: It's a spiritual discipline to work through that sufficiently enough to be able to narrate such events without any hint of "gotchya" peeking through. And I think it's no surprise that you didn't manage that seamlessly. I don't know who could.

SH: There was a kind of getting-at-you.

BB: That's why the rhetorical form you chose makes you especially hostage to that sort of criticism, and then you don't leaven it much at all with displays of shame, or repentance, or regret.

SH: I think that's really an interesting observation. I've never been someone who's been big on shame. I think shame is interesting. I've just never felt it very much.

Regret? It's interesting to ask in what ways regret is different from shame. Shame either happens or doesn't. Regret—you should feel! So, it may well be that I did. But, for example, I say that if I had been born at a little higher class level, hell I could have done something really interesting like being the president of a bank. I could have made a lot of money! But instead, going to college was a big deal. I never regretted any of the "limits of my life." The question is, do you regret moral failure? I've never been much of an activist. I sometimes wonder, "Should I have been more active in the 1960s in the anti-war movement?" I don't know. I don't regret the stances I assumed, or what I was trying to do at that time.

BB: That's interesting, and I wouldn't have expected you to put it in quite those terms. I'm asking about the rhetoric of writing, what it means to have chosen the powerful first person narrative. Some of the problematic momentum that comes with that choice would have been decreased, had you, like Augustine, said "That was a shameful thing I did." Whether you felt it or not, it's an important gesture within the conventions of the memoir. If he does another one, we can imagine what sort of autobiography we're going to get out of another brash Texan, Lance Armstrong, for instance; not only does he seem incapable of feeling regret, but even of convincingly staging it. And of course staging it is a complicated thing. The whole business of writing a memoir is staging.

SH: It is.

BB: Let me reiterate that I've been pursuing this line of questioning in detail because I think the issues surrounding the ethics of writing are crucial for theology today, especially if we're not doing what we're doing in university departments in the near future. If theologians are anything today, they are writers.

SH: Then the question becomes about the genre of theology.

BB: Absolutely, which is exactly what we're trying to get to the bottom of. So if we assume for a minute that the next generations of theologians might try to follow your lead, we need to be clear what it would mean to continue in our own ways the approach that you've called your "mature"[33] way of doing ethics—and in the book you delightfully refer to "theological journalism,"[34] and I like that description a lot. You also have talked about striving to develop a "novelist's eye,"[35] which we've also talked about. If we're going to follow this lead, I assume we can only do so faithfully if we've directly faced the ethical issues that accompany writing about ourselves and other people. I think it should be clear by now why I suspect that faithful writing, especially about ourselves, is tied up with the problem of self-criticism.

It was sensitivity to these sorts of ethical dilemmas that led Coetzee to write his autobiography in the third person. The form allowed him to refuse the judgments about events being narrated which were unavoidably offered when writing in the authorial first person. And here's where I think you're right that you can't force readers to be moral. But you can demand that they do the work of judging the moral quality of the actions of the characters being portrayed, which in this case also happens to be the author. So Coetzee doesn't explain what he did. He only displays the thinking of that character being narrated, when it's needed to make the narrative intelligible, like using lines like, "The boy thought that . . ." Augustine accomplishes this refusal of self-justification by constantly deferring his account to God's judgment. "I was ashamed, I did wrong, God will judge me." You signal your clear awareness of the problem of self-criticism when midway through your story you comment:

> What so often makes us liars is not what we do, but the justifications we offer for what we do. Our justifications become the way we try to defeat the contingencies of our lives by telling ourselves consoling stories that suggest we have done as well as was possible. I cannot pretend that I have avoided deceit in this memoir. But I have at least had a check on the lies I might tell. Being Christian means that I must try to make sense of my life in the light of the gospel, and so I do not get to determine the truthfulness of my story. Rather, those who live according to the gospel will be the ones to determine where I have been truthful and where I have deceived myself.[36]

So you are, like Coetzee, relying on your audience, or asking something of your audience.

SH: And part of the audience are the people in *Hannah's Child*.

BB: Yes. So their reactions are already the first audience reaction, even though you're mediating that to your readers as you tell the story.

SH: Right. I really take the point, Brian, but I am sure I could not have written in the third person.

BB: Right. I mean, did you try?

SH: No. I just couldn't have written in the third person.

BB: It's hard to imagine or it's technically . . . ?

SH: It's technically hard. It's technically hard because how do you write in the third person without assuming an Olympian perspective? An Olympian writes in the third person, but who is able to say what the third person is?

BB: Yeah. And Coetzee is a linguistic craftsman. He's studied the options and absolutely agrees with your worries about the Olympian narrator. That's why he ends up in the final volume of his memoir presenting himself as someone who is being interviewed by a fictional character. The technical issues this involves are mind-boggling. It's pretty apparent how difficult it is to pull it off.

SH: In the great early novelists, the Olympian author was always there.

BB: You're clearly uncomfortable with that. So you're not an English realist in that sense. You are more postmodern than that.

SH: That's right. I mean, Augustine's God is Olympian but then God is God and I am not.

BB: By ending with, "Those who live according to the gospel will be the ones to determine where I have been truthful and where I have deceived myself," you seem to submit that ultimate truth of the judgment to the church. Is that right and is that an improvement on Augustine?

SH: I can't imagine any improvement on Augustine! No. No, it's certainly not.

BB: You know, if you say the church will judge, there's a hope for an absolution of a certain type, or not. And if you say God will judge, you might have to wait till the end. For starters.

SH: You might. I'm thinking in the background there of Matthew 18 and the need to confront someone who you think has done something wrong. So I think that church practice is the way God has given us as a check against our endemic temptation of self-deception. And self-deception is such an important theme for me. Yet self-deception is so hard to characterize because it is not something you do. It's not something you can correct, without help.

BB: Let me press you on exactly that point. There are a few textual indicators that over the course of your career you actually become less self-critical, and more certain about your identity.

SH: I think that's right.

BB: I don't want to flatten out the genuine complexity of your various texts, but I do observe points at which, in practice, you become much more certain about your identity. And this may well be inevitable and appropriate. I'm not questioning that. In our third chapter I am going to raise a speech you made at the 1980 AAR which was clearly self-ironizing, in that you ended by very clearly including yourself in the criticisms that you levied at the guild. You repeat that story in *Hannah's Child*, and you present yourself there as an outsider who tried to be a good Yalie for a while but could never really stick with it because your personality was too forthright and the times demanded more committed engagement than the Yale school allowed was proper for a Christian ethicist. I want to ask a question and make an observation. Let me just ask the question straight and then I'll make an observation after, once you've answered.

Is this an example of the self-deceptions of memory or the truthful confession of the person writing this text in the late phase of his career?

SH: I hope it's the latter and let me say why. It is very tempting for me to play the Southern con, which you know well. I'm just a hick from south-east Dallas, who was raised a bricklayer, trying to make it good in a world that is way over me. So, I'm still just the old boy who is always on the outside.

Bullshit. I'm a person of stature and power. I became powerful through an extraordinarily energetic work habit. As a result, if you are going to be in the field of Christian ethics, you are going to have to deal with me. Isn't that wonderful? I can command your attention, but you can't command my attention. So, it would be deceptive for me to play something that I'm not. I try to be, therefore, as respectful as I can for those entering the guild.

So there is a sense, interestingly enough, that if you are committed to nonviolence, you better be serious, because you are asking people to pay prices that you yourself may not have had to pay, but that you cannot exclude as a possibility. So you have to take yourself seriously, because what you are saying is so serious. So there is, I think, a deeper kind of self-confidence which you may well think is self-righteousness that is characteristic of me at 74.

BB: Just looking at that passage again last night,[37] what was fascinating about it is how it unconsciously displays how deeply the 1960s shaped you, despite the claims you make on the surface level of the narrative. You might well have been put off by the gender-bending, drug-bingeing of the rich hippies, but you took to heart, right at the core of your identity as an academic, one of the central axioms of the 1960s revolution. "It was a time that required you to stand up for what you thought mattered." I was provoked to think harder about your dismissal of being affected by the 1960s by a conversation I recently had with Craig Keen, who said, "That's a lie. That's a self-deception."

SH: I think that may well be right. Those of us who came through the 1960s, I'm sure it left a mark—one, the outlaw mentality that I mentioned was certainly part of the 1960s. I sometimes say that the students that I was teaching—I started teaching in 1968 so of course you still had the 1960s in 1968—that many of the students at that time really were challenging every presumption that was in place about what you needed to be to be a good person in America. Many of the students that I had at that time would buy a van, fill it with brown beans, and spend their life touring around America looking for their counterparts. They ended up selling insurance. I ended up being me. I think that in some ways, I'm more consistent with that 1960s ethos than many of the kids that were going through it at the time. I was coming through just behind age-wise. I never got into the drugs or the sex that seemingly made it so attractive. I think all of that was deeply demonic.

When I started teaching in the 1960s, I would teach a course called "Christian Ethics in Democratic Society," where I had them read the Republican National Convention Platform and the Port Huron Statement side by side without identifying them. I would ask them to describe who they thought had written those statements. And they always thought the same kind of people had written those two statements, because they were so similar. I would have kids challenge me in class when I would try to be defending Just War or something like that. They would even accuse you for even thinking such thoughts, believing you were siding with the enemy. They would call you a fascist pig. Isn't that wonderful? You would have a kid stand up and push it. That's gone. It's not gone in me!

BB: So you tried to provoke it?

SH: I tried to provoke it. It's very hard to do now. So the 1960s—John Yoder in many ways represents the kind of intellectual challenging position that you could get in the 1960s. It's very hard to get it today. So, yeah, the 1960s were a quite extraordinary time.

I was, and am, a very conventional person. I had my head down during those years. I was reading books. I was trying to get a PhD. You know, I really was just trying to figure out if this stuff called Christianity was true. And it's literally true that when I went to Philadelphia to be interviewed by the president of Augustana, to see whether I would be acceptable enough to be brought out for an interview, that was the first time I thought, "I'm going to be a teacher." It had not occurred to me that I was going to be a teacher, that I was going to spend my life teaching! It's good to be a teacher. But that's not what I thought I was doing when I was going through Divinity school and getting a PhD.

The ethics of writing the other

BB: Let's turn now in a last leg of this discussion to explore how you've handled a handful of tricky passages in your own story. I want to emphasize that I'm not playing the tabloid journalist looking for dirt here, but it's clearly important to think theologically about ethically loaded decisions, about what to say as well as what not to say. Because confession or truth-telling about oneself is also a staging of confession, it must take into account the need to avoid betrayals; to keep secrets appropriately.

It seems to me that your relationship with Anne presented this problem in the most potent of forms because you couldn't but constantly avoid at least skirting betrayals. One friend of mine who has mental illness in his family said he would feel betrayed if a spouse of one of his mentally troubled relations were to write as candidly about his family member as you have about Anne. I'm not asking you to go into whether or not Anne's family felt betrayed by your portrayal of her, but I am interested in this problem as a concrete display of your views of the ethics of writing, in this case in relation to the responsibility to keep secrets. If we are to write biographically or confessionally, or even journalistically, we'll inevitably draw others's lives or our life with others explicitly into our theological texts. So how do we do so in a way that does not betray or exploit others?

SH: A memoirist or a novelist, in order to be truthful often has to have an extraordinarily cruel heart.

BB: There is a great German biopic of Thomas Mann, whose family life was just a train wreck, and it shows how his work was a long exploitation of his domestic chaos for his work.[38]

SH: I'm not cruel, which means I may not be truthful, because oftentimes truthfulness has to take the form of cruelty.

BB: Exposure.

SH: Exposure. I just couldn't do that. I don't know. No one has commented on "I'm not coming."[39] The time when Anne tried to commit suicide and when her brother told me, I said, "I'm not coming." I just left that without explanation.

BB: As I read, my inner commentator—who is also a self-questioning son, husband, and father—piped up at that point to ask whether that was a genuine first thought for you or there had been many precursor expressions of "I'm not coming" that preceded it but had been articulated in less dramatic registers. So that type of articulation did open up questions for me, especially having been left without an explanation. But any explanation would have almost inevitably slipped into self-justification.

SH: I use that as an example because it strikes me that someone might want to say that was a real moral failing that should have been more acknowledged. But I just couldn't be drawn back into her life. I had spent too much of time just watching her. I don't remember if I talked about this—I don't think I did—in the memoir. We had started counseling, and she just blew up and wouldn't do it anymore. But after she left, I continued to go to this counselor. She was very good.

BB: You did talk about it.

SH: I did talk about it some, but I'm not sure if I talked about this. Joanne asked me what it was like on a daily basis and I said, "Well, I would watch very carefully Anne's facial muscles" because I could tell an episode was coming because she got a little muscle twitch just above her lip before an episode. Joanne said, "You really lost a job because so much of your life is taken up in that."

I just couldn't be pulled back because my whole life was so orientated to making life safe for Adam, by trying to keep Anne pleased. Those habits were so deep, I couldn't be pulled back into it. But someone could well argue "You should have been."

BB: As we'll be talking about in a later discussion, these questions are very pointed for me—and in exactly the way you have already raised—when we're talking about disability. That sort of enmeshment, that other job—you can't talk about disability without talking about having inhabited that other job, because it requires so many layers of attention and investment, it's almost impossible to understand it without coming to grips with those aspects of it.

SH: Right. Your life is just absolutely taken up with the challenge every minute. I watch you and Adam [Brian's eldest son]. I see how often you have to run up and get him. I spent twenty years trying to say, "What can I do to make your life better?" so that my life won't be so fucking painful!

BB: And that pressure radiates out into everything.

SH: Everything.

BB: So, for instance, one of the ways I'm tempted to read your story is that you were an angry bastard and you said such and such and you stepped on people, not only because you wanted to wind them up or because you'd cut your teeth in the combat of the late 1960s classroom, but in part because a tension in your domestic life was radiating out from that constant watchfulness that you know can end with terror.

SH: Anne had just beaten the hell out of me one day. Not physically, but just verbally. And I was teaching one night, I can't remember the course. But one of the women in the course really went after me about not being feminist enough. And I just took it. But I thought, "Live my life." Let yourself have the shit beat out of you, where you can hardly operate. That obviously doesn't have immediate implications for feminism, it just means that you're working as hard as you can to keep a marriage together with a very wounded person, and that doesn't count for shit. Those are the kind of things that you find yourself in.

BB: Your response then to my friend who said they'd be a little bit uncomfortable if a spouse of his family member wrote in the way that you wrote about Anne is that you had to tell your own story and that you were consciously not cruel to Anne. You excised the story radically and only included enough of her story as you needed in order to make your story intelligible.

SH: That's right. I kept in my mind the whole time, she was cruel, but she was in pain. I wanted people to feel her pain. I think I did that.

BB: I think you did. I think so too.
     Here's another, to me, more puzzling elision. You made three extremely cryptic references to your adopted brother. Was that an intentional leaving-aside?

SH: Yes. Johnny's life was hard. He had five brothers. His mother didn't die. She had abandoned them. My parents took him in when he was around 14. I knew Johnny pretty well. We became, I think, close. But he screwed up his life in some grand ways. He got into some serious trouble. He straightened out and was a good man. There were marriages, however, that shouldn't have happened. I did not see how going into any of that was necessary.

BB: So that's another example of your hermeneutic; it didn't advance your story and it would have been cruel to him, so a few brief mentions are enough.

SH: Absolutely.

BB: That's helpful.

SH: Johnny was drastically overweight. He died early, which is very sad.

BB: Speaking of death, do the deaths of the figures that play important roles in our lives change the moral equation? It does seem to me that it's difficult to imagine you having characterized your mother as you did, for instance, if she was still alive.

SH: Oh I couldn't.

BB: So walk us through how the deaths of the subjects being talked about change things?

SH: Obviously, Anne's death is the crucial one. I could have never written *Hannah's Child* prior to Anne dying. I could not have written the letter to Joel and Kendall about mother, if she had been alive. Mother could be unbelievably manipulative, but she was a good person. There is a sense, again, is it cowardly? Possibly.

BB: You know the old chivalrous Germans were pretty convinced you could assassinate a character before or after they died. So that's what I'm kind of looking at: how do the deaths of the characters change our understanding of what we can say about them?

SH: It's a great question and it's a deeply moral one that we don't think about.

BB: Again, it's not unrelated to the disability issue because I write about a kid who will never speak very articulately about himself, and I do it all the time.

SH: And you create expectations in others about their relations to Adam that Adam cannot control.

BB: Indeed. In a way, I deploy the apparatus that turned you into Stanley Hauerwas, with a defenseless, speechless child. And you can do that with your own mother, who's dead, even though you wouldn't do it to her face.

SH: Death offers the possibility of a certain kind of candor that otherwise wouldn't be possible.

BB: I haven't thought through this, but I've only thought through it in the sense that one of the reasons why I know I can't do what you've done is that I would have to talk about people who are still alive, and I couldn't do it.

SH: I understand, absolutely.

BB: I do wonder whether that is disingenuous or not. Certainly, it's a free pass if they're dead, because then you just don't have to face it. But I do wonder if that is a moral evasion.

SH: I don't know the answer to that. I don't think there is any "in principle" answer to that. It would depend.

BB: The only way I would know how to start—no, I don't think there's a principled answer. But I've done enough journalism, theological and otherwise, that you know when you're about to put something down on paper that came out of someone's mouth, that's going to make them angry. And you make a judgment about whether you should or shouldn't do it, based on a whole range of factors. And that same sort of judgment, it seems to me, is at play when you're writing about your own life, or writing about someone else's life.

You have said that the practice of journalism is not miles away from what the practice of theological ethics should be, and that's where I think I would go with it. That people are going to get angry about what you write about them, or say they said, doesn't seem to be a good reason for or against saying it. As a journalist, the most important moments are when you get people to incriminate themselves in their own words. Since nobody does that intentionally, there is an almost transgressive, outlaw buzz you get as an interviewer knowing they've just dug their own grave and are going to really regret it later, and of course hate you as a journalist.

Hard work and good work

BB: It took me a while to figure out that one of the main reasons I have a hard time distancing myself from *Hannah's Child* has to do with the central role played by the moral unassailability of hard work in the text. I recognize this as a powerful moral ideal in our home Texan culture, which makes me suspicious of my strong attraction to it. You explicitly raise at least one theological worry about the theme at several points in the book, namely, that the person committed to "hard work" can find little place in their life for genuine rest.[40] You also hint at other worries about the overvaluation of hard work, such that it can become an apparatus for assuaging social anxieties, and can make retiring impossible. My question then is this: You often tell us what it is you like about hard work in the book, but what would you say is the most problematic aspect of "hard work" as a term of self-assessment, or of moral assessment of others?

SH: No enjoyment.
   Namely, hard work can give a certain kind of joy, but there is an enjoyment of life that hard work makes impossible because it's so oppressive.
   I think liturgy is pure enjoyment. I couldn't live without it, because otherwise my life would be so determined by hard work.

BB: Would you affirm it as work as well, *opus Dei*?

SH: Yeah, but it's very different.

BB: Can it be hard work, let's put it that way?

SH: I don't find it hard work. I suppose I do . . . That's not quite right. This is very interesting. I hadn't thought about these matters. Sometimes I find the confession of sin hard work!

BB: You might not have thought about how you use the idea of work in your memoir, but I think your prayer "The Good Work of Praise" in *Prayers Plainly Spoken* is very carefully negotiating the central issues.

> Strange Lord . . . make us workers in your kingdom. We want to work, but so often our work turns out to be nothing but busyness. . . . Yet we know you would not have us busy, having given us the good work of prayer. Help us, in our busyness, learn to pray—so that all our work, all that is our lives, may glorify you. In a world that for so many seems devoid of purpose, we praise you for giving us the good work of praise.[41]

SH: What's behind that is an understanding of work as activity in which the end and the means are commensurate. So it is good work because it is restful because the end is not something you struggle to achieve separate from the means.

Why sin is hard work is because the ends and the means are not commensurate in the same way. Though of course, a confession of our sin is prayer, but it also requires a kind of reflectiveness that I think can be quite painful.

BB: My surface question is about the way that the term comes in as a moral assessment.

SH: It's a character.

BB: And a narrative convention signaling a recognition that this or that person is valuable.

SH: But, I mean, hard work for me, in *Hannah's Child* is a character.

BB: Oh, all right. It's an entity in itself.

SH: I hadn't thought of it until you brought it to my attention, but it really is a kind of character. It's just the way my life is formed, to work hard.

BB: Let me take another approach in order to clarify how you think of this "work" character then. I ask this question for our audience, really. Would you say that the academy demands or assumes hard work? It's clear that there are plenty of aesthetes, dilettantes, managers, show-boats, and shirkers who don't even aspire to work hard. This raises the question whether the presumptions about working hard dominant among academics bear any relation to the character, the account of hard work you are emphasizing in the first chapters of *Hannah's Child*?

SH: I really think that many academics are unbelievably lazy! They are extremely privileged and they take advantage of the privilege. I think people in the ministry are oftentimes extraordinarily lazy, and they just don't have the habit of work. They wouldn't know what hard work is. No, I think the academy has got a real problem.

BB: So, there are people who are lazy, but we still need to come to terms with the other side of the equation, with what you mean when you distinguish hard work from mere busy-ness.

SH: I think what we've been about this morning is hard work.

BB: No, this is fun! Preparing is hard work!

SH: And you prepared well. But it's been hard work for me, because you've forced me to be articulate in ways that I hadn't anticipated. One of the great things about hard work is that it saves you from self-fascination.

BB: Let me press you on that, because I sat in this same space 24 hours ago and I begged for money and I worked on spreadsheets and I filled in boxes and I hated every minute of it and it felt soul-destroying and I would be tempted to call that hard work. On the other hand, it made me self-absorbed because I was so angry. But what we're doing now is self-forgetful for me, and that's what makes it pleasurable. It takes immense concentration and self-awareness, but in a manner that pulls me out of myself and into something bigger and more glorious than "me."

SH: That's a hard call, because I think what you were doing with the spreadsheets and all that is difficult work which may not be the same as hard work.

BB: What's the salient distinction?

SH: Hard work means you have a sense that you're glad you're doing it, because it has purposes that are intrinsic to its nature.

BB: I have some thoughtful and serious colleagues who would say, "You gotta know where the money's going and that's part of what it means to live in the world we live in; so you just have not resigned yourself to living in your own world."

SH: That's probably right. I appreciate that.

BB: I mean, some people would have hated bricklaying! Not just lazy people!

SH: I started laboring and daddy paid me 75 cents an hour! I'd be so tired by 11 o'clock in the morning but I'd think, "I've made $2.25!" There was that aspect to it, but it is finally not money, I guess, that sustains you. It's a world that if you're not a part of, it's very hard to describe.

BB: Let me try to more precisely articulate what makes me suspicious about the moralized term "hard work." My first reason for suspicion is that I just find it so attractive. It's the supreme working-class virtue. I very much identify with the father–son depiction you present from your own story, and "hard work" was certainly one of the most potent forms of intimacy I experienced in my own youth. I still find it hard to sympathize with students and colleagues who never seem to manage the discipline it takes to get down to work and persevere until it is finished, who can't, as you rightly put it, "just get on with it."[42] But I'm not bragging about this lack of sympathy because at best it's a microscopic step from there to judgmentalism. So, I worry that the higher the cultural value you assign to "hard work," the closer you come to a form of works righteousness, whether it wears the secular or religious garb. "I worked, so I am deserving."

As *Hannah's Child* progresses your attraction to hard work never seems to fade, but you do begin to raise a few questions about the role it plays in your own life. You call it one of the forms your "self-involvement" takes,[43] even refer to it as an addiction,[44] an anesthesia[45] that allows you to evade introspection.[46] It is very often invoked as a self-evident justification for your attraction to many people, including Greg Jones and even Paula [Gilbert, Stanley's wife].[47]

Your invocation of the term in relation to Paula is interesting, first, because she is one of the few women to whom you ascribe the trait in the book. It's more obviously interesting because it is the one instance when you attempt to depict the transition that you never made with your African American bricklaying laborers—from the communion of the work world into the communion of churchgoing.[48] It's fascinating to observe a transition in *Hannah's Child* from the almost liturgical invocation of "hard work" to an increasing use of the term "good work." The new afterword ensures that the book now ends with these two pregnant words. I'm sure this wasn't an accident, even though you've just tried to hint that it's somewhat accidental. Can you walk us through what you feel is at stake in the progression in the text from "hard work" to "good work"?

SH: First of all, I'm telling my story and I'm not recommending hard work. I do increasingly recognize the ambiguities surrounding it. I didn't really think of it, Brian, so you are a very perceptive reader that sees that I am moving from hard work to good work, probably because I don't do hard work anymore!

BB: Except for this morning.

SH: I do mainly good work. I tend to think I have this kind of discrimination: Hard work means you've got to use your hands. Good work doesn't necessarily mean you have to use your hands. So, there's a physicality to hard work that may not be present in good work. Hard work can be good work.

BB: Surely that runs afoul of your own theoretical perceptions?

SH: It does, it does.

But I guess I think I really have deep sympathy with men—and it's usually men—who are having to do work that is really hard, that few people appreciate as something important to have done. I think about the people that pick up our trash. It has got mechanized but still I think part of the wound of the work is no one appreciates how important that kind of work is. I tend to think about hard work as sustainable if it does build a certain kind of community.

There is a racial aspect to hard work. I think one of the most important formations for me was that I was the only white guy laboring. When you are a laborer—I do this in *Hannah's Child*—you are a slave to the bricklayer. They're the enemy! I really got to know George Harper. George let me know him. And Fred. So, I got a sense of what it meant to be African American before civil rights that really gave me a stance towards the civil rights movement that I really think I wouldn't have had if it hadn't been for those kinds of work experiences.

Work, race, and the church

BB: I think we'll leave the gender aspects noted in your last comment for later, but let's follow up the point you've opened up about race. I think it's worth following up because a close reading of the text can sometimes make it look like "hard work" is being drafted in at sensitive points to do work that you typically ascribe to the church. I think race is one of those sensitive points. You are well aware of the linkage of "hard work" with racist attitudes, that there is often a linkage made between "hard work" and "lazy minorities."[49] That's obviously a sentiment that is one of the major drivers of race antagonism and fascist political rhetoric right across the modern Western world, even today.

At one point you seem to suggest that in the community of hard work race was rendered irrelevant in important respects. You offer the example of your drinking from the black men's drinking cup when circumstances demanded it, "not to challenge racism but because I was thirsty, in a hurry, and did not give a damn."[50] You and I both know this is not quite true. Such acts could not but be direct challenge to racism in breaching the hygienic taboos to which you allude in recounting your mother's scolding for this behavior.

SH: African American restrooms.

BB: My grandfather lived his whole life in south Texas, working in a refinery, and in that refinery they had three colors of porcelain on the drinking fountains—white, brown, and black. Breaching those cultural boundaries could not but be direct challenges to racism in violating the hygienic taboos on which this system was defended. So, if, as you've often said, acts are understood to be more determinative than intentions, this act did in fact challenge institutionalized racism. Why then are you denying that it challenged the status quo?

The way you position this discussion of race furthermore suggests that in the community of hard work you didn't draw on your privilege as a white man in a segregated society, being "a white guy who did the work of blacks."[51] I'm not trying to suggest with this line of questioning that you are to be faulted for not having been some sort of freedom fighter for racial equality before the movement had even begun, but I'm not quite sure what you are saying about what you learned about race in the community of hard work, and I'm hoping you can flesh that out a bit more and explain why you want to deny that it was racially transgressive.

SH: Because the continuing forms of segregation were assumed. It was still the case that when some of the laborers with whom I worked came to the house, they came in the back door. My father, who became increasingly sympathetic with

African Americans as he aged, did not want to mistreat them. Nonetheless, he could not break out of the habits of segregation. I remember once a young African American was hired on the job, and my uncle Dick was laying brick. The young laborer called him Dick, rather than Mr. Dick. Mr. Henry, who was the mud-maker, took the young laborer out with a shovel and said, "Nigger, I'm going to beat you up if you ever call him Dick again. He's Mr. Dick." Those are the kind of stories we grew up with. They are shit. Absolute shit.

The "hard work" commonality meant you could not help but see that young laborer and Mr. Henry and George. You called an African American Mr. Henry and it showed. It was a remarkable glimpse at seeing the humanity of African Americans that we couldn't develop.

I'm sure that resonates with you.

BB: Absolutely. And when you're young you don't know how to tell what's going on. You notice it, but how do you name it?

SH: I mean, you went to integrated schools.

BB: I did.

SH: But I didn't. My schools were segregated.

BB: Interesting. For me living on the next page of the story the dilemmas surrounded the fact that Brock is between Bernard Battle and Pedro Delgado. I lived in a very unstable equipoise between the three "races" rife with a racial tension whose incipient violence was barely under the surface. So the old order had broken down but no stable new order had really arisen. And that was tough, a tough world.

SH: Oh it was awful.

BB: Which is why the place of the community of hard work in relation to the place of the church seems to me really important to touch on. As you've just said, your dad became increasingly gentle in a way that radiated out from the comradeship formed in the crucible of unbelievably hard work. But, you also note, "He, like all of us, lacked the practices to know how the community formed through hard work could be carried forward in other aspects of our lives, but he also knew the sadness with which we must live in the absence of such practices."[52] You're presenting the crucible of hard work as a forum in which the community of comradeship is formed and that challenges the habits of racist society.

Now we come to the sharp end of this question. Given the cultural context, it would be almost unthinkable for Mr. Henry and George Harper not to be Christians. If I'm wrong, I'll be very interested to hear the story. If I'm right, according to your narrative, both your father and his black laborers were Christians, but that wasn't the crucible in which their community and comradeship was forged. We have black Christians and white Christians spending most of their time in the place called "hard work" and becoming friends here in a localized sense, but not in any way that they could be "carried forward in other aspects of their lives."

SH: I remember when my grandmother died. The whole family gathered at granddaddy and grandmother's place. Mr. Henry and some of the other laborers came. They sang a spiritual at the family gathering. It was very moving. But of course there was racism all the way down, still functioning in that way.

The suggestion is that I've never in my work sufficiently addressed racism. I don't think that's right. I have written quite a bit about it, as a matter of fact. And I've tried to do so in a way that doesn't give you the kind of crude egalitarianism that says we're all the same. That kind of egalitarianism doesn't repeat the complexities of the histories that need to be told and lived. And then, part of the problem is that to write about race as a white man after the 1960s, I think, is very difficult. You don't want to assume your voice is the voice that should be heard, rather than the voice of African Americans about it.

BB: I'm guessing that you would admit at the same time that your own cultural origins made that transition especially complicated. I have in mind the way race defines "Texan pride" as you so humorously and poignantly describe in the essay, "A Tale of Two Stories: On Being a Christian and a Texan."[53] Even there, hard work is a central figure. You avow being proud of your ancestors, not only for being interesting, but for being hardy, and note that "my grandfather's and father's hard life as bricklayers has taught me that the great gift of hard work is independence and pride."[54] Texans, you observe, are used to being different, so being part of a countercultural church is not as unthinkable for us as it might be for other Americans more wholly identified with the nation. But that dissenting posture comes at a price, and that price is racialized. "We Texans have little ability to know how to admit our failures, cruelty, and our tragedies . . . The way we hide our sins is to turn them into a banner."[55] What's fascinating about this passage is that you end up placing the term "Texan" as the label for a tragic narrative sustained by violence. This is theologically to situate it in a significant sense as something from which we need to be redeemed. This sheds a much more potent light on your conclusion that "I think I have every right to claim I am a Texan, but I feel less sure to claim I am a Christian."[56]

SH: It's interesting. Last week, a young man came down from the University of Virginia who is writing his dissertation on James Cone and myself. He had seized on that claim that I make that to write as a white person about racism is quite difficult because the African American story is not my story. I said, "I did say that, but I'm not sure I should have said it." It isn't my story, but that doesn't mean that a white person doesn't have the obligation to write as a theologian about what it means—I take Ferguson[57] to be a reminder of this—what it means by the very fact that we're white that we have a privileged position that African Americans do not have. It is important to negotiate that and to say why that's a perversity that we need to make clear and to repent in a manner that helps us not be possessed by the inextricability that we are racist. To say more about that, that's what I would say.

BB: I think I found it a striking passage given how tightly it intertwines hard work as admirable with pride—"being Texan" was the way we named that set of themes. What is far less often admitted is that the whole complex is married to a culture of evasion of culpability that takes its own local configuration. So, when asked to cash out the darkness that accompanies the name "Texas," you cash it out as the sin of racism.

SH: The reference to the "banner" is about Greenville, Texas, and Paris, Texas. When you drove into those cities on the main highway and got to the center of town, there would be a banner right in the town square that said "Greenville Texas: The blackest land, the whitest people." It was unapologetically there. African Americans would be standing on one side of the town square and whites would be standing on the other. African Americans knew they were not to come over to the other side. When I was in seminary, my mother, who was from Kosciusko, Mississippi, was driving back to Mississippi with my father. They went through Greenville and mother sent me a postcard with that banner on it! I mean, she did it with all innocence. But, that's how inured you were in it. The banners are clearly down now. I kept that card in *Dogmatics III/4* for years, just to remind myself.

BB: In a way, it's equally as remarkable that you would develop an analysis of the blindness of one's own local culture. Would you say that card was the spark?

SH: Quite possibly. I think more the spark for me was working everyday with African Americans. African Americans and I did the same work. We depended on one another.

BB: The last thing I wanted to ask about race has to do with this problem of what appears and what doesn't appear in your memoir. You do talk about race during your time at Augustana, your first job that lasted three years. You were involved with the African American student movement. You advocated for the hiring of the first African American faculty. And you even made the contentious argument that this ought to be done even if it required lowering academic standards. But what you don't do is mention that you were involved in very similar issues for many more years at Duke, which had acute problems in this territory. You were part of highly contentious debates about the hiring of the first black faculty at the divinity school.

SH: That had already been done. That was well done by Bill Turner, my great colleague, and several others. Duke was integrated. But it doesn't mean we don't have a hell of a race problem. White privilege is a reality.

BB: It's got to be talked about.

SH: It's got to be talked about. It's got to be challenged. When Sam Wells first came to Durham, he was coming over for supper. So he was following me in his car, since when he left he wanted to be able to get back on his own. I pulled up at a stop-sign and there was a car in front of me with an African American lady in it. She was obviously lost. A car turned and she stopped him. It was an African American male. They sat there five minutes as he was trying to explain to her how to get to where she was going. And when we got home I said, "Now Sam, what you just experienced is your first lesson in racism." I said, "If that woman had been white in front of me, stopping in front of me to get directions, I would have honked her to go on!" But I said she was an African American lost in a white community, asking another African American how to get where she was going. I said the last thing in the world I was going to do was to honk at her to speed up. But that's racism! Once you have it, how you ever break through it is just a constant challenge. It's at that kind of interaction level. I mean, the politics and economics are very important, but how to negotiate all the time is just heart-rending, I think.

BB: So the not writing about it at Duke was in part the inarticulacy of not knowing what else to say in addition to what you'd already said in the memoir about your race experiences on the work site and Augustana?

SH: The problem that America confronts is the failure of the success of the civil rights movement. African Americans allegedly have won. King has his own holiday. Civil rights are in place. African Americans can move to the suburbs, have two cars, three TVs, and worry about Jews moving in. So we get to say, "What was a little slavery between friends?" What does it mean for a society to come to terms with a wrong that was so wrong that there's nothing you can do to make it right? I've always been deeply sympathetic with reparations. The question is how do you provide reparations without it harming those that receive them? The arguments that are now being made by people like Jennifer Harvey[58] explain why reconciliation is the primary strategy whites want to use to fix the relationship between whites and African Americans. But she makes the strong argument that reconciliation will always reward the powerful. I think you can give a richer account of reconciliation that may not involve that, but she argues strongly for reparations. I'm very sympathetic with that.

You know Martin Luther King's phrase that 11 o'clock on Sundays is the most segregated hour? How do you ever deal with that? If I were an African American, I'm not sure I'd want white people coming to my church.[59] They'd take over. Those are the kind of things I think about.

BB: Let's close the circle of this conversation by bringing it back to writing. One way to acknowledge white privilege is to resist writing too much about black people. Or if you don't know what you're doing, don't write about it. This would seem to connect again to the problem of writing as a form of work. It seems to me that it's important to come to terms with the question of how writing—even theological writing—can collapse from a good work into a hard work or even mere busyness. Do you know how we would recognize this collapse?

SH: No. I don't think we do. Also involved there is audience. I mean, writing is at once for an audience and creates an audience. I can't imagine being a white man writing for African Americans. Maybe for, but not . . . I can't imagine . . . I guess the word I'm struggling with is "with."

BB: Does that sort of blockage . . . You've often connected those sort of blockages and death. I'm wondering if our attitude toward death has something to do with the transition from writing as a good work down into a hard work, into not work at all and an evasion.

SH: It could be.

BB: Let me wrap this up provocatively by reading this passage which you quote from MacIntyre in *Naming the Silences*.

> If I have work to do in the world, the time will come when it is done; and when that time comes it is right to die . . . Each of us is permitted to occupy a certain space in time, a certain role in history; without that particular place and role our lives would be without significance. To recognize that it is our particularity and finitude that gives our lives significance can save us from being consumed by that terrible and destructive desire to remain young that preys on so many Americans.[60]

Does not writing about race mean you are ready to die?

SH: Yes. I think yeah. That's a lovely way to put it. Let me put it this way: I think the recognition that I do not have that much longer to live means there's nothing I can do to make up for what I haven't done and that is an appropriate acknowledgment of what it means to have a life close to death.

I'm not deeply tempted to think that somehow I've got to do something to make sure that I've done everything that I need to do to be well regarded. I'm not terribly tempted by that. I've done what I've done. It was the time that I lived. I'm very grateful for the time that I've lived, with its limits that have been limits in my own life.

BB: So in MacIntyre's language, the time can come when the work you have to do in the world is done, but does that mean that you'll stop writing?

SH: No. It is interesting. I like *The Work of Theology* that is coming out. I like the book on the Holy Spirit I've done.[61] But I find myself right now in a period where I'm not writing that much, and I'm not sure what I want to write. I mean, I've never done a lot of writing that I want to do. I've always done what people ask me to do. People continue to ask me to do things. I find myself increasingly drawn to writing that isn't within the intellectual problematics that we currently inhabit. I'd like to write something more like *Hannah's Child*! That's what I think, but I'm not sure what that means.

BB: I've heard you recently agree with Hans Reinders when he admitted that writing a novel had spoiled him as an academic writer, to which you said, "It was writing

Hannah's Child that spoiled me." Even if you don't know what's next, can you tell us how *Hannah's Child* reset your sensibilities as a writer?

SH: First of all, *Hannah's Child* reminded me that I am a writer and that writing *Hannah's Child* meant I could work on style and what style was appropriate to the subject. I say that *Hannah's Child* is someway between Dashiell Hammett and Hemingway because the sentences are short and punchy. I think academic writing is plodding, and it is hard to return to that. I think one of the reasons that I like sermons is that it is a different kind of writing.

BB: But given all we've talked about rhetoric shaping accounts of theology and life, that admission can't be entirely innocent, can it?

SH: No, no it's not. I made a rhetorical move recently that I really liked. I think I had said something like, "I try to make clear what I think, which involves the presumption that thinking is something you can know." Now that kind of turn is a rhetorical turn that is important, that people don't hang on to, but it is meant to be hung on to. People rarely attend to those kinds of moves.

BB: But if we do hang on to it, we can say that diagnostic traffic runs both ways. The guy who finds out he can't write academic prose any more has in your own terms just criticized his own life in very precise ways. A criticism of the grammar of his own life has been exposed by an unease with his prior literary output. To have written a book that you can't go back from has also to mean a shift in the way one is inhabiting the world.

You've recently beautifully explained why the theologian can never retire. Identifying with Barth you note that he "retired from teaching, but he could not retire from the subject that had gripped him from the beginning, that is, Jesus Christ."[62] You also perceptively note that it was this same fascination that had driven him out to explore so many domains of human experience, a roving, joyful promiscuity of interest in God's creation with which you also identify. I've always admired this in both of you: your sense that most contemporary theologians are not really brave enough to write theology in the tradition of our greatest precursors. I want to thank you for daring that. I mean it as a genuine thanks, which emboldens me to follow it by scolding you for having written this sentence later in the same chapter: "I confess when I think about the diverse topics I have addressed it not only makes me tired but it elicits in me a sense of embarrassment."[63] You're allowed to be embarrassed about having been dragooned into a witness for Jesus Christ, but not about where it has taken you, or are you?

SH: No, but what I'm embarrassed by is the range of subjects that I think I can make a judgment about! That's what I was indicating. What I find so remarkable about Barth is how the Christocentric center means, for Barth, that nothing human is foreign. There is a kind of humanism that pervades his prose that I should like to think, in some small way, I am gesturing toward too. I always say that my greatest strength is that there's nothing I'm not interested in and my greatest weakness is that there's nothing I'm not interested in. Theological reflection means you've got to reflect on it all.

BB: What that stance means is that you don't let yourself make the move that so often happens in theological conversations in which we say, "Oh, I'm just bracketing out those other complicated issues." You're forcing us to consider that as essentially an evasion.

SH: Oh yeah, I don't bracket anything out. No brackets!

BB: And that refusal to bracket out the complications, combined with your commitment to speaking about what people asked you to, is inevitably going to land you venturing judgments about things that are beyond your "expertise," isn't it? You're going to constantly be pushed several steps beyond where you're comfortable, especially if in addition you're committed to articulating the truth as you see it about a particular situation, even if you haven't done all the background research you would have liked to before the time comes to speak.

SH: And hope that a friend can tell me when I've got it wrong!

BB: I do hope that this project will serve a role in the work that you say is still open to you. I hope that our conversations will serve to make more intelligible for many what you mean with the description of rest:

> [I]f you have said anything well, you will discover new challenges you had not anticipated. You may not be sure how to go on but you must try. This can be very tiring, because like most people I would like to find a place to stop, or at least rest for a bit. A form of rest is available if you understand rest to be activity in which the end and the means are commensurate. Theologically the name for rest so understood is worship. Worship, moreover, is but another word for prayer.[64]

I hope that these conversations will make that sequence of words more intelligible in a fashion that is also commensurate with the actual content.

SH: Yeah, I think it has. It is fun. I've enjoyed it. I couldn't have done it if it weren't fun.

Chapter 2

CONTINGENCY, VIRTUE, AND HOLINESS

October 12, 2015

The discussion now turns to the metaphysical presumptions of Hauerwas's ethical thinking, foremost among them the God–creature distinction. This chapter sets the stage for several subsequent investigations of how Christians are to understand what it means to be creatures who cannot transcend their reliance on God's care and self-communication. Preliminary investigations into how this distinction positions the task of Christian ethics are pursued by asking about the role of revelation in the thought of Aristotle and Thomas Aquinas as well as the Old and New Testaments. Questions raised here about how these distinctions position divine and human agency and day-to-day Christian ethical thinking will be revisited in later chapters.

Contingency and Aristotle's social conservatism

BB: Let's move on to explore the ways you bend and co-opt language as it is being used in contemporary discussions and even in the texts from which you draw inspiration. In my view you often do this more creatively than most of your opponents and even your fans have recognized.

As our discussions unfold I also want to ask questions about how best to understand the relative weighting of different strands and themes in your work. We've been trained in different enough traditions that I find some aspects of your work to be difficult to penetrate and I want to take the risk of admitting the points at which I simply can't figure out what you're doing. I can probably even put that more strongly by saying that there are some black boxes in your thought where a lot of work seems to get done, but I can't figure out how you get the results you do. The risk of pursuing these moments of incomprehension is that we might end up not being intelligible to one another. But it's also possible that we will discover some exciting new insights, and at the very least I hope airing my perplexities will give you a chance to address perplexities that others also share about how your thinking works.

Let me begin with a simple question: Why are you so interested in contingency?

SH: I'm not just interested in contingency. Rather I assume that contingency is the bottom line for all thought. When I say I'm not interested in it, I assume that it begins with "In the beginning." Creation is a narrative of the contingency of all that is, because all that is is finite because God is infinite. So the ultimate contrast is between God and all that is.

I question in *Sanctify Them in the Truth*[1]—and I think this has not been noticed by anyone—whether the nature/grace distinction was a distinction we really wanted to sustain. I came, finally, to the conclusion that nature names all that which is not God but exists by the grace of God.

So, nature is a category fundamentally shaped by the language of contingency that begs to be displayed by creation. Now all that involves very strong metaphysical claims; all that is is contingent. "That all that is did not have to be" absolutely begs for narrative display, because you cannot show that all that exists exists by necessity. It exists, fundamentally, because of God's humanity in wanting us to be in existence. Thus the emphasis on contingency is a theological claim with metaphysical implications, that is, we can only know who we are by a story. The narrative is required because the relationship between contingent actions requires a narrative to be made intelligible. Contingency is the heart of so much that I do.

BB: Could we then say that, conceptually speaking, there is nothing other than God and contingency? If moral reflection can't desire to escape contingency, to confess this is no warrant to leap the gap from the contingent to God.

SH: Of course.

BB: What seems to me crucial to note about this starting point is how in the metaphysics that results, time is given a much more prominent role. Only amid the sequences of contingent happenings that constitute creaturely existence can we know and respond to God.

SH: I worked hard on the chapter in *The Work of Theology* on time,[2] because, as Augustine observed, most of the time we think we know what we are talking about when we talk about time until we try to say what we think it is. As Augustine observed, time is not the past and it's not the future and it's not the present. But I think of time, fundamentally, as an aspect of everything that has duration and so demands narrative display for it to be rightly known. This is why time is constitutive of life itself in a way that invites the necessity of truthful stories.

BB: Why does such a claim unsettle people so badly? An extraordinary number of attempts have been made to erect a solid bridge across the gap between God and the contingent.

SH: It's the hunger for certainty. But contingency means you can never have the certainty that removes the knowledge that we are contingent beings. Many people find that an extraordinarily frightening set of claims, but I think it's an invitation to enjoy life as God gave it to us, namely, to take joy in the very fact that we exist. And that joy is an invitation to others to *be*, quite literally.

BB: It is very illuminating to suggest joy as the Christian answer to the search for rational certainty so characteristic of modernity since at least Descartes. This raises the question of how the joy that stabilizes Christian action is to be understood. Sometimes I wonder whether or not you feel the abyss that's under human life, which, for instance, is on the surface in a thinker like Nietzsche but doesn't seem to appear in Aquinas at all. It seems to me that if we really believe it's contingency all the way down then our living is suspended over a sort of nothingness and sustained only by God's merciful hand. We affirm this each morning in morning prayer, of course, taking up the psalmist's words: "Our days are but as grass. We flourish as a flower in the field, for as soon as the wind goes over it it is gone and its place will know it no more" (Ps. 103:15–16). Sometimes I think our vocation as theologians and especially as ethicists should make us especially aware of the ephemerality of our creaturely existence because we occupy such an odd and easily unseated position within the dominant rationality of the academy—even though we ethicists have developed our own potent ways of evading that vulnerability.

My main question, then, has to do with how the certainty you are talking about relates to your fondness for Aquinas. On the surface his world exudes a coolness and stability that seems to rest on the stability of his rational apprehension of God. In this sense it seems the antithesis to Nietzsche, whose whole account of joy is designed, like yours, to imagine what "going on" looks like if we do not try to base certainty on the illusory quest to find and understand the foundations of reality.[3]

SH: I don't think that's a right reading of Aquinas. I think Aquinas is a very open-ended thinker. The *Summa* is "looser" than it seems. By "loose" I mean he had the ability to reflect on a huge range of subjects without thinking he had to get it all absolutely right. The disputational style means you can always add another objection, which may really be an objection.

How I think about these matters is you can never get used to routine in a way that you lose the very wonder that we exist. I always think of Chesterton's example in Orthodoxy about the difference he discovered when he left behind his scientific education.[4] Of course, he didn't literally leave it behind, but he saw its limits. In science you believe a thing is green because it is filled with chlorophyll. But what he argued is that what you needed is a child's view of leaves; namely, isn't it wonderful that the leaf is green when it could have been purple!

That kind of wonder at the sheer difference of things is what I've tried to elicit. Obviously Hopkins is in the background, how he understood the sheer *thatness* that this is the way this is to be. Allegedly he got that from Scotus, but I just think it's a beautiful, poetic insight. That "isn't it wonderful that it is green because it could have been purple?" is the start of a narrative. That, I think, is very important.

BB: The background to this whole discussion we're having is a question about how what we say relates to whom we are saying it. I was provoked by Jonathan Tran's question to me at Baylor six months ago about the place of conversation in the doing of theology. That has been a useful question to me because I now realize that if we agree with you that it's contingency all the way down, then it's contingency all the way down in our own tradition.

SH: That's true.

BB: Well that means the scholastic impulse to get everything all lined up and in order is fundamentally an illusion.

SH: Yeah, absolutely.

BB: Which leads us to the conclusion that in fact the only way we can do theology is dialogically. Like yesterday, I appreciated your feedback on my lecture that you didn't think there was enough Christology in it, because I'm confident that I could, in the light of feedback, put as much in as necessary. A much under-discussed aspect of what is uniting the way you and I and some other people like Hans Ulrich do theology is a deep awareness that the space of theological argumentation is very fluid and that what we choose to emphasize for a given audience in a given moment is a constant judgment call. You have to get the acoustics of the different claims you present orientated to one another knowing that they can always be put together in a different way.

SH: Right. That's the reason why you never finish. You never finish!

BB: Let's bring in MacIntyre at this point, because you so often draw on him when discussing these themes. I am thinking of passages where he points to a game like cricket in order to illustrate the contingency and narrative structure of morality. You can only know what counts as a move in a game if you've noticed the rules and social space that is the game, but that is only the *condition* of an appropriate play in the game of cricket. This displays why ethics can never tell you what *you* should do. MacIntyre usually concludes these sort of examples with claims about our contemporary state of moral inarticulacy. He says in *A Short History of Ethics* "[W]e can imagine a society in which traditional roles no longer exist and the consequent evaluative criteria are no longer used, but the evaluative words survive."[5]

SH: It's great you discovered that quotation, because of course, that quote is the beginnings of what climaxes in the beginning of *After Virtue* with the disaster, and all you have left is fragments. He was thinking that in *A Short History*.

BB: Yes, it's very deep in his thought, and you picked it up very early. It is a view that shaped the metaphysical position, as you've just set out, in which time, contingency, and narrative position ethics—a positioning you and MacIntyre share. Perhaps this helps me to understand what's at stake in your correction of how I'm reading Aquinas, because in MacIntyre's account the decline of narrative into freewheeling, leftover, fragmentary moral language assumes a rapidly changing social context as its premise. Thinkers who experienced life and thought as undergoing rapid social or conceptual change have to be very creative in framing their language. I think we see this in Machiavelli or Nietzsche or contemporary thinkers like the pragmatists or Phillip Bobbitt. So I can see how a MacIntyrean reading of Aquinas would warrant a "looser" reading of Aquinas's work.

That said, even though Aristotle admits that theoretical reason is engaged with "that which could not be otherwise,"[6] he has little use for using that knowledge to frame ethical judgment. This loosening of the connection between theoretical and practical reason is a plausible point at which to locate his attraction to an ethics that is almost entirely framed as a response to local contingencies. One gets a very different feel for how these two forms of knowledge locate ethics in Aquinas. That's where my confusion is coming from that has prompted me to ask why you are attracted to thinkers who want a domain outside of time from which to gain some ethical orientation.

I'm getting now that this is what you are disputing—in fact you're not interested in Aquinas as a thinker with a metaphysics of stability because you don't think he has one. But it is hard for me not to read Aquinas as permitting historical change in certain aspects of his account while very stringently ruling it out at the most important levels. You can argue with me about that reading of Aquinas, but that's a pretty obvious way to read him, as so many natural law thinkers have done. At least the rhetorical positioning of his theology assumes the stability of the eternal essence. Modern thinkers like MacIntyre, influenced as he is by Marx, differ here quite radically in seeing historical change as utterly fundamental to all thinking, especially to ethical thinking. How would you position yourself in relation to the language of metaphysical stability?

SH: As you observe, I started reading MacIntyre when I was working on my dissertation. His essays in the philosophy of social science about action were particularly important for me. I probably borrowed at least as much from him as I did from Murdoch about the centrality of activity for how one thinks about communities of the virtues. I think Alasdair's "historicism" is very close to how I think about these matters. Underneath both the development of his understanding of the virtues and of the situation that we're currently in is an account of action as activity that resists the idea that you can survive the world in which we currently exist.

I read Aquinas like Alasdair. He reads Aquinas as a thinker who always assumes that he is engaged in an ongoing inquiry which presupposes an objection can be made, given the disputational style, which may transform the whole article in terms of what is said to be the "agreed-upon." The *Summa* so looks like everything is a set piece, but you have to remember that the *Prima Pars* has to be read in the light of the *Tertia Pars*. Then Christology has to be brought forward at the beginning, and so it is going to be much messier than is usually assumed to be the case, because you think, "Aha! You set it up and you prove the existence of God and then you can say something about the

Trinity and then you can say something about human acts, and so on." I think he didn't think he was establishing grounds that way. He was just beginning in the middle.

I learned so much of this from David Burrell. That he was beginning in the middle had everything to do with David Burrell's location of Aquinas on action, that it is Aquinas's understanding of act in which the means and the end are inseparable, forming activity that shapes the habits that become the virtues that help us acknowledge that God is God and we are not. So I see Aquinas working in a much looser fashion than so many Thomists.

BB: Which would, for instance, make you resistant to taking the Treatise on Law[7] as an apparatus for bridging the contingent and eternal?

SH: Right. First, the Treatise on Law is not the Treatise on Natural Law. The contingent character of the law is clearly on display when he talks about, for example, justice. What kind of punishment do you give to someone who's stolen a sacramental vessel in contradistinction to just stealing someone else's cup? Aquinas knows the very description of the seriousness of the actions of stealing a sacramental vessel depends on historical circumstance! It is how custom informs the nature of law that is at the heart of the Treatise on Law. A moral conclusion about the seriousness of stealing a sacramental vessel, in comparison to just stealing a vessel, depends on the practices of the church that are not written in stone, so to speak. They are discoveries that help us better be faithful. I just don't read Aquinas as trying to turn morality into "that which cannot be other."

BB: Might that also suggest that, in the Treatise on Law, the eternal law could be understood as the premise of the practical reasoning we might be doing, but it doesn't produce the content?

SH: Right. Exactly. Who wouldn't want to avoid evil?

BB: A claim that is both materially empty and yet formally crucial.

SH: Right. It's very basic but it gets you started. It doesn't tell you what to do.

BB: Would you see that as similar to the role played by the beatific vision in the Treatise on Habit?[8]

SH: I hadn't thought about that at all, but it makes a lot of sense to suggest that.

BB: Let's go back then to the other two sources in this discussion, MacIntyre and specifically MacIntyre's reading of Aristotle. Then I want to bring in the New Testament.

MacIntyre has been such a strong influence on your understanding of virtue that it is easy to forget that he had a remarkably robust set of criticisms of Aristotle. The most important of which is that Aristotle was incredibly culturally conservative, and he wasn't this incidentally but essentially.[9] Because he defined the highest form of life as that of the speculative philosopher, he was bound to defend the ethics and politics of the privileged classes. And he in fact lived out this ethic by tutoring the son of the ruler who was in the process of destroying the political community as he knew it.[10] So not only was he a "quietist in terms of political activity,"[11] but he was the sort of "ego-centered"[12] "prig"[13] who could suck up to the ruling patricians, and humorously in a British context, as he makes these criticisms he explicitly, and pejoratively, links this attitude in Aristotle with the modern ideal of the English gentlemen—who one imagines made up a significant part of the audience of one of your favorite novelists, Trollope.

SH: Trollope was not read primarily by English gentlemen, because most English gentlemen were too stupid to read. Trollope was read primarily by women, like most of the eighteenth-century novelists, and Trollope knew it and certainly tried to write for them. He had a very sympathetic view of women because they either had to be married or their lives were over. As a matter of fact, it's not accidental that MacIntyre made Jane Austen the heroine of *After Virtue* because he likes her calculated anger. He doesn't think Trollope is anywhere close to that. If you read a book like *The Way We Live Now* you can see Trollope really juxtaposing the kind of social order represented by the great English craftspeople and farmers who were Trollope's real heroes. The latter were challenging the growth of an industrial civilization. So Trollope, while certainly a long way from Marxism, could be read as at least not unsympathetic to some of the Marxist themes in MacIntyre.

It's interesting that I don't think he would write that passage in *A Short History* about Aristotle being the ultimate prig now. I think that he has a richer understanding of Aristotle. But all of that is but side comment before addressing the issue of whether his very way of thinking about the nature of the virtues doesn't play into the hands of establishment people who want to keep the craftspeople in their place. And the answer is: Probably.

In Trollope, one of my favorite characters is Madame Max Goesler in the Palliser novels. They are oftentimes called the political novels. No one knew where she came from exactly, but she was from Eastern Europe and she seems to have come from an established family but she looked quite Jewish. She is the ultimate exemplar of the gentleman in Trollope, and I think he knew this. One of the characters in *Phineas Finn* is the Duke of Omnia, who had never done anything other than be ready to serve the Queen, because if he had done anything, he might not have been ready if the Queen had called! And the Queen never called! But he wanted to marry Madame Max Goesler because he saw how admirable she was. Trollope's making fun of the upper classes at that point, I am sure.

BB: I take the essence of MacIntyre's early criticism to be that it is almost impossible to read Aristotle's theories as anything other than justifications of the ruling classes, given his high emphasis on practices in shaping the virtuous life. What, in the shortest form, would be your retort to that complaint?

SH: That it doesn't have to be.

BB: Where's the seam we can pull apart to separate his account of virtue from this elitist politics?

SH: That the servant knows the master better than the master can ever know the servant. That's Hegel's master/slave relation. And I think that's certainly true.

BB: The structure of that answer strikes me as not unlike your way of reading Thomas. Many people might have looked to the beatific vision and the eternal law as ways to make the leap out of the contingent into the eternal, and to do so would parallel a reading of Aristotle that understands him to be presenting philosophy as something done by a little club of the elite looking to expend their leisure time usefully. Aristotle himself seems to be of two minds about this end-point.

SH: In terms of Aristotle scholarship, it depends on what you do with Book X and the whole emphasis on contemplation. I think Book X doesn't fit with his account of the virtues. The contemplative thinking about "that which cannot be other" bonds with other contemplative thinkers who are also thinking about that which cannot be other. I think this is Aristotle's attempt to beat contingency. It was necessary because he didn't have a politics that he knew he needed.

BB: In terms of not actually being in a *polis* that satisfied his own criteria of a good polis?

SH: Right. So the emphasis on contemplation was the escape from the loss of any politics that was sufficient. Amélie Rorty fairly persuasively argues that it is anomalous that Book X exists at all when compared to books IV, V, VI.[14]

BB: That reading makes a lot of sense. And it would be especially anomalous when *Ethics* is supposed to be Part I and *Politics* is Part II. Book X could also be read as the off-ramp if you're not going to ever get to live out the politics.

SH: Right. Exactly. That's exactly right.

And in Book X, if you think of VIII and IX on friendship also as a way of trying to provide an alternative politics—a politics that should exist but doesn't—then contemplation is the way to try to survive outrageous fortune that might kill a friendship. If both friends are determined by that understanding of contemplation, then there's the possibility that even if you are beset by outrageous fortune you can maintain your friendship.

BB: Could you comment further on one of MacIntyre's other more fundamental criticisms of Aristotle; that he was constitutively narcissistic? At least in the *Short History of Ethics* this criticism is linked with the accusation that Aristotle has an essentially Pelagian blindness to the If problem of misguided desire.[15] Sometimes it sounds like you would want Christians to embrace what MacIntyre calls the basic question of ancient ethics, "What am I going to do if I am going to fare well?"[16]

SH: I think that's a useful heuristic question to get people under way to have a reflective stance vis-à-vis their life. While it may invite a kind of narcissism, any strong enquiry into what makes our lives worth living can suggest some very critical reflections about how we are living. Therefore, what makes a life *eudaimonistic* is not a question that Christians must avoid because what makes a life *eudaimonistic* can be something as simple as you will never be *eudaimonistic* if you try to avoid the suffering that having strong moral convictions will probably entail. That's an invitation to strong judgment about oneself that is compatible with being a Christian.

BB: Does it admit the debate or ought we to admit the debate, "Maybe I'd fare better if I didn't have strong moral convictions?"

SH: Well, that's one debate that would be well worth generating, if we could! I do think that people are afraid of having strong convictions today.

BB: Life certainly seems to go more smoothly in at least the short and middle term with less strong convictions. How else would utilitarian and consequentialist modes of reasoning become our dominant modes?

SH: It's clearly a bourgeois ethic! Or at least the way it works out most of the time. It's a bourgeois ethic that asks how I can get through life with as little suffering as possible, given the fact that there is nothing that I deeply care about. My problem with those kinds of lives is, "God, how do you stand the boredom of it!" If we weren't Christians, Brian, what would we end up doing? Drinking, screwing, and dying!

I think that you see the results of the attempt to avoid strong convictions in the avoidance of having children today. I've always regarded the debates around abortion as a failure to get at what's really at stake. And what's really at stake is people's lack of confidence that they have lives worth passing on to future generations. So, abortion really is a nihilistic practice that says we're not going to impose the meaninglessness of our lives onto future generations. That's really a very sad result.

The supposed lesson of the Wars of Religion was that if we could just get people to not take themselves so seriously, then maybe they wouldn't kill anyone. Well, they end up killing their children. I have a lecture I used to give on the yuppies as the monks of modernity, because the yuppies really have an ascetical discipline; they would rather have a boat than a child. So they discipline themselves not to have children exactly because why would you want children when you would rather have a boat? What strikes me about such a way of living is it is just so sad.

I regard one of the great moral witnesses of the last centuries as refusal of Jewish people to let Christian persecution stop them from having children. That they would have children in the face of Christian hatred was an extraordinary faith in God, because it's not that you've got faith in your children turning out OK, it's that you have faith in God, who would have the Jewish people be for the world a sign that God will not give up on us.

BB: Let me raise a theme that I suspect is going to remain an important subtext in our discussions to come: to what are we committing ourselves as Christian theologians or ethicists if we embrace Aristotle's approach, however re-formed?

Let me continue my strategy of asking the obvious questions by simply noting the distance between Aristotle and the New Testament. Commenting on the destructive factionalism in the Corinthian church, Stephen Barton has highlighted how the hierarchical social assumptions which permeated Greek understandings of wisdom and ethics were bound to generate the sorts of factionalism we see in early Christian contexts like the Corinthian church.

> Insofar as this kind of wisdom [of the elitist Greek philosopher] reinforces the hierarchical, patriarchal, and factional nature of ancient society as a whole, it is conservative of the status quo, and, in some of its expressions, quite pessimistic. On the other hand, to the extent that a particular tradition places its emphasis on revelation and inspiration, there is the possibility that wisdom of a more innovatory and even countercultural kind may take shape.[17]

I'm guessing you'll have some worries about this contrasting of the inner conservatism of Greek ethics with revelation as the fundament of a countercultural politics. How would you recast the issue at stake? Again a cursory reading would suggest that it's not too controversial to suggest that early Christianity was habitually more countercultural than the Greek philosophical tradition in its late iteration that Aristotle represents.

SH: And of course the influence of Platonism or neo-Platonism being so strong.

BB: In the early church?

SH: Well it was somewhat influential in the early church, but I am thinking primarily about someone like Augustine and how strong the neo-Platonists exercised their influence on him. They taught him the essential distinction between the transcendent One and all that is. There's a wonderful passage where he says, "I could have just stayed a Platonist, but they knew not the humility of the Christ."[18] So it was pride, interestingly, that allowed him to locate what was wrong with both the neo-Platonist—they didn't know Aristotle very well—and what would later be criticisms of Aristotle. It wasn't some cosmological picture, it was how that picture legitimated a certain kind of pridefulness that the Fathers, I think with one voice, called into question.

Of course, the Greeks had no way of accounting for revelation. But what's revelation? Your mother told you about Jesus. It's an invitation to be drawn into a life that was otherwise unimaginable. What it means to say revelation is what Barth emphasized, namely, that the knowledge of God is God's knowledge. So that's the way I think about these matters, Brian, and I think probably I've never made it as clear as I should.

Did anything I just said surprise you?

BB: No. It didn't surprise me, but I think the utility of this conversation is connecting things together so that certain moves that you've constantly assumed and draw upon get forced to the surface. Your quip that revelation is your mom telling you about Jesus may help to answer questions that many have had but not been entirely clear about how you would answer. And yet I still suspect there's an important grain of truth in Barton's position that deserves further comment.

If habit is all we have to say about the formation of the Christian life, how do we explain the wacky things that Christians got up to doing very quickly in the first century? But if we say they started doing those things because they heard some stories from somebody else and those stories captured them, then we can call that capture revelation and we don't need to invoke some sort of special stage-lighting for any of that. But it remains the case that there is something different going on that makes the New Testament countercultural witness function but which is not admitted in Aristotle's world.

SH: That seems right. Basically, with Aristotle and Plato both, how can you imagine that which is transcendent showing up in this man Jesus? That couldn't be imagined.

BB: It's just impossible.

This question was provoked for me by Carlo Natali's account of Aristotle's social location. He lays out how Aristotle's philosophy was an intervention in complex intergroup disputes about what it meant to be a philosopher. Socrates had really created problems for those who wanted to be philosophers by being so politically subversive. In order to protect their communities of study, philosophers thus faced a struggle apologetically to defend their way of life as not undermining the political authorities. Natali points out that Aristotle becomes what MacIntyre calls a prig because he is part of a third generation that had developed very nuanced ways of regularizing and defending these little groups of people who look like nothing more than associations of wealthy people forming little clubs that aren't producing anything and are talking in ways that threaten the governing powers.

SH: I'm not sure I entirely agree with that account of Aristotle. Aristotle was as impressed as Plato was that the Athenians killed Socrates. So he knew that there was corruption in the social order in which he found himself, and I think he was deeply attracted to Sparta.

BB: I'm happy to agree. The point that I am trying to bring forward is slightly different. Aristotle's distancing himself from that earlier Greek tradition makes him look distinctly like a secularizer. The reason why Socrates refused to take payment for his teaching was that he understood his teaching of philosophy to be compelled by the gods. It is not overstating the case to say that for him philosophy was essentially *witness*. How could *he* take money for *their* wisdom? Now clearly there is a god functioning in Plato's work in a very obvious way, but there is none of this talk of co-option by the god. In Aristotle's view of philosophy, "in contrast, there is no tendency at all to missionary proselytizing, to conceiving one's choice of a life of philosophy as a witnessing involving not only narrowly intellectual work but also the entire personality of the subject."[19]

On Natali's telling Socrates looks a lot more like Jesus than anything Aristotle wants to call philosophy.

SH: That was seen by the church Fathers. They compared them all the time.

BB: So again, the question is how he understands wisdom and practical reason to relate to revelation. This is in addition to the question of how his practice shapes him as someone who is not really very countercultural. And we still have the third question about how to read his "secularizing" impulse to say that ethics demands our taking responsibility for our lives—with any talk about the gods understood to be undermining the taking of moral responsibility.

That's the opposite of Socrates, whom, as you say, Christians admired.

SH: All that seems right to me. I don't have any commentary on that.

Subversives and prophets in Israel and Greece

BB: OK then, let's continue this discussion by taking up a little-known biblical story in which we see how many of Israel's institutions were ordered by the assumption that revelation was a regular part of communal life.[1] I'm proposing probing your understanding of the relationship between natural and revealed theology by discussing an entertaining version of what seems to me to be an entirely characteristic biblical vignette in 1 Kings 22:1–28.

It's war time, and the king of Israel is looking at the storm clouds gathering, knowing that soon the enemy troops will be coming over the hillside. As the kings tended to do, he asks the prophets what the outcome is going to be if he takes up this particular gauntlet. All the prophets cry out in one voice, "Go ahead! You'll be victorious, so get on with it!" The king has only one more question: "What about Micaiah? What does he say?" And the prophets say, "Well, don't ask him because he never says anything you want to hear." So the king calls for Micaiah to ask what he thinks. Before Micaiah goes in to the king, the other prophets take him aside and warn him, "Look, we've already signed off on this one. You need to tell the king what he wants to hear." But Micaiah says, "I'm not going to do that. I'll tell him whatever the Lord gives me." To add to the comedy value, when he comes before the king the king says, "What's going to happen?" and Micaiah says, "Well, you're going to win." The king suspects that can't be the truth so he asks again, "Really?" And then Micaiah comes out with a suitably bloodthirsty account, which includes the death of the king and scattering of Israel's armies. And, he concludes in a sort

---

1. This is one of the sections, flagged in the Introduction, where the words on the page can lack the dynamism and urgency of the conversation as it flowed. Brian's tentative and speculative tone is met by Stanley's enthusiastic responses that are clearly prodding him onward.

SH: The image of the sheep being scattered!

BB: Yes. The theme of God's people being scattered on the hillsides so regularly taken up by Jesus in the Gospels is palpable here. And of course the king is pissed off about it, and he throws Micaiah into prison and decrees that he will be given only bread and water until he comes home in peace. And Micaiah's last line is fantastic: "If you return in peace, the Lord hasn't spoken by me."

    I want to read that story as articulating a set of premises that differ dramatically from Aristotle's intentional minimization of the role played by the *daimon* or any orientation of human action by oracles. Israel has a very, very different starting point. Because they have such a different starting point, they've had to develop a whole set of practices and institutions for discerning the spirits. Because this has become institutionalized in such highly elaborate ways the stage is set for the sort of conflict we see in this passage, not only between the different prophets, but also between the prophets and the king. The God of Israel was understood as an agent who had constantly to be reckoned with, and was *expected* to speak, though obviously not terribly often, or you wouldn't get false prophets being so bold. It seems to me that one of the implications of denying that interplay is to falsify the biblical witness at important points.

SH: Let me ask you: isn't there something else going on here? The king of Israel would like the king of Judah to join too? Jehoshaphat, right? Does the prophet Micaiah come from Judah or Israel?

BB: Oh man, don't ask me historical critical questions!

SH: Think of the various bands of the prophets; then think of Amos's "I'm no prophet nor the son of a prophet." These were set, institutional roles in Israel, obviously. And what you had to say depended on whether you were in Israel or whether you are in Judah.

BB: So Israel is not immune from the Constantinian problem?

SH: Exactly! That's what I was trying to consider. Is Micaiah uttering revelation in a way that is different from natural knowledge?

BB: I think Micaiah is a participant in one of the strands of Israelite practice that clearly included obscure divination practices we can't fathom like the Urim and Thummin. These sanctioned versions of divination were presumed not to be beholden to the many false gods, but were ways of listening to the one true God. Micaiah very clearly takes the role of the prophet and doesn't promise to produce revelation, but promises to invite revelation and then is happy to put his hand up and say "I have received revelation." And to stake his life on it. This looks to me like an example of what we've just called in our modern parlance "acting on the basis of a strong moral claim."

SH: And then we have one prophet saying one thing and then another said another until a spirit came forward and stood before the Lord, saying, "I will entice him." "How?" the Lord asked him. He replied, "I will go out and be a lying spirit in the mouth of all his prophets." Then the Lord said, "You are to entice him, and you shall succeed; go out and do it." So you see, the Lord has put a lying spirit in the mouth of all these your prophets; the Lord has decreed disaster for you.[20] There's an intimacy between Micaiah and the Lord that's really quite something! They were plotting together!

BB: I read Micaiah's presentation of the oracle as very similar to the opening drama in Job where God and the tempter debate his fate. The tempter is plotting with the Lord and Micaiah is just relating that tale. The oracle is that he's overheard this interchange, he's had a vision of this interchange.

SH: Is the knowledge of the false prophets in this story natural knowledge?

BB: I think we have to say that they do not have knowledge. They are playing with the trappings, much in the way we can ask questions about charismatic ritualism today. They are pretending to possess the oracle, speaking in the genre of Oracle Speech, but they have no oracle.

SH: And they are suck-asses for the establishment!

BB: It plays straight into the Constantinian game, because if you don't really have an oracle, then what else are you going to do except dress nice, sound articulate, and try to speak with assurance as you tell the king what he wants to hear? The drama assumes both the premise that the king needs the oracles and that there are institutions set up both to receive the oracles and to govern and that those can collapse in specific ways, ways that you yourself have emphasized. What I want to bring into view is the question: What are we doing when we say we need to speak back to power if we, in principle, deny this sort of revelatory engagement?

SH: Well, we don't want to deny, in principle, such revelatory engagement. Do we? Neither you nor I, I think, could say, "What I've just said is, 'Thus saith the Lord.'"

BB: I wouldn't do it, for a range of reasons I think we would share, and I'm worried about our tribe of theologians being attracted to the role and many of the mannerisms of the false prophets depicted here. That's a big part of why I'm interested in what sort of content the Christian ethicist is supposed to be conveying. And more personally, I can't explain the way I've lived my life without being pretty convinced I've once or twice had the Lord rap me on the chest to say, "This is what I want from you."

SH: I don't think I think that though! I don't mean to suggest that I think God hasn't been present to me and made me more than I ever could have imagined I could be, in terms of having a role that has been important for other people, which I take as a great, great gift. But I've never felt that intimacy. I understand that people do. I don't. I just thought maybe that if I had that kind of intimacy I wouldn't necessarily be a theologian.

BB: What do you think you might have been?

SH: I don't have any idea. I might have been a bricklayer! Paula has that kind of intimacy. Timothy Kimbrough does. I think Clark French does, my rector. It just doesn't come to me. That's not anything I regret, it's just the way it works. Now how to tell the story? I have to believe God has been present when I was fourteen or fifteen and called me to the altar to dedicate my life to God. I certainly think God was there, but I don't feel it.

BB: The reason it seems methodologically important to have this discussion is stories like this one from Kings remind us that the people of God present us with a rich ecology of modes of engagement with God. The community could not exist as a community and be directed if there wasn't that diversity. In the most fundamental sense only Jesus continues to perform the roles of prophet, priest, and king. Otherwise, those are pretty separate roles. We might even speculate in a natural theological vein that the biblical traditions draw together traditions of sensitivity to God in a manner not unlike the collections of sayings co-opted from the other nations by Israel to form the wisdom traditions.

There is no reason to deny the phenomenon of wisdom traditions among the nations nor to make the opposite move, to say that Israel's wisdom traditions were somehow just collations of worldly wisdom utterly unaffected by revealed religion. The latter is the more common mistake. I strongly suspect it is this ecology of sensitivities to how God makes the people of God who they are that is behind what appears to be an oddly detailed picture of the body of Christ that Paul develops in 1 Corinthians 12. On what grounds does he come up with this account of the many gifts sustaining the faithful community he now calls the body of Christ if he's not re-presenting a Christian account of the tradition of Israel? For those of us thinking about how the church should live today, the implication seems to be that we need to be careful not to universalize our own place in that ecology by the way we describe the Christian life of faith. There are not an infinite number of roles in the ecology of the body of Christ, but it *is* quite diverse, and we're all tempted to say that our experience explains how it works.

SH: A very deep challenge! A very deep challenge.

But that's fun, how to think through a passage like that.

I always think, how remarkable it is that the people of Israel could tell such extraordinary stories that were not complementary!

BB: I'm sure we agree that it would be a delight if we could have Christians today who could be counted on to say, "Don't go ask him! You know what he's going to say to the ruler!" But such stories are a challenge to those of us who could be called on in that way and yet are totally unpracticed in thinking about our relationship to God in a manner that would allow us to have the certainty Micaiah displayed. That's just an observation about where we are. It must be a dangerous place for the church to be, that we're not certain about what God asks of us at specific times and places.

SH: I agree.

And, those people that seem to have that, we distrust. Can you think of anyone you know that has it?

BB: Given our location at the end of Christendom I would expect that anyone who publically claimed divine inspiration already to be ruled out as someone I'd point to in answer to your question. Maybe that's illegitimate on my part? I do believe that it has got to be right when Paul says the proof of the presence of Christ is action in Spirit and power and that where that does not exist, the story is over for the church. So I'd be inclined, and I'm totally speculating here, but I'd be inclined to be looking for people who seem to make witness-like movements with wisdom and some graceful assurance. I don't imagine that they would be free of internal turmoil and doubt as they do so. But your question points to why I sense that the problem of acting with certainty remains a burning one for Christians in a time when the only available public stances seem to be cynical-irony or propagandic-demagoguery.

SH: What do you make of Sam's arguments in *God's Companions* that the church is called to be prophet and priest, but not king.[21] Only Christ is king.

BB: I think I'd be inclined to say Christ's occupation of those roles is inalienable.

SH: For the church?

BB: Our priesthood is always, at best, a representation of Christ as priest. Are you OK with that?

SH: Yeah, I am.

BB: All the reasons that I think would lead you to deny that a human political authority could be said to be the ultimate ruler I think apply to the prophet and priest. That is a decisive complication to Israel's position, because they understood themselves, for salvation historical reasons, not as *mediating* prophets, priests, and kings but as *being* God's chosen prophets, priests, and kings.

SH: People do not notice, but in *The Peaceable Kingdom*, the Christology I developed there was in terms of the prophetic, priestly, and kingly offices. Even when we use the language of incarnation, prophet, priest, and king make clearer why Jesus is the recapitulation of Israel.

BB: Yes. And I think we need to use that Christological hermeneutic when we speak about the work of the Spirit.

SH: Oh, I'm sure.

BB: But we typically don't at all.

SH: Those are very good suggestions.

BB: If we start this way, all of a sudden the different institutions in Israel start to make a lot more sense. So the wisdom seers were those who had developed institutions of receptivity to the Father and the Son as Creator and the priests to this God as Redeemer. The prophets developed a sensitivity to the Spirit. The scribes discerned this God in Israel's stories and texts—but Christians confess that all of them were discerning the working of the one Holy Spirit.

SH: Sarah Coakley's systematic theology[22] is a very promising account of the third person of the trinity. There are moves she makes using Troeltsch I am not enthusiastic about, but I became convinced before reading her that Romans 8 is really the central pneumatological text on which we need to concentrate.

On MacIntyre and becoming holy

BB: Let's begin to wind down this conversation by asking how you would summarize the influence of MacIntyre on your work?

SH: Massive.

One: Alasdair helped me diagnose the world in which we're living. He also helped make clear that in order to think about the nature of the moral life you need to know something. He uses analytic philosophy but he knows as much as Hegel! It's quite extraordinary. I think that he also taught me how thought that has the ambition to be truthful probably has to take great risks. He's taken great risks. I admire that.

He wrote a letter for my retirement that I treasure. He said, "I am writing this letter to say not only how very grateful I am for all that your work has meant to me, but also how important it has been for so many in so many areas that you have presented a theology whose relevance could not be ignored. Most theologians make things too easy for unbelievers. You have succeeded in presenting them with a theology that it is very important for them to reject, if they are to avoid a peculiarly painful self-questioning. And most theologians make things too easy for believers too. Your work makes it clear how difficult it is to be a genuinely self-questioning believer. It is a remarkable achievement." What a letter.

Alasdair is such a big-brained guy. He can pull it off in a way that I know I will never be able to, but I can use him to help me pull it off.

BB: With this language of risk you've put much better the vulnerability of our work as ethicists that I was trying to name at the opening of our conversation today. You simply never know enough to talk about what people should do in a given place and in a given time. Anything you say can just be torn to shreds immediately by counterfactuals. One of the retorts that drive me nuts is if you say something like, "This is an unjust and destructive practice and we shouldn't do it," then you'll get "Well, there's a lot of good things we should embrace about that practice."

SH: Absolutely!

BB: I've always thought that the temptation in those sorts of judgments is the cowardice that underlies always being willing to say, "Well, I know some nice people."

SH: To people who make those kinds of retorts, I always want to say, "Do you think I'm stupid? Of course I know that! But that's not the way the argument is working."

I think, too, they don't get that if you say X about Y, it is oftentimes not a description so much as it is an invitation to be identified with that claim.

BB: Also, the "Do you think I'm stupid?" is tied to the observation that for most people who say, "I know a lot of nice white people in Ferguson," it is a type of false consciousness. False consciousness is the great enemy of any talk about morality. So the epicycle of argument that says, "Well you said X is bad but there's a lot of good in X" is inoculation against any investigation of false consciousness.

SH: That's a wonderful way to put it.

It's interesting to ask what's the difference between false consciousness and self-deception? I suspect they're closely aligned.

BB: Do you have a good answer?

SH: Well false consciousness is a Marxist category that implies we have a stake in ideological formations that keeps us from the acknowledgement of the world in which we find ourselves. Self-deception is more a complex phenomenon that involves our failure to spell out engagements that we enact. We do not spell them out because if we spell them out we would have to recognize that who we think we are is not who we are.

BB: I thought you didn't believe in definitions!

SH: I thought those were descriptions, not definitions.

My problem with definition is that it invites the notion that there is an essence to a word and I don't think there is an essence to a word. The Oxford English Dictionary gives you histories.

BB: Stories. It provokes narratives.

SH: That's much closer to what I want.

BB: So you think that self-deception is a more determinative than false consciousness because it offers us a way out?

SH: I don't know I want to say it is more determinative than false consciousness. They are both a dominant reality for us.

BB: All right, let's move from talking about your sources to open up some further questions about your own understanding of virtue that I am sure we will be discussing later at some length.

In *Christians among the Virtues* you insist that the key to keeping a Christian account of virtue Christian is a robust eschatology. I would at this point, again, refer to my reasons for pressing the question of content and method, because eschatology plays hell with method! You then criticize MacIntyre's account of virtue as too formally philosophical in that it need not end in any particular concrete community. The Christian story, in contrast, necessarily culminates in the communion of the saints, and thus the eschatological community must be understood as grounding any workable account of Christian virtue.[23] How does this positioning fit with the Aristotelian claim you regularly make, that "true happiness is possible only retrospectively"?[24]

SH: Because eschatology works primarily as a way of making retrospective judgments about what God has done. I suppose a better word might be providence. If you think of God's providential care of us, we always want to turn that into having some sense of where we're going, when in fact you only know where you've been retrospectively. So eschatology is a reading of God's work among us to save us from ourselves by giving us something to do. We only learn later what we've been doing. That's how I think I understand this relationship between a positioning of Aristotle and true happiness is possible only retrospectively as an eschatological claim.

BB: I'm reminded with that answer of Walter Benjamin's angel of the future who moves forward only by looking backward toward the wreckage of history.[25]

SH: It's a powerful image.

BB: Is that close to what you present?

SH: I think so.

BB: It's eschatological, then, in the sense that the Kingdom of Heaven is present but it's not pointing you over the hill to the next turn in the road?

SH: I think that's right. I think that's right!

The eschatology is the invitation to understand that God has never abandoned people and part of not being abandoned is you understand that time is on your side, finally, through God's good grace.

BB: That makes a lot more sense of your insistence that our current existence can by definition only be an artefact of God's care historically unfolded. This locates eschatology primarily in human activity of naming past actions as God and as real in the present in the sense of a "having been made aware" that can be taken as evidence of the work of the Spirit. How then does that fit with repentance and moral progress?

Another point you make in *Christians among the Virtues* is that "[i]t is the common testimony of the saints that as they draw closer to God, they are increasingly overwhelmed by the knowledge of their sin."[26] I think this is an accurate observation about much of the NT witness. But I wonder if it is an admission that creates more problems for a theory of virtue than you typically admit. Even in your formulation here there is an odd juxtaposition of two sorts of progress that are in some tension with one another, namely, progress in holiness, as measured against God's holiness, and progress in the saint's awareness of sin. This is a tension that is only heightened if we introduce, as you do, questions about how congruent our wills are with God's will.[27] My question, then, is this: can a Christian theory of the virtues work without claiming to make some progress in holiness?

SH: Well, I'm a Methodist so the question is, "Are you going on to perfection?" Going on to perfection is a development that always makes us acknowledge that sin is that from which we cannot will our way free. Sin is not so much what we do, it is more to be possessed in a manner that makes us enjoy our sin. I'm not surprised at all that the saints, exactly because of their holiness, are able to acknowledge and describe how they are possessed by modes of life that impede their holiness. Their holiness makes it possible for them to acknowledge that.

So, progress in holiness? I think that's a phrase that we cannot give up.

BB: Would you put your hand up yourself then and say, I'm holier now than I was 20 or 40 years ago?

SH: Should I trust myself to know that?

Holiness surely involves having a worry about whether I could know that. I think I'm wiser.

BB: Is that another way of saying more virtuous?

SH: It's a way of saying that I'm more grown up than I was, when I was younger!

I'll tell you, I think what I've discovered is the trick is not to know God, but to love God. I hope I've grown in that.

BB: That answer makes me less clear about whether we should agree with Aristotle that the task of ethics is to become more virtuous. Maybe it would be best to put this more concretely. You are famous for your cursing, and even justified it in your memoir as a way of resisting being co-opted by the pretentions of the academy.[28] And yet you no longer curse much these days. Would you cite this as an example of your becoming more holy and/or virtuous?

SH: No, it's just growing up. There was an article in *Lingua Franca* in which the big title was "Foul-Mouthed Theologian,"[29] and I just got tired of having that as a reputation. You would go out to give a talk and people would just be waiting for you to say "Fuck" at some point.

BB: It's like going to NASCAR for the crashes!

SH: I thought, "I don't want to live that way. I don't want to live with those expectations. It's just silly." I decided there were certain words that I cannot use.

I can still say them, but I cannot use them. I don't say "Goddamn," I don't say "Fuck you." I'll still say "bullshit," but that doesn't sound to me like it's very foul. I think I've been pretty good at restraining myself from that. It is true that when I grew up, working on building sites, that kind of language was just normal. "Goddamnit! I need some fucking mud on this board so get down here!"[30] It was just everyday language. It was part of going through Yale that I just didn't want to discipline myself to be a successful academic. That's silly in a way. I don't think it made me holier, I think it made me a bit more grown up. I've never liked, by the way, the judgment of some people that say, "People that use foul language have a limited vocabulary." Bullshit! I've been around some people who have extraordinary vocabulary who still need to say "Fuck you," so I don't think it is necessarily that. There are class presumptions involved all up and down those questions as well. I certainly don't think it made me more holy. Holiness, after all, is so associated with people who have learned to live in the most uninteresting place possible because they are so pious. How to have an image of holiness that is not confused with being squeaky clean is a challenge.

BB: Indeed. It's Pharisaism. It's having fences and fences and fences around the law. That's where "no dancing or drinking or sleeping with girls that do" came from; we're going to stay as far away as we can from things that might be bad. It now sounds like your unshakable commitment to the particular narrative means that, structurally speaking, the fact that narratives almost inevitably have surprises and ironic turns and unpredicted forks in the road and curves around which one cannot see, that's the deepest sensibility organizing your imagination of progress in virtue and holiness.

SH: Holiness, for me, is usually embodied in people who just know how to go on in the face of great difficulty.

BB: That's good. And I think your formulation "I think I've been pretty good" does hint that you've had to make an effort at reforming old habits?

SH: Yes, I did.

BB: But it doesn't sound like you would narrate that in the register of faith, in the sense that it needed repentance?

SH: No, I didn't really think it needed much repentance.

BB: It's useful to tease out how these things fit together. A lifetime of taking pleasure in colorful language is not given up in one fell swoop. So was it that you set your mind to it and just stopped?

SH: Yes, I did. It was pretty cold turkey. I made the decision, and I didn't fall off the wagon very much.

Chapter 3

Temperament, Habit, and the Ethics Guild

October 29, 2014, and October 12, 2015

The conversation now turns to questions about whether the theology and practice on display in an early academic performance by Hauerwas are explicable within the terms of his own account of virtue. It uncovers how significant aspects of his early position developed under the influence of the teaching and example of Paul Holmer, one of his professors at Yale. Previously little noticed parallels between Hauerwas's deepest theological instincts and the theologies of Kierkegaard and Barth emerge as well as how these instincts were combined with a Wittgensteinian account of language to yield Hauerwas's distinctive understanding of the task of Christian ethics.

Temperament and habit

BB: A decade after *Character and the Christian Life*[1] first appeared you wrote in the preface to the second edition, "I learn the most from others by attending not only to what they say but how they say it."[2] I'd like to begin our conversation by exploring how well you think such an approach illumines your own work. How close did you come in your early work to running afoul of the charge you make against Barth's ethics, which you then took to "exemplify a position whose substantive insights are constantly in tension with the conceptual categories used to express those insights"?[3]

I'm obviously putting the point provocatively, but I want to start by exploring this hypothesis: that your interest in offering a new approach to Christian ethics by retrieving an ethics of character simply doesn't describe very well what you actually were doing as an academic ethicist, or at least didn't describe what made your early work so powerfully provocative and, for so many, attractive.

Let's take as an example of this point your 1980 AAR talk in which you develop an early version of the thesis that religious ethics is really just about America.[4] In that talk, you set out a remarkably detailed typology of the main schools of religious ethics as it existed at the time in dominant American graduate schools. Such a performance seems to me to be difficult to explain in any direct way as emanating from any ethic of character that I can make much sense of. The paper is full of wit and wicked mockery and I can't imagine that it wasn't explosive when delivered before your peers and colleagues. It is a style that has caught a lot of peoples' attention, and emulated by some of your students and admirers.

For example, you suggested that each of the most important graduate schools for producing people with graduate degrees in ethics has a story that makes its students participants in an extraordinary adventure. Thus at Harvard the task is to help the rest of the world understand the significance of the voluntary institution and along the way develop an ethical theory such as the ideal observer meta-theory to defeat relativism and utilitarianism. In the process you now have a theory that accounts for the relation of religion to morality and why it never rains in Albuquerque. At Yale you learn that the central question is a question that can never be answered, "Why is religious ethics religious?" Union turns out people ready to take action which, means you probably do not trust Harvard or Yale people. At Chicago you learn the social sciences are crucial for discovering the signs of the times though it is primarily by reading the *New York Times* that one finds out what is going on.

Of course, each of these characterizations is a simplification, but one that cannot be denied. You seem to have a talent for that kind of work, and this speech is a paradigmatic instance of what has made your work most eye-catching. Would you object strongly to a reading that viewed this performance as something more than the defense you developed in your doctoral work of virtue ethics can account for?

SH: I think what I meant about Barth struggling against his conceptual machinery is that often the command language doesn't provide him with the conceptual tools he needs to negotiate the specific issues he takes up in *Church Dogmatics* III.4. That III.4 is bounded by his accounts of Sabbath and prayer is, I think, not contradictory, but certainly in tension with the language of command.

So, the question for me is whether the emphasis upon character would be analogously in tension with not only my more concrete casuistry, but with strong claims I developed about the church and how the church is the locus for giving an account of theological reasoning about the nature of the moral life. That could easily be the case. For example I always shudder when I'm introduced as someone who represents "virtue ethics."

I think character and the virtues are a secondary theme that I hope has allowed me to express how God's grace actually makes all the difference for how we understand our lives and how we must live in the world in which we find ourselves.

I used a word in that last sentence that I rarely use: "grace." I rarely use the word grace because it is oftentimes so associated with a generalized account that God accepts us. I worry that that generalized account too often does not do justice to the complexity of the narrative in which we should find ourselves embedded. As a result, grace is separated from Christology. Obviously, God is a God of grace, but that grace comes through the engagement of God with God's creation through the calling of Israel and the people who follow Christ.

So, those last claims I just made, I suspect—the language of character and virtue—must serve rather than be directly thought to be what I'm all about.

BB: That's already helpful. Let me follow up on one part of that observation by simply noting that Barth makes a not dissimilar point at the beginning of III.4 that I read as an indication that he's aware of the difficulty that you've pressed on him. What I have in mind is his provocative emphasis on the importance of ethicists daring to descend from the realm of general rules into the level of concrete observations about our here and now.[5]

For me, the reason I want to focus on the relation of the AAR speech to your early theoretical work is that it seems to me that the AAR speech is a paradigmatic act in this sense: it ventures a judgment not about general truths, but about the configuration of truths here and now. In doing so it explicitly presses the question, "Who are we?" and "In what location are we talking about ethics?" In order to appreciate how ahead of the curve you often were, historically speaking, it is not possible, in my view, to underestimate this aspect of your work. I think this sensitivity to the location of moral argumentation is visible throughout all the domains in which you tended to work.

I'm not proposing that you have to be historicized to be understood, but it does suggest that what you must never do when reading "Hauerwas" is to reduce your "message" (again in scare quotes) to a general program such as virtue ethics. This is in any case how I teach students to read your work. But in order to pursue such a reading meaningfully we have to grasp the methodological implications of performances like this AAR speech. We have to resist, on one hand, pigeonholing such acts as only of local relevance and, on the other, the quest to distil them down to a general message for every time and every place, which they would be if they were the "product" of some general method, as virtue ethics often purports to be. These seem to be some of the main ways that your work is falsified by various readers.

What I believe we're offered if we attend to this AAR performance is an instance of your presenting a particular non-universalizable judgment about a local context which has bite precisely to the extent that it names a reality that exists in the world, or at least can be recognized by the other people that you're presenting it to. This is why it still does not seem entirely clear to me how, even if we understand character to be a second-order concept, you are linking becoming a Christian with acquiring a character in any direct way in your early work.

You work with a toolbox, as every thinker necessarily has to. Put more pointedly, it's difficult for me to call the guy who pigeonholes and mocks the whole discipline in such a pointed and profound way someone that I should describe as having good character. On another level it is also difficult to see how any apparatus of character formation would have generated the guy that could make that speech. So I'm just trying to understand the role and power of naming situations in real-time, as they exist, and the connection of that naming with your emphasis on habit and formation.

SH: Let me try it this way: actually what the development of character names is the acquisition of a history that I'm ready to own. I used the language of character because I was unable to understand from Aristotle how to give an account of the unity of the virtues. I thought that character named how we are constantly engaged in being formed by what we do and do not do in a manner that gives a kind of coherence and integrity to our lives. Singleness is a word that invites many mistakes. But singleness suggests our lives are sufficiently coherent to make sense retrospectively of what we've done, in a manner that allows us to go forward. I take it that that singleness is embedded in the story we acquire through baptism. That gives us a narrative that makes possible the narration of our lives without self-deception.

Of course, one of the things I was trying to challenge in my early work is the idea that our lives are made up of decisions we make from one time to the next. That presupposes that those decisions are not necessarily related. And what I was trying to do was to remind us that though we live our lives prospectively, the most important things about us morally is retrospective judgment. We constantly must try to understand what we once did when we thought we knew what we were doing, but as we look back on it we now understand that the descriptions that we used to give us a sense that we knew what we were doing were clearly mistaken and we now need to redescribe our lives in the light of what we now are.

Now, that's a kind of formal description of what it means as a Christian to come to terms with the fact that, as we look retrospectively over our lives, we discover that what we thought we were doing virtuously is sin; and how we must claim that as us by confession and the willingness to be forgiven. Because forgiveness is a hard and dreadful thing. It means I must be ready to acknowledge that I don't get to make up the story that is my life. God gets to tell me who I am. It's that kind of move that I was trying to make.

Now, I suppose, what I was doing in that AAR address, besides having a lot of fun . . .

BB: Which it was! It's very funny.

SH: Actually, the background of that was there was a joke that was told when I was in seminary that if you asked a graduate of Union Theological Seminary a question, when Niebuhr and Tillich were there, the Union graduate would think just for a minute and say, "The answer to that question is 'One, two, three, four, five, six, seven, eight, nine, ten.'" They could always rattle off the correct answer.

If you asked the same question to a graduate of Harvard Divinity School, when James Luther Adams and people like that were in ascendancy, the Harvard graduate would think for a minute and start to say something, think for a minute, start to say something and then finally say, "I just don't know the answer to that question."

If you asked a Yale person the same question during the time of H. Richard Niebuhr, and in a way as Gustafson continued it, the Yale person would think for a minute, start to say something, think for a minute, start to say something, and then finally say, "I don't know the answer, but if you have these presuppositions, these are your alternatives!"

That's how we were taught to think. Namely, you expose all the alternatives. I tried to be a good Yale person, but I just have too many strong convictions to simply do that kind of analysis. I want to try—for myself and for anyone else that is interested—I want to try to understand how we are supposed to live, as Christians. And that means that it is not just, "Let me show you these propositions, given these alternatives."

And of course that's what is so offensive because Christian ethicists are supposed to be conceptual, we are supposed to clarify concepts. It's not clear that we are supposed to say, "Well, I think that was wrong!"

BB: We're not supposed to be ecclesial authorities, basically?

SH: No. But I think we do have to say, "Well, I think that was wrong. And if you want to be this kind of person, you can't do that anymore."

BB: This is all helpfully advancing toward the clarification I was looking for. Two points seem worth following up. The first is: you were trained like all those other people. You were trained in certain skills, certain habits of putting questions, and the reality is that the training does not account for the fact that you somehow were able to take a step back and start to watch how the landscape was put together. If all of our grad students did that, then we could just go and sit on the beach, right? It's one thing to teach people to come to terms with a literature. It's another thing for them to be able to turn and watch how people are deploying that literature and then use that insight to bend the discussion in different directions to advance some penetrating insight into their current landscape.

One of the reasons that move is so complicated is that we're implicated in it. That's what is so brilliant about the AAR performance in which you characterized the various schools of Christian ethics (to be treated in the next chapter). In fact, I wonder if your closing line of that lecture does not raise a question about the explanation you've just given me because you don't say "this is wrong" but end with a classic deflationary gesture, "But then that is what you would expect a Yalie to say!"[6]

SH: I'd forgotten that is how I ended the speech.

BB: If we take traditions as the forum in which we learn to think and name the world, it seems to me that your own academic tradition, the very tradition that you are questioning, does not offer you the resources to mount the challenge to all the dominant streams of academic ethics that you are prosecuting in the speech. It certainly doesn't explain your predilection for favoring strong moral positions because, as you've just pointed out, it's pretty resistant to making such strong claims directly.

SH: I assumed that part of what it meant to become a theologian is you ought to have something to say. I probably was insufficiently trained out of that presumption.

I sometimes observe that when you graduate from Yale, it was like . . . there was an old TV show years ago and this guy had a long six-shooter and he went around the West taking jobs for doing justice. It was "The Gunslinger" or something like that. He had a card that said "Have gun, will travel."[7] When you graduated from Yale Divinity School it was like you had a card that said, "Have conceptual skills—will serve anyone"!

I appreciate the conceptual skills in which we were trained, but I thought I ought to have something to say. To have something to say, you have to be at least willing to be accountable to some community. That's part of why the emphasis upon the church is so important to me. It's a matter of accountability. And of course, I draw from what I've learned as a Christian, because I personally don't think I have all that much to say. But what I do have to say, I have to say because I'm a Christian. So, I try to say to Christians what I think Christians should say to one another. That of course, makes me a very bad academic!

It's worth recalling that I was already at Notre Dame when I did the AAR speech. I don't know if I mentioned it earlier but Adam came with me to New York. I thought not only could he see New York City but I also thought it was important for him to see what we do at these conventions. There was a special on some kind of cereal, so that if you saved up enough box-tops you got a special deal on an airplane ticket. We saved these up and we bought an airplane ticket for Adam to go to the AAR with me. He was in the room when I did that. I think he must have been six or seven years old. I did this event at the AAR, and the rest of the time we took a Gray Line tour around New York. Dick Neuhaus was nice and invited us for dinner with a lot of others. Paul Ramsey was there and some other folks. Then, on Sunday morning, Dick was the Lutheran pastor of an African American church in Brooklyn, and Adam and I went to that. It was a lovely time.

BB: Let me summarize where I think we've gotten to, and you tell me if this is right. You would understand your use of the language of character as pointing toward the activity of thinking through your life as an early academic and the landscape in which you were working, in light of your prior baptism. This gave you a certain distance and perspective from which to engage in critical scrutiny. Character names your engagement in that self-critical operation.

SH: All that is—I think—right. But it is more articulate than I could be. It is more articulate in this way: when I wrote my dissertation, when I was twenty-seven or twenty-eight, what did I know about Christianity? And so, though the narrative you just gave is one that I would like to think has some truthfulness to it, I think even when I wrote *Character and the Christian Life* as a dissertation, I didn't see as clearly as you just articulated it—the ecclesial implications.

So, though I did the last chapter on Wesley, Edwards, and Calvin (and of course Barth), I wasn't much of a Christian. I think one of the things that I would say is that by assuming positions that I didn't know I was assuming, along the way I've had to own the fact that I'm a Christian, and what that means for increasing conceptual clarity.

My teacher in college, John Score, wrote his dissertation on Wesley and in particular, Wesley's field preaching. Wesley is so often associated in American Methodism with the Aldersgate experience. But you can find in his journal, not long afterward, he's all in despair again. He's not sure he's a Christian. It was John, my teacher, who argued Wesley became Wesley because he went and preached in the field. He was very uncomfortable doing it. People came forward and converted after his sermons. Wesley was in absolute amazement. But it meant he had to own what he had done.

That's the way I look at much of my work. It probably was more Christian than I was, maybe am. But in the process, I have had to become what I've written. I don't regret that for a minute. But it is a way of saying; never think you know what you're doing.

BB: That's very rich and I'd like to follow it up later. But now let me press the point we're discussing one step further. If I'm understanding your biography correctly, the claim that you believed that you should have something to say doesn't seem to have grown from your childhood ecclesial context. So, again there is an interesting ambiguity in your narrative.

SH: I don't know where that came from, that I thought I ought to have something to say.

BB: What about Texas? I mean you know: Don't stand up and open your mouth unless you have something to say or you're going to get shouted down pretty quickly.

SH: Yeah, I guess it could come from there.

BB: Fascinating and important questions about ecclesial identity are starting to appear at the edges of this line of discussion. You said that character is a way of learning how your baptism allows you to understand your life. Could it even be that the fact that Christians are baptized allows them to come to terms with the fact that their own main-springs did not come from the baptism?

SH: Yeah, that seems right. I try to remember with all the language about character and the virtues that we always remain mysteries to ourselves. We're not quite sure where our fundamental dispositions come from.

William James (whom I love) thought temperament was one of the fundamental characteristics of what makes us who we are. Temperament is not something you become. It's something you are. It's a mystery where it comes from. My temperament has always been one fueled by an energy that thinks my life ought to make a difference. That can be very dangerous, but that's who I am. Probably, I think it's shaped how I worked as a theologian.

BB: That's a pretty provocative comment for a guy who has so often stressed the role of habit in ethics. It sounds a lot like you are suggesting that habits channel temperament, but that our God-given temperament is the essential force of who we are. In other words, temperament here seems to be very much in the driver's seat of what constitutes character, and habits are a modality for shaping it, but they don't actually create character.

SH: I think that's one of the places, again, where I don't have to choose between temperament and habit. It depends on what you take temperament to be. For example, is gregariousness a temperament? If gregariousness is temperament then temperaments seem closer to character than we have allowed.

BB: The contemporary language is of introvert and extrovert. I don't know what's at stake in the difference between those two sets of terminology, but I can recognize that distinction.

SH: If by temperament someone is an introvert, that will color all their behavior. Temperament colors all behavior. But it also invites a kind of formation that is about the acquisition of habits. For example, an introvert has to develop the habit of patience with themselves and patience with other people, to hear what other people have to say, even though they oftentimes seem not to be hearing anything at all! So I think temperament is very important for the kinds of habits we produce.

BB: Is your suggestion that human beings have temperament and therefore they are going to need habits, and you're resisting saying that character is the product of one more than the other?

SH: I do want to resist that, that character is the product of one more than the other. I often observe that I was just born with happy genes. It's a kind of temperament. That can be both good and bad. By becoming habituated, you hopefully will acquire the dispositions in a way that saves you being a fool, because being happy can make you a fool pretty quickly.

BB: I'm imagining here the commonsense sensibility that you can tell kids from each other. The forms of affective energy that they are born with will get swung one way or another, and habits are a good way to talk about how that happens. The fact that we can talk so readily about distinguishing children's temperaments—and also how it is possible to see in the old Stanley who doesn't have a cell in his body from the young Stanley but can still be said to have the recognizable temperament he had as a child—all points to a pretty definite role for the temperament. I'm just trying to get the role of habit in the formation of character clear. I'm not sure I'm entirely convinced that the two are equally formative in real life. In real life, it looks like some people are born with a kind of energy that could have been used for good or ill. They need to move it toward good, but you can't make a dull person energetic.

SH: Is dullness temperament?

BB: Low wattage? What's the best term for somebody who is lethargic? Choleric? Disinterested?

SH: Well you would oftentimes call them lazy, but they wouldn't necessarily be so. Oftentimes, I think people confuse what appears to be sexually disciplined people with people who just have low libidos. But if you've got a high libido, you probably better develop some habits that will help you not make a fool of yourself. I don't want to say that temperament just provides the necessity of certain kinds of virtue, because that makes it sound like it is an instrumental thing. But I do think the difference between temperaments offers some people the necessity of developing certain kinds of virtue that are not the same in other people.

Take someone that's shy. With someone that is shy, you need to develop the habit of knowing how to greet someone who is new. I think that that's a great challenge, and a good thing.

BB: All right. Good. This is useful now, because that formulation would then suggest the reason why you can't prioritize temperament over habit is that a virtue-account works on the basis of a picture of balance and unity so that if you are below the mid-line, the habits that are needed to make you virtuous are going to be the type of habits that force you to be more energetic. But if you are above mid-line, you are going to have to be calmed down. There is therefore by definition always an equal contribution being made by both to the character and the habits of any person as displayed in their action at any given moment.

SH: That all seems right to me. One of the tricks is that if you've got certain kinds of temperaments, shyness, for example, then you might not develop the habits necessary to acknowledge the existence of others because your shyness always led you to think that you needed to make some kind of encounter with the other in a manner that would be controlling, where your shyness wouldn't be detected. But then, that means shyness is being habituated in ways that are perverse. How to negotiate those fundamental ongoing challenges is the problem.

BB: That seems useful at the most commonsense level. It's the sort of account you need to make sense of parenting multiple children, where you need to recognize their different palettes of temperament in order to appropriately teach them to become mature young adults.

SH: That's exactly what I was thinking of, and it is interesting how the language of character, which always needs to be carefully monitored, probably elicits that complex relationship between our temperaments, our biographies, and our habits and, in that way, our virtues. We're so tempted to deny that or forget it, and it is so important.

BB: This seems a good moment for you to walk us through your position on the question of the unity of the virtues. In a pregnant footnote in *The Peaceable Kingdom* you write:

> There is a crucial relation, not often noticed, between [the authority of Scripture within the church] and the question of the unity of the virtues. For I do not believe that the virtues form a unity, either for individuals or communities, since there is no single principle from which they can be derived or ordered....

> Indeed, the very diversity of the virtues, and corresponding lives, is required if the church is to have the resources necessary for being faithful to the many-sided tale that constitutes "Scripture."[8]

You repeat years later that you don't believe in the unity of the virtues in *Christians among the Virtues*, but then admit that you still need to do more work on it.[9] What's at stake in this assertion, and do you feel you have gotten much further with explaining what seems to be an important but not very widely held position?

SH: Boy, I didn't know what the hell I was talking about when I wrote that sentence in *The Peaceable Kingdom*, but I do know how to respond about why I think the question is important. That is, the individuation of the virtues is an extremely important task. I don't think just the four cardinal virtues are all you need—gentleness, generosity, humility—to name just a few we always need. We need the diversity of the virtues and how they are interrelated in a way that courage doesn't overwhelm patience, because if you are too willing to go into battle then you probably are not courageous. Courage has to be schooled by patience and so on. What I think these kinds of considerations do is help you understand why it is that often the diversity and conflicts between the virtues in the same person remind us that we are always on the way. We're not there. That's why I think the issue of the unity of the virtues is important.

BB: And that is tied to a question of scripture's collection of the stories of the church through the ages along with Israel. Is that because they display the virtues spread out across many lives?

SH: Yeah, right.

BB: I'm still left not entirely clear about what the unity of the virtues means.

SH: It means that one virtue is not overdetermined in relationship to others.

BB: We don't subcontract the virtues among different people, because that's not how it works. Nor should we aspire to having every single virtue in equal proportion.

SH: That's right. And different people will have different presentations of the interrelation of the virtues. So, one of the things I have not done, and I won't do, is talk about the importance of temperament. Temperament makes a good deal of difference about how our lives are shaped. William James is really good on this. Therefore, that you and I have aggressive temperaments means that the way the virtues will work in relation to our lives will be different to how it works in Stephanie's [Brian's wife] life, and so on.

Is provocation a virtue?

BB: If we return to the AAR speech, it's hard to read it without thinking of Kierkegaard or Socrates. First of all, you're refusing to do typical academic work. You're staging a confrontation of a certain type. The panel was ostensibly about the future of Christian ethics, a topic that is annoying enough to want to evade. But what you do with it is to press on your audience painfully accurate descriptions of their most precious beliefs, but leavened with a good dose of humor.

The question it seems to me that you are forcing your audience of academic ethicists and theologians to consider is whether the practice of the guild might be a little dishonest or at least a pretentious form of tribal self-absorption. What you're clearly doing is challenging settled habits and narratives. It looks like you do this without offering any alternative habits or any alternative at all really.

Your performance looks like what Stephen Webb has called "unstable irony."[10] It doesn't aim to offer an alternative, but simply unsettles problematic certainties, from which the utterer doesn't exempt, in this case, himself. I've already mentioned the way you end—"This is what you expect a Yalie to say"— an admission that you are part of the problem as well. As we're unwinding what you mean by the idea of character, we've now arrived at a highly nuanced account that stands quite a way from most common usages.

SH: I don't think at that AAR I had any alternative other than being myself!

BB: How do you mean?

SH: In the sense that I acknowledge I'm a Yalie, which is certainly true. It was also the case that as someone that was teaching at the University of Notre Dame, I thought that I was part of an ecclesial community that gave me some standing, both to serve Catholics and Protestants, which may have been a deep illusion. But I thought there was a conversation going on within Catholicism in which I assumed I was a participant.

BB: That liberated you a bit from the guild.

SH: It did liberate me from the guild. But I knew I wasn't a Catholic moral theologian, though I knew a lot about Catholic moral theology. I thought at least I was about helping students discern where we were today as Christians. That discernment drew on fundamental theological claims that you couldn't make the judgments you did without them.

That is really important, in that one of the things that I started doing, and I think I learned it from Reinhold Niebuhr, is to think of Christian ethics as a form of journalism. Journalism is about helping us locate the stories that are implicated in our lives, that are so close to us that we don't notice them. Part of what I was doing in that AAR speech was helping people locate those stories within the various graduate schools.

BB: Sorry, which stories?

SH: Like Ramsey carrying on the deontological flame.

BB: So people doing Christian ethics, in those different places, will have been thinking "It's all about Ramsey" etc. They may have only just noticed it, but you were trying to set that realization within a larger landscape.

SH: Right. So what I was trying to do was a kind of journalism to help people locate stories that had already been instantiated in their lives. These stories often took the form of theories whose home was the modern university.

BB: Was that born of frustration at their not serving the church or because you wanted to fan to life a different sensibility? What drove your challenge?

SH: I guess I did it because I thought it was a strange topic to begin with. So, I just wanted to do it in an entertaining fashion that was still academically interesting. I mean, as you've found, almost no one's ever commented to me about what I did at that time.

BB: And why do you think that is?

SH: I think in general I remain a kind of turd in the punch-bowl. He's there. We would prefer he not be there. But at least one of the ways that we can deal with it is to play like he's not there. The best approach is to kind of ignore him.

BB: You'd be in a much better position than I to make the judgment. It does seem to me that you end with what is presumably one of your early trial runs of the charge that American Christian ethics is finally all about America. Just the sort of claim that was destined not to be embraced by anybody who was actually in the audience.

SH: I'm sure they think, "That's the kind of generalization that Hauerwas is famous for, but it clearly should die the death of a thousand qualifications." And that I refuse to let it die the death of a thousand qualifications they just won't forgive me for. I think I've made the case—it's a pretty good case.

BB: Do you think that you've made the case in the sense that you've made a multifaceted enough argument from published texts and cultural observations that it can't be refuted anymore?

SH: I think that's right. I think that's right.

BB: So why didn't anyone "believe" it?

SH: Because they want to be powerful. So that they can be sure to "do some good." They want to be able to do Christian ethics in a way that whether you are Christian or not, you will be compelled to think this kind of analysis is important. Therefore, to emphasize the distinctiveness of Christian convictions as necessary for the display of the Christian life is a challenge for many who think that Christian ethics is fundamentally committed to showing that Christians can be among the most progressive forces in our culture.

I don't believe that.

BB: You still think that's the besetting sin of the discipline?

SH: I do.

There are many good reasons for that. I think that it cannot help but constrain what it is we need to say.

BB: So you have, even though you have been trained in this tradition . . .

SH: Oh, in terms of the discipline I represent the treason of the clerks.

BB: You're not only a traitor. You have, inexplicably, found your way into that traitorous position, but against the grain of your academic tradition. I'm not sure we have or can get to the bottom of how that might be explained.

SH: Do you have any suggestions, Brian, of how that can be explained? I mean, I understand in many ways, I won.

Given the alternatives within Christian ethics that now if—I know it sounds presumptuous, but this is what Gerry McKenny recently said to me—if Walter Rauschenbusch dominated in the early twentieth century and Reinhold Niebuhr dominated for thirty years after World War II (within and after it), I dominated the past twenty years of Christian ethics, setting a good deal of the agenda. I don't know how to account for that. I mean, I've written a lot. But a lot of people have written much, and they haven't changed the conversation. But I changed the conversation.

BB: I like the Wesley analogy. I think it's very evocative. Wesley is a character whose life isn't easily narrated without using some of the same terms that you've used. What he accomplished and how he understood his own biography don't match up, one-to-one.

SH: Samuel Johnson observed that he thought Wesley was an interesting man and he could have some very interesting things to say, if you could just keep him still! You couldn't keep Wesley still. You can't keep me still, similarly.

BB: Part of the reason I wanted to start where we're starting is that I agree with you that you won, as you say, in the sense that you really wanted to say something and what you say somehow had the force of reality with it. It's not because you reproduced Aristotle or Thomas accurately, and it's not because you revivified virtue ethics. It's because you pulled off performances like the AAR speech, which could not be erased from people's memories. And you did it in such a way that it was humorous enough to keep them from checking out and it was self-deprecatory enough for them to stave off, for the time being, the self-protective evasion that this guy's just a self-absorbed asshole. As your theological language has gotten thicker and thicker . . . I would narrate your staying power in a similar way to Barth's: on my reading he knew that he needed a sharp negation of his own theological culture and training, and he discovered Kierkegaard who he then deployed to destroy his own team.

SH: In the Romans Commentary?

BB: That's right. And then he spent the rest of his career figuring out how to say something more constructive without losing that properly destructive critique of religion.

SH: He says, in a little essay on Kierkegaard, that every theologian needs to enter the school of Kierkegaard once.[11] He knew he needed to move in a more constructive direction, just as you've said.

BB: And he did it through Christology, as you've often emphasized. He insisted that you can't say more about Christ and the Trinity than it is proper to say, so the theologian must not say too much. That's a set of methodological affirmations with some potent constructive scope. I think you've harnessed his basic presumptions effectively. Similarly, there's not really anywhere constructive to go if you start with this AAR speech. It's a pure challenge, a pure negation of all the options offered by the status quo. But you managed to find your way from that stance into a theology that people could run with.

What I'm feeling around for here is how you came somehow to be attracted to the apocalyptic disruption of time that is so evident in the works of Kierkegaard and Barth. Even though it takes you most of your life to figure out how to describe the ways in which this has inevitably made your work ironic, it seems like you are finally able to do this only retrospectively in the chapter from *The Work of Theology* entitled "How to be Theologically Ironic."[12]

I still don't think we have gotten to the bottom of the question of how you were liberated to take the stance you have taken to strike this pose you strike with all the distance from the guild it assumes. And then, why did this deployment of that distance seem to make sense to you? I've recently had several newly published books from your teacher Paul Holmer fall into my hands.[1] David Cain's description of him makes him sound a lot like you. "Paul Holmer lived and *was* a dialectic of earnestness and irony. Irony perhaps had the edge—perhaps because of earnestness. His mouth was a runaway, somewhere between a scowl and a smirk—or not between but *both*."[13]

SH: Your question raises two different challenges for me. One is: How does someone who is emphasizing the significance of character for the need of a settled self to acquire the virtues that will give one a life that makes the events in our life a sense of wholeness stress the apocalyptic, which is always the disruption of wholeness? That's always a tension.

---

1. The discussion of Paul Holmer's work in this chapter was unplanned. Brian had a hunch that reading some of Stanley's old teachers would be useful and Phil Ziegler, his colleague at Aberdeen, had some of his books in his extensive library. Brian borrowed those books the day before this interview was set to happen, and he stayed up late into the night, like a teenager with a new PlayStation game, to keep reading. The interaction between Brian and Stanley on this material is therefore best read in a startled tone. Brian had no idea Holmer had left such an indelible mark on Stanley, but Stanley didn't either! In the final subsection of this chapter, "Holmer, language, and ethics" the astonishment at finding this forgotten influence is most clearly on display. Beyond using exclamation marks, it is impossible to note on the page, but that discussion, in person, was marked by side-splitting laughter.

BB: Let me pause you there. As Holmer, in his *Grammar of Faith*, puts it, we are "in a very deep and comprehensive sense 'worldlings,' and it takes a breach of habit, of disposition, of thought itself, to recognize ourselves as truly children of God."[14] So you do have, from the beginning, this breach motif.

SH: Right. I don't think that's incompatible with a stress on the importance of the development of character that makes possible a continuity of self that can pledge itself to be faithful to others and one's own life, always open necessarily to others challenging us about whether what we think we've been doing is in fact what we've been doing. Self-deception is such an important category for me. But you can't locate self-deception with the aid of others, if it is the matter of fact that you don't have any sense of continuities. So the apocalyptic and the continuous are not necessarily contradictory.

BB: If self-deception is a central category, not only are they not contradictory, they are necessarily implicated.

SH: Right. That piece that David Burrell and I wrote on self-deception using Albert Speer, that's really an important essay for me.[15]

Then the second level of your question, as I understand it, concerns the implications of apocalyptic for giving an account of how I challenged the normativity of ethics that fundamentally is about making the way things are be the way that things ought to be. Is that right? The bottom line is apocalyptic which means "it did not have to happen that way" (Wittgenstein).

BB: My deepest question is how do we account for the enduring, ironic, humorous distance that allows you to keep making these anti-Constantinian performances, let alone the larger critique? How could being trained at an Ivy League university *liberate* you from the status quo?

SH: In the sermon I delivered recently at Holy Family, I gave an account of what I took to be Constantinianism, and then I said, "That is a status whose quo is not long for this world!" I thought it was a nice line.

Apocalyptic is not "We must change the world the way Jesus wanted us to do." Apocalyptic is "Jesus changed the world, now let's learn to live in the light of that change." So that sense of apocalyptic I picked up from Barth early on. That fundamentally challenged the presuppositions of Christian ethics, which was fundamentally about "We Christians can change the world," rather than "Witness to the change the world has undergone in Christ." That certainly provided a different stance for me.

BB: You then would endorse a reading of your work that would see that your explication of the ironic character—in a theological sense, not in a postmodern sense—of much of your writing . . .

SH: I can use the postmodern!

BB: Yes. In a way, my question has been malformed from the beginning in the sense that I said habit does not explain ironic performance very well, so if that's the case, then maybe another reading would be: not only did a guy like Holmer display a character with which you resonated, but he also gave an account of the permanence of apocalyptic disruption that is behind this type of criticism of what you came to call Constantinianism.

SH: He didn't call it that, but what I think you are suggesting is that his style—and the content that made his style intelligible—was an expression of a kind of apocalyptic character and wouldn't have needed necessarily to call it that.

BB: Exactly. To put it in simplistic terms, your critique of Christian ethics in America being only about America becomes far more intelligible as you played out the training you'd received from somebody who had studied Kierkegaard really closely. The same Kierkegaard whose theological work was essentially one long attempt to pry Danish Lutherans out of their confusion of Christianity with Danish high culture. You could therefore say that Kierkegaard was all about Constantinian critique, even if Holmer didn't put it precisely that way. But Kierkegaard never deviated from the message, "Danish culture is not Christianity."

SH: But he did put it that way. I had Mr. Holmer for Kierkegaard my first semester in seminary. I just read a ton. I remember thinking that Kierkegaard seems to be one of those figures who you stay with for your whole life or you read sporadically. I chose the latter.[16] But Mr. Holmer had many disciples that chose it for their whole life.

BB: Yes. Was *The Grammar of Faith* something that you heard as lectures?

SH: No, but I read it. What date is on it?

BB: 1978.

SH: Yeah, I read it right after it came out.

BB: Well, one comment he makes, were a student to hear it repeatedly and imbibe it, would make a disengagement from the academic games in the way you were much more intelligible. Here he describes the different ways we might read the Bible using a Wittgensteinian language game account.

> My point is that it is one kind of game in which the telling of the story is done only to fill out the account of Middle Eastern history, and quite another to tell it in order to make the reader a part of a community of faith, Jewish or Christian. In the former game, one addresses curiosity, one serves the interest of being accurate, and one provides an explanation of how people got the way they did, granted their time and circumstances. For the moment, let us call even this historical accounting an interpretation.
>
> But when I tell the story, maybe the same story, even down to the details, so that one will emulate the ancients' courage, live their virtues, eschew their vices, find their law, and seek their God with might and finesse of spirit, then I am doing something quite different. Another game is being played.[17]

SH: Yes, I just think all that is just right.

BB: Reading Holmer has given me a sense of how exciting it must have been to be at Yale at that time, and also some of the emphases other than narrative and virtue you seem to have picked up there.

SH: There just seemed to be so many constructive possibilities. You would make a mistake if you said, "Oh yes, narrative is everything." Mr. Holmer and Mr. Lindbeck never did that, but there were some graduate students who only learned how to make those short-stops.

BB: My constructive interest in these conversations is to try to set up some barriers to those truncated kinds of reading which are legion, as you well know. I have no antiquarian interest in going back to this period nor do I want to produce a genetic account of how Hauerwas got to be "Hauerwas." I'd just never come across Holmer until now, and he seems to make your early academic stance seem much less of a totally novel invention and more of a riff.

SH: If I've won, Brian, how do you understand the victory? Is Gerry McKenny right that I put the church inextricably at the center and that there's no going back from that?

BB: I think that's right. And along with it, the way you locate prayer and worship at the heart of your Christology and ethics. I suspect things would have developed very differently if you hadn't hit on the idea that Christology and ethics are to be explored from the position of prayer and worship. You eventually present that idea in the chapter "Why Christian Ethics Was Invented," and it structures the material in the *Blackwell Companion to Christian Ethics*.[18] That seems to me an intellectual jump that had to be made in order for you to have changed the agenda so sweepingly, and which you found your way through.

SH: That had so much to do with contingency. When I was at Notre Dame, I taught undergraduates primarily. When I taught Christian ethics, *The Peaceable Kingdom* is what I did. That was Notre Dame; where else could you do it?

BB: So you needed an ecclesial context to come to the conclusion that you've got to have an ecclesial context?

SH: Right.

And then when I went to Duke—this is literally true—I didn't get the significance that I was going to a seminary. I did not get it, because at Notre Dame we were a Department of Theology that taught undergraduates, taught MA students, taught PhD students, and then taught in the seminary—it wasn't a separate faculty. It hadn't occurred to me that I wasn't going to be teaching undergraduates anymore.

When I recognized that I would be teaching people preparing for the ministry, I thought, "Well, I don't want to teach Christian ethics the way that I did at Notre Dame, because these people are going to spend the rest of their lives with their primary identity as people who celebrate the Eucharist." And so

I thought, well, I want to be able to teach in a manner that they are able to own that in a manner that they never ask, "What is the relationship between what I do on Sunday morning and what I do in terms of the formation of Christian people as people who don't lie?" So that's how the course was created around the liturgy.

BB: To explain one more piece of my own reading of your work, I think what we see in the AAR speech is an implicit criticism of the discipline as a whole which gets cashed out in this moment in your career because, as you've said, you are coming to be much more clear that theological ethics should be helping people to understand how to make decisions, rather than what most ethicists were doing at the time, which was to major in second-order criticisms of the defenses people were making of the decisions they made. At several points in *Character and the Christian Life*,[19] you are putting those criticisms in pointed formulations.

If we take the AAR piece as representative, your career seems to open with a sharp criticism of the very obvious deficiencies that result when we reduce Christian ethics to second-order debates about ethical method—which is in fact, technically speaking, an engagement in second-order, or even third-order criticism!

SH: I've always hated the distinction between meta-ethics and normative ethics. Goodness gracious me!

BB: You appear to have been backing out of your own tradition at that point, feeling your way toward a way to begin to speak in first-order language. That you managed this has to be understood as one of the conditions for your having "won"—if the theologian is allowed to talk about winning at all. You quite clearly and very early grasped that the second-order discourse was not, in itself, sufficient to serve the church. And I think that's got to be right.

SH: Yeah, and that I think was really shaped by the influence of Wittgenstein and how reading Wittgenstein with Mr. Holmer made such a difference for me thinking that first-order language is not to be explained by some other language. So, I think I've become increasingly clear about that—though it was there early on—in the last ten years.

Holmer, language, and ethics

BB: Let me try out this biographical hypothesis: you picked up, or honed your anti-Constantinian stance in the heartlands of the Constantinian educational establishment because you had teachers who channeled a seriously anti–status quo Christianity from another place and time. You say that you hadn't heard his lectures on virtue in your little essay in *Wilderness Wanderings*, but they're now out in Volume II of his published works.[20] There you say you didn't know he was working on the motifs of "virtue, narrative, memory, vision, and description"[21] but that you were both following up hints from Wittgenstein and his followers, making it no surprise to you that the two of you wind up interested in virtue.

The way you later situate the virtues within the Sermon on the Mount clearly makes a lot more sense when we see how Holmer positions the virtues within an apocalyptic framework. In the essay, called "The Case for the Virtues," for instance, he says:

> I am arguing that moral philosophy, in the enthusiasm for a kind of safe meta-ethics and theory-talk, has not only failed to achieve that vaunted scientific neutrality and objectivity it aims at, but it leaves out something central to the moral life. Inclining apparently to avoid moral trespassing and seeking above all to be scholarly, not admonitory and didactic, the ethicists, philosophical and religious, have left out what is crucial—the primary ethical stuff. For the depiction and pursuit of actual virtues, the terribly homely business of learning how to be polite in difficult circumstances; always prompt; courageous when threatened; temperate when zig-zagging looks right; "just" when advantages lie in injustices; these and more are the achievements, the habitual achievements, that make up the virtues. Without these, there simply is no primitive working context for the moral life. Surely, there is, then, no clarity about moral concepts either.
>
> The oddest thing happens when wanting, wishing, and seeking get concentrated in our life histories. For by these and their virtues our lives make sense. Rather than the virtues being an alien imposition, it is the case that a life characterized by steady wanting, persistent desires, long-term loves, tempered likes and dislikes, etc., is also a rational life.[22]

It now, again, is becoming much more intelligible why in your dissertation you were trying to get together virtue and Barthian apocalypticism.

SH: I probably wasn't as clear about it as you have made me out to be!

BB: Even if you weren't clear, could you narrate, after the fact, the configuration of functional certainties that allowed that trajectory to emerge?

SH: I think that I have always had the tendency to go with what seemed to me to be right, even though I wasn't sure how you could put it together. That was going on in *Character and the Christian Life*. It's still going on.

BB: Given this discussion, would you retrospectively be able to ascribe the influence that shaped that text as more to one side of that equation or the other? Namely, this Kierkegaardian account of virtue and, on the other side, the Lindbeckian narrative?

SH: I think the Lindbeckian narrative was more determinative in the dissertation than Kierkegaard.

BB: In your piece on Paul Holmer in *Wilderness Wanderings* you say:

I recall that we had the following exchange numerous times.

HOLMER: There's a distinction to be drawn; learning about the things of the faith is not the same as learning to be faithful. But, if that seems too patent, it might be said that theology is the learning of faith, not the learning *about* faith. Thus the distinction is drawn with the help of two prepositions, *of* and *about*.

HAUERWAS: But where do I find this language "*of*"?

HOLMER: You read the Bible.

HAUERWAS: But some people tell me to read this part of the Bible and other people tell me to read that part of the Bible.

HOLMER: Well, you need to read a larger context.

HAUERWAS: But some people tell me that this is the larger context, and other people tell me that that is the larger context. What do I do then?

HOLMER: You need to ask your pastor.

HAUERWAS: Some people tell me I should ask this pastor and other people tell me l should ask that pastor. How do I know which pastor to ask?

HOLMER: Stanley; are you sure you are praying enough? And by the way, what is it that you're afraid of?[23]

SH: That was a real conversation! It happened in many different ways, but it was a question and answer that we went through a number of times.

BB: My suspicion is that this is an example of how you become a Christian because the church, through its various members, kept forcing unpalatable truths on you.

SH: Yeah, that's true. I've always maintained that I am a Christian because friends force me to live a life that makes the description "Christian" make sense. I think that is the way salvation works. I often say that I declare myself a pacifist before audiences, not because I like the language of pacifism—I don't—but I let them have any presuppositions they want about what pacifism is because it is better than the alternatives. And by creating expectations in them, I have some hope that they will keep me faithful to what I know is true, but I have no confidence I'm able to live it. Now that's also how I think about being a Christian. Other people make me a Christian, and God does that through other people. When I say things like, "Outside the church, there is no salvation," that's what I am referring to. You've got to have a mediated faith. That's how we have some hope of escaping some forms of self-deception.

BB: I think it's remarkable that you actually had teachers at Yale who played pastoral roles.

SH: They didn't call it that.

BB: But saying, "Stanley, are you praying enough? And by the way, what is it you are afraid of?"—that's not an academic question!

SH: I guess it's not but it was in an academic context, so I thought that is what you had to do!

Gay Noyce was a lovely man that taught fieldwork. I took a course with Mr. Noyce on "Justice in the City" or something like that. He saw me in the hall my senior year and said, "Stanley, what are you going to do next year?" And I said, "Well I've been accepted into the PhD program, so I am going to stay." He said, "I usually try and talk people out of going into the PhD program and instead I try to suggest they ought to go into the ministry. But I think that's what you ought to do—you ought to go into the PhD program!"

I thought, "Well, that's good." That was pastoral.

BB: That might have also been prophetic!

Did you know that Holmer wrote an essay called "Something About What Makes It Funny"?[24]

SH: I did know that, but I think I forgot to go back and read it when I wrote "How to be Theologically Funny."[25]

BB: Did you ever hear him do that as a student? I'm asking the genetic question now.

SH: I don't remember if I heard that or not.

BB: The essay is genuinely funny.

SH: Is it?

BB: The one that did make me laugh out loud is: "If you miss the customs of language, as many of us do so often, then you miss a fundamental ordering agency, too. 'Have you ever smoked after sex?' the young woman was asked by the solemn family-life researcher. 'I don't know,' she said, 'I never looked.'"[26]

SH: I've been told my chapter on how to be theologically funny isn't very funny, but that is!

BB: The other one I find incredibly funny also features an analytical insight that is very insightfully put. He's talking about context again: "After Khrushchev's five-hour rambling press conference, James Thurber reported: 'Great oafs from little ikons grow.'"[27]

So it is a Wittgensteinian account of laughter that we get here. I think it explains quite a bit about your approach in the AAR speech, whether it was intentional or not. He says, for instance,

> We have to say with Dostoevsky that what you laugh at will often be more important than a life-attitude. The laugh "shows" what language cannot "say." So, though the objective state of affairs has to be there, it is also the case that the quality of the person, the manner of his subjectivity, also counts a great deal.[28]

His basic approach is to say that if you can get people to laugh it is a more powerful argument than just straight linguistic argument because of its signification in time and place.

SH: And you share a way of life! Laughter presupposes the creation of common judgments that the laughter itself reinforces. Laughter is a crucial practice for the manifestation, as well as the creation, of community. That's really very important!

BB: This is where it gets really interesting, because this AAR speech both provoked laughter and there was a deep division between yourself and the audience.

SH: People could not help but recognize themselves in the characterizations and they laughed about the characterizations, usually about the characterizations of other schools but then when their school was characterized, they didn't necessarily laugh. But the recognitions were there that made it possible for this not to be a violent act.

BB: Yes, because otherwise you would have stood up and listed their deficiencies?

SH: Right!

BB: Another passage:

> When Robert F. Kennedy projected the possibility that Martin Luther King, Jr. might someday be President, his brother John said: "But do you think the country is ready for a Baptist?" Part of what is meant by a sense of humor is the capacity, for that is what it is, to practice a little detachment, to live a moment of *ataraxia*, amid a life of ardent endeavor, and thus to be able always to put things in a different light.[29]

I see this as the connection with your late essay on irony.[30] My driving question is how best theologically to narrate this link, and your late explanation is that irony results from the eschatological light Christ sheds on everything. But what Holmer is offering you is, in Kierkegaard's terms, the step before real faith. And he's explicit about that. Humor is close to faith, but it is not faith. And that seems not terribly far from the character Stanley Hauerwas, who seems at this point in life to be close to faith but not quite at faith. That's why Holmer is asking the student Stanley the questions he's asking him.

SH: I think that's terrific, but, the Hauerwas at that stage is closer to humor than faith! I'm not sure he's that much different now. I've always felt about half Christian and I'm never sure if I don't enjoy being Christian more to thumb the nose at those who aren't and who are arrogant about it, or whether I am really Christian.

BB: Listen to what Holmer says about that boundary:

> For it might be that humor sometimes is a disguise for the hiddenness of one's faith, just when one is not prepared to go the next step and suffer

openly for Jesus's sake. One sees how it is, Christianly speaking, but one does not effect the transition to discipleship—and then humor is an incognito for deeper things that one is not yet obedient enough to make plain. Under such circumstances a sense of humor is not an accidental feature but is really a part of a judgment about how things are. Amid the suffering contradictions there is a way, God's way through it and out of it; and that makes a life truly worthwhile.[31]

SH: Boy, I should have read that before I wrote "How to be Theologically Funny" because that is exactly what I think and what I was trying to express! I was also in that essay using Cohen's joke book,[32] which is Wittgensteinian to the core. That paragraph you read is both Kierkegaardian and it is also Wittgensteinian.

BB: What I found most poignant about it is that I do think that there is an internal development to the character called Stanley Hauerwas and that this early version is very funny. Yet even this almost-Christian version who is very funny is driven by an eschatological sensibility. Kierkegaard's "almost-there" is somebody who sees the fractured-ness of the world under the light of eternity but is just not able to embrace it. But I suspect that as your life has unfolded you have come to a place that also lets you identify with the last sentence, "Amid the suffering contradictions there is a way, God's way through it and out of it; and that makes a life truly worthwhile."

SH: I hope so, because what makes a life truly worthwhile is having some hold on the truth, the ability to be non-bullshit honest.

BB: Having something to do. "Worthwhile" seems to be truthfulness with purpose.

SH: There was at Yale great resistance to Mr. Holmer, because they thought he was an anti-intellectual.

BB: He writes beautifully.

SH: He was a Pietist of sorts.

BB: That's the essence of it. He was side-swiped by the fundamentalist debates; that if you are an outspoken believer, then you must be on the wrong team in the Ivy League?

SH: Well of course, he wasn't anything like a fundamentalist. But where someone like Gustafson would be very hesitant about their Christian convictions in university councils, Mr. Holmer was not. He was a member of the Swedish Covenant Church, which were the Pietistic Lutherans. The people in *Babette's Feast* were Swedish Covenant.

BB: Did you ever hear anything from Holmer on preaching?

SH: No!

BB: You'll appreciate his essay "Indirect Communication: Something about the Sermon (With References to Kierkegaard and Wittgenstein)."[33] I found all this material incredibly illuminating because he really is in the territory of Barth, in that you need to make sure you don't say more than you need to say. He even mentions what Kierkegaard got from Aristotle, which runs like this. Kierkegaard learned that,

> There was a great concreteness, a host of specific cases, kinds of speaking—dramatic, persuasive, pedagogical and more—that were discussed. The discernment was very rich on the interweaving of style, of grammar, of the speaker's very manner, with the words he was using. Furthermore, what was being said and to whom it was being said and by whom it was being said began to loom up as Kierkegaard read Aristotle. All of these considerations mattered. This was the kind of specificity that Kierkegaard needed almost as an antidote to the generalities of the philosophical culture that otherwise nurtured him. He read Aristotle, not as a scholar forever remembering what Aristotle had said, but as his real teacher who became an occasion, and a vanishing one at that, whose pages caused him to see something for himself.[34]

SH: Notice that what Kierkegaard is reading is *The Rhetoric*.

BB: That's exactly what I wanted to discuss. He starts by talking about what Aristotle taught Kierkegaard—concreteness and the role of rhetoric—and then he turns to Wittgenstein:

> Wittgenstein thought with dogged care and a consuming passion on some questions that were very close to Kierkegaard too. Language and reality, words and the world, what can be said and what cannot—that large range of questions was never long alien to either thinker. And against the highly generalized views of Hegel and his followers, Kierkegaard began to piece together some criticisms of the ontological philosophy, of the new logic, of the notion that all the kinds of human endeavor (religion, art, even politics) were like approximations, good tries, in the direction of a truth that could only be stated in purely philosophic concepts. He, therefore, had to think in a new and cryptic way about words, concepts, logic, reality questions. He described that odyssey variously as out of the complexity, into the simple; out of the aesthetic, through the ethical, into the religious; out of the manifold, through the philosophical, into the simple again. But he did all of this because things religious were so malformed, so mistreated, and so mimicked in the new profundities. Historical learning frequently was combined with mistaken logical and conceptual rubrics to give a learned gloss to deeply personal and strenuously Christian matters.[35]

SH: Hmm. Hand me *The Work of Theology*.

> I need to explain, or at least try to make clear, my understanding of how we do not control the words we use because that is the fundamental presupposition that runs throughout this book. I think it was from Wittgenstein that I first had some intimation that we often say more or less than we think we say. Richard

Fleming observes, an observation I take to have Wittgensteinian roots, it is no easy thing to, "attempt to find ourselves in the complexity of the systematic order of our words, the words that we share." We are never free of failing to mean what we say. Thus the necessity of saying, "What I really meant to say was X not Y."

That the words we use are not our words means we in fact often lose control over what we mean when we use them. Writing, which is one of the crucial sources of thought, is the struggle "to try to mean what we say using words that are not our own. We find our life fated in the language of our ancestors, in the language we inherit from them . . . Hence to understand what words mean we must understand what those who use them mean." But, of course, we must remember that those to whom we look for understanding what we say or have said may not have understood what they have said.[36]

That's just my continuing commentary on the passage you just read!

BB: Reading back now, it's uncanny. In the course of describing the sermon Holmer comments,

> Seemingly, then, the language when it works well 'shows' you the logical form but does not picture it; and perhaps, too, a happy life with its intrinsic reward shows one the sense of life. Language does not do everything. Here it is as if one must be quiet while the happiness of one's life bears out the sense.[37]

SH: It's lovely. It's right. This goes to the complaint that what I do in sermons doesn't seem to add much to the academic theological treatises. This is the reason why! I'm trying to say, "Watch the language and what it's doing."

BB: Exactly. Actually, when I read this passage from Holmer, I thought again about you having several times reiterated that a life like Jean Vanier's is the best argument we could make for Christianity.[38] Some things have to be shown. When Holmer says, "Here it is as if one must be quiet while the happiness of one's life bears out the sense," the sense of the statement that Jesus is Lord is carried in that life. That's very helpful to me because I think one of the reasons that *With the Grain of the Universe*[39] is a little bit off-putting to some is that people don't know what to do with the claim that if the church is not virtuous, Christianity doesn't mean anything. You put it much more eloquently than that, but that basic claim sounds to many like Jesus would be up the creek without a paddle if he didn't have the church.

SH: Right! If the church cannot produce a Dorothy Day, then there's got to be something wrong, there's got to be something not truthful. But we do!

BB: I did my doctorate in London right behind an Australian who became a dear friend, Andrew Cameron. Many years after the fact he confessed that when he first met me in London, he was shocked that I'd said, "Well, I came over here to figure out what this Christianity stuff is actually about." I only later realized that this was the most important reason why very early on I resonated so strongly with your work. Your diagnosis of the hermetic isolation of Christian language was just so obviously right. When churchy language is not genuinely theologically determined then it becomes a self-referentially vacuous way of talking when you are around church people that is essentially not about the Christian God because it is so quickly colonized by political agendas or other idols. I had enough sense to see that among those who confessed to be Christians there were a few that had such substance that the language must mean *something*, but what that something was simply wasn't evident to me. This doesn't seem so different from the guy you are saying can tell a good joke at an AAR speech but is getting told by his own teachers, "What are you afraid of?"

I think I'm starting to figure this character out!

It looks pretty clearly like Holmer was the one who taught you to refuse to look for meanings "behind" first-order Christian language.[40]

SH: I could have learned it from Wittgenstein!

BB: Didn't the two come together? Have you ever committed that story about Holmer and the historical seagull to the record?

SH: No!

BB: I don't think I can resist the temptation to have you tell that story again, because it perfectly encapsulates the convergence of Kierkegaard and Wittgenstein in Holmer.

SH: The story is that Mr. [Paul W.] Meyer, who was a wonderful New Testament scholar—I'd had Introduction to the New Testament with Mr. Meyer and Wayne Meeks was the teaching assistant—and Mr. Meyer had accepted a position at Princeton Seminary. He and Mr. Frei were always very close friends. Mr. Meyer, at his leaving event, gave this lecture on the search for the historical Jesus in the common room at Yale. He went through all the Robinson stuff and that kind of thing. Very detailed. He gave a modest defense that Jesus is pretty much who we see he is in the Gospels, but he accepted the phrase "historical Jesus."

When he finished, Mr. Holmer got up immediately. He was a huge man. He said, "Well, I just don't understand what all this stuff about the historical Jesus is about. I just got back from Salt Lake City, and the Mormons there have this huge obelisk with seagulls on top, because when they first got there, they planted their crops. They were just about ready to harvest and this flood of locusts came in. They were going to eat all their crops up and they would starve. They prayed that God would send them deliverance. And out of nowhere came these flocks of seagulls and ate up the locusts." Salt Lake City is a thousand miles from an ocean, so he said, "Now, they could bring in ornithologists to see if there were migratory possibilities of seagulls doing that. And they could find historians to see if there were records of this happening in other places. But they don't do that. Instead, they build this statue to the seagulls. They don't have a problem with the historical seagulls. Why do we have a problem with the historical Jesus!"

3. Temperament, Habit, and the Ethics Guild

Mr. Frei went ballistic. And of course, Mr. Frei was not unsympathetic about some of the fundamental points about where you get the notion of the historical Jesus from. But it was a classical confrontation. That's how Holmer got that reputation for being a Pietist.

BB: It's the truth of the matter, for him, clearly. His refusal to look for supposedly "deeper" meaning is ultimately a position on issues of linguistic reference. The reason he refuses meaning, he says, is:

> It's one thing to see that language, even religious language, has a meaning. It's another thing to see that it's true. A point to remember is that without the concepts, no one can speak at all, for every language must be there before we can say anything. We all speak a language that's spoken and it's only within that language that words have their meaning.[41]

SH: It's great!

BB: So from the beginning you were trained to resist breaking things down into supposedly more fundamental meanings. As we've seen, that connects to a specific style of critique of academic analysis. And where it ends is, again, pretty familiar:

> Therefore, the religious words are vain when nothing follows their usage, when the individual does not seem to know anything about the matters to which they refer and the way of life to which they are born. Then we can say, sadly, that people do not know what they are saying. To teach them that is one of the theologian's tasks.[42]

SH: Goodness. You wonder where I came from! Boy, that is it!

BB: One other question about this universe of thought in which you are so clearly deeply formed is whether this makes rhetoric the basic discipline in theology?

SH: I want to say yes. I'm not sure if I know what I'm saying when I say yes, because I don't want to give the impression by saying yes that it's all just words.

BB: Well, presumably the starting affirmation is that the fundamental conceptual domain of Christian theology is not, for instance, logic or dialectics.

SH: Right! Though, one of the things rhetoric does is expose the logic of our language, though it itself is not logic.

BB: Grammar is the discipline of naming the logic of our speaking.

SH: That's right. So yes, I think theology is fundamentally rhetoric. In the first essay in *The Work of Theology*, "How I Learned to Think Theologically,"[43] I use Garver's wonderful book *For the Sake of the Argument*[44] as a way to develop this point about rhetoric. So much of rhetorical analysis turns out to be an ongoing investigation of practical reason. Just like you cannot separate Aristotle's ethics from his politics, you cannot separate the rhetoric from it either.

BB: I think this is all extremely helpful. You recount in the essay in *Wilderness Wanderings* that Mr. Holmer was mortified that you were going to study ethics.[45]

SH: Absolutely! He came up to me. I was at the mailbox. He said, "Hauerwas, what's a good man like you going to do next year." I said, "I'm entering the PhD program in Ethics." He said, "Ethics? Moore killed ethics in 1903 with the *Principia*! Ethics is nowhere! You ought to be in Philosophical Theology." I said, "Oh, I don't think so Mr. Holmer."

BB: In "How I learned to Think Theologically," you then go on to explain why you took this position, and I think that few people have grasped how fundamental this affirmation is for your thinking overall. A lot of the mystification I see among all sorts of readers of your work, and I don't just mean the undergraduates, has to do with the fact that this account of language and grammar *is* ethics.

SH: It is ethics! Right!

BB: In other words, you don't need to set up a discreet discipline of ethics because there is nothing beyond the form of analysis that is "ethical" because it's concerned with the language we're already talking and the lives we're already living. To separate talk about ethics from talk about truth or anything else is to already have lost entirely. This is how Holmer's *The Grammar of Faith* puts it:

> It will be altogether salutary to remember that words, even the Biblical and the Christian's words do many things besides "communicate." Once one trains oneself and then perhaps teaches others to be open to the multitude of purposes served by that language—some conveys, some commands, some pleases, some stirs up emotions, some entices thoughts—then and only then will adequacy be done both to the religious life and simultaneously to life itself.[46]

SH: Does he footnote Austin there?

BB: There's not a footnote within pages of it.

SH: That's "How to Do Things with Words,"[47] which was also influential.

SH: I have a question. It's lovely to have this opportunity to interact and I wonder ... I mean—the very fact that you claim me as a friend creates a difficulty for yourself, because that puts you in a position of allegedly identifying with the guy who won. Yet, you've got your own work that needs to continue. How do you negotiate that? I mean your agenda isn't necessarily mine, my agenda?

BB: I'm sensitive to the question you're asking. The reality of the matter is that I have not come to where I am by taking any of the normal routes into the guild. So I'm not hostage to a patronage network that would punish me for making the wrong friends! For instance, though I've been heavily involved in the UK Society for the Study of Christian Ethics, I have not made it to an annual meeting of the Society of Christian Ethics in the US.

SH: Oh I see. Good for you.

BB: I did apply once to have one of these "breakfasts with the author" when my technology book came out. I thought, "It's my second book. Somebody must have heard of me over there." I got turned down. I thought, "OK. Well, I'll go when I have an excuse."

And the British Christian ethics scene is relatively discrete from that scene, and I'm not sure people on your side of the Atlantic are paying much attention to it. I mean, people probably read the journal intermittently.

SH: They do.

BB: The discourse over here is sufficiently dense and rich that I don't really need to bank on recognition in the American guild. Being on the margins, being a stranger and outsider gives you a real freedom to think—which of course comes with a constant temptation to escapism. I've heard stories about your students being blackballed from positions just because other academics know they are your students. I'm just thankful I'm insulated from that by working in a sufficiently out of the way academic context.

SH: I think that's happening less now, but it's still the case.

BB: It's a familiar story. My own teacher, Colin Gunton, was a very dominant figure in all kinds of ways, and when he died, he was not there to tend the political garden and it collapsed very quickly, and many of his students suffered. It was hard to watch. Dominant figures inevitably produce backlash, and I think it just has to be admitted that people have other agendas and there is a certain amount of *ressentiment* from those who feel like they've not been able to have their position persuade people. But I do think that ultimately what you've exemplified is someone who wants to say something, despite the fact that in our conversation today we've talked more about method than I would want to do in the future.

SH: I agree; I was thinking the same thing.

BB: We'll find our way there. But I definitely agree that if we don't have something to say that hits the ground and lets the gospel shine light on people's lives, we're just in the wrong business. And if we're doing that it is by no means my responsibility to protect myself from the backlash against your success.

These things are all very ambiguous anyway. The people who've found their lives impacted by the light you've shed on their ethical thinking will recognize both the differences between us and the similarities we share in that we seek to shed the same light, I hope. The approval of the guild—there is nothing I can do about that.

SH: I'm always impressed by how much contingency shapes what we do. My going to Duke Divinity School was such a contingency. It made me rethink stuff, and this kind of thing. What do you think is the largest contingency that you've faced?

BB: It's hard to list the contingencies that have most decisively shaped me, but a first sketch would run something like this: I'm not a Vietnam kid or a Korea kid, but an Iraq war kid. You weathered the sexual revolution that kicked off in the late 1960s and is now just firmly bedding in, but I was born into the new world. That's one of the reasons for my sense that some of the most difficult contingencies for Christians today are those we live through in the domestic domain. I've had . . . I can say this because of our shared cultural background—you know the expectations that surround the first-born son in Texas—Adam being my introduction to parenthood was always going to be a challenge to those old patriarchal scripts giving his learning difficulties and life threatening episodes. I've gone through some pretty harrowing years in an ecclesial context that has often felt dramatically thin and a long way away from the comforts of a home culture and a family support network. I'd have to think through more how such contingencies might have played into my convergences with your theology. But the fact is that such a story is characterized by a vulnerability that makes me pretty aware of the need for the Lord's oversight and care in very tangible ways.

SH: I was—in the list I thought—he is going to have to mention having to operate in a different culture!

Do you think you would have had the same focus on Luther if you had been in America?

BB: No. Definitely not. I mean, I came to Luther studying with Hans Ulrich. In fact, *Singing the Ethos of God* was my attempt to work through my heritage as a Bible-belt evangelical who had been trained as an English theologian but was trying to come to terms with German theology. That's why at the middle of that book you find Augustine and Luther. And of course, it was Barth who taught me who Augustine is. So, it was in the course of that period that I realized that Luther wasn't who I thought he was. At points that I didn't really expect, he was actually doing what Barth had taught me to understand as theology in ways that—I shudder to say it—might expose points at which we can and ought to be more theological than Augustine was. But to this day the only Lutheran churches I've been to have been in Germany, and in German.

SH: And those Lutheran churches, at least if my experience was the same as yours, would turn you against Christianity forever.

BB: Well it helps that probably my German is not as good as I'd like it to be! I understand best those things that I can read, and much of what I experienced was very theologically rich. I mean, Luther wrote their hymns and shaped their iconography in fascinating ways I'd not encountered before. My attraction is certainly more to Luther and a minority theological tradition that still takes him seriously than, to Lutheranism, which can certainly be off-putting.

Most of the churches I attended worshiped in liturgical forms which were recognizably on the traditional Western pattern, so I could sense . . . you know, I learned during my first five years in England what you say you learned in the Lutheran church when you were teaching at Augustana,[48] that weekly Eucharist was wonderful, and that the standard form of the Western liturgy was rich and highly theological. Going to Germany I could clearly see it as the same basic Western liturgical tradition. That would obviously not be true everywhere, and I've certainly seen that there is lots of terrible culture-Protestantism in Germany which proudly carries on the heritage of liberal Protestantism.

That's why, in hopes of rebalancing the emphasis, in our next conversation I want to turn to what your position means for the inner life of the church. In an important sense, these questions about temperament have to find their expression in the church and from there flow out to outward-facing questions, such as discussions about pacifism. The inner-facing questions come first though, so it is important to explore in more detail how you imagine peaceable living coming to life and finding its form in the ecclesia. I want to go to the horizon that you have evoked of the small practices and try to think through how you engage those theologically.

Chapter 4

ECCLESIAL POLITICS, PEACEMAKING, AND THE ESCHATOLOGY OF WORSHIP

October 11, 2015

> *This conversation culminates in the claim that Christian liturgy is the determinative space for the ethical formation of Christians. Here God's apocalyptic time may be encountered in a particularly dense manner. The chapter probes how Hauerwas understands the processes by which entering this space and being impacted by this alternative time is ethically formative of Christians. What role does our body and bodily practices play in our incorporation into political communities? In what sense are we formed by remembering and being claimed by surprising others, such as our neighbors and the saints? We are offered here a fine-grained exploration of Hauerwas's eschatology of peace and the ways in which he understands it to be born in and received by the community that is the Christian church.*

Practicing dying and the politics of the church

BB: Before we can turn to consider your talk of just war and pacifism, we must consider a more fundamental insistence: that the most important thing we can say about the church is that it is a body of people living as a peacemaking community. Most people know that this is one of the most original and important insights in your work. At the same time, it has also often been said that you have been more preoccupied with refuting the malaises of liberal democracy than developing a thick account of how the church is to live as such a peacemaking community. What seems clear is that your earliest forays into talking about war and politics already contain the main terms that will continue to characterize your views for the rest of your career.

In your 1985 essay "Peacemaking, the Virtue of the Church,"[1] you argue that peacemaking is the cardinal characteristic of the Christian community. It requires the truth-telling that provokes constructive conflict and lives out of an assurance of God's forgiveness and the confession that humans and their institutions were not created for violence.[2] The postliberal emphasis on understanding the church as a cultural-linguistic community in need of traditioning through distinctive practices appears already to have offered you a concrete picture of the way in which the church is political, both internally and toward the world. Could you explain to us the genesis of this strong emphasis on peacemaking so early in your career? What might come as a surprise to some is that in this essay, at least, you clearly rest the argument on a biblical meditation, on Matthew 18.

SH: I suppose that beginning teaching in the midst of the Vietnam War meant war was front and center for everyone's agenda. The influence of Reinhold Niebuhr was also strong and then I read, before I left seminary, Yoder's *Karl Barth and the Problem of War*.[3] When I got to Notre Dame in 1970 I went out to see him and got a mimeographed copy of *The Politics of Jesus*,[4] and I got *The Original Revolution*,[5] which has the great essay "Peace without Eschatology." That's where I think I got the emphasis on the importance of how to think about peace. I think somehow I intuited early on that the great problem is knowing how to characterize peace, because we just seem to know what violence is but we're not sure what peace is. Partly what I had a sense that I needed to do was to help people see peace. That related to the Murdoch moves. Matthew 18, of course, is the central text for the Anabaptists. What I thought I saw there is not that Jesus says: *if* you think someone has wronged you, you *might* go to confront them. He says: you confront them.

I took that to be a deeply political claim because most of the time we prefer not to confront people who we think may have wronged us, "Better to get along by going along," or "I don't have time for that." But I think Matthew 18 is a signal text for the formation of a community.

BB: Let's explore then how you understand this peacemaking church to work, both in theory and in practice. You don't begin to explicate in detail how we might understand peace as the church's politics until midway through your career, and you begin to do so in earnest the more clearly you see that American Christians simply could not distinguish the United States from the kingdom of God—as cashed out in America's evident embrace of capitalism, democracy and empire, to name some of the main subheadings.

Your several attempts to find levers with which to pry Christians up out of this confusion come together in a particularly powerful formulation when you are attacked for your response to 9/11. Drawing on Augustine's account of the two cities, you point out that any account of Christian patriotism worthy of the name must spring from the recognition that Christians have divided loyalties. When we have only one loyalty, to the nation, we can no longer resist the modern state's insistence that we make sacrifices so that it can survive:

> I think...the way Christians committed to nonviolence as well as Christians not so committed can best serve this land called America is by refusing to be recruits for the furtherance of American ideals. Let us rather be a parochial people. For the only way we will be saved from the temptations to serve the universal

ideologies of the empire is through the concrete relations that make our actual lives possible. The lives of the people who worship at Holy Family Episcopal Church in Chapel Hill, North Carolina, have first claim on me. Whatever loyalty that abstraction called the United States may have will need to be tested by the effect it has on what I owe to those that worship at Holy Family and how what I owe to them puts me in contact with Christians around the world.[6]

A lot is loaded into this last sentence which points to the heart of the problem of forging the peace that the church receives.

Could you walk us through what you are envisioning here? What kind of interactions are you committed to at Holy Family that allow you all to be better citizens and patriots? I'm looking for some concrete examples of how this works on the ground in Holy Family. How have you lived Christianity as a tactic rather than as a strategy, as you often put it?[7]

SH: Obviously I can say that what I think we have at Holy Family is preaching in which we are told at once both how we often are unfaithful to the gospel, but at the same time that exactly as we help one another locate our unfaithfulness, we become an alternative which otherwise wouldn't exist for the world.

This may be too personal, but I regard it as something as simple as: many people in the congregation take pride—and I use the word carefully—in the fact that I am there every Sunday. They know that I am here in Aberdeen and when we go to church in St. John's in Aberdeen that that interconnection between Holy Family and St. John's in Aberdeen is a basis for peace. Even if Scotland revolted against America, as Christians we couldn't kill the people we've learned to be friends with at St. John's. So the interconnectedness of human lives—I used mine as the example but there are many—is God's way of forging peace among us.

BB: Does training Christians how to die also help?

SH: I certainly do think training people how to die is part of what we do as Christians. We do that, of course, every time we baptize an infant.[8] At Holy Family we had a very prominent member of the church who was a young woman lawyer; she was in her fifties. She and her two children and her husband were very involved in the church. Then just out of the blue, she dropped dead one day. The church was devastated. We immerse, and our baptismal is in the shape of the cross and it is about ten feet by six feet. Her husband had the good sense of bringing the casket to the church the night before the funeral and we put it on the baptismal and we vigiled it during the night, like we vigil the Eucharist on Friday of Holy Week.

That was a really decisive event for the church and it has continued to shape how we deal with funerals, oftentimes. We don't vigil everyone, but if the family wants to, we do it. I think it also makes possible the ability of people to talk about dying with one another. It has been a decisive event for the formation of the church. It's interesting how these kinds of things happen. And you have to remember it, because we are a transitional church near the University of North Carolina, so a lot of new people come in and out. That is a very important practice for us.

BB: I was in London during a few landmark events—9/11, but also the Queen Mother's death—and as an American I couldn't but be struck by the vigil culture. People here in the UK understand the public rituals that sustain public mourning. It's culturally very different from the way Americans do it. You've certainly opened up a set of connections that should allow churches and pastors to be thinking about how death is celebrated and mourned and lamented collectively, as part of what it means to be a peacemaking church. Collective mourning is not disconnected from the way we play out aggression and rivalries.

SH: I say America is a country—allegedly the strongest country in the world—that runs on fear. September 11 was the day when "they came to us." Our presumption is that if we just have a big enough military, we can make ourselves safe from the world. The other side of this fear is the faith that if we just get good enough at medical technology, we can get out of life alive. So, fear of death is a motivation that is deeply perverse in America.

BB: The connection, then with your vigils at Holy Family is that, precisely because it was a precipitous unexplained death, it could have been a trigger for fear, the fear that is connected to the aggressive medical fix-it-at-all-costs culture but also an aggressive foreign policy stance. Therefore, the vigil, in your view, is a way of the church concretely positioning its members to not be swept away in those two trajectories?

SH: That's right.

BB: Is that the kind of thing that is going to have to become more widespread and more intentional if, as you've taken to saying lately, in one hundred years Christians are going to be known as a people who don't kill their children or their elderly?

SH: I hope so. I know that sounds odd but I think we are increasingly moving to that culture. I mean, abortion is killing your children. And as you know, I think that is not just, "Oh, I'm not ready to have this child." I think it is, "I don't have anything worth passing on to a future generation." How you continue to encourage people to continue the habit of child-having is really going to be an interesting challenge. And I think the elderly are going to increasingly desire from their own self-interest to not live as long as their children might want them to live. I think there are some real challenges coming down the line on this.

BB: I totally agree, and I'm guessing that you also don't mean that they get more serious about contraception or that they get more organized about saving for paying for their retirement homes for their parents.

SH: I refuse to join the AARP![9] I don't think you ought to have a lobby around ageing. I do think it's interesting that one of the developments that is beginning to occur is the presumption that ageing is a disease. I think that's very dangerous.

BB: In *The Work of Theology* you provide a history of retirement as a new invention.[10] Along with it comes the leisure industry and inevitably it generates a type of

SH: I'm not sure confronting the fear of death does. What does defuse them is a society that has some recognition that it lives on wisdom that can only be sustained by the memory of people who have made mistakes on which the wisdom depends. Therefore, the elderly are robbing themselves and their children of that wisdom just to the extent that they think once they turn seventy, shuffleboard is the purpose of life.

BB: With you I lament and am often angry at the superficiality of the old people the baby boomer church has produced. Part of that superficiality is not being able to recognize their mistakes, or the mistakes that they do narrate being absolutely trivial. That superficiality has to be the bad fruit of some earlier mistakes. It sounds like you think one of the earlier mistakes is a lack of truthfulness.

SH: Stories are the work of memory through which we learn how to retain the complexity of our stories from one generation to the next. That we now think we can live without the story means exactly that the elderly have nothing to do.

BB: And they think they need to stay out of our way and not be a burden.

SH: That's right. I say the worst phrase in the world is "I never want to be a burden." I mean, you should want to be a burden! That's exactly who we are. We are burdens for one another.

BB: I've always been intrigued by the Old Testament's language of sitting at the gates. That seems to me to be an institutionalized way of letting discernment continue to operate within the community, carried by people who've made the mistakes, so they actually have a social role that forces them to do what you are asking.

SH: I think it may be true that that's a central image informing Oliver O'Donovan's work on judgment, particularly in *The Desire of the Nations*.[11] In that sense I am very persuaded.

BB: There seems also to be an associated evaporation or collapse of any social location in which elderly people are encouraged to collate their life stories and hand them on via discernments.

SH: The lack of intergenerational interactions within churches is a deep failure.

BB: Surely that's beyond a failure. That's a destruction of a tradition.

SH: No question.

BB: It's a tradition that is no tradition, as you often said. So, vigil would be one way to foster collective memory. What else?

SH: I think having a columbarium is useful. You get to remember who these people are. You get to touch these stones. They are all saints! On All Saints we read the name of every person that has died in our church, from the beginning!

BB: Again, another trans-Atlantic discovery: Upon about ten minutes' reflection it occurred to me how obscene it is that we quit burying people in the churchyard. I mean, what possessed us?

SH: I don't know, space maybe? I suspect it was money?

BB: Or hygiene? But of course, then you are going to have to start thinking, "Well church isn't about having dead people around. It's not about remembering the dead people in this church."

You know, standalone graveyards in Aberdeen grew from an inter-ecclesial dispute. Near the end of the seventeenth century the Quakers wanted to opt out of the habit of Christendom of burying everyone but suicides and those who were executed in the churchyard, for reasons you'd recognize as anti-Constantinian.[12] But you and I were born into a world that couldn't even imagine what might have been at stake in such a debate. The distance between those two situations looks to me like a picture both of the structural collapse of memory devices in Christendom, and also how the processes of secularization began in the church.

SH: It's interesting how very basic practices like that make it hard to tell your story.

BB: I actually started thinking about this in earnest when Adam was sick and I thought, "Where are we going to bury him?" I asked John Swinton, "I don't know how to do this but I'd like him to be buried around here, in a churchyard." Thank God he was able to keep that answer to himself, but he said he would do it, would do the preparation for us.

SH: We're going to be cremated because that's a necessity if you're going to be in the columbarium. Do y'all cremate around here?

BB: Yes. It tends to be more a part of the secular environment but it is highly streamlined for efficiency in a way that seems to undermine its memory-keeping role.[13] To be cremated, to be put in the basement of the church is not the same thing as being cremated in a conveyor-belt ceremony lasting fifteen minutes each and then having your ashes scattered in a beautiful place. These questions need to be thought through at several layers.

Do you have any truck with the early Christian argument, as recounted by Augustine, that you are dead and you are gone but there is a reverence owed to the body? His conclusion, therefore, is that you bury the body.[14]

SH: There is a reverence owed to the body, but I don't think that Augustine's conclusion follows. I certainly think that it is important for later generations to know where to come. I assume that if God can put together the bones in a Church of England churchyard in the resurrection, God can put together the ashes.

BB: But Augustine's point had nothing to do with that; it had to do with how we treat dead people.

SH: I think that's serious, but I think there is a reverence to the ashes.

BB: There's no one definitive Christian position on this topic, which is why we can have the discussion about all sorts of proposals and practices and can disagree with Augustine about burial. But it's called *Christian* theology because it's a way of asking how we should reverence the body that God gave to the person called Stanley after Stanley is not there anymore, simply because God created that body to be part of Stanley. Reverence is an enculturated activity, and even if you wanted it, I wonder if it would be irreverent to follow the current trend of spreading your ashes alongside your favorite running path.

Wherever we come down on such issues, it's continually exciting to me that we Christians have our own matrix, our own grammar, in which to discuss such issues. I'm passionate about having discussions among Christians that seek ways to respond to our present that have integrity within the language of our theological inheritance.

SH: I think that's right. Again, it's going to be particular in particular places.

BB: I'm remembering the conversation we had about armed guards in churches and Christians having concealed handgun permits. It seems like we could expect that set of commitments, given your emphasis on truth-telling, to yield some pretty blunt conversations.

SH: It could. I haven't had them. I don't know who at Holy Family owns guns. What I do know is that when I speak at Holy Family, I try to be relatively quiet, because I don't want there to be any confusion about who is in authority at Holy Family. Clark French, our rector, and Sarah and Paula are in authority. I don't want anyone in the congregation to simply think because I'm smart and I'm a theologian that I know more and therefore I can undercut the people in the ministry. So I try to be very careful. Though Clark encourages me to preach and speak at various times.

But what I try to do when I preach, or when I speak in the Adult Forum, I don't go directly at people and say, "You gotta get rid of your damn guns!" Rather, I try to start with the question: "How do you even start thinking about that as Christians in a way that may be persuasive for people?" One of the tricky things about having strong convictions that are embodied in the sermon itself is how the sermon can become a form of violence, just to the extent you state positions that you know are challenging people but they have no ability or opportunity to respond. How you take a strong position without it being coercive is one of the challenges I face.

BB: Harking back to the Matthew 18 passage, would you understand the way in which you've framed that answer to be an example of how the Anglican church in your time and place is thinking about the same problems that the Anabaptists were historically addressing through the ban?[15]

SH: Absolutely.

BB: That sounds like an affirmation that what Mennonites are doing when they are very serious about discussions that can lead to the ban, ought to provoke an inter-ecclesial response that might run: "that may be more violent than I'm comfortable with."

SH: Right. The Mennonites don't do Matthew 18 very often anymore.

BB: Oh really?

SH: It's a very big problem.

BB: Would you see that as a slip-back from speaking truthfully?

SH: Absolutely!

BB: Not that we Anglicans are the paragons on that front!

SH: Right!

BB: That's helpfully concrete in all sorts of ways, not least in reminding us that the way we speak to each other is a crucial forum for ecclesial ethical formation.

You've recently observed that your stands on these kinds of issues have occasionally led your students to forget that timing and patience are constituent components of the pastoral task. The most infamous interactions seem to have occurred when newly trained Duke pastors immediately removed American flags from the churches to which they had just been appointed. What do you think was the disconnect for these students, who had so clearly grasped something important from your teaching and yet had missed an important subtext? What exactly was the subtext that they missed?

SH: Namely that before you say "You have to remove the flag" they have to have learned to love you. And if they haven't done that, you shouldn't immediately walk in and say the flag has to be removed, because it is an act of violence. The flag for them stands for the loss of sons in World War II and that has to be respected. So it may take you five years to develop the kind of formation necessary for people to see that the flag, at the very least, belongs at the back of the church.

Radically ordinary

BB: Now I want to move to ask you to explain why such mundane activities as thinking about whether you are coercing the congregation with your sermon should be associated with the language of radicalism. In your book with Romand Coles such activities are labeled the "radical ordinary." What does the term "radical" actually mean here? What makes the ordinary "radical"?

You have made it quite clear that you think of *Christianity, Democracy and the Radical Ordinary*[16] as Coles's book, and I take that as read. What's interesting about that book is that the imagination of politics toward which Coles is striving is essentially an attempt to theorize the socially productive unrest of the 1960s.

Coles, and his inspiration Sheldon Wolin, take the civil rights struggle and the various grassroots movements of the 1960s to be paradigm moments in recent history in revealing what it practically looks like to push back against the proceduralism of contemporary party political machines.[17] Coles and Wolin attempt to name and describe in the language of political theory what they saw and experienced as the politically fertile moments of the 1960s revolutions. They want to distil its essence so that it can be fostered in our present. You note in the book that you met Coles because your students at Duke gravitated toward him, and saw in him some of the same things that had attracted them to you. But unlike Coles and Wolin, you tend to downplay your affinity for the 1960s radicals and also, unlike them, as you said in a previous conversation, you don't have a deep commitment to democracy as a political form of organization.

I'm fascinated by the journeys of the middle men, your students, who have typically been middle-class whites who have come from churches that were not really politically engaged, or insofar as they were, they were from the ends of the political spectrum with which you wouldn't have much sympathy. They would have been much more likely to have come from churches in which the Reagan revolution would have been lionized and the 1960s revolutionaries or contemporary anarchists demonized. So why do you think the perception in the American, especially evangelical, church that you are "radical" has been so powerful, and how does it relate to the radicalism of the 1960s that so dominates the political imagination of Coles and Wolin? You take a fascinating line in *Hannah's Child* in relation to the moral revolutions of the 1960s. On the one hand, you say you were too conservative to sympathize with the actual activism of the period, but you lament the collapse of the movement into bourgeois respectability—and essentially claim to be a carrier of the spirit of the movement.[18] Could you explicate what's going on here in theological terms?

SH: When I say that I was too conservative, I don't mean that I was politically conservative. What I mean is that I thought the Students for a Democratic Society and the articulation of what they wanted was so individualistic. The account of freedom that they were propounding was right out of the platform of the Republican Party. So, conservative could be another name for radical, just to the extent that you were challenging the primary presuppositions of what people took to be "the left," which I thought was way too conventional.

When I went to Notre Dame I taught a course I had started developing at Augustana called "Christian Ethics and a Democratic Society." I was trying to give the students resources to be able to understand what was going on in our politics and social life that drew on classical concepts out of political theory. When I went to Notre Dame, I ended up having students that Fr. Hesburgh had thrown out the year before for protesting the war out in front of the Administration building. I've already mentioned how they didn't think anything of standing up in class and calling you a fascist pig for even introducing categories of just war to think about the Vietnam War and so on. What a wonderful time to teach! Issues like, "Do we have obligations to the state *qua* human beings?" were live questions. They are still live questions for me. Oftentimes, the people who raised them at that time no longer entertain such questions as important. So that's what I meant by that.

In terms of putting it into theological terms, I thought that in order to get a hold on what was happening, you had to have a counter-community. Of course, I think the so-called New Left at the time finally floundered on not having this sustaining community across time that would give them a place to be other than continually protesting against what they regarded as a deeply unjust social order. So that's how I was trying to think through those matters.

BB: That illumines the genesis of your teaching on political theology and also suggests why you've more recently been sounding more explicitly "radical" notes, as in your recent public admiration for Jamie Scott's *Two Cheers for Anarchism*.[19] You take that book as a good example of how Christians might engage in "foot dragging" "small politics" that introduce an appropriately destabilizing disorder into a violently ordered polity.[20]

This positions us well to ask again the question about the last twenty years in which you and Romand had been in the same institution and had students going back and forth. If we trace the relationship of American Christians from the 1960s through the 1980s—a time when the Moral Majority gained great political power which is now fragmenting—the fact you and Coles were drawn together by having students that sensed a resonance between your interests is at least an indicator that there was a politically engaged cohort of students that were coming through. This was during a period in which the church was, by and large, understanding radicalism in ways you both would resist, such as, bombing abortion clinics.

SH: I moved to Duke in 1984. I had politically engaged students at Notre Dame for a while and then that went away. When I went to Duke it was the graduate students who had come through some of what was still the lingering influence of the 1960s that kept it alive.

What I mean by "radical ordinary" is just helping locate the significance of people who, for example, keep their promises. You can easily overlook that. In Vaclav Havel's *Living the Truth*[21] he tells about one of the times he was arrested and was punished by being sent to be a janitor in a beer brewery. It was a very bad brewery but there was a brewer there who really cared about brewing good beer. He worked and worked on it and he kept being prevented from doing that by the Communist bureaucrats that ran the brewery. So, he went over their heads to the local Communist committee to try and say, "We can do better as a brewery." Of course, the management of the brewery and the committee were in one another's pockets. So they punished the brewer by sending him to a worse brewery! The Communists were smart! Havel comments and says a good society will be one that lets good brewers brew good beer. Now that's radical ordinary.

You could say, "Well, that was a totalitarian context," but the other example I use is when Havel tells the story of the greengrocer who gets with his fruits and vegetables a sign, from the local communist headquarters, that he is to put in his windows, "Workers of the World Unite."[22] Havel says he's got no commitment to the workers of the world uniting and he doesn't believe the communist ideology around that. But he had to put the sign in his window because putting the sign in his window says, "I understand who is in power and I am frightened if I do not put this sign in my window." Havel asks whether he would put up *this* sign—"I'm frightened and therefore I put this sign in my window." I think that's a paradigmatic example of how so many of us oftentimes put signs in our windows that we don't believe, because we're afraid of what the alternatives might be. That's ordinary!

BB: That's of course an aspect of every society in some ways, which is why it's so politically explosive to ask questions like, "Why do you want to put an armed guard in your church?" or "Why do you want to have a gun under your pillow?" In every society fear takes forms that it is very difficult to see how it can be resisted.

SH: Once, at Broadway in South Bend, we had a murder in front of the church and some of our members bought guns. John Smith, our minister, preached a sermon and he said, "I understand some of you have bought guns. But that's what Christians can't do. I want you to bring those guns to me and I will take them to the police department and have them destroyed!" It was straight up! And they did! They brought their guns in! That's ordinary, but it is pretty radical.

BB: We now have two of your most central terms for thinking about the politics of the church in play: "truth-telling" and "radical ordinary." I now want to turn to talk about the third term, "gentleness."

Jean Vanier and the witness of L'Arche lie at the heart of the constructive vision of the politics of Jesus that develops in your mature work, a terminus that had been foreshadowed by earlier skirmishes with medicine. In *Radical Ordinary* you point out that you understand *Naming the Silences* to be your most extended work of political theory.[23]

SH: Do you agree with that? I do say that, but . . .?

BB: I'm only not immediately agreeing because I'm not sure how, precisely, you've arrived at that judgment. I think it is political theory, and I think it is arguably your most sophisticated exercise of it. But *Performing the Faith* might have more pages! And thus is more extended!

SH: I shouldn't put you on the spot. The reason is I think *Naming the Silences* is my most determinative form of political theory and this has to do with its subject being death. We don't notice the very way we teach ourselves about death entails extraordinary assumptions about the political.

BB: That's clearly hinting at your belief that the phrase "the war on terror" and the juggernaut of American medicine both signal types of response to death. If you want to talk about political ethics, you need to go into detail about how to handle the fear of death. That's why I would agree that *Naming the Silences* is your most *sophisticated* presentation of your political ethics. It leaves no stone unturned in saying, "Yeah, I know what is entailed in being afraid of death when somebody gets shot on your doorstep at church." If you think about your child dying of cancer, that's the most global experience of death that we can imagine in our context, and if we can come to terms with what the gospel means for living in the face of such a death we will be much better prepared to face a murder on the doorsteps of our churches.

That's why I think Vanier, again, allows you to talk through what the alternative politics to the politics of death might look like even though you admit that you find it hard to put Vanier's witness into words. Like a Moses who has led people through the desert of liberalism for forty years, you sometimes seem better able to point to the promised land than to depict how it works from inside its borders. The tension is concisely articulated when you write:

> I do not want to become poorer. I want to remain the academic who can pretend to defend those with mental disability by being more articulate than those I am criticizing. In short, I do not want to learn to be gentle. I want to be a warrior on behalf of Vanier, doing battle against the politics that threaten to destroy his gentle communities. Vanier, of course, is no less a warrior, but where I see an enemy to be defeated, he sees a wound that needs healing.[24]

SH: It's a terrific sentence, isn't it!

BB: It's at moments like these that it's clear that you are aware of the danger that your work is easily subverted when people receive it as a challenge and a crusade to establish pacifism, rather than as a sign in the wilderness pointing to intangible practices of living gently in a violent world. Given this danger, what do you think is lost and gained in your attempt to link or equate pacifism and gentleness as embodied in the life of Vanier? In other words, what is the *distinction* you are indicating when you say that Vanier and Yoder, "strike many of the same chords, even if in different keys"?[25]

SH: I think I would worry about the word "equate" in equating pacifism and gentleness as embodied in the life of Vanier. I don't think I equate them, but I want to see gentleness as an expression of peaceableness that is often not seen as such because the vulnerability that gentleness entails seems not to have the aggressiveness I associate with nonviolence.

But I think that they are profoundly linked just to the extent that if it is to be authentic gentleness, it has to be very hard. Another person that I think of as a gentle person is Dorothy Day. She was extraordinary in her gentleness, but don't get in her way when she is trying to sustain the poor! So that's the way I was trying to think about it.

You know I hate the word "pacifism," but partly what it means to link pacifism and gentleness is that I am always trying to find ways of making concrete what peace might look like. So to call attention to Vanier's gentleness is a way of trying to say, "That's what peace looks like."

BB: That's why I was asking about the relationship between Vanier and Yoder, because, theologically speaking, I am tempted to understand gentleness as more primordial than pacifism. One can imagine gentleness having been a feature of an unfallen world and pacifism, with all the out-riders against that term that we both agree on, is nevertheless a pushing-back against ways of denuded human living that are a consequence of the Fall. This is, no doubt, why you have stressed the important distinction to be made between pacifism and peaceableness.

But as I heard you framing it just now, you again seem to be asserting that peaceableness was the larger, or more overarching, category. But I would say that as a reading even of your own work, only if gentleness is primordial can you assert that "the politics of gentleness cannot be a triumphalist politics." And only in terms of your own account could you distinguish yourself from John Milbank by saying, "Milbank wants Christians to win but I think the best we should want is for Christians to endure."[26]

In other words, if peaceableness is in fact a synonym for gentleness, this would render "pacifism" a political institutionalization of gentleness within one domain of human life after the Fall and in the face of various forms of violence. This would, it seems to me, protect Christian pacifism from being trapped in the posture of a crusade by the Constantinianism with which it is by definition in contest. But even on your own terms, in order to make such a claim you still seem to need to say that gentleness is more primordial.[27]

SH: I don't have any strong reason not to agree with that. But I am just wondering why one needs to be more primordial than the other? Primordial, I take it, suggests we wouldn't be able to talk about peacefulness if we didn't have a more determinative category called gentleness. Is that right?

BB: Yes.

SH: I don't know if that's true or not. I think it is a conceptual issue, and I suppose you just have to look at sentences to see in what way the grammar works to say that if you are gentle, then you are necessarily committed to pacifism, in a way that if you're committed to pacifism, it doesn't necessarily mean you are committed to gentleness.

BB: And that's exactly my worry! In so far as people read you as pacifist and think that somehow excuses them if they are not being gentle, I'd like to insist that is not a venial sin but a complete falsification of your work.[28]

SH: Right. That's good.

You know, I'm a gentle guy! I really am. My father was much more gentle. I like the word "gentleman." I like the word "gentlewoman." I think it is a way to be gentle, without gentleness inviting misuse of another human being. That's always a problem. But I think the "gentleman" was one that did not fear being misused, because they would rather be misused than not live a life that betokened people of character.

BB: My other thought is that all the most in-your-face and properly aggressive acts of nonviolence I can think of have to be collective acts, in some way. But it is not aggression that sustains the formation of those collectivities. Collectives only form when we attend to one another in a manner that allows a political community that recognizes shared goods to gain some solidity. This is another way in which it behooves those who aspire to be peacemakers to understand nothing can be built on isolated provocative acts, nor can a peacemaking community emerge in contexts where the basic tenor is aggressive.

SH: That's right. One of the places where you could think about this, Brian, is in marriage. What is one of the most frightening aspects of marriage? The person we are married to learns to know us better than we know ourselves. That's why they are able to hurt us the most; they know our vulnerabilities. I think that there's a certain sense in which it is very important that there be a gentleness between people who are married. It is a learned virtue.

BB: And if we have gained some clarity on this point, it opens up for me a very important further question about how we understand authority. You've hinted at the role of authority in the context of Holy Family. But I'd like to talk a little bit further about authority, and more specifically, judgment. I'm thinking here of the story about your pastor saying, "You guys need to turn those guns in to me." That seems like a classic example of the judgment of authority. So how does that fit with gentleness and peacemaking?

It is clear that Vanier, for example, was an authority figure in the L'Arche movement, and made quite a few sharp judgments, some of which he later had to backpedal from. It is well known that he sent back one of the three initial people he welcomed to his home from the mental institution, and that he repulsed Père Thomas's early intention to welcome all poor people, vagabonds, and unemployed people into the community as well as refusing and sometimes ejecting assistants who were corrosive of the bonds of community.

Can these forms of ejection and resistance be understood as acts of gentleness or peacemaking? And more importantly, how do we say this without affirming that "violence is necessary for the maintenance of a just and secure order"?[29]

SH: You might not want to call it gentleness but you might want to call it acts of judgment necessary in order for us to remain a gentle community. There just are limits, oftentimes, to how far you can go with someone who is fundamentally disruptive and doesn't get it. You can think of it this way: if your brother or sister doesn't repent—Matthew 18—you are to regard them as a stranger. So the ban is the form of a judgment of a community which says these are the conditions necessary for you to be part of our community. Excommunication is not, "You're a sonofabitch. We're throwing you out. We don't ever want to see you again." It says, rather, "You're a sonofabitch. And here are the conditions that would make it possible for you to come back." Excommunication isn't throwing someone out. It's telling someone that they're already living in a way that places them outside of the community and these are the conditions to come back.

BB: I know you have a very sophisticated definition of violence. Would that act, then, not be violence?

SH: I don't think so. I don't know that I do have a sophisticated definition of violence. I usually don't have definitions at all. I think what you have are descriptions that allow you to provide analogical suggestions about what may be violent, but that you don't notice is violent. One of the reasons I don't like the language of nonviolence is that it makes "peace" what is "not violent." That then makes violence more determinative than peace! So if Augustine is right that evil is always parasitic on the good, then peace has to be more primary than violence. You are able to spot violence because you have been constituted by peace.

BB: When you say—and this is a genuine question—that Christians cannot affirm that violence is necessary for the maintenance of a just and secure order, is that a stipulative description which orients thinking? It may be that levying the ban could be an act of violence, in which case it needs to be repented of. But we're constantly asking that question in the same way that you already alluded to, certain sermons could be acts of violence if they are too prescriptive.

SH: Not prescriptive, but dogmatically . . .

BB: . . . unilaterally promulgated?

SH: Right, right.

BB: There is an issue of moral psychology that I'd like to look into at this point. It's related to how we articulate the active and passive aspects of peacemaking. Coles points out how discipleship, forgiveness, and hospitality can all be turned into power moves if the narrative we deploy to define those turns on an act that *we* undertake. This is to situate all these practices as species of the heroic act.[30] We can be disciples, forgive and be hospitable in a heroic mode. Fits really nicely with the superhero Jesus guys like Mel Gibson are looking for. You have made much of the passivity of the Christian who must receive the Christian story and so reject the liberal myth that we have all had to choose a story when we had no story.

But do not some of the formulations in your early work, especially their interest in urging Christians to "form themselves" according to the Christian story, succumb to the foregrounding of human agency that Coles warns is so dangerous? How today would you relate the call to active self-formation that recurs in your earlier work to Vanier's claim that our healing requires little more activity on our part than being willing to actively expose our weakness and wounds to others, supremely to God?

SH: The answer is "Yes." The early emphasis on Christians forming themselves did not do justice to the fact, in MacIntyre's language, that we are at best cocreators of our own lives. I was floundering around trying to find appropriate language to avoid the strong agency language of libertarianism and the equally strong behavioral reductionism associated with those that were trying to claim that human action is always the result of efficient causation.

So I don't know that I yet have an adequate moral psychology, to be able to deal with that problem. But I continue to try. And habit is very important.

BB: That's the domain in which you are trying to work these questions out to your satisfaction, theologically?

SH: Right! Right!

Saints, exemplarity, and advent

BB: On my reading, important strands of your work converge in the essay "Seeing Peace"[31]: the emphasis on particular Christian language and ethics, on the relation of God to the bodiliness of faith, on disability and your critiques of just war. In short, in this essay you are finally able to say, "Look—here's where we see what living with God looks like in its most obvious contrast with the living from fear that drives the idolatry and violence of our secular liberal societies." The aspiration of the essay becomes much more apparent when we notice that you published it in two collections, one which positions it in the discourse of political ethics, and a second time as an intervention in theological discussions of disability.[32] Like *Naming the Silences*, it concretizes your criticisms of the dominance of "statist" accounts of Christian political engagement by way of a thick illustration of how these play out in relation to medical ethics and disability.

What I am trying to point out is that, like *Naming the Silences,* you are again using the domain of disability and our relation to physical incapacity—with death as its outer-horizon—as a way to articulate both the church's distinctive politics as well as to make an attempt more concretely to narrate what it means to call the church a peaceable community. In my view the piece is brilliant and undeniably important. At the same time, it is remarkable that it also remains in the stance of the *observer* of peace. In effect it says, "Look here, and seeing this, you will see an embodiment of God's peace." Namely, look at L'Arche. This is not to deny that this gesture sets up a heuristic with far-reaching ethical import. Look at the world in this way and you are going to see peace. But it is not a "view from inside."

It would be a very different operation if it went where Vanier wants to take us, for instance, with his regular discussion of "second birth." Vanier's way of putting it is more like, "If you want to live peaceably, each of you as individuals should prepare yourselves to make these kinds of passages, should expect and wait for a sequence of invitations to conversion, and when they arrive, you should embrace them as the coming of a new birth, no matter how painful." You say something important, and yet importantly different: "Look at those people over here, they perform peace properly." To the reader, then, though both of you are influenced by Aristotle, you nevertheless have very

4. Ecclesial Politics, Peacemaking, and Worship 111

different ideas about how to invite people into flourishing, and thus how moral exemplars serve this invitation. To use a biblical idiom, I would say that you start with the biblical narratives, and Vanier starts from the wisdom literature.

SH: When I read this I thought, "That's really interesting." I don't know what to say about it. That phrase, that it all still remains in the stance of the observer of peace, that's right. I hadn't thought of that. And then the question becomes: Do I need to be thinking more about how to recommend the disciplines of the process of peace or something like that? Probably.

I think I do that partly when I think about what it means to have a process of confrontation, reconciliation, or confession or acknowledgment of our wrong, reparations, and so on—but that's not really an answer to this very interesting question.

I guess I'm not involved enough in a "peace process." I've always thought of the university as a peace process, because the university should be the place where people are set aside to have conflicts that a social order needs to have short of violence. I want to think I've been part of working for peace as a university person my whole life. But that's obviously also an invitation to self-deception.

BB: It does raise a question about how moral exemplars are placed. You seem to have taken two tacks: the more dominant one has been, "Look over here! This person is doing it right." It's not just Vanier, but he is a common character in that role. But when Vanier himself cashes out his own emplacement in that role, he says, "Look, this is what you are going to face inside of it and these are the important passages to negotiate as a work of faith when you do." But now that you have alluded to having thought about these questions, would you also say that that's not something that you've put on the page?

SH: I have. I can't remember if it is in *The State of the University* or not, but I have tried to say something like that somewhere.[33]

BB: This question first occurred to me (and I articulated it in brief form in my *Singing the Ethos of God*[34]) because it seemed to me that many people who had been inspired by your work were proceeding to say, "If you want to know how to read scripture theologically and in the church, what you need to look for is examples of good practice." And the questions that immediately raised for me were: "What if what I see around me is clearly a mess; and if I see someone who seems to be doing it well, what if I see *what* they're doing but not *how* they're doing it?" What happens if I try and fail to mimic what seems right about what they are doing? Even attempting to mimic a good expositor may raise so many questions that I stall out. Another layer of pedagogy seems necessary. And as Alex Sider has recently observed, it may also skirt some important questions about the moral psychology involved.[35]

Now we could raise all sorts of critical questions about the way Vanier talks about the inner passages involved in spiritual growth, and he's usually speaking about the growth processes of assistants through the discovery of their own anger and weakness. But it does seem to me that at least in the reception of your work, the insight into the inner work that I think your work assumes is not always picked up by your interpreters, who think it is sufficient just to point to examples. Might your growing emphasis on habit be a type of recognition of that problem?

SH: I don't think it is sufficient at all.
I just don't know what more to say!

BB: Let's move on to a related issue then, the relationship of recollection to Advent. One place this question surfaces is in your banter with Coles about being "haunted" by other thinkers. You say that you are haunted by Vanier, and he says that he is haunted by you and Yoder.[36] What do you think is at stake in this rhetoric? More pointedly, what is the relationship between *hearing* and being *haunted*? What sort of agency do we ascribe to the voices that haunt us?

You often speak about remembering, and Coles likes the language of "echoes" of dead voices, a mechanical metaphor that presumably points to our own present will to remember. But does this do justice to the power of figures from the past actively to claim us for themselves, *surprise* us? In the end Coles often resorts to much more active images of those who haunt him, by drawing, for instance, on Walter Benjamin's messianic imagery, which is very active.

In my view Coles can't really say what he wants to say without a *communio sanctorum*. He treats what he hears as so authoritative that it gives his life orientation. It is hard, therefore, for a Christian not to see him as revering his interlocutors as saints, who, though dead, still speak in a very lively way to him. You also often speak of memory and remembering in terms that seem to deny the saints any agency. Do you want to say something different about how the saints "haunt" the Christian than the Zwinglian who says of the Eucharist that we "do this in remembrance" in order to reform our imaginations?

SH: Yeah, I think so. I think that's a nice way to put it. To be haunted is already to acknowledge a moral claim that you cannot help but think is true and powerful, but which you yourself are not sure you are capable of living out. Rom, I think, is haunted by the question of whether he can have what he's learned from Yoder, without believing in God. I'm haunted by his agnosticism because his work and his life are morally impressive as a person who seems to represent what I think we should be, and yet he doesn't have to go to church! So, to be haunted, is to recognize that you are close to being in an epistemological crisis, in MacIntyre's sense. I take it that that's a good thing.

Now, what this means for being haunted by the past—while there are reasons to acknowledge past injustices—but to be haunted by the past through memory is to, again, see the significance of someone in a manner that we're not quite sure what to do with what we have acknowledged. I think that the saints serve that function is clearly something for which we ought to be glad.

BB: And they serve that function because their narratives place tension on our self-understanding?

SH: Yes. We have enough self-understanding that we know they place a tension on it!

BB: It's different then from the Zwinglian remembrance in that we don't call it to mind, but it is the same in that it is essentially happening within the subject, but involuntarily.

SH: I don't know about the word "involuntarily."

BB: Haunting is the appearance of a personal presence we did not will.

SH: Right. But I was also trying to say that you have to be at least willing to acknowledge the significance of that by which you are haunted because that means the acknowledgment that you are so haunted is not nonvoluntary.

BB: OK. The reason that I invoked the *communio sanctorum* is that's an eschatological notion. When we're talking about the stories of the saints we're not talking exclusively in the past tense. Their stories are alive for us because in some sense *they* are alive, alive to us through the Holy Spirit. So, on our own terms, we would be capable of giving some sort of account of the hauntings of nonbelievers, but it would be an eschatological account?

SH: That's much better! That's great!

BB: I put it that way because as I've sat with your work over time I've come to realize how strongly determined my own thinking has been by your two very deep emphases on eschatology and contingency, and on the church as the concrete forum within which the determinative Christian political formation takes place. The main point at which I feel some divergence is the descriptions we're prepared to offer the role of revelation in Christian ethics, which is why I've been, at several points in our conversations, trying to get to the bottom of how you understand the advent of God's saving work in human life. I want to clarify how you understand the activity of claiming our lives from their sinful bondage by clarifying the roles you think listening, receptivity and passivity play in Christian sanctification.

Another way into this question is to explore what Coles calls the "Milbank-Wells" co-option of your work. The co-option happens, he thinks, when Christians believe they must out-narrate or situate the stories that others—supremely nonbelievers—tell within the wider story of the cosmos as Christians discern it in Jesus Christ.[37] It is here that the emphasis that was strong at the beginning of your work but which you've just distanced yourself from—on discipleship as "forming a self"—seems to be in tension with the politics you are seeking in your discussion with Coles. And it's also why terms like "memory" and "remembering" which, like "hearing" and "echo," are politically very important—each of them can be defined in ways that limit the role the other is allowed to play in reshaping our self-identity and so behavior. Coles's complaint about a certain reading of your work parallels his worry about Cornel West—that he overemphasizes prophetic speaking to the detriment of the prophetic listening to living voices which is clearly its basis and should give it orientation.[38] His worry is that West so foregrounds the importance of prophetic preaching that he overlooks that the reason that prophetic preaching is powerful is that it is in touch with what's happening on the ground.

How then would you like us to understand the central role you've given to remembering in your work? How can we account for the work of remembering in a manner that allows us to remain vulnerable to being unexpectedly reoriented rather than closing ourselves off? This amounts to a question about how we "hear our way through the world"[39] as you at one point suggestively propose.

SH: Out-narrating *can* be a Constantinian expression. Yet at the same time, "Jesus is Lord" is a narrative that seems to challenge all other narratives that would identify someone else as Lord. So, if you want to maintain Jesus is Lord, does that require you to be always ready to out-narrate? I think out-narrate in that context is too determinative. You don't have to out-narrate. You may well want to say that this is a story that I think you will find qualifies some of the narratives that make up your life. But it's not so much that you out-narrate but that you provide a better way of life. That may feel like someone's been out-narrated. Some people in our society today will say something like, "Jesus is Lord, but that's just my personal opinion!" You certainly want to out-narrate that and you want to out-narrate what produces that. What produces that are social orders with strong distinctions between the public and the private, where anything you want to say about Jesus is in the private. It's a complex business, in that regard. In part the claim that I want to be a theocrat highlights this complexity.

BB: This leaves me still unclear whether you want to resist Coles's complaint or to grant that he has an important point. Here again, the Cornel West example seems important. The way I'd be tempted to read the answer you've just given is to say that in so far as we want to be out in Hyde Park Corner arguing with other people and constantly seeking the most powerful apologetic arguments in the public square, that's the kind of aggression without gentleness that would typically be associated by Coles with the virulent mis-reading, co-option as he puts it, of your work. Insofar as our practices as Christians are articulate, it is certainly true that the power and indeed the scope of our narrative will radically question other people's narratives. But only in that sequence. So you can say, "Jesus is Lord but that's my personal opinion" because you are in a place and society where in fact power is on your side already.

SH: Probably. Right. And so you don't notice the irony.

About hearing, do we hear our way through the world? You can only act in the world you can see and you can only see what you have learned to say and you can only learn to say by what you have learned to hear. We hear our way through the world, so the ability to recognize what we just heard is really important.

BB: I hadn't heard that particular sequence of thoughts before.

SH: I'd never said it before!

BB: Sequencing those thoughts that way suggests that when you say "hearing" you are emphasizing how intelligibility always comes to us by way of our and the other's activity which is wholly culturally embedded in our place and time. To "hear our way through the world" is thus to take seriously the way the language of our time and place is configured, which is, as we've picked up at several points, very important for you as one of the continuing legacies of the Lindbeckian Yale framework. This seems beautifully to explain comments like this one from Coles—acknowledging that you would not insist on calling this "democracy" as he does.

> Nothing is more important to radical democracy today than cultivating relationships through which more and more people might become a "we" of more resonant bodies: picking up the tones, overtones, and undertones of others; listening and resonating so provocatively that new tones in others are reverberated into being; listening and resonating so profoundly that old tones in others, days and years and centuries gone by, still resound, perform, and ignite within us.[40]

SH: That's Coles's prose.

BB: That's quite a poetic set of phrases. And the description of the coming to being of radical democracy it presents is so evocative that it leaves me suspicious that the politics Coles is after can only really be said of the church. On what grounds does Coles claim the dead speak like this? The community of the church does not rely on a mechanical effect—I'm pointing here to Coles's language of "resonance"[41]—to evoke new and surprising ways of seeing and living, but on a person—Jesus Christ who creates a community that lives in Him through the Spirit.

In the course of your discussion with Coles, when you speak of the agency of Jesus you never go beyond the language of surprise[42] or disruption.[43] This is a typical passage:

> If I am haunted, I am haunted by Vanier. I am haunted by Vanier because my strident polemics on behalf of the church seem so hollow when juxtaposed against the confident, joyful work L'Arche represents. I suspect Vanier would remind me, however, that such confidence is but the overflow of the love found through the worship of the Father, Son and Holy Spirit. To worship such a Lord, a King who rules from a cross, is to learn to live by surprise, because you never know where or how such a God is going to show up.[44]

What is this surprise you are watching or listening for? Is it different from Wolin's "emergent irregularities"?[45]

SH: If I knew what I was watching and listening for, how would I know it was a surprise!

BB: You read Wolin as a little bit overdetermined by his emphasis on surprise as the heart of politics?

SH: I guess that's right. I think what Wolin wants to talk about in terms of tending to our politics, using the garden metaphor, is "I was planting pea vines but I was surprised. I thought they were going to be Lima beans but they came up Snow peas!" That's the kind of surprise that I think we're about.

BB: When you say, then, that worshiping "a King who rules from a cross, is to learn to live by surprise, because you never know where or how such a God is going to show up," you are asking Christians to live by a different, Christologically configured, form of peace?

SH: I think that's a lot of it.

BB: The situation is always not precisely what you expected it to be and you should never expect it to be what you expected it to be. To be a Christian will always mean being prepared to be mobile. Your thinking and action should always be ready to respond to the unexpected.

SH: The cross was not defeat! And that gives you hope to have a garden.

BB: And one of the surprising outcomes of the cross is that it emboldens Christians to say, "I know it seems like somebody getting killed on the doorstep means you ought to ensure your future by buying guns, but in fact that's an abandonment of hope." To buy a gun is to confess, in deed, that "In the end, violence wins." The cross shows us that Christian hope means, "Well, violence wins a lot, but the gospel invites Christians to live in expectation of the surprising overturning of that law."

SH: That's right. And if you don't go down that road, the road you are going down will create possibilities that otherwise wouldn't exist because you are a different kind of person.

The body's grammar and the Christian story

BB: Let's follow up a point you've just made about the relations between seeing, hearing, and acting. Once L'Arche becomes the paradigm of a peaceable politics for you, you are more sharply able to articulate a point which it seems to me is crucial, but which never came fully to the surface of your previous writings on disability: the communicative power of the body.

> L'Arche is the extended training necessary to learn the language of the body and pain. The people who speak that language—a language whose "words" are often gestures of the body—do not need to be explained. They are there—like life. Our task is to learn to listen to what they have to say.[46]

In my experience people find this point a difficult one to understand, and as a result they misunderstand the force of your enduring emphasis on the fundamental ways that language shapes life. "But what about people who don't speak?" they respond. Could you explain to such a reader how this Wittgensteinian emphasis on deeds as the primal basis of words relates to your enduring stress that words, specifically the words of scripture and Christian faith, are the basic matrix of Christian worship and ethics? When you write, "the body has its reasons making action possible,"[47] how do you understand this to relate to the claim that it is the stories of scripture and Christian language that make Christian living possible, or, as you often put it—here citing Cavell on Wittgenstein:

> If you do not know the grammatical criteria of Wittgensteinian objects, then you lack, as it were, not only a piece of information or knowledge, but the possibility of acquiring any information about such objects *überhaupt*; you cannot be told the name of that object, because there is as yet no *object* of that kind for you to attach a forthcoming name to: the possibility of finding out what it is officially called is not open to you.[48]

How do these two articulations relate to one another? You seem to be pointing toward one answer with one of your oft-repeated formulations: "You can only act in the world you can see, but you can only see by learning to say."[49] Also, when you write, "Recognizing and explicitly acknowledging an eschatological rather than a teleological orientation serves as a helpful reminder that the [Christian] story centers on a sovereign God and not on the acting human subject."[50] I'm tempted to read this as a prioritizing of the "Christian story" grammar as deeper than the "body's reasons" grammar, though you do try to bring them together with the image of the disabled learning to dance.[51]

SH: Boy. The first thing that comes to mind is when I was first watching you and Stephanie with Adam and how you learn to read his body and he learns to communicate to you through his body. I think that's appropriately called "language." I think that where you say this is a prioritizing of the "Christian story" grammar as deeper than the "body's reasons," I guess I don't want to prioritize at all. I want to see them as mutually implicated in that way.

There is a kind of natural theology set of claims involved here. When people ask me, "Why should I believe in God?" I say, "Do you like to eat?"! I think the body pulls us into the recognition that God would have us be bodily creatures whose passions pull us into a life with God.

BB: Is there some tension in your work on this point? Sometimes you give such a strong eschatological account of the body that it is hard to know what creaturely nature can add to our theological thinking. In *Christians among the Virtues*, for instance, you say that we can't do much work with the language of human nature in Christian ethics because "Christianity imagines a new world in which we all will be changed."[52] Given this eschatological emphasis, which I find very much welcome, I'm still left unsure what's left for creation to do in your work, or the confession of the world as creation. You don't often invoke creation, but when you do, it is almost always to point to the ways that human bodies present crucial barriers to human ambition and call forth patience from us. We could say that the narrowing of the doctrine of creation to the human body is already a truncation of traditional usage, but that is not my concern here.

My puzzlement has to do with how your invocation of the Christian account of creation operates in explicating the human body and its role in our ethical thinking. There are occasions when you draw on natural theological arguments about the way the body speaks, but with that come some remarkably sweeping caveats. To be a good medical patient, for instance, we must learn what it means that we have been given our bodies by a God who has not done this as an act of power but as a form of providential care.[53] The gift of Christians to modern medicine is to develop the patience that puts us "on the way to holiness as we learn that we are not our own creations."[54]

All this makes obvious sense—we have and are bodies and they make claims on us that because God created them, we should not ignore. But in a footnote you introduce this proviso:

> We are acutely aware, as anyone must be after the work of Foucault, that appeals to the "body" are anything but unproblematic. Recent historical work helps us better understand why Paul could say that nothing was more "spiritual" than the body. Moreover, understanding the body as peculiarly "spiritual" we think has great potential for helping us re-examine the relation of Christian practices and the practice of medicine.[55]

Has the work an account of creation might do decreased in such formulations to a vanishing point?

SH: Let me provide the context for how I think about creation. In effect, I am reacting against the Calvinist isolation of creation from redemption in a way that they think legitimates talk about common moral knowledge. Such knowledge is used to make possible their ruling other people in the name of what we *really* know, that other people don't know.

So my worry has been with that use of creation to underwrite a natural morality that is not disciplined by Christological considerations. But I do think that the body—remember Wittgenstein's comment that the best picture of the soul is the body—is crucial for helping us be drawn into a recognition of how at once the body enriches our life and at the same time beckons our death. That is a condition that opens up our ability to acknowledge through God's grace what it means to be a creature.

That's a big deal, to acknowledge that you are a creature.

BB: I grasp and agree with the complaint about the severing of the body from a Christological grammar, but I hope I can press you to further clarify *in what way* the body might function, as you seem to need it to do, to offer resistance to our misconceived desires. I want to ask that because it seems we are entering a new moral world in which a fresh set of arbitrary boundaries—I say fresh because there have been many arbitrary boundaries that have been tied to the body—are being drawn at the moment about how we can and can't understand our bodies to exert a moral claim against our desires. There are entirely warranted concerns about skin color overdetermining our moral perception, and there is a parallel absurdity of going the other way around and screening it, absolutely, from all moral deliberation. In the wars about sexuality the status quo position has become that the body cannot and should not impinge on morality or on our desires at all.

Yet, we still, in common language, speak as if the anorexic or the self-harming person should question their desires to see their bodies as they do. Both analytically and pastorally, concepts like gender dysphoria collapse if we don't admit the moral force of the body's own forms of organization. But I am still not entirely clear how you would understand such claims to be theologically grounded, if you think they should be?

SH: I'm always hesitant about the phrase "theologically grounded." Do we mean theological convictions to know that we are bodily? No. But the way we are bodily invites theological construal to show that our bodies are modes of communication with others in which we then discover that the body in which we live is not the end of our body, but that we are embodied through others. That opens up a vast range of reflections about what it means to learn your body is a gift, socially.

BB: You would be resistant, then, to narrowing the question of the body's claim to what makes you feel good or just the doctrine of the creation. *That* and *how* the body makes a claim—that has to be understood through the whole fullness of Christian faith?

SH: Right.

BB: How does that clarify why we think that the self-harmer should stop, or that their body is telling them that they should stop? Is that type of argument in a different universe from somehow saying that our bodies should impinge on the way, for instance, we marry?

SH: No. I take it that the body shouting out not to be harmed has continuity with "male and female he created them."

BB: But even that passage itself corroborates your point since Jesus cited it. It first appears in the creation account but then it is reiterated in the Gospels and it has come to us through scriptures transmitted to us by the people of God.[56] So we're invoking the whole biblical narrative when we cite that phrase.

Nevertheless, here as in other places you've tended to emphasize the asymmetry between creation and eschaton. Because of God's difference in kind from all creatures, knowledge of God cannot be extrapolated on the basis of observations about creation alone. This is why the first sentence of the creation story is fundamental for Christian theology: it establishes the basic distinction between God and all that is not God. In the beginning there is God and there is contingency. If we understand this categorical distinction it becomes plain why God cannot be known except by revealing Godself, meaning that for the fallen human, or humanity as we know it, our knowledge of God must always begin with a turn that can neither be reduced to the inner-creaturely vectors of causality, nor does it always flow from what we already know of it. This brings us back, however, to the root images of the Christian life: half of you seems to want organic imagery at the root, and the other half a repentance/turning/disruption imagery (which seems much closer to the cruciform grammar of the Christian life). You have spoken several times about wanting to keep natural and revealed theology close together. Do you want to keep these two sides in equipoise, or do you think that the division between them is illusory, or do you lean toward one side more than the other?

SH: I think I prefer repentance, turning, and disruption because they are more narratively deep terms than organic growth. It depends on how each life is displayed in that way. If you think about the "little flower," she didn't have anything to repent of! It was all organic growth.

BB: Let me go back to your comment about my relationship with Adam, who has taught me an immense amount about embodiment, being someone who doesn't speak and someone who I find it very difficult . . . well, I always say he doesn't really speak, because he does articulate some very unintelligible pidgin words. In fact, I know what he wants. I often know what he is thinking. He has a few signs. We get along pretty well. So that looks a lot like the body has its reasons. When he is in pain, he can't articulate that but his body articulates that, so that's how I understand that part of the phrase.

You've been to church with him and seen him take Eucharist. He doesn't go to Eucharist because he's hungry. In fact, he never, under any other circumstances, takes one drink of anything. For him it's clearly not even a quenching of thirst, though every once in a while he does have to have the cup wrestled away from him! You'll understand why questions about his relationship to the source of his being are raised by that activity, given that it is hard to imagine him being catechized in any intellectually substantive way, and it's impossible for me to imagine him saying the creed or even articulating the name "Jesus Christ."

That's why I think it is difficult to avoid making one of the two grammars deeper than the other, because we can't say that he's eating because he's hungry. It therefore can't be *that* bodily desire that's drawing him to the Communion rail. It looks a lot more like he is choosing in a Wittgensteinian grammar to embrace a role within a social order. Now does he rationally know that the Communion is Communion? It would be hard to believe that.

SH: Do you?

BB: I believe he is "taking Communion" not just "having a sip of wine." But I also can talk about it and be appropriated into it through the medium of language in a way that he can't.

SH: So you do it for him?

BB: I think of going with him to church every week and us being in a tradition where it's a physical thing to eat and drink and move around the sanctuary as both worship and catechesis. I know I confessed his faith for him at baptism, and I can't say for sure but I think he might well commune for himself. I think he probably has been incorporated deeply enough into the Christian story because he's part of a liturgy and he knows how it works and he knows what comes next and he largely willingly embraces that, which is about as much understanding as I would expect from anybody else in the entire congregation. Last Sunday the server didn't give him the wine and he just stayed there at the rail until she came around again! He knows what he's there for, and it's definitely not lunch!

SH: All that is the body being shaped by habit. The story is shaping him. Probably it's that basic for you and me!

BB: It's true, it's true.

But at least to make sense of what is happening on Sunday morning, could we say that what we believe is *really* going on there is organized according to the Christian story? Without the story being basic, how could we even say what the habit is that he's acquiring? How could we even raise the question of what his body is telling us in receiving the habit of worship as part of his body's grammar? We have to recognize that the grammar of his body *as body* is not pulling him to the Communion rail. Remember, he's not hungry! Or probably better, he's hungry, it's lunchtime after all, but he knows *this* meal isn't going to fix *that* hunger. But I do believe it satisfies his habituated expectation of what should happen in church.

SH: I trust your judgment on that better than I do mine.

BB: I think we were feeling our way toward some terribly important insights, insights, incidentally, which have come to me in the wake of Stephanie and me having gone down the path opened up when you and John Webster confronted me in public a decade ago with the challenge that leads directly into all these questions: "Why haven't you baptized Adam yet?" It was a much needed push at the time, for which we are both grateful. It was just the right thing to say, and it has been incredibly theologically and existentially liberating in light of his scrapes with death and the oddly prophetic role he constantly seems to play.

The point at which you've gone most deeply into the engine room of the politics of the Kingdom, unsurprisingly, is where we began this conversation, at the point of the problem of learning to speak truthfully.

> [I]n the interest of being good citizens, of being civil, Christians have lost the ability to say why what they believe is true. That loss is, I want to suggest, a correlative of the depoliticization of the church as a community capable of challenging the imperial pretensions of the modern state. That the church matters is why I resist using the language of "belief" to indicate what allegedly makes Christians Christian.[57]

What is remarkable about this formulation is that it might have been written at any point in your career, but happens to have been written very recently. As you note in the introduction to *Performing the Faith*, it took you several tries fully to explicate your understanding of this constructive alternative, as the reason why you needed to take this route only became crystal clear late in your career.

> Pacifism and nonviolence are inadequate to describe the kind of peace that should be characteristic of Christian worship. Pacifism is just too "passive" and nonviolence is too dependent on being "not violence." We can only begin to understand the violence that grips our lives by being embedded in more determinative practices of peace—practices as common and as extraordinary as prayer and the singing of hymns.[58]

We've heard why those might be called radical ordinary practices. We are left, then, with the clear insight that the problem of sanctification revolves around becoming people capable of speaking the truth.

We practice worship because it is here that God enters into our time, as you put it in *Performing the Faith*.[59] You begin to stress that the practice of worship is central because you have noticed that people were beginning to turn your Lindbeckian account of narrative into an apologetic strategy, which would run something like, "[W]e're all storytellers anyway, so Christians should tell the Christian story."[60] Because the practice of worship reveals the rupture between the time of God and of the warring nations it provokes in us an intensity of awareness about the quality of time that allows us to place our words more truthfully in the time and context in which we utter them, which is the condition of any truthful speech. We must realize where we stand within the landscape of salvation history when we speak if we are to speak truthfully. We learn this in worship alongside more mundane skills of respectful and attentive listening, reverence toward others, receptivity toward God, and, in them all, patience.[61] In this way Christians are incorporated into God's story,[62] learning "to see in the sheer 'thereness' of what is: God's work."[63] This is peace, which is "but the name given to a life of virtue in which what we do is not different than what we are."[64]

Does this sound like an accurate description of your most developed formulation?

SH: Yeah. I was going to say I didn't have anything to say about this, but just as commentary on your locating that quote about the loss of our ability to think what we believe as Christians is true is due to depoliticization of the church as a community, I think that's an insight that very few people have gotten hold of. Namely, that our humbling of the epistemological claims of the Christian faith is not the result of challenges from science or of historical critical developments about the Bible or Darwinism, but it really is the depoliticization of the church. As a result, we cannot avoid the presumption that what we believe as Christians are always subjectivistic impositions on reality. I just think that set of claims hasn't been taken up, and I think they are pretty good.

Hexis and worship

BB: OK. Let's look at one last set of themes that illumine precisely how worship reforms a Christian polity. A set of connections emerge in the late essay "Suffering Beauty" that seem to me to lay bare the most developed account of the politics you want us Christians to learn. Here is the central claim: "Ethics and liturgy but name different ways of specifying the practical wisdom of the church about the everyday practices necessary to constitute the life of the church across time."[65] Because all creation did not have to be it is contingent, unlike God, and in addition, we know this because something else happened that did not have to, the incarnation. In order to begin to reason about what we Christians should do means that we need to be inculcated into the grammar of God's manner of being in the world. This is where aesthetics and poetics come in, because "the cross, the epitome of human cruelty and ugliness, is quite literally the manifestation of God's beauty—a beauty that we cannot possess but only suffer."[66] Liturgy is the school of Christian reason because it is the ensemble of practices and words that have coalesced as Christians who have come before suffered this particular beauty. This is why there is no one right liturgy, only liturgies which "fit," which suffer and display and introduce us into God's own specific beauty in our own places and times.

You position Aristotle's account of *hexis* as the heart of this account in "Suffering Beauty."[67] For Aristotle, we acquire skills of the type that go with the activities that we are learning: the carpenter learns to "read" good and bad wood, and you extend this insight to say that the Christian worshipper learns to see God's time in its relation to human time because of the tenor of the liturgy in which they worship. This move seems to give a special prominence to liturgists, theologians, and pastors who should be thinking about the shape of Christian worship. They must configure the gathered worship of the church to bring worshippers to receive and enact a formed appreciation of what is just and beautiful: a "good" liturgy is one that reveals to us the aspects of God's story that allow us to live in our times and places in a manner that is good.[68] I read this as your most complex explication of your oft-repeated claim that "the church makes the world the world." In short, "the beauty, the goodness, and the truth of our liturgy is tested by our being sent forth. If we are not jarred by the world to which we return, then something has gone wrong."[69]

Is *hexis* the animating center of your mature understanding of Christian ethics, and if so, how does Aristotle's conception of *hexis* help us to understand what is going on in Christian worship? It's really a passing reference that is not often repeated, but it seems in this essay to place the term so close to the heart of things that it seems like you are, at least at that moment, holding up his understanding of *hexis* as the conceptual explication of how we're to become re-politicized as Christians.

SH: I guess I think that. But I don't know that I thought that until you asked me!

The first way you asked the question—"Have I got you right, and is it right to claim that this is the animating center of your mature understanding of Christian ethics?"—I wanted to say yes to that.

BB: But then I turned it around to ask you for a little more about *hexis*. "For our actions to be actions that make us virtuous we must act according to right reason."[70] Right reason is being distinguished from theoretical reason in dealing with the contingent. I take it we can understand liturgy as the place where the various contributors to the liturgy of the church have arrayed a set of practices and speech-acts by which we can be habituated with the right habits it would take to perform Christianity outside of those walls. Some of the central themes are foregrounded in passages like this one, from *The State of the University*:

> Vocabulary is everything. Few tasks are more important in our day than teaching the language of faith. . . . All Christian speech is to be tested by the one work we have been given as God's creatures. We call that work "liturgy," which is the work of prayer. And when we . . . learn the joy of the work we have been given our work will be sung. Indeed, the language of the Christian, the stories that make us what we are, must be sung because the language of our faith is the very act of witnessing to the master who shared the gift: Father, Son and Holy Spirit. Christian education begins and ends in the praise of God.[71]

SH: I guess that one of the ways to develop that—and it has to do with the body that we were talking about earlier—namely, liturgy fuses bodily movement with language, and the bodily movement itself is language, in a manner that makes it possible for us to be who we seem to be. That's a big trick! Being who you seem to be. I seem to be a Christian and I hope I am. I think I am most nearly who I am when I'm worshipping with other Christians.

BB: I guess I started thinking hard about this several years into attending an Anglican church and getting to know some people that I found to be both strident defenders of a specific liturgy and deeply embedded in it, habituated to it, and who were incredibly dislikeable people on so many levels.[72] So part of the question concerns the way liturgy can become fetishistic and therefore close people off. Another part has to do with how to understand the responsibility this places on the pastor to either explicate or reconfigure liturgy to break-up that fetishization. And a third part is the theoretical question about how it could be that doing something that's the same for 500 years could actually prepare us to decide that we weren't going to have IVF even though we desperately wanted our own biological children.

SH: Right.

BB: There's no one answer to that, right?
We've obviously not nailed down all the aspects of this question, and I have to admit having long found the complications involved off-putting—it just seemed

very difficult for me to understand how going to church was like learning to build a cabinet. There seemed to be too many disanalogous moments involved. But what I think I find increasingly attractive is the way your approach emphasizes connections between Sunday and the life of the Christian during the rest of the week, and that the origin of Christian ethics is fundamentally in earshot of God in the communion of saints. As you very nicely put it, when I am together worshipping with other Christians, that's really who I am.

What it also does is to refocus what we take to be the most important human acts which serve God's sanctification of the church. In other words, it answers the other problem we worried about a few questions back: the problem of using too much active language about "making myself conform to the narrative Christ."

I'm seeing one more important advantage to this position: the demotion of the theological ethicist. The ethicist is not the consultant offering principles for the church to enact to make it more just, and not just because we tend to speak primarily to the highly literate. It is the ministers and shepherds of the church who have the real capacity and power to make the church better. They should be thinking about how to configure and perform the liturgy of the church in a manner that displays for the congregation the aspects of God's cruciform beauty that they need to grasp in their place and time. This is to understand the minister/worship team/elders and so on as servants of a liturgy that is by definition mobile because the truth of Jesus Christ is polyvalent and our contingent settings present uniquely configured challenges. I think this is a powerful and attractive vision, some parts of it are still left to work out, but the heart of the vision seems to me right on the money.

It may even be more powerful than the *Blackwell Companion*, a big book animated by this insight, was able to convey. I found it really interesting that Coles and I both agree that understanding your turn to worship is important for understanding your mature work because it allows you to think more concretely and constructively about Christian ethics. But he thinks that this turn is a problematic one, at least as it is carried out in the *Blackwell Companion*.[73] I think he's right to note that in some of the chapters your understanding of worship seems to be rendered too hermetic, as if liturgy was a "resource" to be mined for ethical derivations. To conclude this conversation, I was hoping you would comment on whether or not you think the *Companion* did justice to your account of the essentially contingent and responsive dynamism of Christian liturgy and its nature as the crucible of *hexis*?

SH: I think it's probably the best shot so far but I have the sense that it's only half there. That's because we didn't have many precedents to even begin to think that through. I think that in so many of the chapters there is a sense that you had to try too hard to make it work, and if you have to try too hard, it doesn't work. I think the introductory essays that Sam and I wrote are really good and important. I think that the rest is really uneven. Some of it's really good; some of it's just OK.

BB: Given your explanation of the animating vision behind it that we've just worked through, is it even theologically legitimate to break up the liturgy into constitutive moments and ask what their ethical implications are?

SH: Yeah, boy, that's a really good question! And my first immediate response, which is therefore critical of the *Blackwell Companion*, is no, it is not legitimate to break it up. What do you think?

BB: Having contributed a chapter,[74] I'm certainly also to blame if there's a problem! I had the distinct benefit of being in the second edition and having had the time to think about the first edition. As a result, I positioned what I had to say about the topic I was assigned, disability, as one that ought to be evoked by every moment of the liturgy. I suspect as well that there has to be more to say than that. But in a way it's our own foreshortened vision that makes us think it hasn't been done before, because it's the way the Church Fathers and Mothers did by far the bulk of their theological thinking. But the fact that we can't recognize what they are doing has to do with the fact that they weren't putting it back together in discreet ethical treatises. What they certainly weren't doing was reflecting on the implications of each liturgical moment. You said as much in your introductory chapters. But the problem remains for us, and it is related to the problem we have been discussing in relation to scripture: Is there actually a method for saying which scripture applies right now, to this question?

SH: No.

BB: Exactly. We agree on that. And so could we ever say which moment of the liturgy is determinative for any ethical question?

SH: No. No. But you could make some arguments and I think the language would be "fittingness." You could show that there's a kind of "fittingness" about certain movements in the liturgy with certain kinds of moral questions.

BB: This account would allow us to say that the *Companion* worked as well as it did because enough people contributing to it intuitively sensed the truth of the claim that liturgy causes us to see things about the world. Starting here allowed them at least to be able to come up with some very penetrating examples. And when they were asked, "Could you write on the Offertory?" they had been taught by the liturgy as a whole to look around them to find something that could be connected in a meaningful sense to that moment. What sparkles about the book is the incredible range of unexpected examples of countercultural witness that it arrays. Would that be a better way to put it?

SH: The whole point is we're training ministers. The book is the attempt to defeat the presumption by those in the ministry that what they do on Sunday morning is something called "worship" and what they do on Monday is something maybe called "ethics" or "politics." If you can just begin to defeat that, at least you've made some small progress in the church reclaiming its significance.

BB: And you've seen me trying to play that out in my lecture in St. Andrew's Cathedral.[75]

SH: Yeah, in the class! That was exactly showing that you can't separate worship from ethics. I mean, you were in the damn building!

BB: Part of the reason I did that came from another critical impulse, which was that one of the circles that was never going to be squared in the *Companion* was its ecumenical framework.

SH: Yes, that's true.

BB: If *hexis* is an important way to put what we mean when we say "Christians are formed by worship," then of course those traditions that have a golden eagle as the lectern, which is over on the side, and those traditions which have a Plexiglas pulpit up in the front and no lectern at all, are going to have a different view of what's going on when they interact with scripture.

SH: They certainly are!

BB: That's going to have direct ethical implications.

SH: That's right!

BB: What I learned from that way of putting things is a heuristic for watching whether the practices that make sense in the other six days of the week are organizing your liturgy, or vice versa. Do you change your church service because you saw something that looked cool on TV or do you learn to view TV through what you learned in worship? And it seems to me that woefully few ministers can enter into that logic. If we ask this question—which is usually depoliticized by being called a question of "mere aesthetics"—it can become very revealing about how we think worship, and the world, should proceed. These are not the sorts of simply aesthetic debates about worship style that are so clearly unresolvable and so destructive of community when understood in isolation from their political import. We ask questions like, "Why would we want to throw away the lectern that looks like an eagle for one made out of Plexiglas?" in order to expose sub-theological rationales, such as "it just looks cooler"—meaning, more like what we see on TV.

SH: I tell you, the deepest worry that I had about the *Blackwell Companion* is that it is obvious that it was a book that Episcopalians put together, that is, Sam and I. So, ecclesially, it is much closer to Episcopal life than anything. And I worried about the implications for African American worship. And I suspect they could make some really interesting interventions to say, "You guys don't do this . . ." For example, the participation of the congregation in the sermon is quite wonderful, and we don't know how to do that. It scares us to death.
Push back on it!

BB: If a conversation could get going that was articulate about the way particular liturgies are forming particular church-political communities, then it would have been a successful project.

SH: Yes. It would have been better.

BB: Well, I'm tempted to say there is no successful landing of such a project; I'm not sure that dictionaries or encyclopedias, for all the reasons that MacIntyre points out . . .

SH: I just don't trust definitions. Notice I never use that language, it's always description for me.

BB: There's the genre problem, but you also have to keep from falling into either liturgical disputes or comparative religion. I think what you've done is very sensitively positioned to keep it from falling off on either side. I actually wouldn't be calling for a replacement volume, but I would like to see a much more robust conversation, which would yield people who could say, "Well we used to do that in liturgy and now we do something different because we saw we had a pastoral issue about how our church was living in the other six days." That could be really exciting.

SH: Somebody else is going to have to do that! Well, good.

Chapter 5

ARE CASUISTRY, NATURAL LAW, AND VIRTUE METHODS?

October 12, 2015

> *Bringing the deep grammar that animates Hauerwas's work more firmly into view, the conversation now examines more closely his reasons for deploying familiar virtue ethics terminology in idiosyncratic ways. Discussion focuses specifically on his use of the language of casuistry and natural law. His formulations of these terms, it emerges, often lean away from common usages due to the force exerted by several Christologically oriented presuppositions. This opens further questions about the tensions that exist between virtue language and some of the central trajectories of Christian theology. Discussions of temperament and repentance lead into further examination of how Hauerwas understands the mechanics of habit formation and character reformation.*

On casuistry

BB: Let's move on now and talk about how you situate some of our main terms as you deploy virtue language. I want to pick up specifically on the terms "casuistry" and "natural law."

I really like the ways that you've been emphasizing the unsystematic nature of Aristotle's thought, and I have also appreciated your pinpointing of the moves that you believe, from a Christian point of view, we have to say that he has clearly gotten wrong, such as his emphasis on the pride of the magnanimous man or the ways this pride commits the virtuous person to sparing his friends his suffering.[1] To iron out those kind of problems you don't try to draw his ethics more tightly together with his metaphysics, though every once in a while you do draw material forward from his politics.

SH: I also think that he didn't connect his metaphysics with his ethics! So I'm not doing something that he wouldn't have done.

BB: As we've already discussed, I've tended to read Aquinas as a systematic thinker who clearly presents a much more integrated picture of virtue and its relation to God and all things, and that has tended to make me understand him as having a strong interest in hiding the tensions in Aristotle's thought and in presenting him as more systematic than he is.

I think until now I've understood you better on Aristotle than I have done on Thomas. But the underlying point would be that you don't need to present Aristotle as a systematic thinker because the real roots of your theology are your beliefs about narrative, and a specific narrative at that.

I hope the discussion thus far has made it more obvious why my reading of your work privileges your assertions that you are not essentially about defending any general method or concepts such as virtue. In my view it is also safe to say that your various projects have not been driven by traditional doctrinal concerns. In other words, you don't derive ethical claims from doctrinal claims.

SH: That's right.

BB: At root, narrative seems to lie closer to the animating heart of your thought than any other notion and the reasons have also become pretty clear why this is not narrative understood as a general philosophical notion, but is about *the* narrative, the Christian narrative. Put more strongly, it looks a lot like Aristotle and virtue theory offered you a set of tools that were sufficiently academically respectable to perk up the ears of the academy at the time, but were sufficiently pliable for you to be able to configure them according to your interest in seeing lives shaped by the one true narrative, the Christian narrative as contained in scripture. Because that's what you believe is keeping Christians Christian in any substantive sense. Was virtue theory allowing you to fill out how that narrative actually touched the ground in human lives?

SH: Yes, that's right. And to anticipate the next question about casuistry, the narrative is tested by the kinds of reflections it requires in which you discover, casuistically, the challenges that living out the narrative presents.

BB: Putting off casuistry for one more minute, I'd like simply to note the implications of your affirmation of that description. I appreciate it because there will be a lot of people puzzled by your resistance to being called a virtue-thinker. There's barely three pages where the term doesn't pop up in your work!

SH: And I almost never use "virtue theory" as a phrase, or a theory of the virtues in which it sounds like, "Oh you've got teleological normative ethics, you've got deontological normative ethics, and you've got virtue theory normative ethics." I just think that's a stupid way to think! If you want to do typologies, OK, be a Frankena,[2] but I just think that's a stilling of the mind, because obviously teleological and deontological grammars are part and parcel of how you think about the virtues. I just have never found those kinds of typology useful.

5. Are Casuistry, Natural Law, and Virtue Methods?

BB: Frankena's typologizing of ethical methods is obviously a divide-and-conquer approach. It is part of what has often made analytical philosophy so arid—it forces either/or's that are obviously alien to practice.

SH: One of the things about "my work" that I think is part of the problem of understanding me is that I had Frankena's ethics memorized. That I wrote a critique of it is important,[3] but no one today reads Frankena's ethics!

BB: I must have been at the tail-end of people trained on it. But it no longer packed any punch. I may have been coming from a more Yoder-like ecclesial traditioning, but it didn't evoke enough of a living life-world to catch my attention. It was interesting enough conceptually, but what could you really do with it? I felt the same way about the very similar approach dominant in medical ethics—Beauchamp and Childress[4]—which was no less lifeless but was still the orthodoxy in that discipline.

All that said, you still regularly and relatively systematically draw on important aspects of virtue theory and think within a lot of Aristotelian categories. The crucial problem in grasping the core of your work is getting the grammar that unites and brings coherence to your various methodological appropriations. Getting the relation between narratological method and the specific narrative foundations of your sensibilities straight, and understanding their relation to virtue theory, begins to allow us to understand how you, or a good reader of your work, can spot a misappropriation.

Back to casuistry then! In your 1995 article "Casuistry in Context: The Need for Tradition" you point to the following passage as one of your favorites in Aristotle's *Nicomachean Ethics*:

> Prudence apprehends the ultimate particular, which cannot be apprehended by scientific knowledge, but only by perception—not the perception of objects peculiar to one sense, but the sort by which we perceive that the ultimate figure in mathematics is a triangle; because there too there will be a halt. But this is a perception rather than prudence, although it is another kind of perception.[5]

I can't claim to understand that passage, but I'm attracted to how you explain it. Words like "murder" designate acts that are in principle prohibited. In the resting of ethical reasoning on prudence, Aristotle bars us from going behind such terms for more determinative reasons. If we refuse to question the demand laid on us by the term, we are pressed forward into questions about whether this or that act should be counted as murder, that is, as an intrinsically unjustifiable act. "[T]he attempt to explain or to give a further reason why murder is wrong has been one of the besetting temptations of modern moral philosophy," you comment:

> Fearing that if morality is based on the "intuition" that murder is wrong then such judgments are arbitrary, it became the philosophical task to find a single principle that could "ground" such "intuitions." That is the reason, moreover,

that modern moral philosophy has tended to corrupt our morality through the attempt to give reasons when no reason is required.[6]

What is missing in modern moral philosophy is precisely the tradition-embedded historical specificity emphasized by Aristotle.

> [A]nalogical reasoning about cases (e.g., what difference, if any, does it make that conception occurred in a rape) depends on the prior description [of what will be counted as homicide, in this case abortion]. That description . . . is dependent on a tradition that sustains the practices necessary for that description to make sense. As a result, casuistry does not end with the problem of the "perception of the ultimate particular"— it begins there.[7]

This is one of the points where I am just left in the dark. What is "the perception of the ultimate particular"?

SH: It is the ability to make judgments based upon the descriptions that are necessary if the story is to be the story that shapes my life. An ultimate particular, for example, is the naming of an action such as suicide. The reason you don't offer the kind of arguments that are involved in the quotes you just read is that if you say, "Oh well, there's nothing wrong with suicide," then you have lost the ability to display the narrative over your life that Christians should hold. The judgment, therefore, that you have the description "suicide" is that the narrative requires you to be a community in which we do not abandon one another. It's so complex; there are many different forms of suicide. But that's what I am trying to think about. You might say, "Couldn't you just call suicide self-determination?" Then, you would no longer be in the Christian world, no longer in the world that is determined by what is Christian. You could live in a world of self-determination, or self-life-taking, or whatever you might want to call it:

"Oh Joe is no longer with us. He self-life-took."

"Jeez, that's too bad."

You see the difference if you called it suicide? And that's the ultimate particular.

BB: So the ultimate particular is a judgment of a specific act retrospectively? Am I hearing you right?

SH: Yes, largely. You can also think of it for prospective acts in so far as you can envision what you are going to have to do and you might say, "Is that adultery?"

"We were just satisfying one another's animal needs?"

"No, that's adultery."

BB: I'm still not sure what the term "ultimate" adds to particular. Here's what I think I'm hearing: this particular act, for us to understand it rightly, must be understood as gathering all the other layers of all the other narratives that make sense of every other domain of our lives in order to make this moment intelligible.

5. Are Casuistry, Natural Law, and Virtue Methods? 133

SH: That's a lovely way to put it.

BB: So it is "ultimate" in the sense that it is actually the right thing to do right now, given who I am, and that "who I am" is a narratival construct?

SH: Right.

BB: OK. That helps us to situate why you think talking about those acts should be referred to as casuistry. You've consistently insisted that Christian ethics and indeed all ethics are ultimately bound to do casuistry.[8] I've never been very sure about what you mean by that claim, a bafflement only compounded when, very typically, you introduce caveats like, "I am suspicious of appeals to casuistry as a good in and of itself."[9]

My first interest, then, is in having you talk through how your insistence that Christians embark on casuistry was a move within the contemporary discourses of modern philosophical and theological ethics. From where I sit your criticisms of rival ethical approaches are very clear and persuasive. You're attracted to a reformulation of the term "casuistry" because you think it is the best way to overturn the "quandary ethics" that was dominant in the 1970s and 1980s. How many ethics students were treated to the thin gruel of highly artificial "runaway trolley" type cases that were supposed to show how certain basic moral principles could in this manner be discovered that would be able to specify the content of our main moral ideals? What constitutes "murder" was always under scrutiny in this context. Is it murder if you decide to let the train go down the tracks to kill a human being rather than 500 rare llamas or something like that?[10] Of this landscape you typically levy a complaint here that seems dead on the mark:

> Just as the pseudo-languages of modernity carry imperialistic presumptions that any language can be translated into English, so casuists like Albert Jonsen assume "casuistry" to be a common practice subject to common comparison. Such a "casuistry" would be so abstracted from the practices of any community that it could not pretend to do any serious work.[11]

This is exactly the point: given the reality that everyone was using the language of casuistry in a manner that was incapable of "doing any serious work," why did you decide to agree that everybody should and indeed must keep doing it, but that they should do it in the different way you proposed?

SH: Because I think that analogical comparison of cases is part of the kind of narrative display that is intrinsic to a community thinking through its basic convictions. Analogical comparison is classical casuistry in terms of how certain judgments are made less or more important by discovering how knowing that X is wrong helps me think about Y.

BB: OK. Let's clarify why the term casuistry best describes analogical reasoning. If we go back to a previous conversation, you said, "I think I am wiser than I used to be." I can imagine that meaning, "I have seen a lot more things and have a lot more stories and therefore . . ."

SH: ". . . I know better how to keep my mouth shut!"

BB: Or I can say, if someone is proposing we do X, relevant stories immediately spring to mind. That seems to me constitutive of talking about wisdom. What's casuistry describing then, given that?

SH: Well you could say experience, I suppose.

BB: Is it just a formalization of what a wise person does?

SH: Sure. Probably.

BB: If we are admitting that wisdom is possible, it sounds like you would say casuistry is a way to formalize it and therefore make it better?

SH: It's a way to share the wisdom with a wider group.

BB: In *The Peaceable Kingdom* you wrote, "Part of the problem with the 'old morality,' particularly in Catholic moral theology, was its concentration on 'act descriptions' as representing an 'objective and thus universal morality.'"[12]

SH: One of the untold stories is the importance of Kant on modern Catholic moral theology. Particularly among the Jesuits. At times they seemed to be trying to reproduce Kant.

BB: Your account of casuistry was not only pushing back against the Frankena-style liberal typologies then, but also a type of Roman Catholic moral reasoning explicitly named "casuistry" that worked by way of comparing acts within a framework of universal reason. Does this mean that the essence of your retort was that, yes, we need to compare acts, but we do it within the matrices of narratives rather than universal rationality?

SH: Right.

BB: This makes more sense of why one of your earliest discussions of casuistry looks a lot more like your having become fascinated by a community with some unexpectedly thick routines in their practical reasoning. The essay "Reconciling the Practice of Reason: Casuistry in a Christian Context"[13] leaves me with the strong impression that there you were less interested in establishing the inescapability of casuistry and more interested in exploring the richness of the Mennonite community's processes of collective moral reasoning. You are especially attentive to how Scripture and practical reasoning are related in contingently specific ways to shape the community's moral sensibilities, on the grounds that, "I have stressed that rationality is a communal process which involves Scripture and virtues, as well as judgments about particular practices and their implications for other aspects of our lives."[14] The momentum picked up in the Yale community of reasoning is having the effect of pushing you toward

5. Are Casuistry, Natural Law, and Virtue Methods?

a community whose moral reason is simply thicker than what you'd learned in Texas Methodism.

SH: Why do I have to choose between the inescapability of casuistry and exploring the riches of Mennonite community?

BB: You don't have to choose between those. When you say casuistry is inescapable, what you mean is that ethical perception is organized by communal language and there are thicker and thinner communal languages. So casuistry is almost a reference to the intergenerational transfer-medium for wisdom. When you saw, at least the textual descriptions, of Mennonite life you thought, "Hey, that's what I've been talking about, and it's better than what I know!"

SH: That's the example of the Amish dealing with having a child killed and how they reasoned about that?

BB: That's right.

SH: I think practical reason and casuistry absolutely require concreteness and that was what I was trying to do with the Amish example. I think you are right that I am drawn to communities that have thicker language. I think the law is an interesting resource for reflection on practical reason. I find case law absolutely fascinating.

BB: Law would be, formally speaking, the classic paradigm of the sort of casuistry I've been raising questions about. That's part of the reason I want to make sure we're clear about what we are talking about because I am not sure that Christian ethics is structurally parallel to law.

SH: No, it's not, because we are not clear on what the paradigmatic cases are from the past! You need that. Catholic moral theology is closer because they've had the confessional, but they are losing that.

BB: You've now given us two senses in which you use the language in a very precise and defined way. Today the language as you've just set it out also differs from contemporary thinkers—I'm thinking here of Nigel Biggar and Oliver O'Donovan[15]—who also think that casuistry is mandatory, but precisely because they have an account of universal truth or universal moral principles that you reject with your emphasis on narrative and contingency. Could you at least say now that your account of casuistry flies in the face of the most widely held understanding of the term in both Protestant and Catholic ethics over the last century?

SH: I don't know. Probably. I am sure there were people that were doing it better than I thought it.

BB: I don't mean this pejoratively, but it now looks to me that the issue is how idiosyncratic your usage is. I think this discussion raises an important observation about your writing. You very often open discussions by saying that you are a proponent of an idea that sounds very much like a general technique that can be deployed by any philosophical or theological thinker. And in the conversations in which you are defending this idea, that is in fact how everyone understands its meaning. But you then go on so strongly to emphasize that if this idea or practice is going to be *Christian* it needs to be permeated by the content-rich *particularity* of the Christian story that you end up inverting the typical understanding of the term.

In *The Peaceable Kingdom* it looks to me like that's what's going on with the term "casuistry." You insist that the morality of a community is not derived from its basic principles but arises from its common practices. You then explain that casuistry is the work of testing how communally held moral prohibitions are tested against our ongoing experience so that the basic narratives of the community are challenged and renewed.[16] Casuistry then is not the specification of universal principles, but the *self-critical revision* of a community's understanding of its own narrative.

SH: Right. You got that exactly right. The self-critical revision of a community's understanding of its own narrative; think of what a pro-choice position does to understanding Mary's "let it be." That's the way I am thinking about these kinds of matters. The idea that abortion is just a pro-life or pro-choice? No! It exactly involves the willingness of Mary to let it be.

BB: The way you just adduced that example within the flow of our discussion of casuistry gives us a perfect example of a black-box to which I earlier said I wanted to draw attention. I don't think there is a method that can give us a principled recipe for making the connection between the biblical narrative and the contemporary narrative of abortion that you've just made. This is where I see your criticism of the abstraction of modern casuistry to hit the ground—any proposed casuistic method for making connections between ethical concepts and moments in the biblical text can only work at such a high level of abstraction that in the end it can do very little real work. There is no moral or hermeneutic principle that demanded the connection you just made.

And you are clearly not deploying the classic casuistical method, saying, "Let's look at all the different scenarios that might have occurred around a conception that have a bearing on our responsibility to carry it to term or not." Instead you've displayed a fertile and creative movement between two narratives. I can see how your comments about the ultimate particular would lead you to say, "Well you have to take all the narratives into account." But casuistry can't possibly mean comparing all the narratives.

SH: True. Oh Absolutely.

BB: But you would affirm that it is what has allowed you to make what is, to my mind, a highly creative link that cannot be formalized?

SH: It's the disciplining of the imagination and its exploration, right? Because imagination is at the heart of casuistry.

BB: When you are doing casuistry like you just did it, you'd surely admit that it would be the last thing in the world most of us would associate with the most well-known deployments of the method today, such as Germain Grisez's *The Way of the Lord Jesus*?[17]

SH: Grisez is another Kantian reconstituting of Aquinas! I just always thought that was a deep mistake!

BB: Even though you've agreed with my summary of what you're doing with casuistry, I remain suspicious that when you are making self-criticism central to the business called casuistry, you do not generate moral knowledge of the sort that all the other casuists think they are by doing what they call casuistry. You seem not to expect moral knowledge or principles to accrue incrementally as the casuists typically assume it should. What you are calling casuistry strains instead toward a conversion, a substantial reorganization of perceptual order. You don't get into building hierarchies or deep layers of specification about moral claims. You're looking for highly imaginative connections like the one you just made between abortion and Mary, and once you've made them, you don't keep returning to complexify them. I suspect you'd also resist doing that in principle because you want to protect the individual who explores the concrete implications in their own contexts. Thus you assume that the connections *themselves* do substantial ethical work.

This is still looking to me like a particularly creative co-option of the language of casuistry, rather than a proposal that we can't avoid it. I wish we all did what you've just shown us! But I think it's much more free and less methodological than people are right to expect from anything like classical casuistry.

SH: It's clearly very free!

BB: My reading would be that you follow a not dissimilar procedure in your appropriation of the term "virtue" in *Christians among the Virtues*. Is that right?

SH: Maybe.

BB: I know this is asking a question that will be hard to answer, but I'll ask it anyway: Do you have any sense of why you find this argumentative structure so attractive? We all have to do X. Here's how I understand doing X. On close inspection, it may look very different from what everybody else thinks?

SH: I see casuistry as an imaginative testing that goes on all the time.

BB: And in that, you're following Aristotle's lead when he starts with, "This is what people say about things . . ." and never then says, "There's nothing to what they say." Instead he brings together various claims that are commonly made in order to discover what is true about each of them. Might this be a way to explain why you've approached the widespread usage of the language of "casuistry" and "virtue" as you have?

SH: I think that's right.

BB: It looks to me like we could say the same thing about the way you have used the language of "natural law." Not only are Christians basically bound to engage in casuistry, but also, you suggest:

> This kind of [casuistic] testing can be constructed as a way of showing that some kind of natural law assumptions, at least in a qualified form, are integral to Christian ethics. For "natural law" really names those moral convictions that have been tested by the experiences of the Christian community and have been judged essential for sustaining its common life.[18]

Again, do you think others use the term "natural law" like this?

SH: I don't have any idea.

BB: But it sounds like you would still stand behind that formulation?

SH: Yeah.

BB: I hear in that quotation resonances of your earlier comment about the relation between eternal law and common law.

SH: Right. Earlier I said that I thought that the nature/grace distinction is a distinction that is necessary for theology in so far as nature names all that, by God's grace, is not God. Then "natural law" is the drawing on the discoveries constitutive of what it means to be people so shaped. It is largely the discovery of collective wisdom across time.

BB: You couldn't even search for collective wisdom across time if you did not begin with faith that such an entity could be sought and that entity names natural law.

SH: Right.

BB: Your developed account of casuistry in *The Peaceable Kingdom* runs like this, and here I think you might well want to revise it:

> What I mean by casuistry, then, is not *just* the attempt to adjudicate difficult cases of conscience within a system of moral principles, but is the process by which a tradition tests whether its practices are consistent (that is, truthful) or inconsistent in the light of its practices in its behavior. In fact tradition often does not understand the implications of its basic convictions.[19]

That passage raises at least two obvious questions. First, does not the "just" in the first sentence not again reaffirm the traditional definition of casuistry as an operation within a framework of "general moral principles"? Second, and in my view much more interestingly, this account of casuistry seems essentially focused on deconstructing moral certainties rather than resolving problems of conscience. It thus inverts the etymological linkage of "casuistry" with "problems of conscience" by suggesting that casuistry should *generate* rather than *resolve* problems of conscience. Because it is primarily a self-critical activity of practical reason, you emphasize that we need to notice how often the mere fact that we are thinking about making a choice at all reveals problematic fractures in our moral traditions.[20] Is this description really an attempt to repair, or is it more a move to blow up the language of casuistry in all its familiar uses? It certainly looks a lot like you've tried to replace its content with what is typically labelled self-reflexivity.

SH: It probably is an attempt to blow it up. Casuistry, classically, was so associated with the Penitential tradition. It is extremely useful for people undergoing confession to be able to describe what has happened or what they have done. So part of the problem is how casuistry depends upon patterns of authority that we simply don't have in Protestantism. Yet, I would like to think that the examination of conscience is important. So I suspect I called attention to casuistry as a way of trying to gesture to that and probably didn't make it explicit.

BB: One of the reasons that casuistry came to my attention in the first place is that it has been offered as a way to repair Barth's ethics. I formulated this question for our discussion when you and Gerald McKenny surprised me in research seminar here in Aberdeen by immediately agreeing that the way to fix Barth's ethics is to make him a more consistent casuist. This aligned you with the proposals about how to deal with the tensions in Barth's ethics proposed by David Clough[21] and in a very different way Nigel Biggar,[22] which focus around how his much debated *Grenzefalle* cases are going to be approached. My own reading of Barth aligns him much more closely to what you did a minute ago—he is an artist at making connections between the biblical narrative and contemporary language. I still haven't figured out how making Barth more casuistical fixes his ethics.

SH: But Barth does casuistry all over the place.

BB: In your terms?

SH: It's close. Think about one of my favorite spots from *Church Dogmatics* III.4, on monogamy:

> A final observation may be made in connexion with what was said at the beginning of this discussion about monogamy as an institution. On the mission field the Christian Church and therefore theological ethics is continually faced by polygamy. We can leave on one side the historical question whether this is to be understood as "original"—whatever that may mean—or as a product of ethical decadence or social necessity. Polygamy is in any case an institution over wide areas. It is rooted in custom, ruled by written and unwritten laws, and lived out as a fact. And the possibility cannot be ruled out that it might again become an institution in other areas. Now obviously this cannot alter the content of the divine command in the very

> slightest, and in proclaiming the latter the Christian Church must not be guilty of any deviation or suppression. Equally obviously, however, it has not to proclaim more than the divine command. Its function is not to establish, maintain and defend one institution against another. It has not to play off European as against African and Asiatic custom, jurisprudence and practice. It cannot overlook the fact that the institution of monogamy offers not the slightest guarantee that the divine command of monogamy, which is its only concern, will be kept and not transgressed.[23]

Now that's a casuistical set of reflections. You may be in a polygamous marriage, but you may have the command of monogamy!

BB: I have to agree with you. That's one of several passages that demands that you do more theology to even make sense of it. I'd be tempted to say that the obvious way to go would be in the direction of the discussion that we just had in terms of murder. Monogamy is, in the New Testament, a term as irreducible as murder.

SH: Right, absolutely, the Ephesians and Colossians texts.

BB: Right. So Barth is trying to ask what situations can still be connected to that axiom and he's thinking through all the different trajectories that might come into play about that question.

SH: Of course, everyone is going to say, "Oh he's thinking about his own situation."

BB: Sure. And the minute that's introduced it provokes the standard criticism that casuistry gives you wriggle room to do what you want to do anyway. Another way to put it would be to say that what we need to do to fix a passage like that isn't to admit that we're all doing casuistry but to say, "He shouldn't have started doing casuistry here because he was in no position to penetrate his own self-deceptions given his life-circumstances!"

The way you end the chapter on casuistry in *The Peaceable Kingdom* seems to me to solidify my claim that you are in fact blowing up the language of casuistry, and here it is the telltale scare quotes that what you want to call casuistry is something totally different than the activity everybody else means by casuistry.

> Casuistry, therefore, is a necessary activity for a people seeking to be faithful to the kingdom of God across generations. It cannot, however, be the province of a small group of "experts." Moral reflection and reason is the activity of a whole community. Often some of that community's best "casuists" may not even be those who manifest the strongest rational skills. Those with intuitive gifts may simply "know" better than they can say what the gospel requires of us. The church must be a community of discourse so that the moral significance of such people is not lost because we fear the prophet.[24]

Could you give us an example of what you are imagining when you affirm the place of this nonexpert casuistry. What does it look like?

5. Are Casuistry, Natural Law, and Virtue Methods?

SH: When I read that, a very strange example came to me. During the Cuban missile crisis, there is a film that shows Kennedy with Bobby. One of the generals says to him, "We have to bomb them" and Kennedy said, "We're not that kind of people. We don't do murder!" I thought, "That's an interesting casuistic judgment."

BB: Why call that casuistry?

SH: Because he had the description right.

BB: He wasn't thinking about how this fit with other possible cases. It was immediate. It was certainly a judgment and yet was just as clearly not the result of a process of casuistic reasoning. In so far as casuistry is comparison of cases, that's not how it looks.

SH: So casuistry is obviously more than the comparison of cases.

BB: Could we call it virtue?

SH: Right. If you want you can call it prudence or wisdom. I tend to think it has to do with naming. When you are laying brick and someone says, "Goddammit! You can build lead faster than that!" I tend to think of that as a casuistic judgment.

BB: In that case, it would be knowing the person and knowing the job and knowing the conditions and using all that to make a judgment that this person is slacking.

SH: Exactly, that's what I meant.

BB: What the passage I just read brought to my mind was the old uneducated saints around my church growing up, to whom I have to credit much of what you would call my capacity to know the ultimate particular, to the extent that I possess this capacity. Of course, they believed things that I couldn't possibly believe now, but it's only at my peril that I criticize their explicit beliefs if I don't recognize their capacity for performing acute discernments.

    The way they marshalled arguments relevant to specific questions or situations was often characterized by those kinds of shocking links to the biblical narrative in ways that did not compare cases but portrayed a deep awareness of the nesting of narratives inside of narratives and the cross-linkages across a range of narratives. Crucially, this ended in judgments of the type, "it all meets *here*," as lightning strikes, so to speak. They weren't stuck on the task of description of "biblical content" without having a way to derive a sense of the claim scripture was making in the here and now.

    It reminds me of an advertisement that's in the theaters over here at the moment, in which somebody throws a ball through the open windows of two cars passing each other going in opposite directions. They'd probably practiced a million times, but all you see is that they have become skilled at "doing the thing" when the time has come. When you witness it, you just realize that to be able to pull it off so superbly they have to be seeing more of what is going on in other planes of reality than I'm grasping!

SH: I suppose one of the things to which you are appealing is how people with memories of precedence face implications they are willing to draw out for other areas of life.

BB: So for you to talk about a seemingly novel social organization like, for example, social media, could only be premised on a sort of casuistic rationality?

SH: I don't have a big stake in sustaining the language of casuistry. I have a stake in doing the kind of work that it seems you need to do to live well.

BB: And I don't have any stake in getting rid of the language, but you've so consistently insisted on its necessity that I wanted to get to the bottom of what, precisely, you're asking of us with this enduring insistence, not least because the way most people understand the term seems to cut so much against the grain of all that you have said that is so familiar.

You make a related but conceptually distinct move when in the same chapter in *The Peaceable Kingdom* you indicate that one of the reasons casuistry is inescapable is that moral discourse is the way we (including Christians) must justify our actions in public. This is a separate consideration. I've been asking about the internal dynamics of Christian reasoning that you call casuistry but you also say that it's a part of the *public* nature of Christian moral reasoning.

> No matter what narrative we find ourselves in or what virtues we have acquired, we do find ourselves having to make choices that require justification. "Quandary ethics" may have overlooked the significance of character and virtue for the moral life, but emphasis on the latter cannot relieve us from the need to justify our moral discussions in a consistent and non-arbitrary manner.[25]

Could you explain how you understand this idea of "justified moral claims"? The formulation takes us into the problem of negotiating the differences between the Christian narratives and other public narratives.

SH: Well let me give you an exemplification. Once I was giving a seminar in medical ethics to the residents at the University of Chicago Medical School.[26] The week before they had someone come in and they had discussed abortion. They had come to the conclusion that because their job was to do what the patient requested, they would perform abortions. I said, "Oh, well, let's consider the possibility that you are rotating through the E.R. You are at Cook County, that's right by the lake. Someone is brought in who had tried to commit suicide in Lake Michigan but it is cold and they didn't drown in the appropriate time and they are rescued. They have a big plastic sheet on their chest that says, 'Please do not resuscitate. Please read the following: I have been studying Seneca most of my life and I am completely convinced that suicide is our most determinative human act. And I've always loved Lake Michigan so I've taken the opportunity to die in Lake Michigan. Please read my psychiatrist's statement below, which certifies that I am completely sane. Please do not resuscitate.'"

And I said, "What would you do?" And they said, "We would resuscitate." And I asked why and they said, "Well, our job is to save lives." I said, "What right do you have to impose your role specifications on someone that doesn't want them?" And they said, "Well suicide, you know, is just wrong." And I said, "Where did you get that description?"

We debated and debated for an hour or more and they finally came to the conclusion that if the guy was brought in one time, they would resuscitate but maybe for a second time they wouldn't! People forget how dependent you are on language like "suicide" for shaping medical practice.

That would be a place where it matters that we Christians don't take our own lives and we feel the obligation to live our lives out in the face of suffering as a gesture of our commitment to one another. So that was a nice example of how a Christian narrative would bump up against a public narrative that had become incoherent.

BB: But your way of putting it is that we're not relieved from the need to justify our moral discussions in a consistent and nonarbitrary manner. To say that Christians believe in suicide, that's not a justification.

SH: No. That's odd, grammatically. You don't believe in suicide. You think suicide is an appropriate description of actions that we are to never perform. So it's not a belief in something, it's a description. We can justify that description by telling the story, a story that narrates why we do not believe our lives are our own and what it means to be a baptized people and so on. If you don't have those stories—that your life is not your own—you find that through baptism. Then you have some basis for not using "suicide" as a description.

BB: Once again, the story that you've just told about your discussion with the doctors, along with the discussion about Barth, displays what is at stake in getting casuistry right. Not least because in both cases it looks like the core reason for the Reformation suspicion of casuistry is once again being displayed. The doctors ended up jettisoning any meaning to the term suicide because they said, "If you come in enough times, it's not suicide." And Barth seemed to be doing something not entirely dissimilar in his discussion about polygamy.

The Reformation worry was diverse. The first was that casuistry is theologically problematic because moral reasoning can never justify our actions. Only God can judge whether in fact an act is good or not, so moral reasoning can never make our actions the right one in ultimate terms. Second, if we stick to wanting to be holy, then it's a paralyzing burden laid on casuistry if it has to go on until the *holy* act is discovered. The danger the Reformers seemed to be most worried about was that always in one way or another, casuistic thinking has to downplay the problem of holiness, which is obviously important to you. As you presented it, casuistry seems to create and open up moral problems. Can the operation of casuistic thinking really make us consistent and nonarbitrary on one side or should we worry, as the Reformers did, about it deflating Christian ethics in the way we saw it doing with the doctors and with Barth?

SH: Just to follow up the points you have been making, casuistry has often been associated with the question, "What's the minimum I have to do to continue to think I'm doing the right thing?" I'm trying to show that it pushes you to the maximal. But obviously that depends on the community in which the casuist stands and what is demanded. The whole tradition of development of the casuistical manuals was really pointing towards the task of increasing holiness, so it wasn't just the minimal, although that was certainly there too.

I guess I just want to say that if it is used as a downplaying of holiness then we can have no use for it.

BB: For Luther at least, the question of casuistry is very close to the heart of the matter because his theology was born from the paralysis that came with a maximal search for holiness: "I want to confess everything." If penitential casuistry was really going toward the maximum, then no one could be more serious about that project than Luther was. While still in the monastery, the young newly ordained priest would stop in the middle of a service to go to confession so as not to sully the holiness of the mass.

The conceptual question is how to keep the eschatological urgency and the emphasis on the progression in holiness that you clearly value *and* keep casuistry, because casuistry in practice very often or almost always had the opposite effect.

I think this takes us back to my opening statement that I'm after the center of gravity in your thinking, because it seems like, ultimately, as you've said, you're not wedded to the language of casuistry and certainly not in the way you're committed to narratives and thick descriptions of character. I think what's become obvious is how important it is that acts are understood as always resting on traditioned perceptions about what is going on. And what is needed when moral language seems to be going off the rails *may* be casuistry but what it *must* entail is better and richer description, whether by means of doctrinal or biblical access points to the one narrative. You seem to open the door to that approach when you say, "If descriptions narrate the heart of the casuistical enterprise they will be found only as part of practices that give our discourse life in the first place."[27]

That emphasis on keeping our discourses alive seems to me the crucial observation to make. The old saints making links between narratives; that's what keeps a tradition alive.

SH: That's what I call casuistry!

On natural law

BB: In *The Peaceable Kingdom* you set out a remarkably sweeping set of objections to modern natural law approaches to Christian ethics. Your sixth point reads:

> The "natural law" starting point for Christian ethics, even in the updated form of "Christian ethics as human ethics" ... ignores the narrative character of

> Christian convictions by forgetting that nature-grace, creation-redemption are secondary theological concepts only intelligible in relation to the story of the God of Abraham, Isaac, Jacob and Jesus.[28]

This formulation flies directly in the face of the very reasons why Christians seem so powerfully attracted to a virtue theory of Christian ethics today, or the resurgent form of virtue theory among Christian ethicists and public theologians, which seems very interested in allowing the nonbeliever in on the ground floor of ethical theory. At the same time you also play directly to that same desire a few pages later when you say—and I don't think it's the first time you've made the point—that "Christian ethics as such is not in principle methodologically different from other ethics, for I suspect all accounts of the moral life require some appeal to the virtues, principles, and the narrative display of each."[29] Are we seeing the pattern we've just been discussing, where the first two terms here are dispensable, or contingent aspects of your thought, but the last is essential or irreducible?

SH: That's a good question. The crucial word in that sentence is "methodologically," obviously in terms of content. And content, of course, determines method. So the sentence is probably a generalization, which to be accurate would require much more qualification. I think the virtues and principles are going to be hanging around, whether they are made articulate or not. But clearly it's not *just* a narrative but *the* narrative that's going to make a difference.

What I'm questioning in terms of natural law is the assumption that we all share in a rationality that produces an agreement about what something called morality is that ethics can explicate as a natural law that can be applied to all people. I just think that's a mistake. Therefore, in that view, the Christian ethicist doesn't have to do theology, they just have to do natural law.

BB: Comparative religion or some version thereof?

SH: Right.

BB: Let's follow up your passing comment in the last answer about the way that material content shapes method, because a prominently placed passage in *The Peaceable Kingdom* seems to me nicely to display the deep tension created by your consistently heavy weighting of Christian material content in relation to the formal categories in which it is apparently being presented.

> For the church to *be* rather than to *have* a social ethic moreover means that a certain kind of people are required to sustain it as an institution across time. They must, above all, be a people of virtue—not simply any virtue, but the virtues necessary for remembering and telling the story of a crucified savior. They must be capable of being peaceable among themselves and with the world, so that the world sees what it means to hope for God's kingdom. Such a people do not believe that everyone is free to do whatever they will, but that we are each called upon to develop our particular gifts to serve the community of faith.[30]

Your presentation often appears to suggest that we should read the language of virtue as carrying the fundamental grammar of your point in this passage, but it seems to me that your conclusions almost always spring from your emphasis on staying within the "Christian narrative" and the practices of Christian communities. Here again, however, there also seems to be an implicit invocation of divine agency attaching to the logic of the "spiritual gifts" which the end of the passage emphasizes. The material picture of the church is therefore fundamentally, essentially even, determining the meaning of the language of "virtue."

How widely would you say that this Christologically organized account of virtue is shared in the Christian ethics guild today? I can imagine that very thoughtful users of this language, like Jennifer Herdt and Eric Gregory, for instance, might prefer that you not dilute too much your claim that Christian ethics is not in principle different from other ethics.

SH: That's right.

BB: That's why it seems to matter quite a bit how much traffic is traveling from your starting point—which is the material content of the Christian narrative—to your virtue ethics framework. Going back to the discussions we just had about whether or not Aristotle is capable of being countercultural, the question of the relationship between method and content is the territory on which the countercultural force of your work as a whole is necessarily going to be worked out.

SH: What do you think the implications of that are for how I understand Jennifer's and Eric's work?

BB: I think Jennifer, as I understand her, tends to want to make natural theology play a more significant role than you do. That has implications for how we understand our task and audience as theologians. Eric wants what we're doing to be much more supportive of what you would call a Constantinian politics, though he is more sympathetic to your theological method. So, the two ways in which each might invoke you as an ally raise different sorts of questions. The point is that, in so far as your work has a coherence, its coherence depends upon your resistance to the claim that the methodological continuities between Christian theology and other philosophies is anything other than accidental.

SH: Right. Well put.

BB: Let me put it a little more strongly, then, drawing on your recent description of the role irony plays in your work: the reason why you are constantly inverting terms as defined in common usage ultimately springs from your irreducible sense that all visions of public (Constantinian[31]) time are challenged by the apocalyptic time of Jesus Christ.[32] Methodologically speaking, it is a position that sits uncomfortably with the quest to form deep alliances with thick accounts of virtue in which natural virtues are granted strong claims to be genuine virtues, as well as every position that is comfortable with or wants primarily to shore up the political status quo.

SH: That's right. You could say the differences are Christological, but your way of putting it is just right. There is a new book by Patrick Clarke[33] and what he shows is that Aquinas on courage is Christologically determined.

BB: Let me take this chance to clarify what you mean by suggesting that your account of the virtues is Christologically determined. In *Christians among the Virtues*, for instance, the Trinitarian account of Christian obedience you offer is very compressed. It is as compressed as it is impressive. But occasionally the compression of your presentation leaves us wondering how your theological claims are operating, and the Christology you assume to ground your understanding of virtue is an obvious example.

Breaking with some traditional Protestant sensibilities, you regularly describe Christian virtue as a form of *imitating* God.[34] But you also seem to oscillate between wanting to insist on a strong *distinction* between Christ's action and the Christian's action,[35] but that doesn't put you off occasionally using the language of *participating* in Christ. Other times you deploy formulations reminiscent of Kantian ethics, presenting Jesus Christ as being the *condition* of intelligible Christian action.[36] On my reading your best formulation is "we are made participants, and actors, in God's story."[37] Do you still want to keep all of these formulations running?

SH: Probably. One of the things that hasn't been noticed is the argument in *The Peaceable Kingdom* where I suggest two things Christologically.

Of course "very God and very man" and the incarnation is a necessary expression for what it means for Jesus to be the Son of God. But I use "prophet, priest and king" to explicate Jesus's ministry as a way to show how Christ recapitulates all of Israel's history in a manner that is Christologically very constructive. That's the old Reformed move.

As part of that, I then try to suggest, and I've done it in numerous places I believe, how the very fact that we are now conscious of the fact that you only know Jesus through the lives of his disciples is a Christological point, because it is Jesus who pulls you into his life in a way that his life is thereby illumined.

So participation is obviously the determinative category for me, for how you think about the relationship between discipleship and Christology and what it means for Jesus to be the one who can call you to participate in his life. He's able to do that because this is the second person of the Trinity.

BB: And you're using the language of participation here as a claim about narrative, not as an account of the ontology of being?

SH: That's right.

Habits and repentance

BB: Let's explore the relation of the language of character to the language of habit. What I worry about in relation to habit language is nicely expressed in your own narrative. It seems counterintuitive to claim that on the one hand we must come to terms with our own lives retrospectively, which means that we spot continuities which in real time we couldn't have named, and then adding that we can address the aspects of our lives in which we still need to be sanctified by altering our habits. How will I ever have a clear sighted enough view of my deficiencies to fix them by cultivating better habits? This is one of the reasons why I wanted to talk about the AAR piece. If you had explained your reason for that attack on the guild by saying, "I knew this guy, this uneducated Christian friend of mine and he said that he experienced the discussions of academic ethicists as offensively obtuse and told me I was a fool for playing the game," then we'd have found a vector to explain how you came to speak against the guild—on his behalf.

But I just can't see how this intervention, which is a very specific sort of intervention, explains the emphasis that you lay in your very early work on the generative force of habit, which I read you as having returned to stress again late in your career. This matters to me because if we can't see that intervention for what it is, I don't feel we can really appreciate what you've done in your work. And that seems to me a pretty important thing to be clear about.

SH: Well I think of habits as skills. And they are the kind of skills that if you get good enough you no longer have to think about what you are doing. Like a bricklayer never thinks about how they cut the mud off the board in order to have a lengthier spread down the course. That can look like routine, but it entails ongoing judgments, given the challenges of different kinds of brick, that you must learn and relearn. There are routine habits, but the routine habits themselves, if they are to be good habits, must be ready to be enhanced by the challenges that they are the result of being well-formed to begin with.

So, habituation is skills that form our bodies. How we speak is habit and the tongue is body. The tongue transforms other habits which mean habits are never just routines. Habits make change possible. And our lives must change, because often the habits that we rightly acquire are betrayed if they are left at the place that we acquired them.

BB: The place the analogy pinches for me runs like this: "OK, in the AAR speech he's explicitly not only undermining the habits of his own guild, which are comprehensive and deep habits, but he's including himself in that." I'm trying to picture how the analogy with the bricklayer is working. "What we must have then is a bricklayer who has been given straw and has been told to build twice as much on a sticky brick that is soaking up the mud. Furthermore, it's not even a brick at all, but is an unstable type of stone." What I'm observing is a performance that represents a step change into another register beyond the habits inculcated by the very guild being criticized. That step change is what gives the criticism force. We can either explain that step change by saying that the habits are from blunt Texas talking and that is interfering with the habits of the academic guild. Or we can say, as you want to say, that it's from the ecclesial world. But I think that's a hard sell.

SH: I like what you said about it might be just blunt Texas. I just do not see why that is a problem.

BB: At the end of the day you have to go home and look your people in the face, and if they think you're just pussyfooting around all the time, you can't face yourself in the mirror.

SH: But I often say, and Brian you know, as a Texan, which you happily claim—not quite in the same way—we oftentimes confuse candor with honesty.

BB: That's good, yeah.

SH: They're not the same thing. I oftentimes use candor as a defeating mechanism. It may be dishonest.

One of the things that kind of reflection about candor and dishonesty represents in terms of my own life is if I won, it makes me extremely uncomfortable to be Stanley Hauerwas. I find it very hard to identify with the person that sits in a room and intimidates students just by being there! I keep trying to think, "Look I'm just trying to get through the damn day! Don't make me something more than I am." I suppose it's inevitable but that sort of thing is just very uncomfortable for me. It's not that I'm modest or humble. It's just that I think the way that I've tried to work is a gigantic cry for help. To make me more than I am defeats the kind of community I hope my work invites.

BB: There's an obvious interpersonal discomfort that goes with being the center of attention all the time. But I also hear a worry about the political deformation that comes with fame undermining your own stated ecclesial vocation.

SH: Right. That's right.

BB: Do you—as a senior to a junior scholar—is that just a fate that must be dealt with?

SH: Yes. The answer is yes. Right. The answer is yes. I think it's just a fate that you have to deal with.

BB: Is that because we live, at least in the Western world, in a celebrity culture?

SH: That's partly it. And I think in terms of our work, you can be easily as hurt by your friends as by your enemies. Your friends can overemphasize one aspect of what you think must be carefully qualified. I think a lot of people are attracted to my work because they think, "Aha! Assertive Christianity rises again!" But that kind of taking account of what I've been about betrays what I think is the fragility of Christian claims within the world. And so, you want to be careful that you write in a way that people get at once, a sense of the Christian recovery that I hope I've been about, yet at the same time, appreciate why that recovery is always going to make you ambiguous about yourself.

BB: I've always appreciated that constant undertow in your work, the expectation that being a Christian just makes you a fugitive thinker by alienating you from the collectives organized around other loves. It puts you crossways with every other polity, and that is right. This is an uncomfortable thing, especially if you are implicated. But I think I can see how the fame, the celebrity dynamic very quickly, taken second-hand, ends up falsifying the core of your work.

SH: Right. I think it certainly is in danger of doing that.

Let me say, I just thought about something about the habits. I don't think you ever become courageous by being courageous and developing the habit of courage. You become courageous, oftentimes without knowing that you are, by being willing to have your life exposed, for example, in intellectual work, to people who are smarter than you, yet you must still try to say what you think needs to be said. The virtues ride on the back of practices without which there would be no virtues at all. And that's habitual formation that can be a resource when the time comes. So, it's the kind of activity that forms certain kinds of virtues that make the habits that are appropriate to the virtues not be stultifying.

BB: So habit is a second-order description of how we could make the claim that the Texan is uncomfortable in the academy and that discomfort can fuel critical intervention. It is one nomenclature for capturing that conflict.

SH: Right. That's right.

BB: These are questions that connect in fairly obvious ways with your descriptions of the Christian life as a journey. On a journey we move forward and develop without knowing where we will end up, unlike the less interesting "trips" we undertake to achieve specific and known ends; basically, errands. My concern then is how you understand these metaphors of life-development to connect to the central biblical theme of repentance. In repentance I renounce my old ways of proceeding, confessing them to be wrong. And we can feel compelled to repent of an old habit even if we don't know how to go on, and we might end up in such a stalled position for some time—when we refuse to do evil but don't have an exemplar of how to go on faithfully. I'm thinking here of when your preacher said, "Give me your guns."[38] That's an invitation to repentance, in theological language. It's a theme of obvious relevance for gender and race issues. In other words, the radical ordinary seems to proceed by way of feeling confronted that something is wrong and so refusing to do that thing anymore rather than seeing a winsome display of Christian virtue. And it's often exactly at the moments that we think we need them that we don't find them, at least in my own observation.

In my view the biblical language of "the path" admits this capacity of repentance to block our lives, as when the psalmists pray for God's word to "lighten my path." I suggested in *Singing the Ethos of God* that we are offered in the Psalms all the exemplars we need, but not of the actions of the Christian, but of the articulated and prearticulated inner movements and more specifically the movement of love as it is embodied in speech to God—prayer. We have all we need of those exemplars if we are to faithfully receive the way forward in the midst of the perplexities of our lives.

I'm raising this point because this path imagery isn't the cyclical law–gospel oscillation we find in Gilbert Meilaender, nor is it a command ethic, which seems to be the only theological alternatives you consider as rivals to a virtue account of the Christian life understood as a journey in *Christians among the Virtues*.[39] Could you explain how you understand repentance to work within your journey account? This is obviously connected to the epistemological question I pressed on you earlier[40]—How wedded are you to the claim that Christians should *know* they are making progress in the Christian life?

SH: We tend to think that the moral life is prospective, namely we always think, "How do I get it right in the future?" when in fact the most powerful form of our lives is how to make sense of our lives retrospectively. We think, in terms of prospective decisions, if we just get clear on fundamental principles and what the facts are, we'll get it right. And then later we look back on those decisions when we thought we knew what we were doing and have to say, "My God! How could I have done that?" Well, you must take responsibility for it if you are to be who you are. And that means you must be able to repent in a way that the past becomes your past. So repentance makes possible our acknowledgment that when we didn't know what we were doing, what we did was wrong and we must take responsibility for it. Otherwise, you will not have a self. So that's the way I think about repentance.

BB: That's very helpful, and it connects with a couple of threads that we touched on already. For instance, we have already discussed the role exemplars play. In our discussion of the difference between your descriptions of L'Arche and Vanier's descriptions of L'Arche, the question is raised, "How do I actually learn to do that thing which you just described, which is also central to the Christian life?" I've suggested one way to think about it is to learn the community's languages for expressing love to God. Vanier tends to speak about it in terms of passages. But how would you see your own work having directed us to understand how we go about that business, other than just saying, "You should" or "Look at your past, think about it. If you want to do better, don't do what you did before. We'll call that repentance."

SH: What usually messes us up is not what we do but our need to give justification for what we do. So one of the disciplines of the Christian life is to learn that I do not have to justify my life, but rather, I can acknowledge I've lived a life less than it should be. And yet, I don't have to go on reproducing that. That's a form of repentance that I want to say is crucial for our being able to think that we have lives worth living.

BB: That's the line that I've often seen in your work. I'm wondering if it works like this—just let me feed it back. It seems to me that the condition of having that thought that you've just described is that I see vividly before me the effects of my actions on someone else.

SH: Right.

BB: So, in fact, there's a perception. We could refer to that as a revelation because you have been doing that all along, it just never occurred to you and it never appeared to you as morally relevant or you had strong internal rationalizations and deceptions to keep on doing it. So the questions of how repentance happens internally is going to be tied up with something that broke in on us to reveal a whole pattern of thinking and behavior as needing to be given up. And that looks a lot closer to some of the biblical language about the dependence for sanctification on the work of the Holy Spirit.

SH: I'm sure that's right.

BB: Recollection then, and the reorientation of the will by thinking about how to act differently do, in fact, in your own presumptions, rest on the ongoing activity of the convicting and convincing Spirit.

SH: This all sounds so something-that-happens-to-a-person, but I think it has deep societal implications. How does Germany come to terms with the Holocaust? It's my impression that they haven't. But the kind of youth that Germany seems to be producing, namely, people who have no strong convictions because strong convictions result in the Holocaust, is not sustainable.

BB: I think there I would have a slightly different reading.

SH: Tell me.

BB: I think the reason why Germany is a big exporter of live-in assistants at L'Arche and for the same reason holds the whole Camp Hill organization together has to do with a very strong moral awareness: "We have a strong belief that we don't erase human beings because they are 'sub-standard.'" And that actually plays out directly in abortion policy as well. It is not easy to get an abortion in Germany. Another really striking experience for me in Germany was when Hans Ulrich, in a lecture, projected the pictures of the participants at Davos[41] up on the wall as a way of pressing the question of who actually rules the world and the role economics plays in that process. Here was this row of giant heads on the wall, of those anodyne political portraits.

You could hear the air go out of the room because of the sense that "we Germans have learned and internalized that you don't project the faces of political figures on the wall and we don't adorn our clothes with national flags, and we actually aren't quite sure if we even want to cheer for our national team at the World Cup." This is not the same as a strong moral position, but there are certainly morally loaded forms of recoil that have shaped the institutions of current Germany in very specific ways, which, as you'd expect, also yield the reticence so derided by the American establishment to joining the "coalition of the willing" to send troops around the world.[42] Those all do seem to me at least partial forms of repentance for exterminating human beings, not necessarily a fully developed response to how we deal with the guilt from the larger complex and all that went along with it. I think that's probably what you are seeing.

5. Are Casuistry, Natural Law, and Virtue Methods? 153

SH: I see. Well, my example may be bad but I am fascinated, for example, by the American genocides and slavery, because what do you do when what was done was so wrong that there's nothing you can do to make it right?

Well, most of the time you forget it.

That's both true of those that benefitted from it and for those that were subject to it. To remember slavery and genocides without such memories becoming justification for further violence would require a very thick account of repentance.

BB: Let's keep digging into how this account works, looking forward in time. Surely recognizing sin retrospectively must help us develop insights and internal disciplines so that we can begin to look forward and see a situation before us as presenting a temptation? You have occasionally suggested that something more has to happen than "mere" habituation, which is not capable of doing all the work that needs to done in order to spot and properly respond to temptation *as* temptation.[43] I use the language of "internal disciplines" because you quote psalms that clearly do not work without there being something going on within us that is "behind" our habits, or at least there must be some sort of non-habituated space in which we can recognize our habits as needing correction, or can at least observe and respond in faith to our being badly comported toward the events in which we are involved.[44] Can the retrospective diagnosis of sin do all this work? If we say that it must, it would seem that we cannot expect to find ourselves in the position of crying out for help from God or our fellow believers—a position that seems pretty quickly to slide into absolving ourselves from moral culpability.

SH: Brian, what in the world would a non-retrospective diagnosis of sin look like? You are only able to confess your sin retrospectively, right?

BB: It would look like, "Oh wow, I'm grown up and powerful enough to be offered something that I've never been offered before, and I shouldn't take it."

SH: But that's not sin, is it?

BB: It's temptation.

SH: It's interesting, the relationship between temptation and sin. Is the very fact that we are tempted already sin? I don't know. I have thought a lot about that, because temptation is also an indication, sometimes, that you are on the right track. I think about it primarily as a matter of memory. Namely, to be forgiven and to accept forgiveness as a form of repentance is to be willing to not forget what you've done, but by remembering you are not justifying. That's repentance.

BB: I have in mind that line that crops up in the Fathers that the sin of the young is lust but it mutates in the old into the sin of power hunger. Now either you retrospectively narrate lust in a way that prepares you to deal with power hunger, or you don't. And I'm not sure you've given me an answer to how that transition might happen.

SH: I think you need to go to a spiritual master, rather than Stanley Hauerwas, for that kind of judgment. I am not at all sure, by the way, that they are right about that. I find lust still an altogether powerful temptation. I've wondered, as a matter of fact, if in growing old and losing the powers that are associated with sexuality means that lust is a form of trying to remain powerful. It gets very tricky.

BB: I mean, that's another way to put it. Because sex is such a basal activity, it can be embedded in the desire to dominate, it can be embedded in hedonism, it can be embedded in exhibitionism. It's plastic, in the sense that it can configure all kinds of practices in a way that we would very usefully call vices.

SH: I once had a young priest at Notre Dame tell me, "Well we celibates can be happily sexually adjusted too." I said, "Don't give me that shit. I'm married." It wasn't true that I was happily sexually adjusted in the marriage because there was no sex in the marriage, but I said, "I've had sex but I wouldn't have the slightest idea what it might mean to be 'happily sexually adjusted.'" What would that mean? What would that look like? Who could claim that?

BB: That's just a shibboleth of our age.

SH: We're too complex creatures for those kinds of simplifications.

BB: Because we're complex, I'm concerned that the first adultery has to be written off in this account as the thing I learned from so that now I don't succumb to temptation in the future.

SH: Well, that's just false consciousness! It seems too obvious to me.

BB: OK, let me give you another banal example. We were both sixteen when we got our first driver's license, and we had our first chance to speed. How would you narrate the reason why we shouldn't do that? There are Kantian reasons and so on, but if we need retroactive experience to answer the question, "Should I speed or not?" where do we go? We're both from Texas; you must have sped as much as I did.

SH: I certainly did.

BB: That's how you develop your linguistic skills! Through talking cops out of giving you a ticket.

SH: I think, one, that the example is banal.

BB: I didn't want to talk about sex anymore!

SH: Well, two, what happened is you scared the shit out of yourself because you were driving too fast and you almost got run over by a train. You begin to appreciate the fact you have to grow up. I don't want to overtheorize these issues.

BB: That's certainly food for thought. But you know we are talking about sex. "I needed to taste the fruit in order to become mature." How does one say maturity is achieved by not tasting the fruit?

SH: I think part of the problem is that we have no way for males to think about what it might mean to grow up without thinking that they've got to find some woman to have sex with. Therefore, I think how to locate the sinfulness has everything to do with male pride.

BB: And that configuration of male pride—and I totally agree that that particular issue is deeply embedded in the masculinity we've inherited—is impelled, we think, by sexual drive, but it is in fact loneliness. That's the only cultural solution to loneliness and we don't do friendship very well.

SH: I say the only *ex opero operans* that we have is the presumption that two people having sex will find meaning in it, irrespective of their not-knowing one another.

BB: Our liberation from that delusion is no easy feat.

Is virtue narcissistic?

BB: What I find most persuasive about your account of the virtues is your insistence on the particularity of human life and the seamless integrity of ethics in living, which you defend against the formalism and individualism of modern ethical discourse.[45] As the saint of both modern ethical formalism and individualism, Kant is often the placeholder for your criticisms here. You find Aristotle useful in allowing you to insist against this modern tradition that Christians are always political and always shaped by friendships because they are always part of the church.[46] You therefore understand virtue language to be especially valuable in the contemporary West in "displacing those ideas about morality that presume the special realm of obligation, ideas that have proved immensely hard to shake."[47]

Your appropriation of the virtue of prudence highlights how differently this configures our understanding of ethics because it extracts us from all conceptions of ethics as the discipline that helps us deal with ethical "problems." It also demands that we attend much more closely to where and when and between whom moral claims are being made or discussed.[48] I find all of this very persuasive and important.

At the same time, there seems to be a countervailing trajectory in your thought. As you often admit, Christians today have been deeply trained to take their own moral orientation from their desires and preferences. If, as we agree, Christian ethics needs to take the emplacement of our moral discussions seriously, it is here that at least one aspect of our being from different generations seems to make a difference. You cut your teeth as a teacher of Christian ethics in an era when the moral conflicts simmering in Western society had come to the surface sometimes in violent yet productive ways. It's easy for me to envy you for coming of age intellectually in the Vietnam era because the youth of today come of age in a world which has managed to contain that open moral conflict by using ways of speaking and living that deaden people to the world in which they live. Sociality means conformity in any age, but powerful technologies and cultural forms have developed that allow political elites to direct attention away from politically sensitive questions. Thus kids today are trained to resist asking certain politically uncomfortable questions, exacerbating the forgetfulness that is intrinsic to fallen human sociality. That's very deeply embedded now, meaning youth in developed, Western Europe are in practice wholly absorbed in the enactment of their consumptive desires.

In light of this context, I can see how a theory of virtue might teach Christians today to attend to themselves in more faithful and Christian ways, but my concern is that, in the end, it can't question the obsession with self-formation that funds our contemporary deafness. How does it connect to a Facebook generation constantly concerned to present themselves as living a happy and beautiful life, a life that is going well?

My question then is this: How can virtue theory in whatever form you want to defend it turn us outward, making us better listeners and more responsive instead of loud broadcasters of our version of the truth? I ask this because I think that today Christians, and especially American Christians, have become infamous for just being broadcasters of the truth.

SH: I don't have any idea. I've never seen Facebook. So I have no idea. When people talk about the social media, I don't really know what they are talking about.

BB: Would you recognize that the consumerist era in which "I am the brands I buy" can take a further twist when the brands that you buy need to be presented on your own private peep show.

SH: Yeah, I understand that.

The significant question is whether an account of virtue can help Christians attend to themselves to be more faithful. That is not an invitation for narcissistic self-involvement.

There is a deep importance to what I call "the personal." You and Stephanie have a personal life of which I have no desire to know. If I ask, for example, "What does Stephanie really like in bed?" you would rightly regard that as a violent and inappropriate question that should not be asked between friends. As close friends as we are, that would just be wrong because the personal is a resource that makes it possible for us to share our life with another in a way that isn't everyone's possession. It also makes friendship possible. So, the desire to live our lives entirely by Facebook is the destruction of the self.

BB: It is certainly the case that there are very young kids in school and those who are tasked with pastoral oversight for them observe that the way their day proceeds is organized by what will be projected from it. I once went on a trip with somebody who wanted to see Europe and so spent ten hours a day driving to get a picture at all of the highlights. You go to any art museum or concert and all you see is a forest of phones held up to "record the moment." Because the technology is so cheap and accessible it can accelerate the problematic dynamics you are describing, to the point that the personal actually becomes the *slave* of the public. So I think those are very important observations.

It does, then, bring us again to a finer point, that if the entrapment of the youth of today is, "I want to go do something today so it looks like I'm having a fun day," how does starting by asking them that basic question, "What am I going to do to fare well?" help them out of that?

SH: Have better friends!

I'm serious, because a person that has no resource of self that isn't known to everyone will not be able to be a friend. They are part of "the mass." I always—I know this seems crazy—but I always think of the Nuremburg rallies as pre-social media Facebook; it is where you lose the terrible knowledge of your existence by being swept up in a communal activity in which you no longer think you need a self.

BB: So we can't do without the individual in the end?

SH: Absolutely. But it's not the liberal individual. It's a human being.

BB: To sustain Christians making that claim would require saying that the determinative community that makes me human is my friendships with God and the saints?

SH: I think it makes a lot of difference when you say it. So yes, you need to say it.

BB: What's at stake when you say it?

SH: You've got to be able to say it in contexts where it's not pretension and the price to say it is not forgotten.

Chapter 6

JUST WAR, PACIFISM, AND GENDER

October 10, 2015

The conversation now turns topical, asking how Hauerwas understands the term "just war" to relate to the term "pacifism." He explains why his main interest at this intersection has been to teach Christians to reframe the standard questions around war, violence, and the Christian relation to the state. His aim has been to foster practical habits that make Christians more resistant to unthinkingly sliding into doing and justifying violence. A crucial aspect of peacemaking turns out to grow from theological discernments about the points where national narratives diverge from the narrative of the people of God. Associated questions about violence and gender emerge, and the chapter concludes with a discussion of why the problem of war is most appropriately understood as a problem of false liturgical practice that will only be challenged by a church determined by its eschatological expectation.

Nonviolence as interrupter of national narratives

BB: You have recently commented that in the time you have left you "have the modest ambition to make every Christian in America aware that as a Christian they have a problem with war."[1] Is this a new tack for you? Why has this become more important to you now?

SH: I don't know if it is a new tack. I can't remember when I came up with that. I do want to. I think I put it in an unfortunate manner. It's not that in the time left to me that I would like to convince *Americans*, it's that in the time left to me I would like to convince *Christians*. I don't know that Americans have the basis to have a problem with war, but I know Christians do. It's the kind of strategy that I try to exemplify in other modes in my work; namely, if you could just find one intervention that would make people think twice about how they think about Christianity and their lives as Christians, then a whole set of conclusions might follow that would help us recover why Christ is the center of our lives. That's where that formulation is coming from.

BB: Is your instinct that the war-mongering of America today has become blatant enough that drawing attention to it might get Christians to think again about their Christianity in America?

SH: Yes. And it's also a way to have them think about war more generally. My question—"If a war is not just, what is it?"—is an important question because people think about just war as offering criteria to say, "Well, three out of six isn't bad in relation to this war!" And so they think, "OK, that's enough. We can go ahead and justify participation in this war." I want to press the just warrior, because I think what the work of Ramsey and others suggests is that a war is not a war if it doesn't meet the demands of just war. Why don't you just call it slaughter? You could call it World Slaughter I, World Slaughter II. The very fact that you continue to call it war gives it a legitimation that I think needs to be called into question. That's another part of the strategy of that kind of question.

BB: That helps. A follow-up question in that territory I wanted to ask has to do with the relationship between just war as a moral theory and the sorts of defenses of war that people deploy in a lived reality among their peers. I was provoked to think about this by David Clough, who has thought very hard about the injustice of our relationship with animals. He confessed in the discussion after a paper he gave in Aberdeen at being pained about the large numbers of people who had told him they were convinced by his theological arguments against meat-eating and the tiny numbers of people who actually changed their habits. You also have often remarked that, especially on the topic of war, you don't think people's minds or habits are changed by moral arguments.

Given your long-standing insistence that the American identity is so deeply intertwined with the practice of making war, could you walk us a bit further into how one actually convinces a people so deeply embedded in the practices that sustain familiar lines like: "Well, we've already gotten going with things that maybe shouldn't be called war but have just been called war for a long time now," or "We work in the aerospace industry," or "We need to keep the economy going," and "We do supply the engines that go in tanks but they also go into trucks," etc., etc., etc. We're so far into living the lives those lines indicate that we are brought back to the problem already highlighted by Aristotle: how can you ever become virtuous if your habits are so deeply malformed?

SH: Aristotle says that you won't convince anyone by argument if they are not already on the way, with proper formation, to be able to hear the argument. I think that's certainly true. I think what David Clough says is extraordinarily compelling, because he is challenging fundamentally deep habits. We cannot imagine what it would mean to give up meat. The "How's?" are very significant.

In terms of war you are going to have an alternative dramatic narrative to the dramatic narratives of war, because when you learn, for example, the history of America when you are in secondary school it's basically the history of war. It is a triumphant story of how brave people made ultimate sacrifices in order for the United States to be the United States. It really is a conflict of narratives between what it would mean to be a Christian and what it would mean to be an American, and how you tell those stories. That's really going to be decisive if you are to have Christians take a more critical attitude towards war and actually change how Christians in America regard the fact that America was born of war, in people being killed in the name of freedom from the British, and so on. It's a paradigmatic situation for me, in terms of the kind of conflict of narratives that I think embodies how you think about the nature of Christian ethics and how as a Christian you are pulled into ways of life that are transformative.

I look for small things that you have to start with that are really quite radical. I try to help people notice the significance, for example, of the fact that you don't have a gun at home. It's a small thing, but it has sweeping implications. If I were Clough, I would just say, "Could you start thinking about what it would mean not to eat your cat?" I couldn't eat my cat if my life depended on it!

BB: That's really helpful.

My immediate response is that you're saying that Christians need a new story for our nation, for nations like America. Christians are going to have to begin by admitting that the story of their people is much longer and richer than the story of America, both temporally and materially speaking. A more determinative narrative in fact overwrites the national narrative. But what would be the content of the specifically American part in that wider narrative of the church catholic if it wasn't the war narrative?

SH: Well I think America hasn't come to terms with being a genocidal nation, in relationship to Native Americans. We don't tell that as a part of the story. I don't think we've come to terms, still, with being a slave nation. Basically, we're caught on the presumption that slavery has been defeated by the Civil War and by later developments that challenged segregation. Martin Luther King won. The radical implications of the fact that you are a slave nation and how to make that part of the story is just very difficult in America.

Often I say: if Americans had taken seriously that we were a slave nation, would we be in Iraq and Afghanistan now? The kind of humility that enables the historical acknowledgment that in turn funds a humble posture toward the contemporary world would give you a very different kind of foreign policy than we currently enact.

BB: So in addition, Stan, to the two frames for this new national history—namely, that we would need to tell it in light of the longer Christian history and also in the light of the sins that have marked that history—how might our understanding of time change if we spoke, not of American church history, but rather of the history of the Holy Spirit in America? Do you have in mind any events that might appear in such a narrative?

SH: I wish I could conjure one up because it has to do with what doesn't get told. So the very fact that you knew one would indicate that it got told somehow, but I'm thinking about . . . I can't think about America right now, but if you think about what it meant for the 1989 Revolution in Eastern Europe, it was made possible by what wasn't narrated, namely, people just daily being fed up with not being able to tell one another the truth. I suppose one of the ways of thinking about it in America is that everyone celebrates the civil rights movement, but people forget those generations of African Americans who were terribly treated and stereotyped but who dwelt in the land of Goshen and made Martin Luther King possible. How do you tell the story of that which does not appear dramatic, but nevertheless was absolutely crucial?

BB: That's a nice springboard for a tour of the development of your thinking about how Christians should understand war. Not least because you've ended that compressed line of thinking about how narratives play into the way we enact nationhood by making a comment, not necessarily about policy, but about a decision which has policy implications. It takes a certain type of community to give rise to a Martin Luther King, but in celebrating his life we in effect always focus our attention on the "great victory" achieved by the legislators who enacted civil rights law in response to his witness. I take that as a terse expression of one of your earliest insights in this domain.

I read your earliest work as an extended and careful self-extrication from Paul Ramsey's formidable body of thought about the just war tradition. Your resistance to his position crystallizes around your realization that his whole account is deformed by framing the question of war from the viewpoint of the policymaker. You came to see this move as a fatal reconfiguration of the longer tradition of Christian thinking about war which Ramsey undertook for the purposes of mining it for the moral insights that could be offered to all people of good will. In short, Ramsey rendered Christian ethics a servant of statecraft. In *Against the Nations*, your first major work on the theme, you started to pursue questions of war from an avowedly Yale-informed postliberal position. This meant tackling the issue of war by emphasizing how deeply language configurations shape the ethical characteristics of given communities.

It was because you were already looking for an exemplification of how Christian language can generate a distinctive ethos that you were soon drawn to John Howard Yoder. His account of how the church might start to think about war was attractive because it checked your two most important boxes: it didn't take up the stance of the policymaker, *and* it was organized by questions intrinsic to the church's own language and life: questions of discipleship, faithfulness, and witness. Right from the beginning, themes of witness and eschatology seem to have driven your thinking about how Christians should understand war. By engaging these three interlocutors—Ramsey, Yoder, and indeed George Lindbeck—you able to push discussions that at the time were stalled in policy debates about nuclear deterrence and counterinsurgency warfare in a range of surprising directions. You wanted to "first ask Christians to change their lives rather than ask statesmen to change their policies."[2] Do you think I have this developmental narrative right?

SH: I hope so, but I don't remember! I obviously have deep respect . . . not only respect but what I hope was a profound friendship with Paul Ramsey. He was a courageous thinker and a clear mind. I take my disagreements with him quite seriously. But I don't know when I began to think that it's all important where you think just war is going to hit the ground. Maybe it was during Vietnam? Paul of course had started thinking about just war prior to Vietnam. But it looked like in the development of just war criteria there was a very important issue about whether just war is the attempt to come up with a series of exceptions to Christian nonviolence, or whether justice is always trumping nonviolence in a way that therefore just war expresses the necessity of justice in a way that presupposes that violence will always be a necessity. It's a very important distinction. But I thought Paul gives you the impression that you generate these criteria in one of those ways and then you ask, "Is this war just?" That's a policymaker's question. Therefore, from Paul's perspective, someone that is running the State Department can do that kind of work. That's how Paul assumed that just war was compatible with, if not a further expression of, Reinhold Niebuhr's understanding of political realism.

I began to think that was far too late a place to begin to think about just war. Rather, you have to ask the question, "What would the Pentagon look like if it were a just war Pentagon? What would the American military look like if it were a just war military? What would the American people look like if they were a just war people?" If you think about the dropping of bombs on Hiroshima and Nagasaki, that was murder. I think almost all defenders of just war theory would agree on that. Would the American people be formed well enough that they would rather more Americans die on the beaches of Japan than drop the bombs on Hiroshima and Nagasaki? Those are the kinds of serious questions that just war people have to ask. It seems to me they just assume that they are going to be players in the international relations that are part and parcel of the nation-state system today. I just think that's too late to even begin to make just war operative. I learned from Yoder, and John wasn't being duplicitous when he did this, that part of what it means to take your enemy seriously is to try to think through what they think in as disciplined a way as you can. He spent a lot of time thinking about just war and its implications. In *Christian Attitudes towards War, Peace and Revolution*,[3] the companion to Bainton,[4] he's got some of the best accounts of just war that you can find anywhere. You wish just warriors would be as fair about Christian nonviolence as John was about just war.

BB: I'm sure that a lot of what you've just been saying wouldn't be intelligible for me had I not lived outside of America for so long now. I'm thinking specifically of living in Germany, where their national narrative was radically reshaped by the defeat in World War II, and people don't have guns in their houses and you can see people's visible recoil from contemporary saber-rattling in public, whether from politicians or private citizens. It's remarkable how different it feels than the American world where you cheer in the streets after the assassination of Bin Laden, a sensibility that is sustained by day-to-day practices and attitudes that make such celebration comprehensible. I can see how the public action fits together with the day-to-day practices and the national narratives. You're saying, "What would it mean for Christians not to have guns in their houses?" and trying to show how this would radically alter their knee-jerk reactions to things happening in the public policy arena.

SH: I'm impressed by how the military continues to be, for many young people, the expression of the profoundest moral alternative they think exists. Because to be part of the American military is to be trained to be part of a community in which you have to have a certain moral commitment to protect your neighbor. People are dying to have the kind of community that gives you a sense of moral identity that people desperately want. That being a Christian today doesn't create that kind of danger—that we need one another—is a deep judgment against us, because if we are an alternative to war, we have to be grouped in a manner that helps us live through the dangers that threaten being an alternative to war.

BB: I'm still coming to terms with two things that happened ten years ago during a Sabbatical with you in North Carolina. One was at Duke, when I saw on the magazine rack in the Divinity Library a cover story on one of the major Christian magazines. The cover had a picture of a black-suited security guard wearing the usual sunglasses, radio, and gun in front of the church. It was a whole article about how to go about this. It wasn't, "What a problem this is!" It was, "Now that you've realized your church needs armed security guards, this is how you go about getting some." I had an equally violent recoil when Texan friends and church members told me that they had concealed handgun licenses. There seems to be literally no way to talk about such behavior as a problem. Neither as a practice, nor a theory.

SH: Your best opportunity is to argue it pragmatically. The problem with people carrying guns is that the people most likely to be killed are the people carrying guns, often by their own gun.

BB: But you're opening up a type of theological analysis that also, and more profoundly, asks us to understand every one of those guns as a concretion of our resistance to vulnerable reliance on one another.

SH: Yes, that's right.

BB: That's a potent alternative narration that allows a material object to take a very different iconic role in our self-perception.

SH: To follow up on one of your other suggestions, namely: Did I intervene about war as a way of trying to find the exemplification of how Christian concepts generate a distinctive ethos? I'm not sure. That's certainly a quite reasonable reading, but I don't remember developing that as an ongoing strategy. Certainly later it became that, for sure.

BB: I just want to note that I find this all really exciting because I've always found just war arguments tedious. But around the time of the second Iraq invasion, I realized that no American could be so irresponsible as to ignore how vigorously and continuously we are making war today. American Christians better start thinking about war, despite the fact that it can't possibly be the heartland of what Christians should be about. In an important sense, the question of what sorts of things should and should not be done in the course of prosecuting war is an outer-boundary problem, or it should be an outer-boundary problem. That is why I find your opening criticism of the displacement of just war talk into the politician's policy arsenal very liberating. It is liberating in the same way your talk about medical ethics is liberating, because it exposes why entering the discourses of just war and medical ethics has typically demanded subscribing to a whole range of theologically dubious assumptions. In other words, there's a type of Constantinian critique built into the earliest strata of your ethical thinking.

SH: That's right, but I don't know if I knew it at the time.

BB: I'm not sure how developed it is for you, but I know I was initially attracted to your work because we seem to share a nose that is sensitive to that Constantinian co-option. It's so stiflingly boring in its contentment to supporting the status quo that it could never really rise to the level of being intellectually or morally interesting.

In my view one of the most memorable passages in your Aldersgate sermons is a very concrete expression of this point. It's 1992 and you're on the road, in Oxford, and:

> as is often the case when you are travelling, I had no idea what day it was. I soon discovered, however, that it was the Fourth of July, when the from-my-point-of-view-far-too-enthusiastic person charged with warming up the audience said, "We all know what day it is; let's show the Brits what we are made of." He then had all the Americans stand and sing the national anthem. I was aghast. The [first] Iraq war had just ended, if it has ever ended, in which we, that is, we Americans, began to believe that you could have a war in which no one, or at least no American, gets killed. I was introduced, and before I knew it, I said something like this: "How can you do that? I understand you are in England, and it seems like fun to thumb your nose at the British, but you are not Americans; you are Christians. You are part of a nation that has just slaughtered thousands in a desert. Even on just war grounds, this is not a time for celebration but for mourning. So, please, never do that again." Paula arrived just as I finished my diatribe and was beginning my lecture. She can testify that I had managed to create in my audience a hostility that was quite remarkable even among people who thought that if C.S. Lewis had not existed they could not believe in Jesus.[5]

SH: That's who they were! Boy, they did not like me! They were women between forty and sixty, who if they had husbands, they were there without them. They were absolutely C.S. Lewis groupies! It was run by a man named Stanley Mattson, who was trying to found a C.S. Lewis University. He was getting money from all kinds of people to do this. He wanted to redecorate the Kilns, C.S. Lewis's home.

For what it's worth, I think C.S. Lewis is better than his readers, but his readers just about kill him!

BB: I think it is remarkable how early you had this dynamic running and were able to articulate it, even if you didn't have a fully developed theoretical explication of that insight. In 1985 you could write:

> Pacifism and just war . . . are only intelligible against the background of faith in Jesus as the Lord's anointed. If that faith is missing, then pacifism and just war alike become hollow abstractions inviting casuistical games at best and ideological perversions at worst.[6]

Your analysis demands Christians be continually vigilant in resisting the perversion even of theologically and intellectually serious thought. So here's my hypothesis: You found Paul Ramsey both attractive and deeply worrying, not least because what was most dangerous about his thought was precisely what made it most attractive. It might be worth a little bit of further reflection about that point. But as you wrestled with his position on the two main domains of his writing, just war and medical ethics, you forged a set of insights that I would read as culminating in the words you wrote in your first response to the attack on the Twin Towers: "At the heart of the American desire to wage endless war is the American fear of death. The American love of high-tech medicine is but the other side of the war against terrorism."[7]

SH: That's a wonderful sentence, isn't it! Two sentences, I should say.
  I think that's right. It's interesting that no one noticed that surely there's some kind of paradox embedded in that claim, because how is it that the desire to wage endless war—going to war means you confront death—is the American fear of death? It looks like if you go to war, death is not feared in the same way. But I wrote that exactly to elicit that kind of response because I think just like we subject our medical care to the project of helping us get out of life alive, it is the American denial of death that creates a world of constant fear, because any change in that world looks like a challenge to American hegemony, which is necessary to sustain a society that can produce a medicine that can help us get out of life alive. It is that kind of inner relation that I was trying to elicit. I thought that it is hinted at here and there in Ramsey, particularly in his accounts of medicine. I may have thought that I was learning something from Paul along those lines, and I hope I did.

BB: I want you to talk a little bit more about Paul Ramsey, whom I never met and from whom you clearly learned a lot. When I say what was most dangerous about his thought was also its most attractive feature, I am referring to his seemingly universal tendency to situate theological ethics as the problem of the powerful.

SH: I think that's probably right. I think somewhere, where I sketch what I regard as the development of Christian ethics in America, I suggest that Ramsey is the last representative of the Social Gospel, because he wanted to do ethics in a way that would be an expression, as you just put it, of people in power.[8] "What should a Christian Secretary of State do?" and so on. In that sense, he was providing a kind of disciplined expression of what he had learned from Reinhold Niebuhr, which meant that his theological convictions, which were deep, were not necessarily expressed in his thought about just war or medicine. He was a good friend and I thought the world of him, but I used to kid him. I said, "Paul, your theology, for example in *Patient as Person*,[9] is all in the preface!" It was a kind of natural law ethic after that. He would bristle and argue against it but I think a lot of that is true.

BB: As I'm hearing you, your answer is ultimately a critique of the discipline; in other words, the discipline was allied to power because of the way the discourse was put together. Was there also a sense—and this seems to be demanded by your own Aristotelian commitments—in which the social position of the academic ethicist reinforced that tendency, or made that the obvious way to configure the discipline?

SH: I think that's probably right. In some ways Christian ethics is the last constructive gasp of the dying of mainstream Protestantism in America! Therefore, it is at once an impressive alternative to the presumption that Christians have nothing to give and at the same time a sign that you are in deep trouble.

BB: Let me ask a provocative question now in order to clarify what's at stake in this line of discussion. As someone trained in that tradition, and working in the elite academy, one way to read your attraction to Yoder was that he was not a part of that whole guild. Could we say then that it either actually did or potentially did corrupt Yoder to become part of that guild?

SH: No. John, I think, always remained a kind of outsider to the tradition that you and I were trained in. He wanted to participate and of course he was president of the Society of Christian Ethics, and he certainly wrote in the journals. He wrote engaging some of the expressions of the most substantive Christian ethicists around, but I don't think he ever succumbed to wanting to be *us*.

BB: We'll come back to Yoder in due course. But let's stay with just war for now. Your first developed response to the Christian just war tradition as it existed in the US in the early 1980s was, it is now clear, a critique of "statism." This is the locating of just war discussion as a mechanism for negotiating questions of "just" policy and political judgment. But the deeper worry that emerges as you continue to think about these issues is the reality that the state in the modern world has become a corporate person, an entity that is essentially ideological. I take this to be the case because you begin with increasing frequency to protest the claim that is so often repeated that we must serve the state's survival by making "sacrifices." "We" being citizens, but also including Christians. In my view, this insight confirms that in your hands the postliberal mode of linguistic analysis is a potent mode of cultural criticism. Your attention to watching language constellations allows you to put your finger on some nontheological rationalities that are ethically determinative of a community, in this case of American Christians. Lindbeck gave you a general story (i.e., "all we have is particular stories") that allows you to see the pernicious effect of a particular community's embrace of certain language (in this case, "a" state is "worth killing for"). This critique remains the substrate of all your subsequent critiques of war, on my reading. I think you encapsulate that in a nice formulation in *Dispatches from the Front*: "Americans always want to fight wars to defend such abstract concepts as freedom and democracy, or in a special fit of hubris, to fight wars to end all wars."[10]

This is where it gets really interesting. Though you don't explicitly say this, you suggest early on that Ramsey's approach represents an inversion of the apologetic endeavors of the patristic eras. You say:

> The apologist of the past stood in the church and its tradition and sought relationship with those outside. . . . [Though the Patristic] apologist never assumed that one could let the questions of unbelief order the theological agenda. But now the theologian stands outside the tradition and . . . tries to locate . . . what is essential to religion, in a manner that frees religion from its most embarrassing particularistic aspects.[11]

You've already hinted at this again with your needling of Ramsey as a natural theologian. Where this positions you, it seems to me, looks a lot like a repristinated version of Tertullian's argument in *de Corona*: that the reason why Christians ought not to join the military is that it is fundamentally an *idolatrous* domain.[12]

This move represents a widening of the accusation of idolatry by recognizing the culpability of all citizens in democratic nation-state war making, and you add to that the accusation that the theological guild has succumbed to the Constantinian temptation to "think like a ruler" rather than "think in the worshipping congregation." But the core move looks, from where I sit, very much like Tertullian's; at the end of the day, the problem with being involved in *this* military is that it is organized and sustained by idolatrous language and practice.

SH: I think it crucial in that characterization—which I accept—is what that way of thinking does for directing attention to the "we." As I often say when people say, "Well, what about Hitler? What should we do?" I always remind them, "Who is the 'we' that's asking that question?" It's a way of forcing Christians to recognize that the kind of moral arguments we will develop about war depends, crucially, on who the "we" is and how they are situated vis-à-vis the wider society. Constantinianism inextricably wants to occlude any knowledge of the "we." We're just thinking the way any right thinking person would think. In that sense, it makes you call into question categories like "citizen." Do you know what you're talking about when you say "We are citizens of the United

States?" MacIntyre makes the argument that citizenship is the naming of people positioned in a geography that has a history. Exactly what citizenship in America does is to deny that. Citizens in America are people who are committed to the ideals of liberty and freedom for anyone, and that turns out to be a formula for imperialism, because "we" are everyone! The occluding of the "we" invites idolatry in a way that is completely hidden.

BB: I'm hearing two premises. One is that no Christian theology of just war can afford to overlook the context in which the argument is being made. That's the first premise. The second is that *this* nation and *this* military are irreducibly idolatrous, and that's why Christians shouldn't get involved. That's the connection with Tertullian. The link with Ramsey is: Ramsey denied the second premise.

SH: I think you have to be careful with the second premise. It makes a good deal of difference what you mean by idolatry. Protestant liberalism depended on idolatry being the ultimate sin. That was Tillich who understood it as the giving of infinite value to the finite. It was a generalized way of life that could be true whether Jesus had been raised from the dead or not. For me, idolatry means to be engaged in ways of life that render the worship of Christ incoherent. Therefore, it depends on a theologically specific narrative to be able to locate what you mean by idolatry. But that means that it is certainly the case that often times, being in the military makes it impossible to be a follower of Christ in a way that isn't idolatrous.

BB: Given all that you've just said, I'm dying now to have you explain what you meant when you wrote in your most recent major book on these themes, that "I love America and I love being an American"?[13]

SH: Charlie Pinches has written a lovely book about how it is that Christians have to be at home in the world in which we find ourselves and what that means in terms of family and its relation to the politics in which we find ourselves.[14] I think that sentence about my love for America is a way to suggest that I don't want and I don't think it requires the Christian commitment not to participate in war to mean that thereby I have to ignore the beauty of the American land, which I am deeply moved by, or the generosity of the American people, which is deep. There's a sense in which the energy of Americans is really quite attractive. It's a way of saying "I understand we're all in this together!" I'm not just playing the outside critic. I think that's what I am trying to suggest. I do love America.

BB: It was clearly something you had to say as a preface to the sort of criticisms you were making. Personally I just find it more difficult and maybe it's being from a different generation. I can make the comparison again with the counternarrative of German nationalism, which is if you really took seriously the things you are asking us to take seriously about America—genocide, etc.—it would be more like loving an abusive spouse than loving landscape or loving certain likeable traits, of which there are many. How could you argue that there aren't? Nevertheless, taken in sum, what nationalism means today in America is not what you describe as your love for America. Furthermore, if the narrative genuinely becomes more honest about the dark and the light, what one means by love becomes far more complex, it seems to me.

SH: Absolutely. All that's true.

Paula and I were once in Egypt, and we were to be picked up by a travel company. I think we'd landed in Aswan. No one showed up. We were just absolutely lost! We had no idea what to do! In that context, knowing that there was an American embassy, I thought, "Thank God that I'm an American, so I can get some help." That may be a sign that I haven't taken my own convictions seriously enough, but you have to acknowledge those kinds of relations and not think that you're just being the great lone hero.

BB: That's a helpful clarification of how you mean the grammar of that claim. I think that my off-the-cuff observation about that tale would be, in a similar circumstance, Paul is very happy to appeal to the Emperor.

SH: "I'm a Roman citizen."[15]

BB: "I'm a Roman. Give me what's coming to me!" But it's a little bit difficult for me to imagine him saying "I love being a Roman," or "I love Rome." Part of the reason that I just find this such a disturbing question is that it is hard to me to see how contemporary Americans can deny that they occupy the place of the Romans in the first century. It's one of those very important, very mundane political acts to say, "I love America."

SH: Obviously it's got a lot of qualifiers on it! But Pinches' book is, I think, the primary reason I wanted to make that kind of claim.

Pacifist or just warrior?

BB: Let's move now to another line of questions under the heading, "Are you a pacifist or a just warrior?"

Around the period of the first Gulf War you extend your initial approach by engaging more widely in the material debates around contentious just war problems. As you do so you often repeat that yours is not a traditional Anabaptist refusal to serve in any office of the government . . .

SH: I want to raise a question about that characterization. Anabaptists did not withdraw from the willingness to serve. They were kicked out. They are ready to be of service to their neighbor, even in offices of government, though you may not like the way they run things. And then they get thrown out. But it doesn't mean they're not serving.

BB: So the refusal isn't to be an officer in an apparatus which is wedded to force/violence, however you want to talk about that, structurally speaking.

SH: Right. But they will be there in a way that may make many of their neighbors nervous because they think if you have to kill someone, they're not going to do it in order to govern.

By the way, John Yoder has a terrific discussion of Penn and Pennsylvania in *Christian Attitudes towards War, Peace and Revolution* in which he argues that the Quakers really were governing Pennsylvania and because they wouldn't kill the Native Americans, they were thrown out of government.[16] And John says that was not a defeat. That was a victory. The very fact that you are willing to let yourself be thrown out is already a sign of nonviolence.

BB: That makes a lot of sense. As does your settled conclusion that Christians ought to be engaged citizens in modern states, in the way you've just suggested. But because they are not revering the state or being willing to kill, they're "pledged to constantly explore . . . how practices that at one time may have been nonviolent have in fact become violent."[17] I think you display in a very tangible way the implications of this claim in the essay "Whose 'Just' War, Which Peace?"[18] in which you criticize in detail the just war defenses that had been made of the second Gulf War invasion. In other words, the Christian faithfulness to their nations that you call for demands an engagement with the state that in its belligerent moments will probably be viewed as traitorous, given modern beliefs about the citizen's duties to the state.[19] I hear that confirmed by your reminder about how Yoder read Penn. You also observe that already in the fourth century Christians like Augustine knew that Christians can only really be for their nations in a serious way on the basis of divided loyalty—because their first political Lord is Jesus Christ.[20] Only such a church can be a witness to the nations in which they find themselves, provoking and exemplifying how they might be less violent.

This brings us to the critical issue: Is it conceivable that Christians would be part of the forces of the state that dispense violence in any capacity? You've just explained some of the basic conditions of how we might think about that. But recalling the line of discussion we pursued about the idolatrous nature of particular times and places also suggests the more precise formulation you draw from Yoder. You quote him saying, "Is the Christian *called* to be a policeman?" Or by extension a soldier?

He goes on:

> We know he is called to be an agent of reconciliation. Does that general call, valid for every Christian, take for certain individuals a form of a specific call to be also an agent of the wrath of God? Stating the question in this form makes it clear that if the Christian can by any stretch of the imagination find his calling in the exercise of state-commanded violence, he must bring us (i.e., lay before the brotherhood) the evidence that he has such a special calling.[21]

SH: Isn't that wonderful?

BB: It's a wonderful reformulation of the discussion, for sure. And then you observe that Yoder says he's never met anybody who would make that claim. More *should* be making it, you insist, concluding that "I have long argued that neither Yoder nor I are 'sectarians.' We are rather theocrats. It is just very hard to rule when you are committed to nonviolence. But we are willing to try."[22] Given these openings and your often articulated resistance to being labelled *simply* a pacifist, would you have the same resistance to being described as having a particularly fine-tuned type of just war position?

SH: Probably. I think so. Ramsey argued in a much-overlooked but significant book on the ethics of a sit-in[23] that just war is really a theory of the legitimate state formation by democracies. I think that argument has not been appreciated the way it should have been. The theories are so ambiguous that it is hard to say whether you agree or disagree with them. I think my general response to the question of whether the kind of position I represent is to be called pacifism or a just war position is that this formulation of the question invites a problematic response in assuming that I must be one or the other. What that does is make one assume that you know what you mean when you say nonviolence. I think that what Yoder was about was constantly attempting to show us how we are already involved in nonviolence in myriad ways that we need to consistently extend all across life. That's how I think about what it means to be a theocrat, for example, which is also an attempt at humor. I want to be able to govern in a way that a government has done what is necessary to make nonviolence determinative with the practices of the government.

I oftentimes say, if you take the police function that John here refers to, and you tell the police in Durham, North Carolina, that we're not going to let you wear guns because we don't want you to kill anyone, that means we're committed to trying to enact a politics in Durham, North Carolina, in which those called to the police function can be part of that governing aspect of life in a way that they're not tempted to kill anyone. What kind of community do you need to be able to sustain people in that way? Obviously, the lack of concern about people being poor, about how racism continues to produce terrible results for African American males and so on has to go. If a policeman says, "I'm going to carry a gun," you've got to be concerned that people have decided that those problems don't really matter. That's the way I try to think when I am saying "theocrat." I want to rule in a way that puts those kinds of issues before us. But people don't want people like me to rule, because I'm not carrying a weapon.

BB: Is your joke about theocracy also suggesting that you don't take democratic polity seriously?

SH: I don't talk that much about democracy. I'm not sure I know what it is. The rule of the people scares the hell out of me. It depends on who the people are. I think a democratic society is fundamentally about the rule of law, and how the law should protect the least among us. If that's what you mean by democracy, I'm a democrat. But the idea that the achievement of the rights of the individual is the outworking of democracy is very problematic.

BB: It sounds like your main resistance is to claims like, "These are the institutional structures for governing a society that are most Christian and so Christians should support them against all other forms of government." Is it right to assume that you take that position for the sorts of reasons that lead you to worry about Ramsey's statism?

SH: Right.

BB: Judgments about political structures are always ad-hoc. You can make judgments about how governance in your own nation is playing out and you can push it one way or the other, but you would never be a principled supporter of either the monarchical or a democratic structure.

SH: That's exactly right.
  I'm not necessarily against monarchy, you know! It depends on who the king or queen happens to be and how it's structured.

BB: How does this claim fit with your decisive repudiation of David Hollenbach's claim in *Against the Nations*:

> Within time it is simply not possible to embody the fullness of the kingdom of God in a single form of life or a single ethical standard. . . . [Thus] both the pacifist and just war ethic are legitimate and necessary expressions of the Christian faith. . . . The fact that these two traditions have been present within the Christian community for millennia has not been an accident but a theological necessity.[24]

Having flat-out rejected that claim, you've now complicated both sides of the equation in ways that make me wonder exactly what you're rejecting.
  In addition, at some points you seem to suggest that Christian just war advocates and Christian pacifists share an eschatology that allows them to rule some acts out of bounds, even if their survival would depend on their acting. You make that argument in *Against the Nations*.[25] You've also praised contemporary work from the best avowedly pro-Constantinian thinkers like Charles Mathewes and Eric Gregory. And even Yoder, as you present him, often seems congenial to a less categorical opposition toward Christians participating in the wielding of state force. I'm thinking of lines like, "Church and world are not two compartments under separate legislation or two institutions with contradictory assignments, but two levels of the pertinence of the same Lordship. The people of God is called to be today what the world is called to be ultimately."[26]
  In the end you always—I think rightly—stress that the central question is how we read history, but at the same time you make the rather bold claim that those who think that "war is part and parcel of society's histories" are misunderstanding "God's history."[27] However many caveats we might need to make, are we really in the position to say that no soldier has ever been "part of God's history"?

SH: I'm not quite sure how to understand that question. Can we really say that no soldier has ever been part of God's history? I guess, "has never been part of God's history as a soldier?" or something like that?

Let me put it this way, Brian. People oftentimes, as I've said earlier, ask "What about Hitler? Wouldn't you have been a soldier in World War II?" I'm sure I would have been. It's not like the position is saying, "You fought. You didn't. The one that fought is wrong. The one that didn't is right." Those kinds of retrospective judgments do no one any good. The question is not, "Did someone, by being one of Caesar's Legions, become less Christian?" The question is, "What are we to do?" I'm just trying to help us recover why those that fought in Hitler's Legions might have been better off if Christians had offered them a different life. I'm sure we could have! And what now, do we do, as Christians? I just want Christians to be able to say "no." They probably won't do it on just war grounds, but they should be a people who can maintain the kind of critical edge toward the nation-state that helps us keep the war-making potential of those states limited.

BB: OK. That makes a lot of sense. I think what I'm after is how we can get to the place where that critical edge is being worked out in church practice. This is the condition for getting believers who would bring before the community the claim that "I feel called to be part of this police force now." I still have your line in *Against the Nations* in mind: "I've argued that war is part and parcel of society's histories, a necessary part that provides them with their sense of moral purpose and destiny. The problem with those histories is not that they are devoid of moral substance, but that they are not God's history."[28] If we take that point seriously, then it seems like we'll never get the critical church practices you're after because we've begun with a denial that any Christian could ever bring before the community the claim, "I feel called to be part of this military or this police force now." We've said that in principle, one could never make such a claim. And that seems to evacuate the critical edge.

SH: What Yoder taught me is that what Christians have got to want is the creation of conditions for conscientious participation! Most people going to war are not conscientiously participating. They are just doing what it seems like everyone assumes is to be done. Therefore, no one has the ability to say "yes" unless they have the possibility of saying "no."

BB: Is the grammar of saying yes intrinsically tied up with the promise of glory?

SH: I don't know. It certainly seems to be a deep temptation for people to think it is glory. That's a real, real problem.

BB: I think that trying to sustain a *critical* relationship has got to be the crux of the whole discussion.

SH: Part of what was behind *War and the American Difference* is a judgment that we're not going to get anywhere, critically, about the ethics of war until those of us committed to nonviolence find a way of showing that the commitment to nonviolence is not a denigration of those who have conscientiously participated in war in the past. Though I wish they hadn't, it is not for me to judge them, saying, "You did wrong. Those that are nonviolent did right." What is crucial, it seems to me, is for those that are just warriors and those who are committed to nonviolence to recognize that we're all implicated in the war-making power of the nation-state. Therefore, it is not like the pacifist gets to suck their self-righteous thumb against the people that go into the military, but that both those committed to nonviolence and those committed to just war are people who are caught in a societal situation for which an alternative simply doesn't seem to exist. I'm trying to take the Us-against-Them out of the debates about nonviolence.

BB: Are you sticking with the complaint about Hollenbach then, or would you like to nuance that? However you want to nuance the language of pacifist and just war, what he's saying is that both the pacifist and just war ethic are legitimate and necessary expressions of the Christian faith.

SH: No. I do not want to go down that line. That's Jesuit pluralism! It says you're both right. I think that that just leads to sloppy thinking.

BB: The conceptual point would be that you are opposed in principle to arguments of the type that I took Jana Bennett[29] to be presenting that run, "You can't understand celibacy without marriage and you can't understand marriage without celibacy."

SH: So you can't understand pacifism without just war and you can't understand just war without pacifism? I think that's way too simple. There are so many different kinds of pacifism and there are so many kinds of just war, but what's really at stake here is the issue among just war people of whether just war is a series of exceptions from Christian nonviolence or whether it is a commitment to justice which means that you can never live in a world in which you think nonviolence is possible. To say that just war and pacifism are both legitimate within the Christian economy you have to look at how just war is thought to be justified. If it was justified as a series of exceptions, it is closer to thinking that it might be something that Christians can do. If you think of it as about justice and why it is that you must always be ready to kill if you want to live in a world of justice, that's a little further away. That argues more on natural law grounds.

BB: What made me raise the question is that it seems as if the utility and conceptual clarity that you get from refusing to discuss celibacy/singleness in abstraction from marriage rests on a more basic insistence that both are forms of life which for Christians are organized by the question of how to be a faithful man or woman in the light of Christ's witness. Both forms of life are committed to exploring how sexual continence and Christian witness claim the whole of our lives. The position that I've been hearing you just develop sounds similar. Before God and the church, every Christian is called to the one vocation to make peace and witness as a Christian in political society. This is why we can even discuss Christian police. It would certainly be a fatal mistake to say that the pacifist and the Christian policeman were different types of Christian. Insofar as the Christian policeman/solider is Christianly thinkable, it's got to be some type of reflection on whatever the Christian pacifist is after.

SH: That's right. My test case is to say that as someone committed to Christian nonviolence, I am more than willing to join in a community discernment to ask what would be necessary for those called to the police function not to have to carry the weapons. How would we need to be related to one another for that? I think that's a perfectly appropriate way of imagining a possibility for a Christian called to the police function.

BB: The problem then with Hollenbach is that he has a quasi-Hegelian picture of the pacifist and the just warrior producing a salutary conflict that can be counted on to be productive by some presumably dialectical process of opposition. Insofar as we can talk about both of those forms of life as justifiable Christianly, it is only because they are striving after one thing?

SH: Right.

BB: You've emphasized that the heart of the matter is producing Christians who conscientiously engage from wherever they end up in this story. This would seem to come to a fine point in the Christian who would claim today that they are called to be a soldier; namely, that they need to put their hand up to be ready to make, what you call, the "sacrifice of our normal unwillingness to kill."[30] It seems indubitable that this is the crucial theological and moral boundary one must be ready to cross to become a soldier. And when you cross that boundary you have to develop the skills required to be part of modern armies, which are ultimately organized to kill effectively. These are the grounds on which I would never encourage a Christian to enlist.

On the other hand, in agreement with Yoder, it's not clear to me how one could categorically rule out a Christian being called into the military. It goes without saying that Christians entering the army with the views we have discussed should prepare themselves to spend some time in the brig. But for the reasons that you've pointed out in relation to Penn and Pennsylvania, could that not be understood as a powerful witness to Christ's peace? I am thinking of a recent comment of a Navy SEAL, a covert operations veteran, who commented on the murder of Bin Laden: "We were not going to keep bin Laden alive . . . By law we know what we're doing inside Pakistan is a homicide. We've come to grips with that. Each one of us, when we do these missions, say to ourselves, 'Let's face it. We're going to commit a murder.'"[31] Can we imagine a Christian who would say, "I'm willing to sacrifice my unwillingness to kill in order to become a soldier, but I'm not going to murder, kill noncombatants, etc.?"

SH: No. I think a Christian cannot be called to be a Navy SEAL. I do not think Christians can sacrifice their unwillingness to kill. I do think they can be

BB: medics. The World War I example would serve me there. It's interesting that most tasks in modern armies are bureaucratic.

BB: Logistical.

SH: It's logistics. Can you get machinery and weapons and ammunition to the front? That's what wins battles—if not wars—these days. I suppose there are all kinds of positions in the armed forces that are not immediately about killing, but even there you have to worry about participation, even at those levels.

BB: You have to still go through boot camp.

SH: You do. And you have to be taught to kill. I always think about bayonet drills. You really have got to envision the possibility that you are going to drive this length of steel into someone's gut. Man, I don't want to learn that.

BB: You think that the boundary line for Christians should be gaining that practical experience and that imaginative horizon?

SH: Right. I think that hurts you. There's a natural law argument here. I think that people were created not to kill. Part of what it means to be captured by sin is the power over us for people to continue to presume we must kill animals to live.

BB: I've long thought, for the reasons we're now discussing, that we Christians should much more publicly acknowledge the trauma of soldiers returning from the front, and be far more engaged in the rehabilitation of this cohort of human beings who have basically been blindly exploited and now are coming back very much shaped by this practice and this imagination. Putting ribbons on posts and all that business really looks from this perspective to be so superficial a way to "support our troops" that it looks almost willingly evasive.

SH: Exactly. My sympathy goes out to people that have gone into the military and have faced the horror of what it means to kill another human being. There's no way to talk about that. The language I use in *War and the American Difference* is that killing creates a silence that surrounds those that have killed, that isolates in a manner that makes you terribly alone.[32]

BB: I just discovered a footnote in *The Peaceable Kingdom* that offers a remarkable and remarkably dispassionate comment about how we might think about Christians participating in government.

> To what extent Christians can or cannot participate in a society's government cannot be determined in principle, but depends on the character and nature of individual societies and their governments. Most governmental functions, even within the military, don't depend on coercion or violence. It may be possible, therefore, for a Christian in some societies to be a policeman, a prison warden, etcetera. What, however, is crucial, is that Christians work to help their societies develop the kind of people and institutions that make possible a government that can be just without resort to violence.[33]

Is that a formulation you would still take as your mature position?

SH: Yes. I think so. Do you think there's a problem with that?

BB: No, but it was useful to talk through, for instance, how the *type* of military inflects our thinking about the question. If you're going to say that boot camp rules out Christian participation, then it rules out participation!

SH: It probably does, right? There's another footnote in *Against the Nations* no one has ever noticed. I say:

> I'm indebted to Robert and Blanche Jenson for helping me put the matter in this way. For the pacifist is tempted to condemn the state for the necessity of war, but if we do so we but become the other side of the just war position. Theologically we may not know how God can provide for the possibility of a non-violent state, but neither can we act if such were not a possibility.[34]

Who knows what God might produce? It's an attempt to deflate the Weberian starting assumption that the state is always the hegemony of violence.

BB: I think it will be very helpful to continue to probe a little bit more around the edges of this position. For instance, could a Christian be a law enforcement officer if they had to train on the gun range, shooting at human-shaped targets?

SH: No.

BB: So they couldn't really be trained on guns?

SH: They couldn't really be trained on guns. They could be trained on certain kinds of physical response to people threatening violence that would look coercive. A kind of judo? I think that's pretty interesting; that they learn to use the violence of the attacker against themselves. I don't know that that's necessarily a bad thing.

BB: And, as you suggest in that passage, a Christian who was a prison warden or a cop and was in a police force where they were trained for choke holds should quit?

SH: Absolutely. That's exactly right. No question.

BB: That's a pretty robust hermeneutic for thinking these things through. But you haven't really laid it out in this type of detail before.

SH: No. I don't really know what it would look like to lay it out in detail. It depends on the context in terms of what had been traditions within the policing. I think the very development of police—and people forget this, at one time you didn't have police—in London, when they developed the runners, the police in many ways made society less violent. I give great credit to that.

BB: I think the reason I've been thinking about these things is that it seems pretty obvious that the function of a just war theory is to reduce violence. We see that in debates about the militarization of the American police, or over here in Britain, debates about whether cops should carry guns or not. The type of thresholds you're setting up, will by definition, and like you say, perhaps intentionally, exclude Christians from getting involved in the debate at all if the thresholds are set very high. It's the Penn-and-being-ejected-from-government problematic again.

SH: Yoder's focusing on Penn—some people would think, "Well that's such a special case!" But I think it is the exemplary point that allows you to start thinking about these things.

BB: Let's talk now about the warrior's honor, a theme that has already peeked out in our brief foray into the question of glory. I'm going to push back now in the opposite direction. In his book *Borderline*[35] Stan Goff, who is deeply indebted to you and your work, has recently suggested that it's because you've drunk a little too deeply from the wells of MacIntyre that you tend to assume that there must be some salutary virtues in all sorts of habits. While allowing that this is a charitable impulse toward soldiers, as a longtime soldier himself Goff nevertheless thinks you are too eager to grant that the American military as we know it still nourishes laudable virtues like honor. You seem to have just backed off that claim a bit in having apparently ruled out contemporary Christians from being combat soldiers, in that they would already have bought so far into the killing habits that they are beyond the pale—so that's one piece of the problem. Goff's criticism runs:

> In MacIntyre's accounts of goods and practices . . . there is a moral difference between being a good farmer and a good burglar; and I am going to suggest that soldiery is closer to the latter than the former in terms of what it contributes to the common good. My experience of war is that war, as a practice, does not inculcate honor as often as hatred, hostility, cruelty, and the fragmentation of the soldier's personality. Bad soldiers do not make war a bad thing. War invariably makes soldiers do bad things, and we become what we do.[36]

Very similar questions have been raised about the racism and unprofessionalism and corruption that characterize police forces in places like Ferguson.

If I'm really honest, if we're going to get into the game of looking for the warrior's honor, the most compelling depiction I've seen in a long time is Mohamedou Ould Slahi's account of how he negotiated his extended tortures at the hands of the American intelligence community in black sites around the world and Guantanamo.[37] So here's the question then. Are you still wanting to hold onto notions of "warrior's honor"?

SH: I think so. I take Stan Goff's criticism seriously, but I'm not naïve about what war does to people. I was at the United States Air Force Academy a number of years ago, giving a lecture, "A Pacifist Looks at Just War." They have a Philosophy Department, and I was asking if there was much debate in the

American military about the use of aircraft to kill the enemy in a way that ground troops were not susceptible to being killed. They said it was a raging debate, because it is dishonorable to kill without your own life being subject to being killed. It's dishonorable! So, how honor would shape military practice, at least for some people in the military, is taken very seriously. I don't want to deny that.

But then a deeper question can work another way. The Amish, for example—do you know why they used pins to put on their clothes? Because when they were thinking about these things the people who had buttons in their clothes were the military. So they thought you shouldn't do anything that the military did. So they used pins rather than buttons. There's an important sense in which it's right to ask whether you ought to talk about honor at all. At Goshen College they don't give honorary degrees, because it would underwrite notions of honor, which are military. It makes you think about the whole description of why honor becomes the allegedly overriding ethos of the American military, when that's part of the danger, from a Christian point of view.

Of course, I wrote that piece about honor in Trollope and Barth, which I would continue to stand by in terms of the account of honor that I developed there.[38] But, no, it is a very serious question.

Interestingly enough, what is honorable and dishonorable, at least for many people in the American military, has a more restraining effect on war than does just war theory.

BB: I can understand, then, your going to the Air Force Academy and having that discussion as a Christian's attempt to bolster any trajectory you might encounter that resists the further extension of violence. The question from our last line of discussion that is still hanging out there for me is how would you understand your relationship to the people in your audience there who would call themselves Christians, and who would have gone far past the boundary that you say Christians should not go past; by practicing killing.

SH: Obviously my obligation is to try to help them see that they've gone further than they should have! You have to say, "Well, as much as I can appreciate those moves, why are you here?"

BB: It would therefore be a success if there were a few walkouts?

SH: Absolutely. My question in those contexts is always Mike Baxter's question: If you really are a just warrior, when have you ever said no? Keeping the "no" alive is part of what one tries to do.

Yoder and the self-deceptions of nonviolence

BB: Let's move now in a third and more directly theological direction. This has to do with your alliance with Yoder on these themes. Yoder often strikes me as coming dangerously close to espousing Marcionite claims or at least ones with anti-Israeli implications. Consider this passage you approvingly quote in *Dispatches from the Front*:

> Judaism successfully kept its identity without ever using the sword; kept its community solidarity without ever possessing national sovereignty. In other words: Judaism through the Middle Ages demonstrated the sociological viability of the ethic of Jesus. Judaism in terms of actual ethical performance represents the most important medieval sect living the ethic of Jesus under Christendom. Jews are dispensed from becoming "Christian" because of the racism and the anti-Judaism of official Christianity. The story thereby demonstrates, without wanting to, that the way to be a Christian sectarian minority is to live without the sword.[39]

As your own student Tommy Givens has pointed out, what we have here is a depiction of Israel as a historically reconstructed ethical abstraction. Yoder is deploying "the common weapon of claiming to know the true embodiment of the reputable entity of Israel over against false pretenders."[40] He thus puts us in the position of having to ask the question whether "ethnic" Jews are really "unethical" and so false Jews.

I can see why a member of a pacifist minority in America would want to say this, but I don't see how Yoder then avoided at least implicitly condemning the sheer existence of the state of Israel as a falsification of the truth of Judaism. It's not clear to me that he has the authority as a Christian to make that judgment, which is why I'm worried about the anti-Semitic momentum of his argument for pacifism. Would you be prepared to levy the sort of rebuke that Rosenzweig levied at Kafka's friend Max Brod, who as a Jew dismissed all Christian theology but because he liked Dante and Kierkegaard, wanted to label them "Jews dispersed in Christianity"?

SH: Well I have to say I think Tommy is right. I can't help but enjoy John's presumption that Judaism represented a people who had lived how Jesus wanted Christians to live, and it turned out they can survive that way. I think there's some wisdom about that. You just have to get down and dirty about these things. I do think the state of Israel is a real problem, and I take it that to take a side in a debate among Jews will turn on the question, "How do you understand the establishment of a state prior to the eschaton?" So many Jews that are mainly ultra-Orthodox Jews don't like the state of Israel at all, because they feel it is forcing God's hand. I am on the ultra-Orthodox side on that. Though if I were a Jew, I'd want Israel to exist. I think Tommy is right. It's just not the place for Christians to tell Jews who they are. Therefore, some of the things I've said, such as that quote, clearly have to be said much more carefully.

BB: That seems like a substantive shift from Yoder's formulation and I can see how his problem could be rather straightforwardly fixed in the way Tommy suggests, simply by not getting into the game of deciding who is the real Jew. But would that also apply to the way we talk about Christians and violence? This would be to admit that we're not in the eschatological position to say that this Christian in the military is not a real Christian.

Yoder's position also seems Marcionite to me. I think this is what I was alluding to in my earlier question about how we talk about God's history. It seems Marcionite in claiming to know an awful lot about all the possible ways God might work in human history. David, Joshua, Deborah, and Samson are significant characters in the Old Testament, as is Jael who is depicted as an agent of God's protection of Israel when she kills an enemy king with a tent peg. It is biblical stories like these, liminal as they admittedly are, that make me slightly less anxious than some to show, for instance, as students of yours have attempted to do, that Bonhoeffer had to be mistaken in his view that God led him into the plot against Hitler's life. And you've just admitted that if you had lived in the time of Hitler you'd have considered being in the military. This is by no means to suggest that murder and killing are now OK for Christians.

I am at this point rather attracted to a line like Barth's—I can wonder whether God told Bonhoeffer and Samson to do what they did, but I can't really assert with any confidence that he never could have asked them to do what they—and in Samson's case scripture—said God did. You seem more willing to make the further claim, with Yoder, that in Christ we can be confident about what we know God could never do. But that brings up precisely the Marcionite problem in apparently working from a presumed difference in how violence is portrayed in the Old and New Testaments.

SH: Have you ever read Yoder's *Tertium Datur*?[41] He thinks that one of the most determinative ways that Christianity became unfaithful was when it thought of itself as fundamentally different from Judaism. He thought it crucial for Christianity to continue to read the Old Testament, you can call it the Hebrew Bible if you want, because a theological reading of the Old Testament helps the church see how Israel's narrative is her narrative, with all of its unfaithfulness. I think Yoder's readings were really terrific, and I have to think that they're the kind of readings we can continue to give.

The last thing in the world that I want to do is to be a Marcionite. In the piece that I've just done for this conference in Durham in November on Catholicism, I suggest that the deepest challenge before Roman Catholicism is how to start acknowledging the Catholic church's minority status, and how it needs to be able to read its life in the light of the people of Israel, so that it is finally relieved of the problem of being a success. That's what I think.

BB: Once again, the devil is in the detail. Francesca Murphy's commentary on I Samuel very nicely surveys the attraction for Christians in positions in political power toward figures like David.[42] And obviously, David, with all his war-making, is not going to be easily shoe-horned into the critiques you've given of bayonet training. That's one way in which the statist forms of just war thinking got off the ground, with the question, "Let's think Christian about rule by looking at king David." Of course to do this appropriately thick claims will have to be made about the kingship of Christ framing our explication of all rulers after Jesus. Would you be happy to reengage that tradition and think it through?

SH: I think David is a failure. I think what it means for Jesus to be the new David puts David in a very inferior position. This has everything to do with how, indeed, kingship is received through the Old Testament. I think that overall, in the Old Testament the people of Israel came increasingly to the judgment that David was a bad idea.

BB: This is where I have been educated by conversations with Jews, most influentially the former UK chief rabbi, Jonathan Sacks. I ran that line to him and he pushed right back, saying, "Jews don't think of David as an exemplary sinner." As a Christian this surprised me, since I share the sensibilities about him that you've just expressed. But he also explained to me the theological reasons why to this day Israel has a conscript army. They read those Old Testament passages as presenting a mandate for universal conscription, which connects in a surprising way once again with your own position.

The story of David's taking a census for the purpose of getting soldiers can be read as the sort of negative verdict by the biblical authors on David's warmaking tendencies that you and I would find pretty important, not to mention his having been barred from building the temple because he is "a man of blood."[43] When our Christological thinking about these issues begins to have genuine substance, it tends to keep mixing up the boundary between the Old and New Testaments. I can't recall whether you draw on the Bible or Barth when you suggest that if we're going to have armies at all we should have universal conscription, but a Jew can teach us that it's in the Old Testament, even a Jew who resists the claim that David was a flamboyant sinner—which for us means he was also a practiced repenter.

SH: We recently had the lectionary passage about David and Bathsheba and Uriah. I always am fascinated by how it starts, "In the spring, when kings go out to war." It's become routine! It's no longer charismatic. The great figure of Joab. You kill the traitor, even if you kill the king's first son.

BB: Even though he told you not to.

SH: But you know better!
It's *realpolitik* at its deepest.

BB: Have you read Robert Alter's *The David Story*?[44]

SH: No, I haven't.

BB: It's excellent. He shows why it is appropriate to read the whole narrative cycle as *realpolitik*. It's fantastic.

SH: He's terrific. His Psalms book is just terrific.[45]

Gender troubles and structured violence

BB: The Bathsheba narrative raises another set of very ticklish questions about gender. This is more fraught but perhaps even more important territory in raising questions that I think are much closer to home, theologically closer to home and practically closer to home for most Christians. Goff asks the question of how it could be that some of the most famous pacifists we know could have been involved in such blatant exploitation of gendered power differentials.[46] He mentions Gandhi, Martin Luther King, and Yoder, all of whom were highly influential pacifists in the realm of politics, and clearly had various levels of influence in shaping the views and policies of those in government, both directly and indirectly. But each in their own way exploited the institutionalized sexual power differentials that afflicted their age and ours, cashing in their fame by taking sexual liberties with women, often married women. This is exacerbated in Yoder's case by his fulsome theological defense of his persistent exploitation, which, as Paul Martens has noted, was not something he apologized for but which he defended as acts of Christian discipleship and peacemaking.[47] How are we to narrate this paradoxical gulf between these guys having such insight into the role of power and violence in public combined with unbelievable naiveté about power in the domain of sexuality?

SH: I have to say, I was absolutely stunned by the *Mennonite Quarterly Review* on Yoder.[48] I knew about it, but I didn't know the extent of it. Mark Nation has convinced me that I have to write a response in terms of my relationship with John. What he did was just wrong. And he backed it with a stupid theory. I told him once I had found out about his behavior from Ray Myer and Mary-Ellen, his sister, who is Ray's wife. I said, "John, I don't care what the theory was about in terms of your thinking that this was something that Christians could do in a nonsexual way as brothers and sisters in Christ. You couldn't be right about it because you were doing it in secret."

I think that what I have discovered that I just don't know how to account for is John's lack of empathy for the women he was engaged with. In the Tran/Martens/Howell/Cramer article[49] they describe the encounter with the young Mennonite woman who had just had a child and John suggesting that they go to his hotel room and take off their clothes and let him watch her nurse the child. He didn't feel how aggressive and violent that was? Surely, empathy was just lacking! I don't know how to account for Martin Luther King Jr. and Gandhi. But it shows that men have been socialized in ways that are destructive for us and clearly are destructive for women. I myself think that I did not appropriately appreciate the damage that John was doing to women, in terms of my own involvement in that situation, which was clearly on the side. But I don't think that the disciplinary process was as successful as I thought it had been.

BB: I'm glad you've said all that, and I think it was important to have said it. My main interest is in trying to understand how these cases complicate, for instance, the line you were taking earlier that it was the small practices and the narrative that help us to escape our self-deceptions and blind spots. Pretty clearly, these three guys were practicing in their day-to-day lives exactly the sort of violence that they were both highly attuned to and publically denouncing in another register of social order. Drawing an analogy with our earlier discussion, if you want American Christians to be less excited about going to war, they should not have guns hidden under their pillows. What we've got here are guys with guns under their pillows, preaching the immorality of war. And I'm just not quite clear how to hold those two things together?

SH: What you can't hold together is how the same person can do both?

BB: If nonviolence is a hermeneutic for spotting power games, it's not clear to me how these guys could be so clear about the minute movements of power in one domain and totally blind to other movements of power. Or perhaps whether their preternatural ability to sense social dynamics made exploiting them in other domains irresistible.

SH: It's called self-deception, isn't it? I mean, who knows what kind of stories Martin Luther King was telling himself. Yoder had this stupid theory. Gandhi was a Hindu so in terms like this, who am I to speak? I don't know how to account for them.

BB: How might these observations help us think further along the lines you've opened up with your critique of war? Given that the main energy of that critique has focused on the idolatry and sacrifice associated with our particular configuration of war making, I suspect you might have more to say about the misogyny that's so central in sustaining the ideology of war as we know it today. You have written many times about how masculinity and sexual domination can become almost normal, and this discussion has, again, indicated that normality as well as its problematic reach.

Sexual domination can become common sense and has become common sense in many sectors of North American culture. I'm thinking particularly of your drawing on the devastating critique of contemporary American moral thinking by Catherine MacKinnon in *After Christendom*, who takes a position not unlike your critique of Ramsey. If just war talk today is vitiated when we take the viewpoint of the legislator, public discourse around sexuality is similarly vitiated in being so thoroughly aligned with the masculine viewpoint.[50] Could you say more here about ways that the military in the US uses ideas of masculinity in recruitment, propaganda, and so on? Perhaps the military is even recruiting women now using the idea that women can be even more manly than men?

SH: Stan Goff has done that so well. I don't have anything more to say than he has said. I think the male gaze is just as destructive of women as it is of men. I think the relationship Stan shows between pornography and war is very compelling. I've always thought Margaret Mead was quite insightful when she was thinking about Samoa. She observed the great problem with every social order is that women know their power.[51] They can have children. What can men do? They're useless. Women just need them around every once in a while. So men need to have some kind of reinforcement to reassure themselves that they are really important and needed. So they go around trying to show that they can kill one another in order to protect people, to protect "their women." It's just such a destructive account of masculinity. I don't even know if you need an account of masculinity or femininity. But it's there.

As someone who, allegedly, is unsympathetic with feminism, I am very pleased that you noticed my use of Catherine MacKinnon. I am very influenced by her and Shulamith Firestone and that's never been appreciated by feminists. It kind of pisses me off, I have to say. I think I have tried to take feminism very seriously.

BB: Could you give us a few more lines about what you are pointing toward when you say you are not sure we need an account of masculinity and femininity, which sounds like an unfinished project.

SH: Well I've always distrusted those kinds of descriptions because they so invite either biological determinism or social constructivism of one kind or the other.

Men and women have bodies that are specific and also different. What forms that difference takes, I think, is open to unbelievable variation. I don't know that there's any one Christian way of displaying what that difference should look like. I would hope that Christians wouldn't necessarily underwrite the modes of what counts for feminine and masculine in the various societies that they find themselves.

BB: If I am hearing you rightly, it sounds like you think that not only do they never end, but these negotiations about the force of gender should never end. But also, conceptually speaking, one way to end the discussion is to deny that there is a distinction at all.

SH: Right! There is a distinction.

BB: We just don't know how appropriately to acknowledge and respect it. What we do know is that it is patriarchal and imperialistic to have a claim about distinction at all in the new ideology. Such claims ought to be resisted. The so-called rejection of heteronormativity, in other words, you think is a misguided solution?

SH: Absolutely!

BB: Let's engage in some self-criticism. The careful and insightful report by Mathew Guest, Sonya Sharma, and Robert Song has recently reminded those of us in the academic discipline of theology in the UK that our discipline remains largely populated by men.[52] They are looking at academic theology in the broadest sense. There are several vectors that sustain this situation, such as the enduring linkage of the pulpit with men but perhaps even more devastatingly the performance-oriented configuration of the modern academy, which essentially punishes career breaks of any kind in every university discipline.

I'm curious about whether you think there are features of your own work that have played into this dynamic. One that comes to mind is our recent discussion about "work" and "the job" as depicted in the first two chapters of *Hannah's Child*. Do you think that the way we men have learned to think about "hard work" can set up problematics that exacerbate the tendency of the theological academy to be a very masculine domain? I have in mind your memorable casting of the academy in competitive terms in our first conversation when you said, "I won, didn't I?" I am also thinking of your tellingly direct comment in *Hannah's Child* that "Home meant Mother. 'The job' meant my father . . . being taken to 'the job' meant I was becoming a man."[53]

SH: Yeah. What can I say other than that description, "Home meant Mother. 'The job' meant my father," were simply the way things were. To deny that would be to fail to acknowledge that you were shaped by these contrasts that powerfully seize the imagination and are very hard to ever disperse, because I suspect I still have presumptions about that.

Do I think that my own habits reproduce what the report suggests is the male dominance in theology? Yes. Yes. And yet I'm defensive about the recent review that counted up the number of white men I had quoted in my work in comparison to the number of women.[54] I think it was a cheap shot. I do think that the women that have been important for me intellectually—Iris Murdoch, Elizabeth Anscombe, Helen Oppenheimer, I learned a lot from Sally McFague in terms of what she was doing in literature—it never occurred to me to take those people seriously because they were women. I was just taking them seriously because what they were doing was so interesting. Now given the gendered world in which we live, that may be a failure to acknowledge that women are under power differentials that are detrimental to them and you ought to worry more about quoting women because they are women and being in conversation with them because they are women. I am sure my habits are too deep to make that turn.

BB: And the habits point seems to me still to be a very challenging one, because the fact of the matter is that by being in the university, theology partakes in what is ultimately a competitive culture in which silence is death. That makes it pretty hard to have babies. Now, it can be done. But it takes a set of compromises. For instance, the French upper classes appear much more committed to egalitarianism, but they just all have nannies! I think in the English-speaking world, the empirical observation that there are all kinds of power imbalances has not yet been met with an honest accounting of what sustains it. It's been met with a rather superficial policy response; "let's get the numbers equal."

We're talking now about questions that are, conceptually, extremely interesting. We're talking about problems that have arisen due to your positioning as you have traversed cultural changes. Having emphasized the importance of contingency in the doing of theology, this seems like a case where we see one of the difficulties it generates. Your positioning on this topic is markedly different than the one you occupied on the theme of disability. There you staked out a new position that was on the right side of common morality before your time. You were arguing on behalf of those who were soon to be accepted as morally exemplary against those in the moral order of the 1980s in which people like Jean Vanier would be cast as slackers, or at least antitypes to the much sought after Christian leader. That was a nice position to be in, as an ethical thinker and as an academic, and it's a comfortable place. Who is going to trash the guy defending disabled people?

But Christians now are having to learn what it means to be on the wrong side of a rapidly changing moral convention. Nowhere is this more obvious than in the realm of sexuality, which encompasses the problems related to gender violence as well as a long history of violent suppression of same-sex relationships and other formerly marginalized expressions of human sexuality. We are rapidly reaching the conclusion of the first phase of the transition that started in the 1960s with the coming out of marginal lifestyles that had been vigorously excluded for centuries and is concluding with their being near the center of the cultural mainstream. It's a transition from one moral regime to another. It will probably for a little while longer be possible to get away with saying, "It's not clear to me if gay relationships can be called marriage," for instance. But pretty soon this will be seen as by definition a bigoted or an unjust belief and if Christian theologians want to explore such positions they are going to have to do so on the wrong side of the moral, legal and cultural law.

Against this background your situation seems to me to resonate in an interesting way with a thinker like Foucault. He began writing and thinking about homosexuality before the sexual revolution, before the 1960s, but then found the moral and political landscape drastically changing. After it had happened there was no way he could deny the accusation levied at him that his ideas had been formed in reaction to the old repressive regime. A position he had staked out at a time when it was morally challenging position had now been so overtaken by events that it had come in the new landscape to look not terribly different from what had become the conservative position.[55]

I'd suggest that a not dissimilar fate has befallen your writings on disability. I am interested in hearing your reflections on how you've negotiated similar dynamics in relation to your various forays into sex and gender. For instance, you were way ahead of the curve in pointing out the importance of singleness in any Christian view of human sexuality, and in attacking the reduction of the category of the family to biology. But I wonder where this leaves us in a new situation in which reproduction has been so decisively technologized that children can now be rendered a consumer option and procreation can widely be considered irrelevant for our definitions of marriage. What advice would you have for those of us who have to *begin* here?

SH: My basic advice is to say what you think you can say honestly and clearly. I think also the word "courage" is probably going to be necessary, because the demand given the Supreme Court decision for recognition of gay marriage is just going to be a presumption that you just have to accept.[56] I can't accept it, as much as I would like to. If you think that marriage is an institution in Christianity that has a unitary and sacramental end, I cannot also see how it doesn't have the procreative end. It doesn't mean that every marriage has to be procreative. But marriage as an institution does. I am more than ready to acknowledge that gay people can be as good as parents—if not better—than nongay people. The question is, finally, where do you get children from? For me, it's not going to turn on any one biblical text. It's really an ontological question that involves the navel. I just wish that Christian marital practices were sufficient to sustain the acknowledgment of significant gay committed relationships, but our practices are awful, because romantic conceptions of marriage have just destroyed us. And of course, it is analogous to taking the position on disability, early on. I hadn't thought of it. How do you mean that, earlier on, that "this seems to have been the fate of your writings on disability"?

BB: I mean you went into disability primarily as a way to get under the skin of medical ethics. You hadn't really set your interventions up to present a constructive position and it was more than sufficient as a deconstructive position of the medical orthodoxy. Because it was ahead of the game, though, you got trapped, because people read it as presenting a constructive position.

SH: I didn't do it purposefully, to challenge medical ethics. I just started thinking about it because I got pulled into that world and then that followed.

BB: The basic analogy, to my mind, is that with that early work you gained an influence that was not insignificant for a small group of people trying to think about disability theologically and finding few resources. And you obviously had a very similar influence in the domain of sexuality, by making what is now commonplace argument that singleness is not a bad thing for Christians. But as you've noted, that position was essentially directed at the romanticism and over-valorization of marriage. But it may well be that in both cases you had made a sort of Kierkegaard-like critical opening move that you held onto because people weren't getting it. But then other people starting misreading these positions as constructive proposals which they were not set up to be.

SH: I see. That may be true. I don't know.

BB: The question is really about how your impulses can help us to go on, because I suspect it's really going to be more the impulses than the straightforward arguments that we have to use, or develop.

SH: As I look at it down the road, I cannot imagine how the American marital law isn't going to have to acknowledge polygamy.

BB: In even more mundane terms, when you have a National Health System like we do here in Britain, if you legally subtract biological gender as part of marriage law while saying at the same time that every couple has a right to infertility treatment, does that demand legal blindness to the physical bodies involved? This hasn't really played out yet but legally it's already on the cards.

SH: Infertility treatment is expensive as hell.

BB: Well, if you've got three combinations of bodies, then you've got to have three kinds of infertility treatment. That seems to me one of the horizons that your work has opened up, to allow us to begin to pick the material practices apart. Of course, we're already in a world where you can have surrogacy and you can have sperm-banks and you can have transnational adoption. So what's the problem, right? But that's where I see the insight of your saying, "We have to ask about the institution" in the way you did in *Naming the Silences*. What's practically entailed in picking apart the three goods of marriage, institutionally? Well, one thing has got to be the valorization, legally, of all of these technical reproductive aids, because it's not clear how you would . . .

SH: I've been against IVF and IVD from the beginning. I've just never understood why not being able to conceive and experience pregnancy is a medical problem. Why is it a medical problem? It's unfortunate, but there are other alternatives such as adoption. Why is it so important that it be your biological child?

BB: For me this line of questioning simply highlights how difficult it is to conceive how we're going to go on given the intersecting structures of enculturated violence that characterized the gendered horizon of our contemporary world. How should Christians, especially men, navigate the patterns of domination and exploitation in universities that are by no means absent from our own field of Christian ethics? I think I speak for my whole generation when I say that we—both men and women—have been made acutely, painfully aware by the behavior of our elders that the church is just in a total mess on the gender front, and we are all struggling to negotiate a cultural transition away from the settled, and in their own way productive, structures of patriarchy.

It has to be admitted that there was a certain grace and meaning that went with the old "Leave it to Beaver"[57] 1950s world. But it feels like we younger Christians in the developed West are having to get on without any obvious role models in this transition. Of course, there are some insightful and powerful feminist and queer critiques of the violence of the status quo. But by and large it seems to me that much of the theological work about where we might go from here remains to be done, since much of the revisionist theological work to date has attempted various "Troeltschian" decontaminations of the tradition in ways I think we could both agree are corrosive to its integrity.

SH: I think marriage has become such a damned necessity for many people because they intuit that it's their only hedge against loneliness, particularly as they grow older. That puts too much weight on marriage. A marriage is sustainable if it is surrounded and constituted by friendships that allow the partners in marriage to respect the other's distance.

I always rather like the scenes from Victorian novels where the wife is having breakfast and the husband comes in ready to read *The Times*. The newspaper is placed next to his plate. The breakfast is on the buffet but as he gets his breakfast, he suddenly thinks he'll ask his wife how's she's feeling. So he says, "How are you . . .?" And she rushes out of the room because she wasn't prepared for this unbelievable assault on her being.

I think modern marriage legitimates those assaults in a way that makes it feel totalitarian. How to love one another without that loving being an invitation to absolutely evacuate the other's legitimate distance is one of the great challenges before us because we're so desperate not to be alone.

BB: That's a powerful observation that could easily be taken in the wrong way as could my suggesting that there might have been certain fertile aspects of the old patriarchal settlement. I think now you've positioned me to clarify why admitting that might remain important. Women in middle-class and upper-class circles were obviously disadvantaged in some respects in not getting to join the men as they retired to the smoking room while the women would retire to have tea.

SH: And embroidery!

BB: We've heard endlessly the stories in our time of the ways in which someone who wanted to cross from one group to the other would be thwarted in that desire and the ways in which the political power was held by the men who brokered it as they smoked cigars and therefore, women were barred from escaping entrapment in the domestic domain. There's all sorts of negative sides to that.

SH: They wouldn't even let them read newspapers.

BB: That sounds blissful!

But we seem to have emerged from rejecting that boundary into a world, as you say, in which there is one room in which all single sex gatherings are treated as suspect and in which the internal configuration of domestic space has not found a new order. The separateness and the togetherness are hopelessly mixed up now. The profile that I very regularly see is men fulsomely claiming in public that we're egalitarian and we have an egalitarian marriage and still expecting the wife to do the cooking and being frustrated about not being able to go out with their male friends for nights out and the women frustrated that they don't have a very satisfying job or day-to-day life. We're still very much in the early stages of coming to any meaningful new settlement on the backside of the collapse of the age-old games of partitioning space along gendered lines.

SH: I think that's exactly right. The idea of an egalitarian marriage strikes me as utopian bullshit. I can't imagine what that would mean. We're too subtle as creatures for that. How to respect the dignity of one another often means that there will be aspects of the relation that are anything but egalitarian.

BB: Christianly speaking it has to be a gift that the church, both men and women in it, are so vulnerable here. But I think that vulnerability produces an anxiety that is easily displaced into the debates in which we are so angrily embroiled, about protecting the traditional family from interlopers, namely from people with sexualities that are different. As if the disarray of the old patriarchal ordering of domestic relations was the fault of "the gays"! I think the great demonic twist of this historical moment is the lack of exemplars that I was talking about earlier. There seems to be a kind of white-knuckle approach to marriage that came to be the norm over the last thirty or forty years. Christians get married and stay married, no matter how badly we're making it work as a livable relationship. We're going to hang on to something that doesn't seem to be working even though the old patriarchal model is collapsing all around us. The new twist is that the white-knucklers now are being called violently bigoted, and it's just leading to chaos.

SH: It is. I think it's also interesting what it does to sex. We've talked before about how sex becomes so desperate in the sense that it is the one place where people think in terms of the Eucharistic formula—*ex opere operato*—in the sense that if they do it, they believe the act itself will necessarily be constitutive of meaning. And that doesn't work. That just doesn't work.

The question is what it means to be in a relationship where our bodies are not off limits for each other. It's so difficult to sustain. Often, sex becomes located as the only determinative form of touching. It can be quite demonic when that happens. We have to make Christian marriage an intelligible alternative to that.

BB: Especially when the tasks internal to being a good lover in a committed relationship, even when supported by extended relationships, continue to be carpet bombed in the popular culture with narratives in which meaningful sexual activity, to put it bluntly, is connected solely to transgression; either transgression of the commitment of marriage or transgressive enactments of touching. It seems to me that landmines are laid in every one of the exit routes out of the predicaments faced by contemporary couples.

That long detour into the problem of marriage, problems associated with a strong Christian moral affirmation, very helpfully explains how you understand the question, "What am I going to do if I am going to fare well?" in its connection to Christian faith. Specifically in how the Christian faith as revealed through a historical tradition generates strong moral claims that produce or should produce countercultural living. The final result does look very different from anything Aristotle could conceive.

The question seems relevant in our discussion today because it highlights the relation of the narrower discussion about war and pacifism to wider questions about what it means to live peaceably, as we discussed in Chapter 4. But I don't want to leave the topic without asking straight out: Am I missing something here? Is my generation as "naked" before these challenges as we feel we are?

SH: I just wrote down "Yes." I think your generation is. I don't have any advice!

BB: OK, then. Given that answer, I've long had the worry, and this is based on my own simple observations about how my life has run, that we have sometimes to learn the life of faith without the sort of exemplars in front of us that we need to go on. But you often speak as if we can count on having access to exemplars. If then you allow that there might be no obvious exemplars—what does that mean in terms of your own way of approaching ethics?

SH: Well, exemplars may be dead. So, to reach into Christian tradition and discover people who you hadn't anticipated could be of help would be one of the ways to do it. Who knows what you'll find around you that you hadn't anticipated.

BB: The tradition and the stories of the saints allow us to maintain hope for finding practices to make this transition with grace?

SH: And also prayer. Asking God for help would make a difference!

Peacemaking and worship

BB: Let's park these questions about the implications of peacemaking in the context of gender relations and return to wrap up the discussion on war and pacifism by looking at some of your late writings. I've noticed a pretty stark change in tone in some of your writings after 9/11. Your rhetoric shifts from traditional academic argumentation of the type that you once shared with Ramsey and his descendants to the more explicitly first-order language of Christian faith that, as far as I can tell, first appears with your ending of your comments on the first Gulf War with a prayer for God's judgment.[58] Do correct me, but you seem to have put more prayers in print toward the end of your career. This looks like an early example, maybe the earliest example of appending one at the end of an essay.

The iconic ascent of George Bush Jr. to the top of the rubble of the twin towers to call the US to war seems to force your "turn to worship" to take root much more explicitly, much more practically. You insist that no Christian should talk as Bush has, and you say that for Christians silence is much better than such talk in a moment of acute distress. Having said that, you then proceed to say what you feel you can about the attacks on the Twin Towers, and following them with a prayer and a sermon. I'm fascinated by this because I am tempted to read your response to 9/11 as the real *performative* display of what peacemaking means to you, that you promised on the very first page of *Against the Nations* in 1992.[59] In any case, this is how I'd like to read the basic presumption framing your mature book on war, *War and the American Difference*. There you write, "The challenge for those who would worship Christ . . . is to allow what we do in prayer to confront habits that seem to make war inevitable."[60] Would you agree that after 9/11 your talk about war is more often characterized by the rhetoric of prayer and worship than previously?

SH: I think that's right. I think the very mode of analysis in *War and the American Difference* calls attention to what I call the liturgical character of war in the American experience, namely that we have to repeat it in order to assure ourselves that the sacrifice of the youth of the past makes us deserving of the sacrifice of the youth of the present. It is a liturgical exchange. Therefore, the alternative to war is really worship, not some set of principles. It's my way of trying to get us off the dime of the discussion between pacifism and just war and to help us see why it is that though everyone says, "Oh war is terrible" we still do it over and over again. It's my way of trying to help us to see what I think is really there, but seldom noticed.

BB: Given those considerations you can see why the chapter on war and peace in *Approaching the End* feels to me a bit anticlimactic.[61] In it you return to the beginning, consolidating and summarizing in a succinct and comprehensive manner the strongest lines of argument that you have developed against "just war theory" and its intrinsic wedding to modern nation-state Enlightenment based rationality. It is a very useful piece to have in being such a good summary of your position. I only call it anticlimactic because the embedding of your discussion in the language of address to God has given way again to academic prose, to the Ramsey-esque style or at least a style that Ramsey would have been proud of. I'm curious now to ask what made you go back to the older rhetorical stance when talking about war?

SH: Because I was asked to write about it by Graham Ward for the *Oxford Companion to Europe and History*.[62] The venue made the difference. But I was pleased to be able to do it and engage Bobbitt and people like that.

BB: If I was to summarize the trajectory of your thinking about just war as a whole, I would say that it grows from the fundamental assertion that the work of Jesus Christ has been to create a space that the lords of this world do not rule and that this space is the church. In that space we can afford to forgive and be forgiven, to speak and to listen, and to slowly unhand the rule of violence.[63] The task of living peaceably calls for serious thought—as does the task of engaging with those in positions of political power who "hold the reins"[64]—but these are very different sorts of tasks.

SH: That is certainly right; that I hope that what I am about is trying to show how the work of Jesus Christ has been to create a space that the lords of this world do not rule and therefore can give you an alternative history. Of course, what that does is then make ecclesiology so central to the project. My thinking about war is not central to what I am about but is rather a way to elicit the reason why Christology and ecclesiology are so central.

BB: Would it be fair to say that you backed into that latter claim through engagement with war? So the trajectory of your writing is, in a way, the inverse of your conceptual emphases.

SH: Probably. When people say, "Isn't your central work about nonviolence?" I always think, "I hope not!" That just seems to me to get the emphasis wrong.

BB: Well we can certainly unpack why that mistake can do damage to any reading of your work in our next interview, when we consider the role of disability in your theology.

Chapter 7

MEDICAL ETHICS, DISABILITY, AND THE CROSS

March 29, 2015

The central insight emerging from this conversation is that disability can legitimately be understood as the hermeneutical key to Hauerwas's work as a whole. His discussions of this theme are oriented by an emphasis on the cross for any accurate understanding of the Christian gospel and its Christological focus. Several questions raised in previous conversations about the role played by revelation, joy and the Holy Spirit in the Christian life now receive much more detailed answers. Hauerwas also further clarifies his understanding of natural theology as he discusses the role played by the body in medicine, liturgy and L'Arche. This leads to further specification of his understanding of the relationship between natural theological modes of argumentation with eschatology and the work of the Holy Spirit in Christian formation.

Caring, curing, and cracks in the social order

BB: Let's return today to your early work and talk about theology and disability. I'd like to begin by focusing on the book in which you first drew together your writings on this topic, *Suffering Presence*. Part of the reason I wanted to talk about the problem of biography in theology in our first chapter had to do with knowing that I wouldn't be able to discuss *Suffering Presence* without speaking biographically.

This was obvious in the first instance because *Suffering Presence* was a seminal book in my own intellectual formation. I came across it while enrolled in a rigorous medical ethics master's program in the mid-1990s, which included lots of time on wards and weekly ethical grand rounds with clinicians. I learned an immense amount about how modern medicine works, how medical ethicists relate to it, and what it means to do top-level academic work. It was an exhilarating period.

The most important thing I was learning, however, was how liberal theology had become the servant and defender of the medical status quo. I was being taught by Claremont-trained Rawlsian Kantians who were strongly attracted to process theology. What this meant in practical terms is that Beauchamp and Childress's *Principles of Biomedical Ethics* wholly defined what was taken to be a Christian medical ethics. As you know, that is an incredibly conservative text, and it is indicative of the stagnation in the field that when you wrote *Suffering Presence* you were pushing back against the second edition, and I was still chafing against it when I was trained using it a decade later when it was in the fourth edition. I think it is in the seventh edition or something now?

What bothered me is that I couldn't see much evidence that my teachers ever seriously interrogated the medical dogmas that drive the agendas in a top flight research hospital. If you don't question those agendas, you end up serving them. I was watching Christian truth claims being harnessed to support trajectories in medicine and research programs that I was pretty uncomfortable with— baboon to human heart transplants, to give one example, or experiments in harvesting organs of anencephalic infants. Though I couldn't have articulated it at the time, I was learning first-hand what you later came to call the problem of Constantinian accommodation. The real eye-opener for me was to realize how the medical ethics industry had developed very specific assumptions about what type of theology was allowed into the game. Only years later did I come across John Evans's illuminating narration of how medical ethics had been born out of academic theological ethics, but had rather quickly been co-opted by the demands of modern medical systems for routine low-level policy pronouncements.[1]

I found all this pretty distant from the Christian sensibilities I found compelling, and in ethical terms it seemed to be functioning as window dressing for the medical juggernaut. So I think it would be fair to say that from your perspective I had most of the right questions when I discovered *Suffering Presence*, even though the book had only been assigned because we needed to know that a position like yours was "out there," in both senses of the phrase! You won't be surprised to hear that it wasn't taken to be a serious representative of the discipline of medical ethics, given the understanding of medical ethics I've just described.

You can see then why it took years for me to make any sense of the accusation that you were a covert Protestant liberal. You were saving me from the liberals! It took me fifteen years before I was able to pin down to my own satisfaction what I took to be the grain of truth in that often repeated accusation.[2] I relate these stories because I think I've taken a pretty unique road into your work, and I don't think many people today appreciate what you were up to in the "playground of the medical ethicists" in the 1980s. Since not many today are aware of this background, few are prepared to appreciate what you were and weren't saying about medicine and disability, especially intellectual disability.

But I mean, come on, in defense of my first teachers of medical ethics, the position you lay out on the first page of *Suffering Presence* looks a lot like a flat-out refusal of the good faith necessary to have a decent conversation! You're firing away almost from the first lines:

[T]he rise of "medical ethics" is due more to the confused moral world we inhabit than to our technological revolution. "Medical ethics" therefore does not so much solve our difficulties as it reflects the moral anarchy of our times, for it is by no means clear how the practice of medicine can be sustained in a morally fragmented society. Put more strongly, it is by no means clear in such a society what the practice of medicine is about.[3]

Who did you expect to engage you after that opening?

SH: Christians!

I think I expected to engage Christians, and in an odd way I think *Suffering Presence* is now being appreciated. It took twenty-five years. People didn't get what the book was about. *Suffering Presence* was my attempt to do natural law ethics. The great achievement of medicine is contained in the commitment of physicians to care for patients in a way that prescinds all other considerations other than what is good for this patient. Now think about that: you are to care for a patient in a way that prescinds all other considerations? I take it that that is the result of Christian commitment to always respecting the dignity of the neighbor and that the question then becomes whether you can sustain a medicine on those grounds when medicine has been transformed into the presumption of cure, a presumption that is impossible for the physician to deliver.

What I was trying to do was to suggest why it is that something like the church is necessary to sustain what is now the natural presumption that physicians are to care for patients without any other considerations about the value of that person, as suggested by the question, "Should I care for this person because they are more valuable than that person?" No. You need to care for the patient that presents themselves to you, given what you've learned from past patients about how to go on in the face of an illness from which you are not going to get much better. That is an extraordinary commitment that demands support for physicians. From where? I don't see it coming, apart from the church.

By the way, I think besides the Evans book, I also admire Joel Shuman's first book.[4] It was a dissertation that I directed though Joel did not need a director. Using Wendell Berry's phrase "health is community," Joel tries to show that one of the central problems of modern medicine is that the very characterization of illness that legitimates physician intervention abstracts the patient from community.

When people say, "Why haven't you done more, following up what you did in *Suffering Presence*?" I say because Joel did it. So many times I think graduate students and other people say better what I was trying to say, so I don't see any reason that I need to say it.

BB: Because I read *Suffering Presence* so long ago, I expected to find it outdated when I reread it. But in fact I had the opposite experience. As you noted, I'm part of the small crowd discovering that there is more there than I grasped the first time around. I can only say that, though, because it's become clearer over time how that book was primarily an intervention in the field of medical ethics, whose parameters are not very different from what they remain today. I think the diagnosis of the problems of that discourse that you offer in *Suffering Presence* as well as the constructive response that you offer remains incredibly pertinent today. Your diagnosis of what doctors were after from medical ethicists, why philosophers and theologians wanted to get into the medical ethics game, and why the theologians gave away the game from the start[5] are in my view just as insightful as the analysis you gave of the guild of academic ethicists at your 1980 AAR speech. You certainly deploy very effectively a criticism of cultural conventions in our practice of medicine in the way you've done in many other domains. From that perspective, the decision to introduce the problem of intellectual disability was a masterstroke.

It is also evident that you were still feeling your way into how to talk about the phenomenon of disability. Sometimes you are grasping at how best to move the argument forward, and here I'm thinking of your use of Adam Smith's *Theory of Moral Sentiments* and the *Epistle to Diogenetus* to make your concluding constructive point in "Suffering the Retarded."[6] Yet in the time and place, the judgment that this was a topic that medical ethicists needed to be confronted with was exactly right, and to the extent that the discipline continues to trundle along in the liberal-autonomy-informed consent-cost/benefit model vein, this remains a point that needs to be pressed even today.

I can see, however, how people who read *Suffering Presence* for the chapters on disability will have very easily come away with complaints. The first time I ever saw you at work in the American context was in 2005 when I was part of a panel discussing your writings on disability at the American Academy of Religion.[7] I can still vividly remember being shocked to the soles of my boots when a woman stood up during question time and literally raged at you for idealizing the church in your writings on disability. I'd like this image to remain in our minds throughout our discussion today, because the pain and rage of disabled people towards the church is no small matter and looking away from it deadens us. This poor woman had obviously lived through the painful pity and marginalization that people with disabilities can experience in our churches. I'd never even considered her accusation, and by that time I was neck deep in the problems raised by disability myself.

I suppose then that the journey I was making must have paralleled your own—that what you had written as an intervention designed to confront medical ethicists was being read much more widely and taken to be making claims about the lives of all sorts of people that they resisted. Does this trajectory sound right?

SH: Yes. It does sound right. I remember that very well.

BB: It has since happened to me, often, for a range of reasons. But had it not happened to you before?

SH: I don't remember. But I remember that time very well. I don't remember how I responded, but I hope I responded sympathetically and without trying to be critical of her response.

BB: I don't remember your response either, but I don't remember thinking, "Oh I wish he hadn't said that!"

SH: What I think she might be missing is I'm not talking about what the church actually *does*, I'm trying to say what it *should* do. Of course you can say that's still idealistic fantasy, but I thought she didn't quite get that I was trying to make a normative argument, not a descriptive argument. Although that distinction can be obscure.

The fact that I had hit upon disability as important was a matter of sheer contingency. I had met a man named Harvey Bender, who was a geneticist—a fly geneticist—in our Biology Department at Notre Dame. We were on some panel together at Notre Dame. Harvey was serving on the board of the local ARC Group that was running Logan Center. Logan Center was in existence because of Indiana's unbelievably bad care of the mentally disabled. So he said, "Would you be willing to serve on the board?" I was asked because you needed to have people on the board who did not have a mentally disabled child. I said I'd certainly think about it. I had never been around mentally disabled people before. The first time I went to Logan Center I was given a tour. Of course, getting to know the mentally disabled, first of all, scares the hell out of me. I didn't know how to respond to them. They were different. I tell this story—it's true—there was this young, maybe seven- or eight-year-old boy with Down's Syndrome who came up to me while I was walking through Logan Center and put his arms around my neck. I had to pick him up and carry him. You know, I was playing the game, "Oh how are you Johnny?" and this kind of thing. But all I could think of was "How in the hell could I get him out of my face!?"

But at the same time, as I became more involved in Logan Center—and I was on the board for I think seven years—the more I came to the conclusion that you were looking at a crack in our assumed humanitarianism that could not be accounted for without, I thought, strong theological convictions. Listening to the parents talk and getting to know these kids, I thought what I was seeing was a kind of crack in the ideologies of our lives that allegedly are humane. I think most people, if they could choose, would rather that these kids not exist. So that's how I got started reflecting about it.

After I served on the board I then became a member of Protective Service. As you know, so often disabled children are simply abandoned, and the court doesn't know what to do with them so the Protective Service acts as guardian. One of my graduate students was a lovely lady named Bonnie Rainey. Bonnie was the social service staff on Protective Service. I would go around with her to the various residential facilities of kids for whom we were guardians. I just learned a lot.

One of our children was a young man named Boyce. Boyce may have been twelve or thirteen. He was profoundly mentally disabled. He spent most of his life lying in a beanbag. The presumption would be for most people seeing Boyce, they would think "How sad, it would be better if he had never been born." But Bonnie could walk in and greet Boyce, and she would put her hand on his cheek and there would be the damndest smile you've ever seen in your life! You know,

I thought, that's what it means to be human. But you need a Bonnie! How to sustain people like Bonnie is I think one of the great challenges that I try to make articulate.

I think it helps you see at once the glory and frustration of medicine. Most physicians are called to be present to the ill in a way that the ill are not going to get that much better, but you still are present. So presence is really such an important concept for me in that book.

That's how I got pulled into the world of disability, and then started thinking it needed to be articulated. There were aspects of what was going on that needed to be made articulate in a manner that the moral commitments that were constitutive of what we were doing at Logan Center and what Bonnie was doing would not be lost. That is partly what we try to do as people committed to ethics. Ethics is such a silly thing! Do you really think that coming up with ethical theories is going to make people better? Nah! At least one of the things that we must do is to make articulate moral realities that might be lost if we didn't know how to say what we're doing. So, that's part of what I was about.

BB: That's a very powerful and useful way to put it; to say that you thought you saw a crack in our humanitarian assumptions. Obviously, that crack existed in a certain place when you discovered it. And some of that, a lot of the legal standards and the moral thinking surrounding lives like we're discussing have shifted, as have some of the presumptions of the medical ethics industry. I'm interested in helping us think about where that crack lies today, so that we can continue the same sort of journalist-like pointing that you've just so clearly described.

For instance, in *Suffering Presence* you are pushing back against the institutional warehousing of people with learning difficulties by insisting that it is unjust to treat people as perpetual children.[8] The time now seems ripe to reposition that claim since the pendulum seems to have swung in entirely the other direction as those institutions have been dismantled. Now people with mental disabilities are living in community care, which has often left mentally challenged adults sitting in flats by themselves watching TV. They're self-determining adults, so we can just let them live their lives as vacuously as the rest of us do! Even if the institutional world you were reflecting on seems to be gone, I suspect the crack remains here somewhere.

SH: Yeah. What do you think about that, Brian?

Let me say: the reason that I put it back to you is that when I moved to Durham, I had a different set of responsibilities and opportunities and I wasn't hands-on anymore, in the way I had been at Logan Center and Protective Services. I didn't feel like I could write with the kind of immediacy that I did with *Suffering Presence*. So, discovering Jean Vanier—you're absolutely right—made all the difference. I think of myself as a witness. I try to witness to what the witness of Jean Vanier is. Jean helps us discover our vulnerabilities. I'm hesitant to think I still have something to say because I fear abstracting. I fear creating abstractions that make it sound like I'm smarter than I am on these issues. That's why I'd like to give it back to you.

BB: There are quite a few directions I might go with that. But let me make a couple of initial comments. In the first place, the term itself, "disability," is entirely too unifaceted and nontheological. The term "disability" itself I would take to be a political label, in the sense of a designator that's used to funnel resources. In a society that thinks people with need should be given greater support, a label is required for who will get it, and disability is one of those labels. But that's essentially a technical apparatus. There's no theological reason why the people we lump today under that term should be grouped together in any more substantive sense.

I think part of the crack now is that the technical apparatus of caregiving, organized by liberal society, gets to define the field. So the way in which we think we are being humane has shifted quite a bit from the days you're talking about in the 1970s in the US. One thing I think you see in your own story is that terms like "limit" and "sickness" and "mental illness" and "physical disability" and "intellectual special needs" are often extremely different beasts in life. This issue turns up in your memoir, for instance, when you note that "it wasn't Anne's bi-polar disorder but her anger that finally exhausted me."[9]

Now I think I have had enough experiences being involved with charities and groups trying to support people in churches and in life more generally to know that the anger to which your comment points is related both to the intellectual and/or emotional problems of the individual in question as well as the various social pressures that come with living with them in society. It's not like you can parse it out easily. We're in need of much more clarity about what it is we're talking about.

SH: Of course I agree entirely about the language of disability. My way of saying it is, "Don't talk about disability. Talk about Adam." So the name makes all the difference. That means you always need someone to know the name. That hopefully will put a brake on the generalized category of disability. But that's a hard thing to do.

BB: I absolutely agree. Part of the reason I'm fumbling for words here relates to the reality that all the descriptions of Adam I need to deploy in order to make him a subject within the bureaucratic apparatus of disability lie so far from my own language about Adam that it becomes very difficult to even see how the two connect. And in my language I never call him disabled.

So, for instance, even though he really doesn't speak and is mentally delayed but physically fairly active, before he had leukemia, we weren't given a social worker, because he wasn't disabled enough. Then he got leukemia, and of course lots of kids that society finds very valuable get leukemia, so he instantly got a social worker and we got a lot of additional support.

That included getting a handicapped parking badge because when he had leukemia some days he basically couldn't walk. The rule for getting a handicapped badge is that you can't be capable of walking more than 100 meters. But now, as you know, he can walk like crazy! And so we lost our handicapped parking badge. That doesn't mean he's any easier to shepherd through a parking lot. If you have got to park outside, he could dart between cars very quickly and easily.

SH: It scares the hell out of people.

BB: Exactly. But that doesn't count as disabled enough, so what you need to know about Adam, which is how to get him from the car to the grocery store, and back again, only impinges in a very oblique way with what's called disability in the legal system. I have tried to do a little work in various places to explicate my own ways of talking about Adam. But it's a big, big gap, a sort of parallel universe of language.

SH: When I got to know parents through working at Logan Center, there was a wonderful man named Joe Newman. He and his wife had a mentally disabled child. Joe—Jewish—was a fighter. What I really began to value about Joe—Joe really knew how to fight bureaucracy. And I thought at the time, "You know, most middle-class people are absolutely at the mercy of bureaucracy because they don't have to fight it." Joe Newman shares a lot with poor people, who have to learn how to fight bureaucracy to get the food stamps and that sort of thing. I thought, it's very interesting that this is a kind of indication of why it is that bureaucratic rules are so determinative in our social order. That's where I find MacIntyre's analysis in *After Virtue* about why it is that the expert has become the authority in modernity so compelling.[10] You need the expert to reassure yourself that the bureaucratic institutions that you are developing are necessary for social life today. That's why you get social science thinking you can have a distinction between fact and value, which has no epistemological use, other than to develop an epistemology that gives authority to experts who allegedly know what's happening! All that seems to me to be at the source of all these great difficulties.

BB: Another aspect of the crack peeks through in your comment about your journey with Anne, and specifically, the dynamics of the end game of your marriage. Your core assessment is that, finally, it just exhausted you. It does seem to me that the crack as it exists today can in part be located by looking for the exhausted faces. Exhaustion is vastly underappreciated in the theological discussions about disability. Living with it, in our world, for all these bureaucratic reasons and others is exhausting. And churches should be a respite.

SH: I was going to say that church is a respite care!

BB: Exactly. One of the simple lessons that Stephanie and I have been trying to articulate when we talk to churches is when someone with a disabled family member comes into a church, think of it as a moment of respite care for the whole family. Every time they're dealing with the medical apparatus, every time they are dealing with the school apparatus, every time they are dealing with the governmental apparatus, they are having to push that stone up the hill.

SH: I think one of the things that is so hard is that when someone comes to a church and lives with a child or a friend who is disabled, people don't know what to do. So there needs to be a kind of training of what to do. You don't need to fall all over yourself saying, "Oh how wonderful!" No one trusts that. But you can touch their hand.

BB: Yeah, there has to be a way found between just being relieved to have a representative of a marginalized group in the building and the sharp intake of breath upon the appearance of disabled people at the church doors which goes with the panicked thought "We don't know what to do!" We found it most useful to say that if you have a visitor with disabilities or a family with a disabled family member, if there seems to be any distress at all, all you need to do to begin is to say "Hello" and "Can I make this any more comfortable for you?" So again, another one of the cracks is that we are formed by our societies in ways that make that gesture awkward and we're not brave enough to venture it. Every church has the opportunity to learn how to digest that blindness and that awkwardness at least.

SH: Right. Absolutely. And wanting to acknowledge it so at least in that way I know that it doesn't have to be.

BB: You nicely articulate the point off the cuff in a recent interview.

> OK. Well I think what is killing evangelicalism is money, and money is just a name for greed. It's very interesting: most people are ready to talk about lust because they think they know what it looks like. Think how seldom they talk about greed because they don't know what it looks like. This is what greed looks like: "I just had to have it for security." It's an individualism that's underwritten by money, an individualism that says, "I don't need anyone else; I can save myself."
>
> For evangelicalism to survive, it has to put people at risk to need one another, to make them vulnerable. That means they've got to risk their children.... Evangelicalism puts far too much emphasis upon belief rather than creating communities of vulnerability.[11]

SH: That's pretty good!

BB: In the remainder of the conversation, I'd like to meander through some of the internal developments of your thinking about medicine and disability, beginning with this quotation from *Suffering Presence*:

> If any one intuition underlies these essays, it is the recognition of what an extraordinary gesture it is for a society to set aside some to dedicate their lives to the care of the ill. That we do so, I think, is not primarily because we are self-interested and thus want to guarantee that when we are ill we will not be abandoned, but because we are unwilling to abandon others who need help.[12]

Just as an aside, I'm now struck by how close this is as an intuition to the central thesis of Paul Ramsey's *The Patient as Person*.[13]

I have a couple of questions about what might be meant by the phrase "we are unwilling to abandon others who need help." My first observation is that, historically speaking, this moral sensibility is quite obviously a legacy of Christendom. The Greeks and Romans didn't provide healthcare to everyone, and they didn't have any problem with infanticide, so as a matter of historical fact, the condition of being unwilling to abandon anyone who needs help is a claim that only makes sense insofar as we are living off of the legacy of Christendom. I note here again your recent refrain that you think it will be a real moral feat if Christians won't kill their children and their old people. Given that you tend to be caricatured as an opponent of Christendom, would it be right to affirm that we should be grateful for Christendom on this score?

SH: Yes. Yes. When Sam Wells was appointed dean of the Chapel at Duke, I said "Sam, this is of course a Constantinian position. Use it!" First, everything about Constantinianism is not wrong. As I have tried to develop elsewhere, Christianity is a faith that by its very character is going to produce a material culture.[14] The question is whether the kind of material culture it produces will be one that does not necessitate the use of violence to sustain it. I am thinking of something as simple as the development of families capable of sustaining children.

You are quite right that Ramsey in *The Patient as Person*, which is still one of the more incisive books about medicine, pointed out what a great achievement it was for that community called the church to produce people willing to be present to those who are ill and dying. You certainly don't want to lose it, though I think we are losing it. Given the church's loss of status and prestige, that makes you free to be able to use certain forms of Constantinianism, which was the production not necessarily of unfaithfulness, but of what we Christians should be about.

BB: You've rightly pointed your answer primarily to institutional structures that are marked by Christian presuppositions, but I was trying to direct attention to a widely held *moral* sensibility, even among unbelievers. If the hospital ultimately sprang from a few convictions of Christians in the fourth century, that institution is still trundling along, it is also true that there is a waxing and waning of moral sensibilities about *what*, and more importantly *who*, that institution is for. It seems to me that the institutional structure remains relatively stable, but the moral sensibility out of which it grew seems to be trailing off precipitously.

If it is the cracks in our societies where we need to see Christian witness going on, I would point to the last decade of fights in the United States about universal healthcare coverage as one of the cracks that seems to be widening. There is no longer, if there ever was, a consensus among the American people that they should care enough about the health of their fellow citizens to not let them drop out of the medical system. The same trajectories can be glimpsed in the drumbeat of voices trying to privatize the NHS, undermining the solidarity principle on which it was founded.

This seems to suggest it's a problem right across the developed West. You've been talking recently about the dying of Christendom, and I just want to try to flesh out a little bit more of what might be entailed in the discovery that there might be fewer people who are "unwilling to abandon others who need help."

SH: Well of course, people think my identification of physicians as people who are charged with not abandoning the ill is romanticism, and not just because they get paid not to abandon the ill. I'm well aware of that. I'm just trying to hold out a vocational description that I hope they will see is part and parcel of their practice. I try to find in everyday relations—which oftentimes people don't think of as moral—moral resources that are still in place but we fail to see their significance. The very fact that physicians still are trained to be with the ill is a great moral resource because the ill are not easy to be around and often not much can be done for them, medically speaking.

It is often claimed that surgeons, when they think they can't do anything for you, walk away! That means one of the crucial forms of medicine today are nurses! That's why the restriction of the care of the ill to physicians is a mistake. I'm not sure I'm answering your question.

BB: No, that's making a lot of sense because it means that there's never going to be a general prescription. We have to watch the way the language and the tensions in particular practices are laying out. I'm reminded of an argument I had with a Professor of Nursing in California, just a few weeks ago, who, drawing on the moral momentum you were talking about, said, "Well, nurses will always care. Even if doctors get driven by the system further and further away from the patients, you will always have nurses who are hands-on and therefore engaged in general caring for the patient." But in the UK that's pretty directly under attack right now. You can train nurses into a job description that is in practice the repudiation of earlier practices that had been taken to be essential to nursing. Time studies and targets can be used to keep nurses moving and looking after ever larger numbers of beds.

SH: It's demonic. The timing of patient care today is destructive both of patients and physicians. Those working in gerontology—it just takes more time. But they're not going to give them that time. It's really quite destructive.

BB: Again that's another one of those cracks that people with mental disabilities fall deeply into. If they can't handle the examination room or getting undressed in this way or getting there in a scheduled time or getting their story out in thirty seconds, they just don't get the care. If, as you say, we're looking for the practices which really bind people together and carry trust, those are expensive.

SH: I think a lot about driving. Driving is such an extraordinary gesture of trust. I trust you to stop at that line, or that stop sign. It's just a wonderfully cooperative place where our humanity shines. One of my favorite places is Mull. On Mull, before you go over to Iona, all the roads are single-lane. They have pull-overs. You'll see a car coming toward you, some distance away. And then they have to decide and you have to decide who pulls over first. That depends on judgments about where you think the pull-over is and who is closer. I don't want to romanticize, but I just found the people on Mull extraordinarily cooperative! I want to attribute that to their driving habits. Or is it a lot of tourists? But the tourists catch on pretty quick too.

Disability and the meaning of community

BB: To extend that conversation back toward *Suffering Presence*: Would you agree that your discussions of disability in *Suffering Presence* gets a lot of its moral force from its examples, and that the examples you most often give are based in the love of parents for disabled children? The book is rife with stories of parents learning to love nonstandard children, refusing to abort or abandon them to institutions, accepting them as they are, learning to trust their judgments in the face of the tyranny of the expert—in short, being taught by them what it means to live as a community that accepts difference.

SH: I'm an Aristotelian. The just man justices. So how do you know what the just man justice-ing looks like? You've got to give examples! Therefore, practical reason is fundamentally an exercise in exemplification, through which you then provide the kind of reflection that helps you understand why that example is powerful. And that involves locating that example in ongoing ways of life that help you see why you can't have that way of life without these kinds of exemplifications. So example is everything for me. I think *Naming the Silences*, which is *all* example, is my attempt to show how examples produce thought in a way that helps you understand why those examples are so powerful. You can choose certain examples that are intuitive, but it really needs display, in that way. It's interesting. When Jeff Stout in *Democracy and Tradition*[15] goes after me for not concentrating on examples I thought, "All I have is examples!"

BB: I was really struck that in *Suffering Presence* one of your most powerful insights into disability, which you continue to emphasize right through your career, is that it's really unfair to start the analysis of disability anywhere else than with people who have learned to love and accept those people who make most people uncomfortable.[16] Now you've very helpfully clarified what's at stake in putting things that way. And that leads you to reframe the question of how we should "treat" the disabled in this way: "Who do we need to be to take everyone seriously in all their diversity?"[17]

That makes a lot of sense.

SH: The phrase "take everyone seriously" is a terrible phrase though! That's bad writing. What would we need to be to receive the presence of the other without regret—that would be a better way to say it.

BB: Good. Good. I can see the improvement.

If it is true then that these sorts of examples generate the moral force of the argument, then it is going to become very important to understand how they have been located and where they sit in relation to your most closely held priorities. In *Suffering Presence* you set yourself the task of showing us where we should look to learn how to care for one another, and specifically, to care for mentally disabled people. I presume this has to do with the different audiences for whom you wrote the essays in *Suffering Presence*, but what we find is that you direct our gaze to places where you might not have later in your career. For instance, in your discussion of experimentation on children, you espouse Aristotle's view that the family is a natural or primitive institution more primal than the state.[18]

As far as I can see this is the only grounds you offer for your repeated insistence that we (liberal Westerners) have to rely on the witness of the parents of disabled children to help us to understand what care means beyond the limits of the Western liberal tradition.[19] I would be tempted to read this line of argumentation as one you'd be slightly less comfortable with today, but you do repeat it forcefully in the last words of the book, even speaking of the community of the parents of disabled children as a discreet moral community not unlike the community of "hard work" that we talked about earlier, on which other communities (such as the church, presumably) depend in order to be good communities.[20]

SH: I find myself embarrassed that I called the family a community at all. It doesn't strike me that the family is a community. Also I worry that I have made the family too significant, in an odd way, given my views that one of the decisive differences between Christians and Jews is that a Jew's first mitzvah is to have a child, whereas Christians don't have to be parents. That means then that the role of the family is overdetermined if the family is all you've got.

Probably, what I should have talked a good deal more about in terms of that context is friendship, and how friendship reaches out and calls more people in, other than just the family.

BB: Let's look a little more closely at the third part of the book, which is entirely devoted to disability. In this it was a genuinely novel proposal in the context of the literature in medical ethics at the time. Is that correct?

SH: I don't know. There may have been some other things, but I am pretty good about trying to read what one should read and I couldn't find much.

Oh wait I'll tell you! There are people like Wolf Wolfensberger. People I really admired; they weren't officially ethicists.

BB: He was a sort of thinking practitioner.

SH: Oh he was! He was at Syracuse. He was a force of nature! I really admired him! He came up with the principle of normalization. I once told him, "I don't want to be normal—I'm a Texan!" But he was absolutely right. What he meant was that disabled people in institutions should not be robbed, for example, of needing to have their own toothbrush! That was really important.

BB: But such thinkers had a very Balkanized relationship with specialized medical ethics?

SH: Right.

BB: Could we put that a little more strongly; that disability scared the medical ethicists of the time to death because they were all about impressing doctors by making themselves useful and solving their perceived medical dilemmas for them?

SH: I hesitate to make that judgment. That might be the case, but I suspect it was more the general presumption that mentally disabled people always suffer and that is why people would rather that they would be out of sight and out of mind. So, it wasn't intentional. It was just part of the general syndrome.

BB: I also suspect that that there was a Constantinian trajectory at work within the guild of medical ethicists. Why hamstring your status as a discipline by talking about the marginal or hopeless cases in the medical universe? To make the discipline important you have to devote yourself to solving what the doctors think are problems. Their problem at the time I was studying was the old chestnut for medicine in capitalist societies, patients asking for things doctors didn't want to provide. You could say that people with intellectual disabilities do that accidentally, but it's not a glamorous territory and there's no obvious sense in which you can advance the interests of the subdiscipline of Christian ethics by investing in that sort of question.

SH: I think your analysis is right. It's part of a Constantinian project. In Yoder's language it's a neo-neo-Constantinianism.[21]

BB: There's no reason why the objection I want to raise would have occurred to you at the time, but I want to put the question about the book that most bothers me as a theologian, as a Christian, and as a father of a learning impaired child. In general, you take great pains to stress the diversity of disability as well as the diverse reasons that people become disabled. But you seem to end up with a curiously narrow suggestion of how we ought to interpret this theologically: "Prophet like, the retarded only remind us of the insecurity hidden in our false sense of self-possession."[22] I can see how such a comment might be affirmed in a very general sense, in that the mere existence of some people, like the birds of the air and the lilies of the field, can be profitably meditated upon to discover something theologically important. But then you push the argument further, asserting it as a Christological claim about universal human neediness.[23]

Here's the rub for me. This apparently collapses the "message" we expect God to have for us through disabled people to a sociological category, or something coterminous with a sociological category. The gesture seems very close to the move made by John Chrysostom, who once said in a sermon that the beggars at the door of the cathedral preached a sermon every bit as eloquently as he did— that we should be aware that we are all dependent on everything from God and so should be grateful for what we have.[24] In putting the case the way you did, you're obviously in very good company, despite your having inherited it from MacIntyre rather than the Fathers. But isn't that putting remarkable constraints

7. Medical Ethics, Disability, and the Cross

about what we might expect God to teach us through other people, whether they be poor or disabled in some way? I'm tempted to say that it borders on a sin against the Holy Spirit!

SH: I'm not sure I know what to say about that. Is the suggestion that I've limited what it is that God has told us or tries to help us discover in mentally disabled or poor people?

BB: I think so. The language of "prophet-like"—that's obviously revelatory language. But the language of prophet-*like* makes it clear that you are not making a straightforward claim about divine revelation. In the end you seem very close to recapitulating *Dependent Rational Animals*.[25] People with intellectual disabilities teach us that we're really all dependent like they so obviously are.

SH: Yeah. That kind of suggestion is "Well, we can finally make some sense that they exist" and turn them into something.

BB: Yes.

SH: I always try to avoid the argument that you hear often; namely "If we hadn't had Johnny and he didn't have Down's Syndrome, we wouldn't be the moral people we are today!" I'm trying to avoid the use of the disabled and other people like that to make us better people.

BB: You more often make the gesture that they don't make us better people, but we do learn from them what we all share as human beings.

SH: Right! I think that's right.

BB: So it is a move designed to deflate our self-certainties.

SH: I think that's what I'm about. I suppose it was also—the language of "prophet-like"—I mean they do challenge some of our most cherished pretensions, but it is also a way of saying, "You know, we ain't all that different." It's not like they need our help and we're OK. We need help too. Something like that.

BB: I invoke the sin of the Holy Spirit, which I don't do lightly, in part as one who hopes for something more from Adam's fellow church members than "We learned from him because he has Down's." That will be a constant barrier to their receiving the gifts of each member to the body, to use Paul's language, which are constitutive of the body of Christ. Therefore, any gesture that limits what any individual is expected to bring into the body of Christ, or that channelizes it by assuming a cluster of pre-loaded expectations—like "Oh you're poor people so we know what you tell us"—that's a very dangerous statement to make because it doesn't admit the surprises we discussed in our previous conversation.

SH: That's a lovely way to put it.

BB: If we really think there is a prophecy taking place, we must by definition understand that to be an address from God. In fact, then, the sheer fact of the divine address should be more powerfully exposing our dependence, contingency and sinfulness than anybody's disabilities anyway.

SH: What can I say? That's clearly right. The gesture toward prophet-like is a gesture that is clearly an attempt to use the mentally disabled in a way that is inappropriate.

BB: Let me press that admission by adding that, in addition to this narrowing of expectation, the language of prophet-*like* is analogy language. In so far as God wants to break in on us through certain lives, they are not *like* prophets, they *are* prophets. In other words, if we can expect surprises from the weakness to which the cross points then people with all sorts of non-standard bodies and minds might better be treated as privileged conduits of a confrontation that we need.

SH: I made an observation years ago that I am not sure I think is right but there seems to be something to it, and that's mentally disabled people do not regret who they are and we find that unbelievable. That's quite a gift.

BB: Too right. OK then. Let's return to *Suffering Presence*, asking now about the constructive response it offers to the difficulty of maintaining a caring medicine in liberal societies. You set out in the book to reveal the moral practices that do in fact sustain medicine. You want in so doing to shore up islands of what we now call "good practice" amid the fragmenting forces of modern rights-based liberalism.[26]

Your first move is to undermine the "expertise model" and even the "professional model" as grounding the authority of medicine. "Both physicians and patients must learn that each of them is subject to a prior authority—the authority of the body." That's great stuff. Drawing on Pelligrino and Thomasma, you then further specify the authority of the body by saying that it "sets the norm for medicine because it is the 'artist of its own healing.'"[27]

In *Suffering Presence*, you seem relatively comfortable with the language of "natural goods." Looking back from where you are now, if we are going to propose the body as the authority for medicine, and specifically the body's powers of healing, would you still want to describe it with the language of natural goods? Given our previous discussion of the importance of Christians learning to live as if they have no control, perhaps today you might be happier speaking of healing as one of those things which both the medical professional and the patient cannot and should not try to control or predict but must *receive*, and are therefore dependent on God's own working to provide?

SH: I don't trust any account of health that doesn't depend on prayer! So, health is a natural good, but it is a natural good that depends on prayer. I think that suggestion, about the wisdom of the body, is right and it is full of suggestiveness which I did not know how to develop. I'm not sure I know how now. The body is not just the physical outline that we each have, but "body" names, for we Christians in particular, the baptized body, the community. You learn how to name that body, across time, through judgments that can change. There has been a great deal of work, and I have read a lot of it, about the stages of the body and how it is displayed and "constructed"—I always hate that language—but it's not just a given. It is an ongoing discovery through the engagements the body makes possible, making the body what it is. I just didn't know how to do that.

You've done it better than I have.

BB: I wouldn't claim that. But what made me think about this is living on the oncology ward and seeing that the real turning points are first of all entirely out of sight. They have to do with healing. We have to be very careful not to talk about a God of the gaps. But it did seem to me spending weeks and weeks on oncology wards that the thing you're praying for is healing and it was perhaps not really accurate to call it something that the body had. The doctors were trying to kill the body. They lived in hope that it would not be killed. It's of course not a zero-sum game, but how you talk about where prayer goes and what God does, it seems to me can be concretized sometimes. For the leukemia patient, the bone marrow is the zone over which prayer and medicine are both attending.

SH: Wow.

All that seems right. How to spell it out further is really difficult. I've been around the oncology unit. I had a friend who had a son who got a form of leukemia that basically required them to kill the kid to cure him. You take out the bone marrow and radiate it and wonder if you know what is going on.

I do admire those people in leukemia wards because so many children die. You can't personally be invested in every kid. If or when they die they are going to drain you and the work is draining enough. So there is a kind of professionalism that I admire that you need to sustain that work, which also has to do with the body.

BB: We'll return to that in a few minutes. But let's continue chasing the question of where we should be looking to find the communities that can witness to the crack in modernity. In *Suffering Presence* you emphasize that in order for the community of medicine to sustain its commitment to remaining with people who are sick and in pain even if they can't cure them it is reliant on the "dark public" of the church in which people are learning the narratives and practices that enable Christians to remain with people in their pain.[28] That brings us back to the lady shouting her protest at you on this point in the question time at the AAR panel.

What do we do about the fact that the church is often not good at all at teaching us what it means, practically, to stay with people in their pain? Insofar as you are presenting yourself as a representative of the Christian tradition, your example of not knowing how to be with your grieving friend Bob[29] seems to me to point precisely to the problem: Christians no longer seem today to know how to "sit Shiva" like the Jews and like the biblical example of Job's friends, whom you commend. A few might, but as a concrete community, I think it is fair to say that we are not doing very well either with teaching people the narratives and practices of dealing with mourning or living day in and day out with mentally ill or disabled people.

I take it that it is the dismal reality of church life today that leads you to fall back on the "community of the family" to teach the church what its own narratives mean even while asserting as you did so clearly that "the family requires moral direction and support from a community."[30]

SH: Well, I think there's a great moral capital in being stuck with people! What the church can do is help us not regret that we are stuck with people. I mean, you are stuck with Stephanie and Adam and Agnes and Caleb. They are not necessarily people you would choose. Being stuck is a good thing, because we have different temperaments, we have different desires and histories, and we have to come to terms with that. People are increasingly trying to find ways to live lives in which we don't get stuck with people. But you're going to get stuck with people! So I think that's a resource that we need to make more of.

I mean, that doesn't answer the question of what are we going to do to make Christians recognize this!

Obviously, the mobility of our culture makes it increasingly hard to have a context in which we own our being stuck.

BB: Here's then the nub of my question about how we arrest the flightiness characteristic of our late-modern culture: How did you stop asking yourself the question: "Why did I marry Anne?" Is there a difference between Hauerwas's rule,[31] "I don't ask that question," and "God gave this person to me"? What I'm trying to get my hands around is how we appropriately theologically narrate being stuck with people. It was great that you drew our attention to the temptation to escapism that afflicts modern marriage through Hauerwas's rule, but it's a pretty anthropocentric narrative of how we might live into that rule if we only say, "Well, we committed and we are sticking to our commitment."

SH: I never asked myself how I got stuck with Anne, but also I never blamed God. I thought I'd made a promise I had to live out. As I say in *Hannah's Child*, that I stuck it out I don't attribute to any great virtue, because firstly I was afraid of failure and secondly I was worried that if I didn't stick it out, I would lose insight. Isn't that interesting? The suffering had to be part of the power of the position. But again, I never thought of that as something that God was sending me as a test, or anything like that. I still wouldn't think that.

BB: Yet you would simply refuse giving God an agential role in any narration of her being brought to you, and you having promised "'til death do us part"?

SH: That's right. Perhaps some people can do that. I didn't see that I could do it.

BB: That then left you with, "I will make a liar of myself and I will undermine my own integrity as an academic and a person to back down from what I said I would do"?

SH: Yes, right. How did it finally end? And how did I think of it finally ending? She had left but it was when I became convinced that as long as she could blame me for her life, she had no chance to get well. And I was exhausted. It was those two things.

BB: The question of how marriage can be sustained is obviously a burning issue across a wide swathe of contemporary Western Christianity. The sorts of practices we take to be appropriate responses to Hauerwas's rule are therefore very important. For myself, in the same way that you say "I'm not a strong enough Christian to worship at a bad church," I have to say, "I'm not a strong enough Christian to stick with my vows if I think God had nothing to do with my making those vows." I mean, I've made some stupid commitments in my life that I haven't always felt duty bound to play out in every case to the bitter end! But Christian marriage seems to me to be of a different order than many other commitments.

If we are going to admit that God has given us the children we have—and that doesn't seem too difficult to affirm—I suspect this ought to play some role in how we might narrate what is entailed in having come to the point of promising "'til death do us part" before a pastor and congregation in a church. In my case I can't get enough ballast in my own promises to see why I have to stick with every last one of them unless some of them, such as the ones I make at the altar before God, are related both to my responsibility before God and God's involvement in my getting into that situation. I've really appreciated some of the German marriage liturgies that emphasize this point, following Luther's reading of God bringing the man to the woman in Eden as the first wedding.[32]

SH: I simply couldn't think like that with Anne. I just couldn't.

BB: Is that closer to how you might be able to think today?

SH: Yes, it is. But it was a different reality then.

BB: Let me emphasize again that I'm not trying to put you in the position of having to explain what you did in the past. But it does seem that we have to find a way to help Christians today understand how we should understand the commitment of carrying through with marriage vows or other Christian commitments, precisely because you have shown us how important it is to be "stuck with" people and to take that seriously. Every single person who is married, as your rule stresses, sooner or later comes to the point where they say, "Man, what a dumb decision I've made. This is a bad situation. I would be happier out of it." Whatever your biographical experiences—the conceptual point is extremely important to get clear about.

SH: I'm so hesitant in general in talking about God's agency in biographical terms. But I certainly think that the vows one takes before God in marriage are vows that we take before God and that therefore marriage—I don't think it is a sacrament—but it really is one of the essential practices of the church, in which God gives us strength.

BB: We could say that your own explanation about why you stuck with your vows to Anne parallels what we said about the irony of your AAR speech. It was at the edge of real faith, and it was contiguous with real faith, but it wasn't real faith itself.[33]

SH: I think that's right.

BB: And it doesn't mean that it's without value.

SH: It certainly doesn't mean that it is without value. Indeed, Adam and Laura are married and have been married almost twenty years now. With two kids! I am sure that [my son] Adam's commitment to marriage draws on my commitment.

BB: This does shed important methodological light on the disputes going around about the relationships between Christian and pagan virtue. It is a good thing to keep your promises, but it is not the same thing as keeping your vows before God. That's really nice.

What we do in experimental medicine

BB: I think we can explore this point in a bit more detail by taking a detour through your 1990 book *Naming the Silences*, which I also just reread, or should I rather say that I just really read it for the first time. I picked it up years ago and could see that it was an extension of the theoretical insights you had developed in *Suffering Presence* but as you say in *Naming*, "it makes all the difference in the world whether the question of suffering is asked by those who are actually suffering."[34] Before I had children, I didn't even notice that the book focuses on the problem of facing childhood leukemia, and now that I've not only had children, but a learning disabled child who has had leukemia, I feel in an especial position to revisit it and probe the whole theology of modern medicine and the role of church and family in offering a better way.

Could you give us a few words about how you feel about that book today?

SH: I've always thought it was one of the best books I've ever written! It was one of the best books I have written because in it is fundamentally a witness to other people's lives. I thought the way I let people speak, like Wanderhope of de Vreis's *Blood of the Lamb*[35] or the lady who is an evangelical Christian who finally refuses to ask "Why does God allow bad things to happen to good people?"[36] are very powerful.

And the suggestion that modern medicine works as a theodical project to try and sustain liberal social orders because liberal social orders are structured on the presumption that you can get out of life alive; I think all that's really good. I thought the use of Bluebond-Langner at the end, about dealing with kids with leukemia, and how we try to protect them from the knowledge of death, and in the process make their lives worse is a haunting matter.[37]

BB: I agree. I found many aspects of it powerful, but the way in which you saw the oncology ward as a microcosm, or an arena in which the pretenses in which we hide our pain in general are exposed—I find that very powerful. You said that Bluebond-Langner:

> has shown us in an extraordinary way that these children had learned they were dying long before their actual death. Why would they keep such knowledge secret? It is her contention that they did so because they recognized the necessity of their entering into a mutual pretense with their parents as well as the medical staff.[38]

SH: They were protecting their parents.

BB: That's right.

SH: And how they would share with one another knowledge of their impending death in the bathroom? I mean isn't that poignant?

BB: It is indeed.
    You then comment on that point. "Bluebond-Langner's account is troubling not only because of what it reveals about the effect of such pretense on the children dying of leukemia, but also because it reminds us how much our everyday lives are constituted by such pretense."[39]
    In light of those comments I'm tempted to read the woman shouting at you at the AAR meeting as an uncomfortable but truthful embodiment of your own message; that the pain and suffering of illness and disability must not be evaded, precisely because the church too is caught up in these masking pretenses. It too often falls silent when suffering falls on believers. If we therefore seriously pursue your proposed solution—that we learn that our suffering is part of God's own story—it can deeply alienate us from other believers. Tragically and painfully then, we are doubly alienated and rendered mute by our pain which is exacerbated by the incomprehension we face from Christians who don't really know how to sit with us in our suffering.

SH: Wow. It seems to me you may be right, and I haven't thought of it that way. The way pain creates a silence, I think I learned from Ellen Scarry's *The Body in Pain* about torture and how torture works to create a silence that you cannot articulate what has happened to you.[40] That's part of the power of the torture.

BB: I am pushing further into the story you tell in *Naming the Silences*, then, in two directions. One takes us into the normal orbit of medical ethics and the other draws us back into the discussion of the relation of illness and disability. The first connects with your comment about the moral problem of being an oncologist. In one footnote you write:

> But our medical response to leukemia has improved not because of any sudden breakthrough but because of the knowledge we have gained by performing this procedure on that child. Of course, in the process of acquiring this knowledge we have often used children for what are in effect medical experiments, even

though we knew what we were doing could provide them with only minimal improvement. I have asked hematologists how they justified the use of these children in this manner as well as the unavoidability of playing on their parents' false hopes. They usually told me they simply tried not to think about it. We are now in the position of being able to help some leukemic children today because we treated others wrongly in the past.[41]

SH: That's a powerful footnote.

BB: It's quite the comment!

Your observations about the moral dubiousness of combining treatment with experimentation on children remains engaging because it has much wider implications than most people realize today. Every tissue that is removed from our bodies, every zygote produced through IVF, every pint of blood we give is in essence enrolled in the massive experimental protocol that is modern medicine. A long time ago I wrote with Stephanie a piece of theology reflecting on some of our experiences with Adam that is probably the most widely read article I've written. It was entitled "Being Disabled in the New World of Genetic Testing."[42] In it we detailed our various attempts to secure care for Adam shorn of any experimentation. It's really no joke to even make that request. It starts to create friction immediately. So now he has been treated for leukemia and thank God, it looks like he'll survive it. But you still can't get treated for leukemia without being part of an experimental protocol—or it is very difficult to.

So even if we follow your advice and don't evade thinking about it, we're in a pretty murky world here. Our very experienced oncologist was honest enough to remark at one point, "When people look back on what we do today, they'll think we were barbaric."

SH: He was that honest?

BB: He was, yeah, maybe because he was about to retire. I'm pretty sure he was more surprised than we were that Adam made it, which he expressed by saying, "He took a hell of a lot more chemo than we thought he could." But that sort of utterance just proves that the treatment was still in his mind an experiment. A doctor would never say, "Wow, what a surprise that this antibiotic worked." We went to his retirement party just a few weeks ago where he sat on the stairs and took pictures with maybe thirty kids, and all I could think of was the much larger group of patients we knew on the ward who weren't there. The circle of children who weren't there for the picture.

SH: I was talking to one oncologist who said, "You know, we're pretty good now at curing hard tumors." And I said, "How did you get there?" And he said, "Oh we just used the drugs we had. We've had them on hand but we just got better at doing it." I said, "How'd you do that?" And he said, "We experimented on kids." And I said, "Did they die?" And he said, "Yes." And I said, "Did you tell the parents it was experimentation?" He said, "No, we told them it was therapy."

Even if they had told them it was experimentation, many parents of course are so desperate to have their children live they'll say, "Oh yes, do whatever you think is necessary." I do think that what's crucial here is a truthful medicine, in which the parents have some sense that if they want to use these experimental techniques on their kids, that their children may well suffer pain they wouldn't otherwise have suffered and will also die.

I think behind this is that most of us are not sure what we're doing when we have children. And since we're not sure what we're doing when we have children we think, "My God," in the literal sense of Heidegger's thrown-ness, "I've thrown this human life out in the world and I don't know why but I sure as hell don't want them to die on me, because if they die on me I will feel terrible that I brought them into the world anyway!" So if they are sick, I have to do anything I can to make sure they are OK, because it was arbitrary that I brought them into the world anyway. So I think that we oftentimes subject children to what can only be described externally as cruelty, in order to make sure that their death doesn't become part of our life.

BB: On the problem of experimentation on children, you make the comment in passing—this is just a parenthetical question—"Not enough attention has been paid to the ethical issues involved in using animals in research. It may well be that we learn more about what moral issues are involved in human research if we think more about our assumptions that we can subject animals to almost any peril or pain for the good of people."[43] Since I've just been drafted onto our university animal experimentation ethical review panel, I have to ask: has anyone risen to this challenge?

SH: No. I just signed a statement against using animals for experimentation by the terrific animal activist, Andrew Linzey. He's at Oxford, an Anglican priest. I've always admired his work. It's theologically quite good. No one's taken up his challenge. It's really a hard call about whether you want to call for an end to all experimentation on animals, but some of it is just unbelievably cruel.

When you worry about and raise questions about experimentation on animals, then you're always asked, "Are you a vegetarian?" and when you say no they say, "What's the difference between killing an animal to eat it and experimentation?" I don't know that I have a good answer to that. I think there is a certain dehumanizing aspect to watching an animal suffer over a long period of time in order to achieve a scientific outcome. That's a little different from eating the animal. That's about the best I can do.

I think, as Christians, we pray at a meal to thank God for the sacrifice of this life that keeps us alive. I think it would be very interesting to ask those who are experimenting on animals to pray in thanks for this animal. That would be a place to start.

BB: One other very mundane way I'm now thinking it has to start is at least, at each review meeting, to request an accounting of how many animals have been killed in this census period.

SH: They don't give you that?

BB: No. But every protocol ends with killing the experimental animals.

SH: They have to kill them, because most of the time, if they don't kill them, their lives would be hell given the experimentation they've been part of.

BB: A lot of ours are just in diet studies. So, there's plenty that don't need to be killed, but if they weren't killed there'd have to be some place to put them. And that costs money, so we're not even going to talk about that. That position is then defended on nonfinancial grounds by saying, "Well we don't know what the sequelae from these experiments are going to be and we don't want to cause unnecessary suffering."

SH: I bet these are special genetically altered mice?

BB: Many are, and others are bred to be predisposed for certain disease conditions. Half of the whole facility is just breeding.

SH: It's very expensive.

BB: The shocker is: this is a big building, like an aircraft-hanger, and even though half of it is devoted to breeding they still have to ship animals in, mostly rodents. So there must be warehouses where they are breeding incredible numbers of rodents, hundreds of thousands annually. For me the connection with your comment about the inability to distinguish between treatment and experimentation in leukemia points to a zone called "experimentation" continually expanding under our current medical regime while the zone of activity called "treatment" contracts. It seems to me that trajectory is taking place in just about every realm of modern life. Everything you buy now is both a purchase and data for future market research. I'm tempted to think that revisiting arguments like Ramsey's in *The Patient as Person*, where care is sharply distinguished from cure, would be highly complicated.

I remember once watching Oliver O'Donovan getting dragged back and forth across the coals as he tried to defend his reactive principle[44] in a modern nation-state in which financial stimulus is the central part of what governments do.

SH: I really think that governments are legitimated today primarily in terms of their ability to sustain high-tech medicine!

BB: We are in an odd kind of Mobius-strip world in which medicine can then only be funded because it is experimental and going to produce more high-tech medicine.

SH: I keep saying that Americans are committed to the idea that if we just get smart enough then with our medical technologies we will be able to get out of life alive! It's not going to happen.

BB: Taking it back down to the concrete level: even with all the improvements in success rates, leukemia is still a terrible disease to treat because what you are treating is the bone marrow. You can't get to it without a needle or a drill. And you treat it by injecting poison that is so toxic to the body that you have to put it in an arterial vein. If you put it into a peripheral vein it will burn right through the blood vessels and into the surrounding tissue. This means that when the disease is discovered you need both to get the chemo going and to surgically implant a port, so you don't burn up too many of the peripheral veins with the chemo. But the kid at the point of diagnosis is pretty sick, so their immune system is not working very well.

I say all that because I vividly remember sitting on the edge of the hospital bed with Adam on my lap and holding the wound on his chest from where they'd put the port in. I felt utterly desolate watching the incision slowly splitting open because his skin and his blood were unable to muster the strength to bind the wound. I tell this story because leukemia is a disease that leaves no marks at all, but the treatment leaves incredible wounds. I know people would find your comment about the barbarism of those treatments offensive, and yet any truthful account would say that it's the treatment that is so scarring. You cut and stick and poison the kid because the only alternative is their dying.

In *Naming* you comment on Bluebond-Langner's explanation of what this phenomenon means for how children understand themselves. Bluebond-Langner:

> asked each of the children for permission to speak with them. She explained that she was an anthropologist interested in what children thought and did. She notes that the children usually responded by telling her what they had gone through that day—they would, for example, "exhibit their wounds."[45]

That catches your attention, the phrase "exhibiting their wounds." You comment further in a footnote:

> By showing where and how they have been poked and prodded, children present themselves to others as sick and find their self-image confirmed. This is further evidenced by the fact that once children internalize this view of self, they no longer use this strategy, except when meeting someone for the first time and wanting, for any number of reasons, to affect the stranger's view of them.[46]

I think this is all true. But it's also untrue in a sense, when we think about what it might mean for mentally disabled or largely nonverbal children. Adam hurts but he can't verbalize where it hurts. He thus seems incapable of being incorporated within this medical narrative. In this he seems to be more than a canary in a coalmine—another way that you often talk about people with intellectual disabilities—revealing modern medicine for what it is. Because he is impermeable to the mutual pretenses that govern our lives, for him there seems to be no other reality than trust and communion, or its lack. Without a horizon of future or past, he demands presence.

SH: Let me respond to that. I think one of the deepest lessons I've learned from Vanier is how he helps you see that kids know, for example, when their parents are unable to love them because they are disabled. Or that their parents are unable to be present to them and basically abandon them. You may think that children with intellectual disabilities don't get that, but he helps you see they get it. And the pain is deep, deep, deep. That's how he tries to intervene, just to touch in a way that says "You're not abandoned." I think that that's really one of his great gifts.

Therefore, it tears your heart out.

BB: I've only given this much biographical detail because I wanted to concretize what you might mean by the decisions you are pushing us hard to think about. Of course as Adam's treatment progressed we had to talk about what if this one doesn't work or what if the next one doesn't work and at the far end of that is the type of operation to which you've already alluded, a bone marrow transplant. And that basically means that you kill the original bone marrow and you inject somebody else's bone marrow. That's a big roll of the dice, and it's extremely invasive and painful. That's the torturous side of medicine you've already talked about. But what's probably less well known is that you have to be in a bubble during that period.

SH: Yeah, because you are susceptible to infection.

BB: Exactly. Infinitely susceptible.

You could be killed by the basic germs that live on everyone's skin all the time. So Stephanie and I had to talk about whether we would ever do that. Because Adam's reality is organized by presence and touch, and that's the level at which his reality exists, we said we would never go down that road. That might well have been his death sentence or would have been presented as his death sentence.

But that seems to me to be where this hits the ground, ultimately, for us. We knew getting stuck with needles is torturous, but being separated without touch from his parents for six weeks, that would be genuinely unbearable torture in the deepest sense. We refused to do that.

SH: I suppose the only other alternative would have been basically to have him comatose for six weeks, feeding him intravenously.

BB: I think their state is so fragile that suppression of normal functioning—because of course knocking somebody out is really just suppressing normal functioning—in a very fragile body, to risk stress by suppressing autonomic systems would be too risky. But we never really pursued it with the doctors.

Much closer to home, he now has a degenerative eye condition.

SH: Stephanie told me.

BB: Keratoconus, which means that the connective tissue that holds the lens in shape breaks down, and the lens goes very cone-shaped. One has gone very rapidly. There is no explanation for why that's happened. If the other one goes, he'll basically be blind. That would be a drastic change in his life circumstances.

SH: I cannot imagine it.

BB: So, at the level of what you can do about it, you can do a cornea transplant. But that means not touching the eye for six weeks and laying still. It is almost impossible to imagine that.

SH: I was going to say: he's clearly not a candidate for that.

BB: To "stay with who we've been given" is in this sense so draining because you're always thinking, or trying to stop thinking, "Should I be spending more effort hunting for the magic doctor that will do this?" "Are we depriving him of a lifetime of mobility by letting this go?" These are the dilemmas.

SH: I think, quite frankly, to put those questions to yourself is torture. I think you shouldn't do it. I mean, it's torturing yourself. I just don't think you should do it. You've really been good with Adam. That idea that there is someone out there who could do that is fantasy.

BB: Right.

SH: You shouldn't torture yourself.

BB: I admit it, because it's not dis-analogous to the woman who spent all her life wishing she was bigger chested and wishes she could be different. But this is the world we live in, where not only are we not happy to be stuck with people, we're not happy to be stuck with ourselves, and some forms of medicine have seen how stoking that fear will increase demand for their services.

SH: Absolutely.

BB: When our knees go out and we lose half our hobbies, and our eyes go out and we lose our ability to communicate or move around, a good part of our torture is our presumption that everything can be fixed. "Getting out of life alive" may be the chapter heading, but the content of that chapter is the debate running in our head, "Well, I could get these knees fixed."

SH: People keep saying to me that I need a knee replacement. I say no. I probably do, but I don't trust it. Did I ever tell you about that time in Trosly[47] I almost went blind?

BB: I remember you were having trouble with the one eye.

SH: When I came to Trosly, I'd had some bleeding in my viscera. I was sitting there, around the table and the vision went black. So I just thought that was still the bleeding in the viscera. I went back and I told Paula, "You know I think I'd better go have this checked, just to see." I went into the ophthalmologist and the assistant saw me and said, "Oh, you have a detached retina." She said, "How long has this been?" I said, "Three days." She said, "In five days you're blind." She said, "You need to be operated on right now." They just had a cancellation, and they took me directly! I had a band put around my eye. I had to keep my head very still for a week or so. They were calling Paula, and Paula came over to get me! I almost went blind! That was really lucky!

Vanier, L'Arche, and Aristotle

BB: That story reminds me that another totally unexplored vein in this universe is the way that our construal of the power of medicine means that the experience of "Do it now" can hit us very hard. Being told, "He's got leukemia, chemo starts now," is in so many ways the inversion of the way human life has been lived for millennia. You've occasionally noted that our Christian ancestors wished for a slow death so that they could get their affairs in order. Now because we don't want to die at all we can be jerked off-stage into the medical apparatus at a moment's notice.

Let me pause here. There's an interesting wrinkle in your using Vanier as a source that I'd like to hear your take on. You don't have to read Vanier's writings very closely to notice how centrally placed a psychologized understanding of the family is in his works. He often gets his arguments going with a picture of the wound that every human life suffers. He frames this as intrinsically tied to the origin of self out of primal, parental relationships. It is the dominant metaphor he uses to explain not only the healing that core members need but the healing that the assistants should be seeking as being part of L'Arche. He everywhere assumes that every child deserves loving parents and to live in a loving home. That's why he never presents L'Arche as more than a community rescuing the lives that have been refused love. The community of L'Arche is only offering a womb of love and attention that every human being deserves but cannot and does not displace the family. Here's a randomly chosen but I think typical example from *Man and Woman God Made Them*:

> For children to grow and acquire a true inner dignity, it's not sufficient to be loved with tenderness and accepted as they are. They equally have a need to be encouraged, strengthened and guided by a parent or a substitute parent, true and good educators who believe in them and their capacity for growth. The parent or the substitute parent must prove to them that they are truly loved and that he or she is really interested in their wellbeing and development.[48]

I think that for him, given that starting point, L'Arche is an ersatz family and it cannot and does not displace the family. More importantly for our purposes, theologically speaking, this raises some conceptually important questions to wrestle with when we take L'Arche as an exemplification of why the church is a real family. Because at the end of the day, Vanier seems very consistently to draw on a picture of natural affection that I think you grow increasingly uncomfortable with. At the end of the day, as Vanier sees it, L'Arche is trying to provide a replacement for what is fundamentally a communion of natural affection, specifically the mother and father.

7. Medical Ethics, Disability, and the Cross   223

SH: In my writing and drawing on Jean I downplay that a lot. I wondered, and Brian I would be interested in what you think; my hunch is that Freud has played a role in Jean's understanding of family. Do you think that's right?

BB: I'm sure that modern psychology has, whether from Freud or Jung I couldn't say. He seems to read both. He also seems to frame their insights within a remarkably strong understanding of disciplinary divisions. His book on Aristotle describes the different disciplines like this:

> My research into the basis of Aristotelian ethics brought me a great deal of light and helped me to grasp the connection between ethics, psychology, and spirituality. Psychology helps us to understand human behavior and grasp the fears and blockages that are in us, in order to help us free ourselves of them. Spirituality is like a breath of inspiration that strengthens our motivation. Ethics helps us to clarify what is a truly human act; what justice is and what the best activities are, that render us more human and happiest.[49]

SH: I remember that and I thought, "Boy, that's a mistake! Making those kinds of distinctions between the disciplines as a matter of fact."

BB: Of course all of that is held together in Aristotle and Aristotelian ethics. So you're saying that the mistake is to let the modern, positivist disciplinary divisions break that material up?

SH: Right.

BB: That makes sense.

SH: I think his language of woundedness is so evocative because when people read him they recognize that's certainly true. Of course, that the core members are wounded in ways that you can't hide the wound, so to speak, makes his stories so powerful. If it's Freud or not, it doesn't really matter.

BB: He certainly emphasizes across the board that everybody at L'Arche has the wound. And he is very explicit that he himself is first among the wounded. I think that's very important and illuminating. But it is a natural theology. The problem, though, is that if you constantly foreground this wound construed in psychological terms you can never talk theology without referring to the Freudian origin story. And it does trade on a familial presumption that you, in other contexts, very roundly criticize.

Given these criticisms, I'm wondering precisely what the analogy is between the church and L'Arche? Or how do we learn from L'Arche as the church? Or, is the church different from L'Arche?

SH: I think the practice is so rich that the psychologizing doesn't dominate. That would be the way I make sense of it.

BB: What the church learns from L'Arche is that it is an organization that is set up at its base-level to take seriously the fragility and woundedness of every human life and it, therefore, fosters much deeper perception about all sorts of things.

SH: If I were to systematize Jean's writings, theologically he is probably closer to what Lindbeck calls the experiential-expressivist mode of theological reflection than I would feel comfortable with.[50] But, why do that! That's not what he's about. You don't need to systematize him. His theological practice is so much richer than those kinds of typological interventions. I don't see any reason to do it.

BB: The set of linkages that has got me to this line of questioning runs like this. You've criticized medicine because it can't actually situate the doctor or medical professional and the patient on its own natural theological terms. It needs the church. At other points you notice that the church doesn't really handle that question very well, or the question of disability very well, and so you appeal to the example of L'Arche. But the closer you look at L'Arche, the more precise you need to be about how we can learn from it because its founder's explication of what's going on is susceptible to many of the types of critique you have levied at medicine.

SH: I think that's probably true. Do you think it's a problem?

BB: It's only a problem if we don't know what we're looking for. I think some of why I find your writing on virtue hard to finally get to the bottom of is precisely that sort of circular reference. We can never avoid circular reference, of course, but how do we nail down the primary referent? Your points about exemplification seem to be rock-bottom there. How do we know what it is about Jean Vanier and L'Arche that is really crucial to help the church be the church? His pretty steady deployment of natural theological frameworks makes that not a straightforward operation.

SH: I think I've often acknowledged that I do natural theology, I just refuse to do it in a way that makes it sound like it's a prolegomenon before I get theology off the ground.

BB: Have you said anywhere how you understand natural and non-natural theology to fit together?

SH: No.

BB: Could you do that now?

SH: I don't know that I want to, because they are too interrelated.
  What do I mean by natural theology? I mean the discovery and acknowledgment that to be a human is to be destined to die and the implications that follow from that which are worked out in diverse ways. We should not be surprised that we will find those who are not Christians having insight about how to live that are very commensurate with what we think of and how we think as Christians. When I said that *Suffering Presence* is a kind of natural theology, the very discovery that we need people present to us when we're ill, that have

BB: skills, is a kind of natural theology. You then show why it is not sufficient without further theological construal.

BB: So natural theology can't just be an independent operation?

SH: Charity is the form of the virtues! My way of thinking of natural theology is the discovery of insights to live well! Insights are not fundamental givens.

BB: Do continue that line of thought and work us through what's going on in your head when you lecture Jean pretty directly that he needs to work more Christologically, as I have heard you do more than once. That's what I have in mind when I say that revealed theology plays a steering role in Christian reason. There's not really a parity between the two types of theological thinking.

SH: What I mean when I say that is, if you take when we were at Trosly, I don't think Trosly would be sustainable on the healing of wounds without the mass we attended. The mass is more significant than the insights about woundedness.

BB: OK. Because you don't get L'Arche growing up in Vienna around Freudian psychological institutes.

SH: No. Jean would not be Jean Vanier without the formation that he received as a Roman Catholic.

BB: We can argue with him, as you do, about whether L'Arche is sustainable when a secularist or Muslim set of practices replace the Roman Catholic ones. You would want to both say that the practices matter so it won't just evaporate if you do that, but it might not be sustainable.

SH: It might not be sustainable without the articulation of how the Islamic L'Arche is drawing on the resources of the wider L'Arche movement, that is fundamentally Christologically shaped.

BB: That's good.

Let me ask you about one other aspect of Jean's own account of what he's up to, how he redefines Aristotle's account of true friendship. Recall the discussion we had earlier about Aristotle and virtue. This is how he responds to the reality that the type of friendships that he is so focused on at L'Arche are just unthinkable for Aristotle.

> In true friendship, everything—will and feelings alike—is orientated by this concern for the other person. This is the reason for friendship. I have seen the goodness, the beauty of another person and I have been attracted by it. It is then possible to build a friendship on the basis of inequality, provided we don't deny this inequality from the outset. On the contrary, by recognizing it, we can make the bond between us strong and true. We can really establish a form of equality, an equality that's proportional.[51]

I understand his suggestion to be that virtue is the ordering term and is in fact so dominant that it overwrites the concern with power hierarchies that Aristotle assumes to rule out friendship with disabled people.

SH: In Aristotle it is very important to be equals in order to be friends, but the way he puts it is friendship creates a kind of equality. So even in Aristotle, though you are both character friends, and have the virtues, there is the possibility of difference, in a way that language of equality has trouble capturing. I'm suggesting that what Jean is about there, about friendship, is not entirely antithetical to what Aristotle understands about how friendship creates a kind of equality that is possible between Jean and core members. It is the case, however, that I am sure Aristotle would think of core members as natural slaves with whom you just could not have a friendship. For us, that God would befriend us is the fundamental idea that explodes Aristotle!

BB: It's too big a gap between types of beings!

SH: I take it that what Jean is about is witnessing to the reality that God has befriended us through the kinds of friendships L'Arche makes possible. I think that what he is saying about seeing the beauty of the other life is that you see the other life as God's befriending and that makes it. Given our creaturely status, for God to befriend us is more radical than our being befriended by someone who is mentally disabled. That's the kind of transformation that I think Jean is rightly calling attention to.

BB: How is the language of virtue fitting there?

SH: I don't have any idea!

BB: I can see that it makes me a more virtuous person to be friends with people very different from me. And I could see describing it being important, for people that I really can't understand how they are seeing things, to have friends. But can we say that we are related because we will practice virtue for one another?

SH: Yes. I don't know. I just don't know!

What I do want to say about that, however, is that one of the things that so disables disabled people is the assumption that they should have no moral responsibility or formation. Now that will occur in a huge range of possibilities. But just to the extent they are said to be incapable of acquiring habits that are morally important I think does them a deep disservice and is extraordinarily prejudicial. When you care for people, you must care that they can care. Otherwise, you just condemn them to the prejudice of the normal.

BB: I see the force of that line of thinking, and I think it's got to be right. There are also aspects of human will and reasoning here. If ethics is deliberation, then I can imagine people with very low cognitive capacity willing or not willing that they should will or not will, as we've talked about before—to learn to brush their own teeth. They can resist that out of the same perversity that you and I can resist going to the doctor or whatever else. But I'm not clear, given Aristotle's position, and I'm curious about your own position, would that then mean we should also ascribe to them some type of moral deliberation, however attenuated?

SH: Well the easy answer is to say, immediately, yes. But I don't know what that will look like.

BB: I appreciate Miguel Romero's explication in the *Disability Reader* of Aquinas on this topic, who takes the other side on this question.[52] Aquinas says that to be a human being is to be rational by definition, but that some people can be locked inside their faulty bodies. Those people will get their virtue directly, by infusion. It's almost like there's a parallel person in there. I am resistant to those sorts of proposals.

SH: Yeah, me too. The preface that starts the *Prima Secundae* about rationality commits Aquinas to some of that. I think that's unfortunate.

BB: Which brings us to another piece I wanted to tease out a little bit. How should we read Aristotle's account of ethics as an expression of an intrinsic power possessed by the "rational soul"? If ethics is, by definition, thinking about and reasoning about action, there is going to be no way for someone with a deficit to reach the level of moral culpability.

Vanier softens this line by suggesting that the Logos shines in every human, so renarrating how soul is understood. Vanier's way of dealing with the central role played by reason in Aristotelian anthropology goes this way:

> Logos is simultaneously the intelligent *nous* in Greek that grasps principles intuitively and the discursive intelligence that reasons from basic principles. Thus Logos is a light that enables us to contemplate, understand, reason, order, name, control, regulate. Thus the definition of man as a being having Logos could be more faithfully expressed as a being possessing an inner light capable of grasping the light in others and thereby becoming autonomous and steering itself toward the light. Light here, should not be taken in its mystical sense but in the sense of that which is luminous to the mind in the same way that we might say something has had light shed on it when our minds have understood it.[53]

SH: I thought he made a mistake with the Logos language to begin with, as a characterization of Aristotle. And that account of Aristotle's understanding of reason is not right because it does not do justice to Aristotle's understanding of what it means to perceive the ultimate particular, which is fundamentally an exercise of practical rationality. Jean makes him sound more like Plato than Aristotle. But I like very much Jean's revisionist account in terms of being able to see the dignity of the other as part of what is intrinsic to rationality.

BB: So even if it's not easily gotten out of Aristotle, the premise that there is an inner attraction of people of very different stations toward one another needs to be defended in one way or another?

SH: Absolutely.

BB: How would that cause you to either modify or put in a different category the Aristotelian claim that ethics is a type of reasoning that presumably demands some minimum level of rationality?

SH: It is a type of reasoning but reasoning is also a formation through habit, of the body. So it's not like it is up here in the head, somehow.

BB: Thus the L'Arche member who over the period of ten years recovers from institutional life by taking responsibility for brushing their own teeth can be said to have undergone some version of moral deliberation?

SH: Absolutely.

BB: One other related question. What do you make of Vanier's account of *eudaimonia*? He says,

> The root of the word *Eudaimonia* is actually *daimon*, which originally meant the god who dispenses goods. It was a natural progression from "the one that distributes the portions" to "the portions themselves." The *Eudaimon* is thus the one who receives a good share dispensed by the divinity. Aristotle makes little use of the word *daimon* but does take from his predecessors the idea of this element of fortune being indispensable to happiness, indispensable but not sufficient in itself. If the word *Eudaimonia* originally had a passive connotation, in that we receive a good or bad share, it has gradually assumed the meaning of a certain activity—whether we are good or bad is our own responsibility.[54]

How does that sound to you?

SH: Pretty good. I think he's got most of it right. I don't know what to make of the etymology, but he understands *eudaimonia* fundamentally as an activity across time in which we are habituated to receive the goods that are commensurate with the virtues. And that, I think, is pretty close to what he's saying.

BB: If his etymology is right, it sounds again, as we discussed in Chapter 1, that Aristotle is essentially taking the supernatural out of the *daimon*.

SH: Oh that's true.

BB: He does it because he wants responsibility, moral responsibility, to be up to us. But that loops us back around to the question of the relation between natural and revealed knowledge. I just found it fascinating reading Vanier that he flat-out embraces this trajectory of a secularizing account of *eudaimonia* and is explicitly resistant to saying that the gift of the gods is fundamental to the way happiness and moral responsibility are described. And that seems to produce some tension with the earlier discussion we had about "natural" in your theology, as well as reminding us how odd it is to "build a Christian countercultural community" by beginning with a thinker who downplays revelation.

SH: I'm sure that's right!

The sight of the Holy Spirit

BB: I think it would be fitting here to return to do some theology around some personal narratives.[1] I am provoked to do so by a passage that you put at a high point of your impressive little new book on the Holy Spirit. (I am *always* impressed with a short book! As Mark Twain said, "I didn't have enough time to write a short book.") You develop several chapters' worth of theological description of how Christians understand the Holy Spirit and then you wrap it up with this passage, which begins this way: "Stanley witnessed holiness in action at L'Arche." It then continues:

> I have seen the work of the Holy Spirit at L'Arche on a visit with Jean Vanier and his community of friends in France. On a Sunday I saw holiness enacted. The "church" was a converted barn. The mass was in the late afternoon. The congregation gathered slowly. Many were in wheelchairs. A number of core members helped other core members find seats on the simple benches. The mass began with the core members assisting by lighting candles, carrying the cross and Scripture. One young woman danced around the altar. The priest did what priests do in a manner that made clear he rejoiced in what was happening around him. Just as the mass was beginning, Jean came in pushing an elderly core member in her wheelchair. He parked at one of the lower benches and sat beside her. She leaned her head on his shoulder and did not move from that position until it came time to receive the body and blood of the Lord Jesus Christ. I've never seen a more gentle gesture. She and Jean had all the time in the world to be present to one another as the Holy Spirit was making Christ present in the world in sacrament. I'm sure that I caught a glimpse of heaven and the communion of the saints in that moment. The Spirit had come to rest on the body in a manner that was unmistakable.[55]

I found that passage particularly striking, because I was in the same service. But I was sitting in the transept and I couldn't see you and I couldn't see Jean Vanier. And you couldn't see me. And I had a very similar experience of being overwhelmed by the worship that was going on very near me, but in my case there was a young female assistant who had come in with an older male with cerebral palsy or some variety of partial paralysis and mental disability.

---

1. This subsection is another instance where the excitement and the sense of shared discovery that marked the conversation is not well served by the script format of an interview on a page. Stanley has written in the past about how he has standard answers for standard questions. Here, those answers fall away and he is brief, affirming, and to the point in his responses. We are beyond the territory of standard questions and standard answers. This conversation is pursued with a sense of shared excitement at finding agreement over so critical an issue as the role of the Spirit in the Christian life.

They were sitting very, very close to me and I could see that he was putting his arm around her head, and I think he had one of those braces they put on paralyzed limbs that made it look very abrasive. His embrace was as perseverant as it was rough, and it got progressively rougher in ways that made me very uncomfortable.

But what amazed me and was an incredible witness to me was the assistant's patient witness to the love a battered Christ can provoke in a human being. I certainly would have expected her to get up and take him out or handle him more roughly in return, and that just never happened. I found it incredibly confronting. It looked very much like a superhuman level of patience that I couldn't, myself, imagine. So, I find it especially interesting that those two works of witness were happening at the same place in the same time.

The first thing I'd like to ask, then, is: Can we understand both of those as being catalyzed by the Holy Spirit in the way you've explained your own view?

SH: I certainly think so. The fact that the one I was watching was extraordinarily gentle and the one you were watching was threatening violence doesn't mean that the Spirit wasn't present in both. The relationship between the young woman and the core member you described is obviously one that had been developed over time. That she had learned to be patient took some doing, I suspect, if you had talked to her. So what I am suggesting is not that the Spirit just poured out in one way then and there but that it was there from the very beginning.

BB: I agree with you and I think the account of the Spirit that you set up in the book as a whole helps us understand why we can talk like that, because the Holy Spirit is the Spirit of Jesus. We can therefore resist saying that everything is the Spirit because what we learn in the stories of Jesus, Israel, and the church provides us with a theological hermeneutic to discuss what can count and what can be received as a work of the Spirit.

I'm tempted to go one step further, thinking theologically, and to say that your very language suggests—and I'm thinking of the language of "glimpse of heaven" and the "communion of the saints"—you seem to have seen in the activity around you two human beings witnessing to the eschatological final peace. I would be tempted to say what I saw was a revelation of the cruciformity of the love of Christ. Might that allow us to say that some of the diversity that we see in the Christian vocation reflects the complexity of the divine story to which we witness?

SH: Absolutely!

BB: As you say, the peace you saw—Jean Vanier and the core member—was probably preceded by both characters traveling through the rough work of loving in the face of the other's rejection.

Could we not say that the complex Christian story both helps us to affirm diverse moments as parts of the one story, the work of one Spirit, who might

7. Medical Ethics, Disability, and the Cross

also therefore be said to be the author of diverse but definitely shaped and mutually defining forms of life; such as marriage and singleness?

SH: I think all that's right. I don't think I have anything to add to that, Brian. That just seems to me spot-on.

I suppose one of the things we perhaps didn't do in *The Holy Spirit* is emphasize in what way the Holy Spirit creates new alternatives that hadn't been there and therefore you associate the Holy Spirit with sudden and extraordinary developments. I don't want to deny that the Holy Spirit shouldn't be associated with such developments, but I think that it's a mistake to make the work of the Holy Spirit defined primarily by that kind of dramatic, or with discontinuity with the past, because I think, for example, the Holy Spirit is present in the everyday care of mentally disabled people, in a way that's not dramatic at all. I think the Holy Spirit is the everyday rescuing of refugees. Those are the kinds of things that I would think about, along those lines.

BB: The everyday point is a wonderful one. Let's tease that out a little further with another story that has a lot of the same features but with a different but important associated point.

My pastor Isaac Poobalan recently made a poignant observation. He said the previous Sunday he had felt himself being involuntarily dragged by the lectionary to address Jesus's teaching on divorce. This put him in a state of acute inner tension because there was a family in church that day in which the mother and father, long married, had also been estranged for some time. Many people in the congregation knew about this situation and the grown couple's elderly parent and adult children were also there. So you can see the issues at stake. Isaac said he was really struggling, both as a preacher and a pastor, to preach truthfully about this passage on divorce to that particular congregation. I didn't realize this at the time, but he said after he'd preached and we all went forward for Communion, that very family lined up at the altar to receive Communion. And the next person at the rail was Adam. For the first time in two years he reached up and put his palm on Isaac's mouth. It's a gesture that Adam regularly uses to communicate presence, but he'd never done it at the Communion rail. That he did it at this moment in this very service Isaac received, he said, in the same way as Isaiah took the angel who cleansed his lips with the burning coal.[56] He received it as a judging and purification of whatever he had just managed to preach, a judgment that he received as the life-giving touch of Jesus Christ, through the Spirit. Are you comfortable with that interpretation?

SH: Yes. I tend to be very reticent to claim anything that I say or do as the work of the Holy Spirit. I'm not reticent about making those claims about others! Our task is to live in a way that our lives are unintelligible if God does not exist. It was Cardinal Suhard, a French cardinal, who said that.[57] I think that narrative is a narrative that is unintelligible if the Holy Spirit is not who we say the Spirit is.

BB: The reason I've put my question the way I have has to do with the frequency with which you, especially in *Hannah's Child*, want to downplay the immediacy of the Spirit's work and make it an *ex-post-facto* realization. I wonder if it is in fact possible to live the Christian life if there is no tangible divine presence at all. I put the question that way because we now have three stories in which the name the Holy Spirit has been indexed to realizations that could very easily be rationalized away, but which were not rationalized away and therefore became substantive points of moral orientation for the perceivers. It doesn't seem to me irrelevant that the first story came from you, your story about Vanier at Trosly.

SH: Let me just respond to that in terms of whether I provide an adequate way of talking about God's continuing action in sustaining us in this life. There's a lovely essay on me by a Dutch intellectual historian named Herman Paul.[58] It's a very sympathetic account of my work, but he raises at the end whether I have provided a way and have actually displayed how God continues to act. I have been very hesitant to underwrite a generalized account of God acting because it makes it sound like what's really important is we say God acted here or God acted there, when that way of describing what God does then is separate from what God has done in calling Israel and being in Christ. So, I tend to assume that God primarily finds us through secondary causes which can be displayed without God, but that doesn't mean that God is not there. Those are the kinds of issues I struggle with.

BB: If we take on board all the critical points you often make about experience being a nonsense word Christians often deploy to cover some substantial confusions, I am trying to ask a question that allows you to keep all those caveats and protect the agent-centered morality that is so important to you. Can agents actually act if their only certainty is a retrospective one? Where is the certainty coming from that allows us fallen and deluded creatures to act at all?

SH: From the joy that they discovered through the work of the Holy Spirit, making clear that they are not alone. Confidence is a form of joy. So just to be taken up in the activity we're engaged in in a way that I don't ask myself a lot of critical questions that make it impossible for me to do anything. It's really joyous activity, for me. It's like reading a book that is so engrossing you just purr.

BB: Would that explication of pneumatology be a way to theologically read your comment earlier about proceeding in your writing of the Matthew commentary with a Rousseauian hermeneutic of not pausing to go back and second-guess it? An attempt to let joy be the ruling interpretative course?

SH: Yeah, I think so.

BB: Would you allow that to be called a pneumatology?

SH: Yeah, I think so.

BB: Could we then say that there is, built into your most basic presumptions, a necessary role for the Holy Spirit as divine presence?

SH: Yeah, I think so. I wouldn't want to say my commentary is inspired! Inspired is just a way of saying that this is the work of the Spirit, because what is being said is unintelligible if the Spirit doesn't exist.

BB: Yet even within your own virtue framework—how would Aquinas and Aristotle put it—it was not an act hastily undertaken that just happened to work without any real preparation?

SH: That's just luck!

BB: Without the pneumatological explanation, or attempt at explanation, or faith, it would be a totally different act?

SH: That's right. That's exactly right!

BB: Does that account also help us out of the Cartesian search for certainty, and the Calvinist legacy behind it? You seem to suggest this in your prayer "Not Certainty, but Joy" that ends, "We pray, therefore, not for certainty but for joy at the discernment that you have discovered and given us a way to go on in the midst of confusion."[59] Is assurance a cognate term for what you're talking about here? In what sense does this proposal differ from "Be joyful, and do what you will?"

SH: I take it that that's a parody of Augustine?

BB: And more, Fletcher's parody of Augustine.[60] I mean, if certainty is theologically problematic language, and joy is a better alternative language, is joy related to assurance?

SH: I think it is related to assurance, but the assurance is part of a whole web of relations that means it would never have occurred to you to do what you will, to act arbitrarily. The idea that you can validate outrageous behavior because it is undertaken joyously is unthinkable if you rightly understand the context in which joy is possible, or what makes it possible. It's not like God is a cipher! God is quite specific in terms of the kind of God it is we worship. I can't imagine what would lead you to think, "Since I'm joyful, I can just do what I want." There are paragraphs in Barth on this topic, III/4 in particular, that one would wish had been more carefully put.

BB: The methodological question I'm trying to get my head around is how the joy that is clearly an important theme for you relates to the certainty that plays such a dominant role in our modern ways of thinking about ethics. Descartes, for instance, thinks we have to get theoretical clarity before we act because he thinks it is the only way we can ever really be assured that we are acting rightly.[61] That's obviously making several distinctions you don't want to make. But you're just as clearly not saying that joy just plugs into the configuration of considerations Descartes held together with the idea of certainty.

SH: Absolutely!

BB: But that leaves me wondering what joy tells us.

SH: I think of it as satisfaction, namely, that it's a recognition that given the overall formation of the gospel in my life, I seem to be who I need to be. That's satisfaction.

BB: How does that satisfaction relate to the satisfaction of a job well done? How does the global satisfaction relate to imminent, local satisfactions?

SH: I think they are identical; I have to say. A job well done is an expression of a life well lived.

BB: Is life well lived reducible to a collection of jobs well done?

SH: No.

BB: Presumably then you mean life well lived is the target. Joy, real joy, is about life well lived with a central component of such a life being jobs well done. It's hard to imagine a life well lived where all the jobs are going badly. But on the other hand, Christians could well find themselves in a position where lots of jobs or most jobs are going badly. We call that martyrdom.

SH: Right. Interestingly enough, one of the figures that has influenced me on this is John Dewey and his book *The Quest for Certainty*[62] where he really went after certainty as a goal for the moral life. I think on the whole he is right about that. If you think about Jean Vanier, I don't think Jean ever thinks about certainty. Why would he need it given how satisfactory his life has been? Not without pain, not without struggle, but what would certainty add to his mode of existence?

BB: What Jean Vanier has done, a lot of people would have quit. This brings us back to this discussion of how one knows to stick with a marriage, how one configures the thought, "It's going from bad to worse and this thing is going to wreck my life." L'Arche could have not worked in a thousand and one ways, and it didn't work in a thousand and one ways, and yet he stuck with it.

SH: He didn't stick with it because he was certain.

BB: You think he stuck with it because he was joyful?

SH: I do. And for him, the joy was, "I don't abandon my friends."

BB: I'm not disputing that, I'm just trying to figure out how it works, because the other resonance that tends to run for me around the language of joy is it is unpredictable. So, certainty is the antithesis of joy in the sense that if you bank on it, you are going to live a frivolous existence.

SH: Joy happens to you. You don't will it.

BB: Nor is it the superficiality of plain enjoyment. So I can imagine, again, periods of living in Trosly that were dark and in which any description of joy would have been quite a stretch. I'm trying to get clear about our grammar when we invoke joy as giving us the assurance that keeps us going on.

7. Medical Ethics, Disability, and the Cross 235

SH: It's only going to work through exemplification. The idea that you could express it almost as a formula is not going to work.

BB: You would then use that language as a type of external or *ex-post-facto* description of something that we've seen?

SH: I think the *ex-post-facto* is very important.

BB: I get some satisfaction when I notice how much laughter seems to emerge from our research seminar in Aberdeen. I would call this joy, but I'd have to admit that I have not aimed at it. I do receive it as confirmation that the work is going well in the fullest sense. That's the sort of configuration you are looking for?

SH: Right!

BB: Joy names success in the widest framework; moments in which that success is tangible to us.

SH: But I would be a little concerned about that word "moment" because joy has endurance that isn't just momentary.

BB: You don't think of it as a feeling?

SH: No. It can be a feeling.

BB: What is it when it's not a feeling?

SH: It's an all-pervasive sense that my life matters.

BB: So it is satisfaction? It is satisfaction and substance?

SH: What an extraordinary thing: to think your life matters! We are flickers!

BB: Indeed. To say that in front of the Judge is a stunning claim. It also presents an interesting variant on Descartes's problem. He thought "How can I know anything at all?" and in the light of eternity, how can we as Christians be so proud as to say that our life matters? But that God doesn't let us be crushed under our insignificance but genuinely to appreciate it is another way to name joy.

SH: People who aren't Christian, you are born, you eat, drink, have sex and die? What does that amount to? Suicide seems quite rational then to me.

BB: Let's revisit what we're doing when we tell such stories in public, incorporating them into our work as theologians. At your retirement party you made the following remarks about Anne's role in your life as a person, and as a theologian.

"I'm simply not sure how Anne's life made a difference for how I think,"[63] you begin. You continue, "On one hand I remember trying very hard not to let Anne determine what I thought I should say as a theologian." A few lines later you then admit, "I remember worrying if I finally walked out, whether I could sustain the kind of edge I thought I needed to do the kind of theological work I was doing. So I was using Anne to ensure I wouldn't become just another academic theologian. We're such subtle creatures." You admit with the line "We're such subtle creatures" the falsity of your latter worry—that you would lose your edge without Anne. But it must surely also have at least been partially misguided to hope that your life with Anne wouldn't have a strong influence on the theology you did. This leaves us with your opening statement: "I'm simply not sure how Anne's life made a difference for how I think." Is that where you find yourself landing today?

SH: Yes. I still don't know. As I noted before, when I wrote *Truthfulness and Tragedy*, people thought I must be thinking of Anne when I said tragic. But I wasn't. I thought pathos was the appropriate category, not tragedy, in terms of what she was going through and what we were going through. If you think of something like this, which I might have learned: when things really seemed like you just really didn't know how you would go on the next day, I was absolutely sure that my life was made possible by the people that were praying for me. I could palpably feel it. That was really important; a belief in intercessory prayer.

I learned that because I am not a natural pray-er. But I try to pray for my friends. I'm not very good at praying for myself. So all that was something that I learned.

I probably learned how much I depend on friends to see me through. I guess, one of the things that happens to you when you are married to someone who is seriously mentally ill is the isolation of it. Anne would say, "You can't tell anyone I am sick." Most of the time she would claim she wasn't. "You can't tell anyone that I am sick because they'll treat me like I'm sick and that will make me sick." She was very smart. But that would mean that if you couldn't tell anyone that she was sick, then you were trapped in the loneliness of her illness. Just Adam and I knew it. So, how not to let her isolate me from friends, but at the same time trying not to turn her into someone just suffering from mental illness; I had to learn something from that I guess.

BB: An insoluble riddle.

SH: It certainly is an insoluble riddle.

BB: This is the last thing I think I'll say because that's a perfect point of connection. I want to end this conversation by indicating the role that I take disability to be playing in your corpus, or at least, the role that I think future readers ought to understand it to be playing. My thoughts here have been spurred by Jonathan Tran's recent reflection on the story you tell about Anne in *Hannah's Child*.[64] He writes: "I cannot help thinking that Anne Hauerwas has been, rather than being a defeater to Stanley's theology, the subtext that fashions its most subtle contours."[65] He then quotes a long string of your maxims, such as your famous one: "You always marry the wrong person." This leads to the observation:

> Too often Stanley has been read by Hauerwasians and anti-Hauerwasians alike as suggesting a triumphalist narrative to which Anne Hauerwas can

only be a surd in the dull sense, a defeater in the philosophical parlor games we are wont to play, whereas it seems to me that the story to which Stanley keeps pointing us, over against our proclivities to make it a dull story, is the story of the church and its promise and wonder, and what that promise and wonder necessarily entail and constrain in the very logic of its grammar. If the Anne Hauerwas's of the world were defeaters in the story of salvation we call the church, well then indeed it would be dull.

This brings him to make a remarkable concluding suggestion:

> It's an incompletion to ever hear Stanley's story without hearing the role that Anne played in it, just as it's been a mistake to receive Stanley's church without its attending and necessary difficulties. This is the condition of our stories, the very possibility of any triumph we Christians dare claim.[66]

Tran presents your constant engagement with disability as the central internal bulwark in your work resisting all attempts to turn it into a *theologia gloriae*, a triumphant theology, and it does so more effectively than your constant emphasis on pacifism, which can relatively easily turn into a heroic project. So I'd agree then, for Christological reasons, with Peter Dula's response to Tran,[67] which calls for us to make your wrestling with disability to be a hermeneutic key to your work because it demands that church and theology never move past the cross. As Peter puts it:

> Jonathan has taught us something genuinely new about Hauerwas's theology, genuinely new even if it was already there, waiting patiently for Jonathan to draw it out. That is now a challenge for all of us to go back and read Hauerwas with that in mind *and* to ask ourselves about the subtle contours of the theology each of us writes, to ensure that those contours are responses to pain, whether pain as personal as family and friends with mental illness, addictions, eating disorders, or as structural as the legacy of slavery or the fact of patriarchy.[68]

SH: I think all that . . . I hope all that is exactly right. The question that Peter ends with—slavery—is a challenge for how that needs to be taken up, not just by me but by all of us that are white. Probably I have not done justice to the challenge of women not being regarded as human beings and that would be a theme that would need to be taken up in that same agenda.

BB: So it is the hermeneutic key because it demands that the church and theology never move past the cross.

SH: That's exactly right. As you were beginning, I was going to say that the issues are Christological, and in particular it's crucifixion. I mean, the gospel is not a successful story. Or it is not a story of success. It's a story of redemption, and redemption isn't success.

No, I like it. Those passages you read are very important. I think Peter and Jonathan are right. It's been there from the beginning, the difficulty. Now how much Anne is the naming of the difficulty for me, I think I continue not to be sure about. But that there is the difficulty there is exactly right. The SCE Presidential Address that I did was certainly an attempt to get at that.[69]

BB: This line of reasoning would suggest that the pacifist emphasis is a negative condition of your thinking and the refusal to run from pain is its positive condition.

SH: I think that's a nice way to put it.

BB: And that's going to be really hard to sustain in a North American culture designed for success, as you well know. I remember a very beautiful and poignant service in Duke Chapel at which I had heard a glorious sermon at the dedication of the organ, in which Christianity was compared to fine craftsmanship. The next day there was another service with Jean Vanier who wanted to have a foot washing. He said, "This is an intimate thing, because it is a painful thing, a bearing of our woundedness, and I don't want any pictures." That was a battle he lost because the PR value of the moment was irresistible to document. Think of the fundraising potential of pictures of Jean Vanier washing feet in the new Duke chapel! To let our pain show and refuse to run from it will demand some very fine grained adjustments to practice, but to embrace such changes has an incredible reach.

SH: Yes, and it's filled with invitations to deception. To suffer is to invite the possibilities of self-deception every bit as powerful as the assumption that you need to be happy!

BB: Well, Palm Sunday seems an appropriate day to reflect on these things!

SH: I was just thinking that.

Chapter 8

Preaching, Praying, and Primary Christian Language

March 8, 2016

> *This final conversation explores the role of the first order language that has been the primary language used by Christians through the ages: prayer, praise, and preaching. Today, by contrast, modern academic theology most often takes the form of second order discussions about the utility, correctness, and implications of that first order language. Having been one of the few Christian ethicists in the past few decades to have regularly breached that convention in academic theology, Hauerwas explains why he has done so and why he thinks it is important for theologians to draw directly on and deploy first order Christian language. The conversation ends by speaking directly of the links between several themes that have recurred throughout these discussions, laying bare Hauerwas's reasons for insisting that the Christian life should be prayerful as well as marked by the joy and humor that is indicative of the apocalyptic in-breaking of Jesus Christ's rule.*

Learning to write for Christians

BB: Today Stan I'd like to draw our conversations to a close by discussing the literature you've complained that most people ignore; your sermons, prayers, and biblical commentary. There's an irony in ending here that is compounded for anyone who has come across your own stated opinion about this literature: "*Cross-Shattered Church*, as well as *Cross-Shattered Christ*, *Disrupting Time*, and most recently, the commentary on *Matthew*, are books that I consider to be my most important work . . . if you can only read a little Hauerwas, read one of these books. They are what I most care about."[1] I can understand why you would have a special attachment to this body of work as expressing what you "most *care* about," and why you would later add that in these books you've done some of your "most *determined theological* reflection."[2] But how well placed are you to judge this your most *important* work?

SH: The more general response is of course that you are never well placed to be the judge of your own work if you think, as I do, that what you have been given to think is more determinative than your thinking. Therefore, I would certainly defer to others who may well have a different account of what is the most important.

BB: That hints at why you make those claims to explain why you dedicated several of these books to your grandkids. In the hope that they become at least lay Christians, you point them to these texts as what will be most of use to them in their Christian life.

SH: Exactly. I have no idea what it will mean for Joel and Kendall to claim to be Christians, but I want them to have the burden of explaining their grandfather! That's a place to start!

BB: That's a funny thing, isn't it? Caleb has been asking me recently, "How am I supposed to tell people what you do?"

SH: Uh-huh! It's great! I hope they are confronted by someone along the way saying, "Hauerwas? Now I think I read a book by someone by that name that did this or that. Are you connected with that?" And they are going to have to say, "Well, yes, but he was just my grandfather." But in terms of saying "He was just my grandfather," as they get older they are going to have to try to explain what made their grandfather their grandfather and what he cared about.

BB: So the dedication is . . .

SH: Manipulative!

BB: . . . and is also a time capsule that says "Start here"? In a way, the books are dedicated to them because they represent to you the future generations of the church?

SH: Absolutely right. Although I've worried about whether I am a very adequate grandfather, because I haven't gotten to see them so much as they were growing up. But they are wonderful kids. And Adam and Laura are terrific parents. I feel good about them.

BB: Though I think Nicholas Healy's *Hauerwas: A (Very) Critical Introduction* is a misconceived exercise at several levels, having immersed myself in your sermons and biblical commentary of late, I do find one of his observations hard to brush off: that this material does not "add much to what can be found in more ordinary non-sermonic academic productions."[3] The *Matthew* commentary, for instance, is littered with footnotes directing the reader to more extended treatments of themes only briefly introduced there. At the same time, I'm suspicious that my thinking this is to make a mistake not unlike Healy's assumption that he can describe your theology without explicating your ethical writings. My question, then, is what these performances of Christian language *add* to your second

8. Preaching, Praying, and Primary Christian Language 241

order descriptions of how Christian language shapes Christian behavior? As you've recently noted, "Without knowing how to say what you are doing, you do not have the skill though you may appear skillful."[4]

Are we supposed to read your sermons and prayers as the first order performances that make your life and ethical proposals intelligible?

SH: I think it's right that much of what I do doesn't add much to what can be found in more ordinary, non-sermonic productions. That's exactly what it's meant to do. I try to call attention to what extraordinary things we are given to say as Christians and why it is crucial that we notice how extraordinary it is what we say!

That I oftentimes use prayers and collects that are in the Book of Common Prayer is my attempt to show that this is as deep as it can get. The very idea that you need further explanation deeper than what is said there is already to embody an account of language that I distrust. The development of ordinary language philosophy informs how I try to direct attention to the grammar of fundamental Christian speech. Healy's suggestion is that this makes my work theologically thin. That is one judgment I would really resist. I don't think that it is theologically thin. I think it is theologically scattered. But then, I think our language is scattered as Christians and I'm trying to show connections between various things we say.

BB: And the basic procedure for you is always, "Look what you just did"?

SH: That's right. Exactly!

BB: Is it right then to say that you are inverting Healy's complaint by responding that all your "second-order analytical work" has always been a gesture demanding we "Look what you just said"?

SH: Exactly. It's to assemble reminders of the significance of saying Jesus is Lord. That's what Barth does. He assembles reminders by making connections. I tell students to read Barth like a symphony. You start with the major theme: Jesus is Lord. Then you run it through twenty-five different variations. Then you end with: Jesus is Lord. But it is enriching what you say when you say Jesus is Lord.

BB: Barth is a useful example because his work alerts us to the reality that something does happen when you move from the lectern to the pulpit and back again. I've always found Barth's sermons less interesting than his theology. My sense is that his theology, for all its philosophical precision, is really very close to preaching, and his sermons very often sound perilously close to digests of his theological work. But I don't have that same sensation about your sermons.

SH: You know, I think I've never found Barth's sermons that compelling, even the ones he did in the prison. I've wondered if partly that's because he is still so beholden to the European model of the sermon as the exposition of doctrine, somehow or the other. You just don't get Barth's liveliness in the sermons that you get in the *Dogmatics* itself.

BB: Throughout this conversation I'd like to stay in orbit around this question of how the cast of your prose is shaped by your standing behind either the pulpit or the lectern—and I think any casual reader of your work would sense a difference in tone. That's what I want to get to the bottom of today: what, precisely, is the difference between these different sorts of writing and speaking?

SH: The difference is certainly a difference in writing. The sermons and the prayers, I take them as an invitation to try to write in a manner that—I'm hesitant to use the word, but it's what I think—is poetic and to make the language do work by showing connections between assertions that create a world that otherwise would not be seen. It's a question of how sermons and prayers invite a kind of grammar that involves the attempt to make the word beautiful. That is one big difference between the lectern and the pulpit. Although I often want to be sermonic in the lectern too.

BB: When the basic category of theology is witness, it's kind of hard to escape that!

Your earliest forays into publishing sermons came in your 1988 book *Christian Existence Today*. In that book you are investigating the question of how to be a Christian in the university, and you include chapters investigating that question.[5] In the chapter "The Ministry of a Congregation: Rethinking Christian Ethics for a Church-Centered Seminary" you offer a closely observed first-person narrative description of your local church—Broadway United Methodist at the time—as it negotiated several apparently mundane questions, namely, whether or not to celebrate weekly Communion and whether or not to move to a different location or to make a substantial investment in repairing the roof.

The tone and rhetorical positioning of the piece clearly takes the standpoint of an academic ethicist, but it is less clear to me that this is all that's going on in the essay. Your stated aim is to offer a worked retort to the critics who had labeled you a sectarian, and that's obviously an academic aim. But the book's subtitle, "Rethinking Christian Ethics for a Church-Centered Seminary," signals a growing desire to reframe some of the basic assumptions of the discipline of Christian ethics itself. It feels to me like a logical development from the academic who, as we saw in your severe questioning of the main options in the guild of Christian ethics in your 1980 AAR address,[6] is now looking for a more productive way to spend his efforts. For a guy in this position it appears that being given new responsibilities at Duke to teach ordinands may have been a godsend.

The finer-grained analysis you develop in the book of the various tensions and problems that beset the church today, in retrospect, looks very much like the problem constellation that finally finds its answer in *The Blackwell Companion to Christian Ethics*. The line from the problems you describe in *Christian Existence Today* through to the course on Christian ethics you taught at Duke organized around worship[7] to the practical therapy you and the authors of the various chapters offer in *The Blackwell Companion* looks in this light like an entirely natural development. What I find uncanny about an essay you name

8. Preaching, Praying, and Primary Christian Language 243

"The Ministry of a Congregation" is a comment you bury in a footnote in which you portray the *church* as catalyzing this process in having claimed you from your "ecclesial whoredom."[8] Would it be fair to read *Ecclesial Existence* as your first testimony to having been "saved by the church"?

SH: When I first went to Notre Dame, Adam and I worshipped at Sacred Heart basilica. It was a beautiful building, and the liturgy was beautiful. The congregation of Holy Cross was in charge of the liturgy, and the liturgy was always well done. We loved Holy Week. But Sacred Heart was not a congregation. I thought Adam needed to be part of a congregation, so we went to an African American Catholic church for about a year. But the overwhelming presence of the choir drove me crazy! So we ended up at Broadway United Methodist church, and that had a real sense of significance for me. You could say that I began to be more of a churchman again by being part of Broadway. I wrote that essay partly in response to the sectarian accusation but also just to celebrate Broadway.[9] That is to say, the position that I've taken can seem so dramatic. Christians have to be Christians again, and it sounds like I'm calling for some kind of great heroic alternative, when I'm thinking about the everyday simple life of deciding in a congregation whether to move to every-Sunday Eucharist. I think that is an extraordinary achievement. I was trying to call attention to the significance of the everyday when I was doing that essay.

There's a wonderful story about "How the University Contributes to the Corruption of the Youth."[10] I wrote that for Bethel College. It was when Yoder had been dis-invited and I was called in as a substitute. Using Martha Nussbaum's piece on how Socrates really did corrupt the youth, I tried to counter by asking what it meant to be a people capable of forming students in the virtues. So I delivered it, and a young Korean who had become a Christian as part of the Mennonite missionary movement in Korea raised her hand and said, "I don't understand where all this virtue talk comes from. We're not called to be virtuous; we're called to be disciples of Christ." And I thought, "Oh shit." Out of the mouth of babes comes truth! I, of course, said, "Well I'd like to think that the virtues are part of the expression of what it means to be a disciple" and so on. But I thought, "Boy, that's a counter you really have to think about!"

BB: This story resembles another story you tell about how you became a member at Broadway. You say that you became a member because the pastor, John Smith, had the nerve to ask you, in the bathroom of all places, where you went to church. After you answered he responded, "Well then, you sure don't live out what you talk about."

SH: It really happened.

BB: You conclude about that confrontation, "I figured that anyone who would challenge me that way could not be all bad." And then in "The Ministry of the Congregation" one of the pivotal points in the narrative, where you suggest we are seeing the church as it really should be, is the pastor reprimanding you in public for proposing that the congregation take a vote about how often to take Eucharist. In effect, the story is that you learn what it is to be a Christian because the pastor says no to you.

Combined with the story about being confronted by the Korean student, we have three clear examples of the church telling you "No" in a way that both shapes you and attracts you.

SH: I think I say in the essay that after Adam and I had been going to Broadway for six or seven months I came to John and said, "Well this is a good place. I'd like to be a member." And he said, "What is your status as a Christian?" And I said, "I don't really know." I said, "I don't know if I'm a member of any church." So he said, "Well it doesn't sound, to me, like you are a very good church member." And he said, "In order to be a member of the church you have to come to Newcomer's Class for a year." And I did! And it was great! I was in it with two or three other folks and we did a lot of good work.

BB: You also allude to your being reclaimed by the church in *Hannah's Child* but this seems to give a little more detail to what was going on in what looks like a pretty pivotal period.

SH: It's where it happened.

BB: In the midst of the messiness that is church life, somebody pointed the finger at you and said, "You need to shape up and live up to what your words say."

SH: Absolutely. I have great admiration for John Smith.

BB: *Christian Existence Today* also reveals that you are now seriously wrestling with how to subvert the label that has begun to cling to you of being a "narrative theologian." It is this problematic that leads you to the idea of interweaving sermons into your academic essays.[11] The aim of these essays is explicitly to display how you are in fact about the *one* story rather than "stories as method." It was a good strategy, but you seem a bit apologetic as you roll it out: "Since I was trained at Yale I am too insecure to let the sermon stand on its own, so it is followed by methodological commentary."[12] It's a Barth-like sermon you choose for this first experimental piece. Judging from the length and the theological density of the sermon, one suspects that you might have been rather insecure about the congregation who heard it disliking it or finding it impenetrable! In any case, it feels like in this attempt to include a sermonic text in a piece of academic writing what we have is a performance by someone who's still an academic, but who for the first time is stretching his wings as a *church theologian*, rather than an academic defender of the conceptual *importance* of theology.

SH: I didn't say who that sermon was written for. Some of us started worshipping together in the crypt at Duke Chapel. Geoffrey Wainwright was part of it and Paula was part of it before we were a couple. That's where we went to church. Geoffrey was ordained and Paula was ordained, so they could celebrate. But then we would take turns preaching. The texts were lectionary texts that I was given. There were ten or so people there.

BB: Were they all academics?

SH: More or less. Academics, university people, students at the Divinity School.

BB: You're suggesting then that this was an appropriate sermon to preach to a bunch of academics in the crypt at Duke?

SH: Right. I worked hard on the sermon. I think it's a good sermon. I had thought a lot about Babel and Pentecost. I still think a lot about those connections. But then I was asked to write this article for a Festschrift for Mr. Frei. I thought, "Well, that sermon is an exemplification of some of the moves that Mr. Frei makes in *The Eclipse of Biblical Narrative*."[13]

BB: But he never put a sermon in an academic essay.

SH: He never did it.

BB: Why not?

SH: I don't know. I don't want to speculate about that. But he liked it very much and wrote me a lovely letter about the article. In his letter he emphasized the importance of the Holy Spirit. I've lost that letter. I can't find it anywhere, which makes me unhappy. So the commentary was a way to make the sermon appear more academic in relationship to the responsibilities of writing for Mr. Frei's Festschrift.

BB: Did it feel a bit risky trying this out?

SH: I suppose it did, though I thought Mr. Frei would like it. Again, as you know, Brian, I've never had the means to worry about the inappropriateness of what I try to do. I didn't worry about it being a sermon. I am always so taken up in what I'm trying to do that I forget that it might appear inappropriate to some people.

BB: This gives us a bit more of a sense of why you seem to have felt so free to reorder academic conventions in the many ways you've managed to pull off, including the mixing of the usually hermetically distinct genres of sermons and academic writing. It's useful as well that you've pointed out that this was a logical implication of some of the emphases you'd inherited from your teachers at Yale, despite the fact that you are the only one that saw that as a way forward.

SH: I don't know that I'm the only one, but it just seemed to me that what I learned at Yale necessarily pushed me in those ecclesial directions, with the practices that were commensurate with that.

BB: The material content of this first "inset sermon" centers on the importance of the work of the Spirit at Pentecost to reverse the punishment of Babel, through which the life, death, and resurrection of Jesus are revealed as the true creation story. I was surprised to find a move that plays such a fundamental role in your *Matthew* commentary present so early in your work. Having also pulled the same biblical thread in one of my own early attempts to introduce biblical material into an academic paper in Christian Ethics,[14] I can't but be struck by the fact that the Babel-Pentecost linkage was the biblical theme on which you ventured this sermon and its inclusion in your academic writing. I only interject myself here because it offers an illuminating contrast: I end up at Babel-Pentecost as an expression of a long-standing desire to work out how biblical "structures of thought" can be allowed to do philosophical work in theology, while your trajectory seems to move from a set of philosophical points of clarity to the Bible.[15] Some telltale formulations indicate that this is your trajectory, such as the following: "The church is, therefore, an ontological necessity if we are to know rightly that our world is capable of narrative construal."[16] This sort of formulation is a long way from speaking first order Christian language.

SH: I guess that's true. I always kid that Baylor University's motto is "*Pro Texana, Pro Ecclesia*" which I say are the only two ontological realities that matter. To call the church an ontological reality is to say, "How would you know there is a world if there wasn't a church?" What would you be referring to, because the only way that you know that there is some history possible of all existence is because "In the beginning . . ." That is a reminder that there is a metaphysic implicated in the presumption that there is a church that makes the world possible. I want to say that the very presumption of people that you could write a history of the world is a theologically dependent presumption. It's partly a way to remind us that there are truth-making claims embedded in the statement that the "first task of the church is to make the world the world." It's not just a "confessional position" in that way.

BB: I think what I'm trying to tease out here is that the language I've just quoted performs statements about the order of being, and I'm drawing attention to how those statements are uttered within a story in the order of knowing. The order of knowing story concerns a university theologian getting confronted and claimed by the church and becoming a different kind of theologian. I'm proposing that this text is a transitional piece in that even as you are uttering claims about the church in the register of the order of being, the developments afoot in the order of knowing display that these claims are taking you to a new place from which you would no longer be tempted to start your arguments with claims about the order of being.

SH: Yes, you may be right about that being a transitional moment, but I didn't know it, if it was! If it was, all to the good. Of course, I suspect I was still, as I still am, trying to think through the implications of fundamental moves that Yoder makes.

BB: I'm trying to come to terms with a theme we've touched on before. You certainly emphasize contingency and the importance of deep acknowledgment of the order of coming to know in your thought. The reason I feel that some of the formulations in this essay indicate a transitional moment in your thinking is that up to this point you haven't been working very hard in any visible way to serve ministers or the contemporary church. In short, the task of trying to persuade ethicists and academics to alter their methodological approaches is one sort of language game, and trying to teach the church to live *as church* is another. I feel like in this book the tonal change in the prose betrays a shift in your conception of your audience. The language is changing. I don't think that's disputable as a textual observation. You are trying stuff. You are addressing the church directly. Your thinking is coming from the church and going to the church in ways you hadn't really tried before, on my reading.

SH: I'm at Duke! I'm in a seminary! I'm training people for the ministry of the church! When I went to Duke, as I say in *Hannah's Child*, I really hadn't taken in that I was going to be in a seminary. Then I thought, "I've got responsibilities to try to give these people the skills necessary to sustain them in the ministry for a lifetime." So you are probably quite right that that was really beginning to work on me in a way that never would have happened if I had stayed at Notre Dame, where I was teaching primarily undergraduates.

BB: The literature that we're talking about—especially the prayers—couldn't have emerged without this transition?

SH: I think that's right, for sure. The prayers? I never prayed before class at Notre Dame, because I didn't know who was out there as students. Since they were required to take some classes in theology, I thought it would be coercive to ask them to join in a prayer if they, as a matter of fact, were not ready to pray. Therefore, I didn't want to coerce people into a religious act in a context where their attendance was compulsory. So I never prayed at Notre Dame. I may have when I taught in the seminary. I can't be sure.

BB: In any case, for me *Christian Existence Today* is a testimony to how seriously you took this transition to training ministers. This is indicated by the sheer volume of work you begin producing that's very churchy in the most obvious way and distinctly different from your earlier writings, even something like *The Peaceable Kingdom*. Everybody will have noticed that some Christian language, like "holiness," evidently does real work in your earliest texts, but you've started to speak to a different audience. We are now beginning to witness you doing some serious new intellectual work as you begin to ask, "What I am going to say to ministers?"

In shouldering the responsibility of serving the needs of ministers in training you formulate the following assessment: "one of the most profound moral challenges that the clergy face in our day" is "the disparity between the theological definition and the sociological reality of the ministry."[17] It is one of the most painful ironies of your life's work that even though the empirical church has demonstrably been the impelling motor of your increasingly theological thinking, this has never dissipated the accusation that you romanticize the empirical church.

SH: Well, writing the little article on Broadway was a way to show that I wasn't romanticizing.[18] Writing the article on Aldersgate was a way to resist romanticization.[19] People would probably now put those articles in the general category of trying to do some kind of ecclesial ethnography. I wasn't that sophisticated. I was just trying to draw attention to churches doing basic work to indicate that this isn't idealism; this is everyday reality that is extraordinarily significant. The church of Jesus Christ is alive and well in the lives of everyday people whose lives do not appear to be morally significant. But they make all the difference.

BB: You'll remember from the disability conversation the incident we discussed when a woman shouted at you at an AAR panel session for talking about disabled people in the church in what she felt was a romanticized manner.[20] I am lingering at this point because this has obviously been a constant barrier to the reception of your work. I hope we can help people to have a better understanding of the fact that even a slightly more sophisticated reading of your work would show that the empirical messiness is there from the beginning.

SH: Yes. I hope that's right. Then, the kind of article that I wrote when I did the SCE Presidential address, "Bearing Reality,"[21] is a more explicit expression of the difficulty that being Christian creates. It's not like you are suddenly triumphantly saying, "I've got life by the short hairs!" No, not at all.

BB: I like the formulation in the sermon on 1 Corinthians in *Learning to Speak Christian*:

> You think we have got troubles. Try Corinth—a church divided into factions, a church wracked by sexual immorality, a church in which members are but a short step out of paganism, a church beset by class and economic divisions, a church in which some speak in tongues no one can understand. If you are ever tempted to think the early church got it right and it has been downhill ever since, I urge you to read Paul's letters to the church in Corinth. We have never gotten it right.[22]

What do you think is behind the illusion that if we are speaking about aspects of the life of the church that people don't see, then we're not talking about the "real" church?

SH: I believe where Christians, even in deep unfaithfulness, say they are worshipping God, God shows up. That should scare the hell out of us. In the text we had for morning prayer this morning, we read 1 Corinthians 11:30, "Why are so many of you sick and dying?" I really believe that judgment against the church for its unfaithfulness is still a mode of God's care of the world. All my anti-Constantinian rhetoric can give you the view that somehow God has abandoned the Constantinian church. No, I believe the Constantinian church is the church. I'm not going to give up on it, I'm going to try to say, "Look at what other alternatives we've got." So that's what I've been trying to say. Brian, does that make sense to you?

BB: We were in Dundee this weekend and, bizarrely, an art installation on the side of a parking garage brought these questions powerfully to mind. The installation is made up of thousands of little playing card-sized flippers finished in a sort of gold chrome plating, which have been hung like a massive hanging tapestry across three or four vertical stories of a parking garage. Since every one of them moves with every breath of wind that touches them the effect is that you can literally see the wind, in the same way the light disturbances you see on the surface of a still lake reveal the eddies of the wind blowing across it. I find such visions utterly mesmerizing, and I often think about the Spirit playing over a sinful congregation in the same way. So when you say we have to teach people how to see what's there, that's all we are able to talk about—the Spirit playing over all the sinful stuff. It also means we shouldn't be surprised or disheartened that so often all we can see about the church is the sinful stuff!

The problem is to avoid such descriptions not constantly coming across as utopianism—because the sinful reality can often be very broken indeed, and very painful. You seem to have been continually trapped by that.

SH: I suppose that's right, but all you can do is try to show exemplifications, which I try to do, like at Aldersgate church.

BB: It is lately popular to say that what we really need to deal with this problem is to do a lot more proper empirical study of the church.

SH: I'm not against that, but I just want to know what a proper empirical study of the church looks like since I don't trust sociology. It's not that you can't learn much, sometimes, from sociology. But the reductive character, oftentimes, of those studies, I have got to resist.

BB: It's pretty difficult to imagine how they are going to resist being over-determined by the sinful, common dynamics of human life in general, which are, of course, always present not only in the church, but also among the society of academic sociologists, all of whom want to "get results."

SH: Right. I try never to forget that the church is people! And people are difficult.

BB: . . . even though the church is not *just* difficult people, even if that's what it always looks like on the surface.

Observations on method in preaching

BB: It would be great to talk about some individual sermons but I haven't figured out a good way to do that. We could easily talk about any given sermon for a whole conversation. I thought instead I might take the slightly different approach of simply listing some general observations about your published sermons and let you comment about what you'd like in return. Forgive me the length here.

    a) First, stating the obvious, you like a memorable story. Perhaps less obvious is the role played by surprising linguistic juxtapositions at the climax of your sermons. This may be what you were talking about with the poetry. The punchline of a late sermon typifies this approach:

Like the people of Israel, we have been bitten by the snake, and it is not at all clear we will survive. . . . To be raised with Christ means the end of any attempt to passively stare at the crucifixion. You cannot stare at that in which you participate. . . . it turns out that in the process of learning to see, to *really* see, the life we are given through Jesus's death we become a people bronzed and lifted up by God so that the world may see there is an alternative to being captives of death.[23]

b) You regularly comment on the implications of the congregation's current location in the liturgical calendar, and, in general, your sermons could be said to be locating the congregation in God's time. This suggests why you called one collection that includes a significant number of sermons *Disrupting Time*.[24]

c) Third, it looks very much like one of the reasons that you have been criticized for not engaging with the detail of scripture in your sermons is that you normally do not quote scripture directly. Closer reading, however, reveals that your sermons do turn on theologically loaded readings of pivotal passages from the lectionary, and are often directed at refuting contemporary misreadings that you take to be far from theologically innocent. If read charitably we can understand this as a performed insistence that the lectionary rules preaching. You don't repeat what has been read but respond to a text to which you expect the congregation to have been listening. I have a strong suspicion that most of your critics don't acknowledge this performative context, reading your sermons without reference to a prior oral presentation of the scriptural texts.

d) The thinness of the academic discourse of Christian Ethics is pilloried to particularly potent effect through casual unfavorable comparisons with the profundity of the Christian life as depicted in scripture.[25]

e) Rowan Williams is quoted much more regularly in your sermons than in your academic writing.

f) The older you get, the better you get at the short sermon. The exception to this rule is your sermons in honor of people you know at events like ordinations or weddings, which you evidently delight in delivering.

SH: Those are extremely interesting observations. I always take the text very seriously. I am against idea-sermons. What you say in the sermon always has to be dependent on the text you've been given. One of the things I also try to do is work very hard not to exclude the Old Testament text. So I try to preach, as much as I can, in a manner that the text of the Old Testament is seen as crucial for what we're saying in the New. So there is a certain sense that I hope my sermons are really exegetically responsible. That involves why it is that I believe Christianity is a form of Judaism and that I don't say that but I try to show what the implications are for the reading of the text we have before us.

I am trying, always, to be exegetically responsible, though I am resisting the presumption that the exegesis depends on knowing "what was meant" in the original setting. My way of putting it is that if Paul walked in the door right now and said, "What I really meant in 1 Corinthians 11 . . ." we would say, "That's interesting. Sit down and we'll discuss it. You thought you were writing a letter to the Corinthians. We now call it Holy Scripture." How would he know? Paul didn't know he was writing Holy Scripture! So I'm not going to let the historical-critical method determine what needs to be said about what the text is doing or should be doing. I wish people would attend to that, because the way I try to read the Old Testament typologically is always very important.

BB: I have to interject at this point: the question that you always ask about what we would say if Paul walked in the door *is* determined by historical criticism in the sense that he's being conceived as an inhabitant of the first century rather than as a living member of the *communio sanctorum*. Your presumption is very different from one that would say "There's no way for me to write a sermon on his letter without already being in some sort of conversation with this saint who is also my apostle."

SH: Right. All that's right.

It's also the case that I always try to write and preach in reference to the church year. That has to do with time, and how the church learns that the time in which we live is not the time in which all people live. So, the liturgical calendar is very, very important for me.

Earlier you suggested I like a memorable story. I think most of my sermons don't involve stories at all. I was never attracted to the narrative preaching movement. Yet sermons cannot be what they are without being embedded in the story of "Out of all the peoples of the world I have chosen you, Israel, to be my promised people." But that doesn't mean that the sermon itself tells a story. I worry that, for example, when preachers tell the story of "When me and my wife . . ." I always think, "Oh no." That's just an invitation for the congregation to think, "Isn't our preacher clever?" I don't like that at all. I try to stay away from any self-revelations or stories that have shaped my life.

BB: Given this point, it sounds like the first passage I quoted is better read as an instance of something like a figural reading. It is trying to situate *us* as the Israelites bitten by the serpent. Structurally speaking, it appears that it is not narratives that make this link, but figural connections. Repositioning the congregation in relation to the text is more the force of what you are after.

SH: That's exactly right. In the *Matthew* commentary I comment on Herod's destruction of the innocents, "The Herods of this world begin by hating the child, Jesus, but, as Frederick Dale Bruner observes, end up hurting and murdering children. That is the politics, the politics of murder, to which the church is called to be the alternative."[26] When you write a phrase, "the Herods of this world," you are already typologically working to make the story of Herod a story that shapes how we should see the world. That's easy to overlook, but a lot of methodological presuppositions went into writing a phrase like "the Herods of this world"—the crucial word being "this."

BB: It encourages people to look at the events going on around them with very different eyes than we get when we speak in the common language that runs, "Man, there are a lot of incompetent politicians in the world."

SH: Right, that's exactly right!

I never noticed that I quote Rowan Williams so much in my sermons! Of course I am not as smart as Rowan, or as accomplished, but I think there are real similarities between his work and mine. Both of us are all over the map. It must be very frustrating! Rowan knows so much more in terms of the Fathers and Dostoevsky, but still, I feel a deep kinship with him.

BB: Rowan's presence stuck out to me especially having just heard a fantastic paper on Donald MacKinnon by Andre Muller. Andre has been working for years on what will certainly be the definitive biography of MacKinnon.[27] His considered opinion is that Williams is MacKinnon's most obvious intellectual inheritor in the fundamental sense that MacKinnon was seriously committed to resisting premature closure, or closure at all, really. This is interesting because if Williams is getting quoted more frequently in your sermons, it suggests something about the difference between your academic writing and your sermonic writing. Your sermonic writing does feel more resistant to straight conclusions. There is an openness to their texture that seems distinguishable from the impulse of your academic writing to use precision to close down alternative readings.

SH: I'm also a big fan of MacKinnon. I'm happy to say that I actually knew him. Ken Surin put together a conference on MacKinnon. Milbank wrote a paper to which I did a response and MacKinnon was there.[28] I think MacKinnon almost single-handedly saved British theology after World War II. I am sure MacKinnon's work has been a decisive influence on Rowan.

BB: In *Cross-Shattered Church* you briefly raise, but don't really answer, some fascinating questions about preaching and publishing sermons, or the relation between oral delivery and publication, that I'd love to follow up a bit more.[29]

   a) What's at stake in your insisting that "sermons should be arguments"? And what kind of arguments do you mean? You elsewhere suggest that the sermonic form is a better form of argument than theoretical argumentation.[30]
   b) Why do you write dense sermons and "expect my hearers to do the work of hard listening"?[31] I'm curious why you say that.
   c) And third, what is at stake when the sermon, which you call "first and foremost an oral art," becomes a chapter in a book that, you muse, may turn it into something different, a "biblical lecture"? You have certainly expressed significant worries about this transition: "To concentrate on the sermon abstracted from its total setting in worship, to concentrate on a short series of sermons separated from their setting in the whole Christian year, and to abstract the sermons from the church's whole ministry is fundamentally to distort them."[32]

These questions are pressed in the 1992 book you wrote with Will Willimon, *Preaching to Strangers*, which contains some startling comments, beginning with your flat out assertion that "[t]he written sermon is a different genre than the sermon preached."[33] Admitting that you were having trouble getting engaged with Will's sermons in manuscript form, you then admit further that you only got excited to write the book with him because you were "too lazy to go to church one Sunday"[34] and only warmed to the project upon hearing Will preaching on the radio. For a sermon to be a sermon, you explain, it has to engage its hearers, or in this case, you correct yourself, "a" hearer, which seems a rather significant—even if inadvertent—admission from someone who has so regularly emphasized that the sermon is not only an oral act, but an ecclesial act. You then go on in the book to make rather detailed comments and criticisms on the texts of Will's sermons, pursuing in some depth issues raised by details of the text that very few would have been able to catch in the oral presentation—which we as readers can only assume differed little from the written text.

SH: I originally got thinking about the sermon as an oral art in terms of Yoder's *He Came Preaching Peace*,[35] which contains sermons John had delivered in various places, or presentations he later calls "biblical essays." The biblical essay is not the same thing he delivered, although the words may be absolutely the same because the sermon as an oral art depends on presenting the sentence ironically. Tone of voice is central to the sermon. There is a materiality about the delivery of the sermon, which is not the same kind of materiality that is a text in a book. So when I say it is primarily an oral art, it doesn't mean that then when you read it as a written text, there is a deficiency; it just means it is a different thing.

BB: What then do you mean when you say that the abstraction and reification that goes with this transition of the sermon into print is "fundamentally to distort them"[36]?

SH: I am not sure what I meant!

BB: You do note that it is not irrelevant that a single set of identical words is connecting us reading the book with somebody in the church hearing a sermon, but the distance between the location of those sets of words makes a big difference—not unlike the difference it makes to read 1 Corinthians today or in the first century.

SH: It does. When I said that I was having trouble getting engaged with Will's sermons before I heard him on the radio from Duke Chapel, I was only able to listen to him at all because we worshipped earlier at Aldersgate than they did at Duke chapel. So, by the time I left Aldersgate I could get home and listen to his sermon or get it on the radio on the way home. But saying that I only got excited about his sermons when I heard them was meant ironically. I actually enjoyed reacting to his sermons, though I have the impression I really made some pretty significant points about his sermons here and there, but again it's never been noticed. For instance, the point that Duke Chapel is fundamentally preaching to strangers, and therefore Will found it almost impossible to resist the experiential expressivist move that Lindbeck characterized. Here he was, wanting to be in Lindbeck's terms, a cultural/linguistic type, but he ends up an experimental expressivist. He does so because he is trying to make contact with strangers. This is why preaching in our time is fundamentally shaped by the assumption you are preaching to people who are only half Christian. Apologetics takes over.

BB: Do you think the fact that the sermons were also being broadcast over the radio accelerated that tendency?

SH: I would think so.

BB: I bring that up because if it was true that that context produced the expressivist sermon, might that give us some critical purchase on the meteoric rise of the satellite church? The packaging and projection of the sermon that is built into such church models seems to roll the "preaching to strangers" dynamic into the very conception of how the sermon is conceived and practiced.

SH: I think that's really exactly right. You said it before I thought it. I think that's exactly right. Think about those churches that have the reputation of being conservative, like Joel Osteen's church in Houston. Here you have a guy who styles himself on being evangelical and yet the logic of his position is experimental expressivism all the way down. You get, in evangelicals, in their preaching, Protestant liberalism on a stick and they don't even notice it.

BB: Does the way that you have described the transition from sermon as an oral art to text suggest that today the oral sermon is now something that remains to be *achieved*? It's a task, a responsibility to achieve an oral sermon?

SH: That's a really useful suggestion, but I didn't think of it.

BB: Let me give you another example. I have a doctoral student who did a fantastic thesis, never published, on Augustine's preaching.[37] Augustine never wrote his sermons, didn't make notes, and didn't prepare a script.

SH: Some amanuensis was writing it down.

BB: Exactly. That's the only reason we have the sermons today. Ronald Boyd-MacMillan showed how, precisely because they were recorded in that way, we can see that he's constantly responding to the feedback he's getting from the congregation. The mobility of his preaching is starkly displayed in the moments when he gets up to preach after the lector has read the wrong lection. What does he do? He preaches on the lection! Now that's oral performance! But more to the point, he'll say, "I see you laughing" or he'll say, "I see you squirming," and it is very obvious that the tack of his sermon is deviating to follow the paths opened up by the congregation in front of him.

SH: He even says, in several places, "I can smell you; I see it's time to quit." They were standing up in that heat!

BB: I don't have an agenda here other than to say that the observations that you are opening up suggest that our sermons are not freshly cooked because we are overdetermined in exactly the way you suggest by the generic audience and our thinking about the subsequent lifespan of the words we are uttering. Augustine knew he was being recorded, but that didn't stop him from complaining in his sermon the day after Christmas that it was pretty packed the day before but that he's glad that the "true believers" are here today. Ronald also turns up an instance where a miracle happens at a shrine in the side chapel of his cathedral, and that gets incorporated straight into the sermon as well. Even if I can't do it, I can see that something genuinely oral, local and particular is going on that is in no way being co-opted by the fact that someone is taking notes in the back.

SH: I think that's exactly right.

BB: Moving around to the other side of the pulpit, your critical engagement with Willimon's sermon raises the question for me of the proper stance of the hearer of a sermon. I wonder if you would agree that the nightmare of being a theologian in church is trying to quit analyzing the sermon and the pastor's performance, which is often paralleled by the nightmare the pastor is having when a professional theologian is in the congregation as she worries about whether she's being torn to bits or not.

SH: Right. Will is very articulate about that. He suffers most preachers' worst nightmare—having Hauerwas sitting there in the congregation listening to him. But of course, we're good friends. Will is not defensive. To become defensive is to lose the game. He wants to be a faithful preacher.

BB: Your offering Will extended criticism makes a little more sense as something you have engaged as a service to the preacher for your second sermon of the day, the second course of the meal for you, but do you have any advice on whether we should allow our critical mind to start chewing on what the minister is doing in church?

SH: No, I think that's exactly what we should do.

BB: Why's that?

SH: Because the sermon isn't the property of the one preaching it. The sermon is the congregation's reception of the Word of God. You sure better be ready to think that that word should invite some critical response. The idea that the congregation is just passive recipients of the word means that you don't get what the word is about.

BB: I think what I have in mind is a cognate of your refusal to read scripture with the question "What does it really mean?" We are trained as theologians to see the theological skeleton that's holding the language of the sermon together. We are prone to getting very reactive to poor theological assumptions and badly formulated words, and that can make it hard for us to be good congregants. As we just noted, there's a lot of sin and brokenness and superficiality and platitudinousness in all of us and everything, and we can be trapped in seeing that and the critical apparatus is what traps us there. In part, what you've already articulated is that that's not what the church is.

SH: I hope that that's right.

Reading, memorizing, and commenting on scripture

BB: Over the last few years you've taken to regularly pre-empting the question "How do you write so much?" by offering this answer: "because I read a lot."[38] There's a superficial obviousness about this answer that has led me to assume that you are drawing attention to the tendency of fewer and fewer people to read much or deeply, including academics. But in a 2010 commencement address to seminarians you push this theme in a decidedly theological direction.

> [W]hat you have learned to do in seminary is read. By learning to read you have learned to speak Christian. That you have learned to read and speak means you have been formed in a manner to avoid the pitfalls I have associated with the contemporary ministry.[39]

These are not self-evident connections, because we know people who read a lot and aren't formed very deeply by it, and we also know Christians who have learned to speak "profoundly Christian" but are pretty poor and certainly not voluminous readers. Walk us through your reasons for thinking reading is so important for Christians and especially for ministers, and it would be useful if you could relate that to your claim that "[i]n truth I have only come recently to understand that what I have been doing for many years has been teaching people how to talk."[40]

SH: That goes back to the earlier question about how my sermons don't add much to first order language about the faith. I think that theology is constantly about helping us not say more than we need to say theologically. Therefore, there's no substitute for reading great texts—Augustine's *On Christian Doctrine*, for example—that help us to learn the grammar of saying what we need to say about God, and no more. The "no more" is really hard, particularly in times when you are discovering that there are many people out there who are just as good and possibly brighter than you are who won't want to speak the way we Christians have learned to speak. They don't call it "creation," and that makes a hell of a lot of difference.

So I think what I am trying to get at there is the importance of clergy, first of all, and laity second of all, learning to say what needs to be said and no more. An example I've been using recently has been when a minister comes to a family that has just had someone die, people are devastated and so the mother says, "Well, I guess they have gone on to a better place." No! Heaven is not a place! How do you discipline Christian language not to fall into those traps? I think we're not very good at it. Sermons should be teaching the basic grammar of what it is we say as Christians.

BB: I like the answer that you gave very recently, but interestingly it is couched autobiographically.

> Over the years I found that writing was a necessary exercise if I was to be a good teacher. Writing is not unlike the fundamental movements the body must learn in order to play a sport well. One of the ways to learn those exercises essential to the work of theology is by reading. Reading, writing, and teaching, therefore, are not three different activities for me, but constitute inseparable disciplines that make my life as a theologian.[41]

The linkage that is left out in your straight injunction that "you need to read a lot to know what you are saying" is in naming what the *discipline* involved in reading actually is.

SH: Right, and how the grammar of the sentences must work in order to say accurately what it is that we know. The appeal to reading can be so misleading because there is so much to read. But I take it that the fundamental grammar is given in the Bible and it is where we learn to say no more than needs to be said. That is really hard because we want to babble. Babbling is the language that we brought out of Babel.

BB: Only if you spend time, for instance, with the Old Testament do you come to grips with what it means that this text has become scripture, because it is so austere. If something is repeated, it is not an accident. It is only because we trust that is the case that it is powerful.

SH: All that seems right to me.

BB: This is just an observation in passing but reading, writing, and teaching leaves out one piece that was constitutive of the orality of Israel and the early church, which is memorizing. It is clearly the habit that allowed Augustine to preach for an hour or more at a time without notes. He's memorized some outlines and had scripture in his heart and mind. Part of the reason that this came to mind is that I have an uncle in Nacogdoches, Texas, David McFarland, who when he was in a job that had him commuting a bit, would memorize whole books of the Bible.

SH: Is that right? Isn't that great?

BB: What a discipline! And we wouldn't have a Bible if Israel and early Christians weren't formed that way.

SH: It's a great point. I suppose I've ignored it entirely because I can't memorize anything. I just forget it within a week after I've memorized it. But it is really important, and you are absolutely right.

BB: I do wonder what it means that—I don't know if it was the same for you—my mother, bless her, against my wishes for my summer holidays, made me learn weekly bible verses. I'd have a scheduled time to go across the street and say my verse to the elderly neighbor lady.

SH: It was a contest! Wasn't it *Something*-swords?[42]

BB: There were "Sword Drills" where you had to look up the passage. "Exodus 29:3—Go!" But there was also this formalized practice of weekly memorization.

SH: I know what you are talking about. Memorization is important, but not sufficient.

BB: I think this is where your comment about what, precisely, the discipline of reading is about is so important, because it is empirically verifiable that you can know a lot of Bible and cheer at all the points that Fox News wants you to cheer at. That is a habit that is not easily unpicked. I can see the power of your decision to say "I want people to be looking for the Herods," because Fox News wants us to "cheer for good Americans," and if you've got biblical language to hand, it's very easy for it to lead people straight to the wrong places. We took down guys like Saddam and bin Laden because they were Herods, hooray! In your time the churches, if not academic theologians, at least had an idea about what is in scripture, so in your generation the dominant problem was the misapplication of scripture. Hence your infamous attempt to take the Bible back from individual Christians.[43] But it may well be in my time the issue becomes sheer ignorance of scripture even among avowed Christians.

SH: I think you are better off in sheer ignorance than I am with the situation we're in, because it allows cherry-picking.

BB: Right, the gilding of one's own opinions.

This is a good point to move to your *Matthew* commentary. You have never claimed to be anything other than an essayist, and many of your essays over the years have taken the form of extended commentaries on books or essays you think are important. And yet, in the first paragraph of the introduction to your *Matthew* commentary you try the southern con on us: "Few could be as ill prepared as I was for this task."[44] Given your evident facility with commenting on all sorts of texts, from novels to poems to the driest fat books of academic prose, one could just have easily taken the opposite position, that you were the most suitable contemporary theologian to write a theological biblical commentary. What made writing it feel so different to you?

SH: The absolute inexhaustibility of the text. I was just overwhelmed by the depth of the text, and how many different things could appropriately be said. There is a kind of overwhelming about that. I felt a sense of frustration, as well as a sense of "This really is about God!" How to put those together was an ongoing challenge in the writing of it.

BB: Your typical explanations of the incapacity of modern theologians to write biblical commentary run like this one from *Learning to Speak Christian*:

> I suspect theologians' loss of exegetical skill has to do with the diminishment of biblical authority and literacy among Christians in the mainline

churches. How do you make an argument that turns on the exegesis of a particular passage when those to whom you are making the argument have little knowledge of Scripture? As a result, the Bible cannot help but be a resource of 'ideas' that become the primary focus of theology.[45]

It looks like you contravene every claim in this previous explanation when you then explain how you came to write *Matthew*: "I do not think I would have been able even to begin the work on Matthew if I had not been asked to preach on the seven last words of Christ at Saint Thomas Church Fifth Avenue in New York City."[46] Is your point that it was an atypically biblically literate church that provided the occasion for this particular modern theologian to reclaim one of the traditional skills that should be possessed by every theologian?

SH: No. It was that to be asked to comment on the seven last words of Christ forced me to have an engagement with the text in a manner that just scared the hell out of me. It made me attend, and of course in sermons before this I had attended but not in quite the same depth as the sermons in *Cross-shattered Christ*, and confront the seriousness of Christ's crucifixion. It wasn't just "something else." I think that I discovered in the commentary that, in spite of my deep cynicism, God was giving me the gift of love that I wasn't sure I wanted. Writing that commentary really drew on that sense of the overwhelming-ness of what God has done in giving us the Gospel of Matthew. I believe God gave us the Gospel of Matthew.

BB: So being confronted with a different kind of exegetical appropriation or explication of seven sentences forced you to develop a different angle of approach than you had previously developed, even in sermons, and without that *Matthew* wouldn't have been possible?

SH: Absolutely, that's right.

BB: Then I guess we're looking back at your pre-*Cross-shattered Christ* situation when we say that the question of who the modern theologian is addressing as audience is pivotal when negotiating all this territory?

SH: I really think that's so often overlooked; that we have, as theologians, people who are obligated to read us. That is such an extraordinary gift.

BB: At the same time you seem to suggest it is also a temptation because modern theologians write primarily for those in the professional guilds, their colleagues—not those who are obligated to read them but those who read them by choice. And those who read them by choice are a very small minority and are not necessarily even churchgoers. Thus the fact that you were first an academic professional, and as we've talked about with *Christian Existence Today*, are moving toward being a church theologian, begins to give us a better sense of why you could only write a commentary after a process of laborious extrication from the basic expectations of responsibility to your audience, namely, the academic guild.

SH: I'm sure that when you wrote your book on the Psalms you felt the same kind of tensions?

BB: Oh yeah, definitely. Though your having undergone that transition later in your life may position you better to assess our present. What does it mean that exegesis—and doctrine for that matter—seem to have come to play such a minor role in *Christian* ethics? It's the height of irony that a trained Christian ethicist would feel uncomfortable making the transition into what the whole theological tradition would have considered a basic skill!

SH: I think so many people go into ethics because they don't like theology! I think that is an extremely deep problem. We now have people saying, "I'm not a Christian ethicist, I do social ethics." But they still want to be members of the Society of Christian Ethics! What in the hell is social ethics? I think that those definitional attempts to discover a discipline are problematic.

BB: There's a slightly different form of resistance on our side of the pond. One of the first times I met you at a conference in Oxford a very senior member of the guild took you to task for having accepted the task of writing the *Matthew* commentary, since "it eats up too much of your career to do well." It's not the most pressing task, biblical study is background, perhaps important background, for the task you are really expected to do as an ethicist. Even a senior ethicist well aware of how traditional theologians worked still assumes that the academic ethicist has a responsibility to write certain kinds of texts, and writing a substantial commentary doesn't discharge but evades that responsibility. It's a distraction from that responsibility.

SH: It's partly that I do what people ask me to do. And since I don't believe Christian ethics is much of a discipline in the first place, I saw no reason why I shouldn't try to write a commentary on Matthew. I was one of the first to be asked to do a commentary in the Brazos series and once I'd accepted (it also involved friendships) I really began to worry because I had no idea how to do it! But I did it, and I think it's pretty good. I tried to write not about Matthew, but with Matthew, for all the ambiguities of that distinction. But I think it was an important distinction, because almost all modern commentaries are about, not with, in that way. So I wanted to comment on Matthew's text throughout in a way that Matthew pulls you into the crucifixion and the resurrection.

BB: I want to come back to that shortly but let me ask you one more question about what we've just located as the distance of the "discipline of Christian Ethics" from this traditional skill. You write in *Learning to Speak Christian*:

> We are dying—and I mean quite literally we are dying—for examples of what reading Scripture theologically might look like. Scripture, vivified by the Holy Spirit, is the heart of the church. Without a heart we cannot live.[47]

One of your enduring theological judgments has been that the end of Christendom is a gift to the church. Is there a sense in which we could

8. Preaching, Praying, and Primary Christian Language 261

understand this alienation of the discipline from theological exegesis as part of the natural development of the Christendom trajectory, and is there any sense in which it is a gift?

SH: I think yes. I am trying to make candid the assumption that Christian ethics is the attempt to come up with accounts of justice that will allow Christians to rightly order the world in which we find ourselves. That is a Christendom/Constantinian description of the first order. Therefore, part of what I must do is to try to write in a manner that doesn't reproduce those kinds of Christendom assumptions and offers a completely different reading regime. That's hard.

BB: Attempting direct engagement with scripture then, as an academic, is part of receiving the gift of being given a responsibility to try to display a continuity with our forefathers and foremothers within a context in which such work appears to be a disloyalty or defection?

SH: Right! That's lovely put.

BB: Let's go back to your saying that you wanted to write *with* Matthew. Another way you put it is that you wanted to "submit to his discipline" and that you wanted to "retell the story Matthew tells" and also that you are writing a "moral allegory." You summarize your approach in the Preface by saying, "I have tried to write in a manner that the reader is encouraged to discover and make connections."[48] It is not hard to argue that the book is full of marvelous intertextual connections that you make, not unlike the ones we've already discussed about us being the Israelites bitten by the adders in the wilderness or being confronted by the Herods of the world. How do you imagine the links *you've* made fostering the link-making of your *readers*? Are you hoping that they discover additional analogical connections?[49] Or are you suggesting that readers should learn to imitate your exegetical approach? When you say the reader is encouraged to discover and make connections, how does that follow from the connections you've made? I take the point to be something like, you want to make links between scripture and the world today and you want those to resonate and capture your readers. You are not necessarily saying, "Imitate me as a link-maker."

SH: That's right. You want to make connections within the text in a manner that the connections within the text help you narrate the world in a manner that you need continuing instructions not to forget the story that is narrating the world, because the world is going to resist being narrated in that way.

When I preach, I try to preach in a manner that people can discover that what is said helps them make sense of their lives in relationship to the fact of what God has done for us. Preaching is a constant invitation to discover how my life is unintelligible if the God we worship has not raised Jesus from the dead. That's how I think about it.

BB: Would it be useful to clarify this emphasis this way? You are saying, "Scripture tells us where and when we are, so I, as the preacher or the commentator, am not telling you when and where you are." Presumably dispensationalism was already afoot in Texas when you were growing up, but it was certainly very popular in my day, with Dallas Theological Seminary being the national hotbed training people in this theology. Dispensationalism also wants to tell you when and where you are. We're this many years away from Gog and Magog and the Great Beast, and we can calculate how much time we have left before the Second Coming.

SH: When you ask: are you hoping if they'll discover analogical connections within scripture and between scripture and ourselves—that's exactly what I want to have happen. The Scofield Bible was an attempt to expose an alien [dispensationalist] structure of scripture. There was something kind of right about what Scofield was trying to do, even though it was crazy! I want something like that, but not that.

BB: Your introduction also emphasizes that you want your *Matthew* commentary to be read as a text that does not lose the dramatic urgency of the Gospel and therefore want it to "read like a novel."[50] This obviously represents a stark contrast with most modern commentaries. Why do you think it is important for biblical commentaries to hold on to this dramatic tension, or at least yours? Is this an artifact of your long-running insistence that it is a crime for theological writing in general to be boring, or are you saying something more fundamental about commentary, perhaps asking us to reconsider the *level* at which the biblical commentator must conform to a biblical text? Your comments on this point remind me of your assertion of the "inextricably dramatic character of the sermon—dramatic in the sense that a sermon must elicit a response from hearers . . . to be a sermon."[51]

SH: Well, I think when I say that I want it to read like a novel, it's my way of reminding us that Matthew is the story of a life that moves from birth, to conflict, crucifixion, and resurrection. There is a narrative unity to the text that is constantly broken up by our exegetical practices of isolating pericopes. I wanted to write the commentary to defeat those kinds of fragmentations of the text, so that you keep wanting to get to the next chapter to see what happened. That's what I meant by trying to write the commentary like a novel, in a manner that when you finished, you would think, "Oh, that's really exciting." So, in a manner that you see the connections between the movement within the text itself. That we preach on isolated pericopes can result in the loss of the Gospel being a gospel. Again, I am constantly thinking with Mr. Frei's *The Identity of Jesus Christ*,[52] in terms of how the identity of Christ is the narrative that the Gospel itself is embedded in.

BB: That's really useful and as you are speaking it occurs to me that pericope preaching is a very obvious and clearly defensible way of handling the excess of scripture that you rightly called overwhelming. As you've also noted in your own writings, the discipline of having to preach on the same pericope year after year is another way of making that excess in some way digestible. But each of those perfectly legitimate solutions complicate our access to the story as a whole in any meaningful sense.

SH: It's funny. I've just had to preach on the text I preached here two years ago: "And God reckoned him righteous."[53] The text came up again for a sermon for Christ Church in Nashville, and this time I preached about God's telling Abram not to be afraid. I asked, "Why did God tell Abram not to be afraid when Abram showed no sign he was afraid at all?" I reflected on what it means to learn to be afraid.

BB: Is this an extension of your strong impulse that theology and preaching should always have a dramatic tension?

SH: Yes. The problem is constantly how to defamiliarize the text. We're still in a world in which people think they know what Christians think and what the Gospels are about, in a manner that means they cannot hear or read the text without it confirming views that, I think, are not Christian. They will distort our faith. The constant requirement is to try to find ways to defamiliarize the text.

BB: One of the places where your interest in the dramatic character of the text very nicely defamiliarizes a very familiar passage in the commentary comes when the chief priests:

> Ask Pilate to secure the tomb. Pilate agrees to do so and makes a guard of soldiers available so the tomb can be secured. The guard was not only stationed at the tomb, but the stone in front of the tomb was sealed in place. The chief priests, Pharisees, and Pilate assume that a stone can hold Jesus, the Son of God, in place. They have learned nothing from the earthquake and rocks that were split at Jesus's death. They are obtuse, but that they are so makes them unwitting witnesses to Jesus's resurrection.[54]

Now there's some familiar details of the text being made unfamiliar by dramatic formulation.

SH: I think, "Is that in the text?" No. But it's clearly a reading that the text can invite in a manner that isn't an imposition on the text. I always try to defeat speculation about what the text should have meant or could have meant by sticking as close as I can to the obvious. I think that reading was kind of obvious.

BB: It's obvious even though we don't make the connection because we are too familiar with the story. If you've split the temple curtain from a distance and your death has caused an earthquake and the sky to go black, it certainly follows that this is a guy you are not going to be able to hold in by normal means.

I want to follow up the great point you made about trying to capture the unity of Jesus's life. You say, "I follow Matthew's lead in letting Christological reflections be developed while following Jesus through his ministry."[55] I want to ask about the wider implications of this approach. It reminds me of Luther's decision to present the full scope of his mature theology not by writing an *Institutes of the Christian Religion*—a definitive systematic treatise—but by writing an extended commentary on Genesis, which is shot through with exactly this sort of narration of the present.⁵⁶ There's plenty of annoying aspects to it, the way he talks about the Catholic Church and the Anabaptists and all that, but he is constantly making exactly the kinds of connections that you have just been talking about. Theologically speaking I would read this as one important implication of his commitment to let scripture determine which theological themes will be addressed by submitting to the sequence of the divine acts as scripture presents them rather than setting up a systematic order that will order what gets presented.

SH: I was so pleased that you put it that way because it allows me to say I've always been attracted to the way Luther worked. When I was in seminary, I opted out of the Church History course that Mr. Pelikan taught, but I wanted to take some courses in history. There was a man there doing his PhD under Mr. Pelikan named Ian Siggins, from Australia. He taught a course on comparative exegesis in which we looked at the difference between the exegetical practices of Calvin and Luther. I worked on a comparison between Calvin and Luther's Commentary on John. I really loved the way Luther works. I have read a good deal more of Luther's more polemical writings. The concreteness of his theological work is something I deeply admire. You reminded me how strongly I've been influenced by Luther, and most people would not recognize that.

BB: The other resonance that I see quite strongly is that even in his highly structured disputational writings, he was always writing because people asked. That's the only kind of writing he did. He thought that's the kind of writing a theologian should always be doing. Not unlike your own prodigious output, the volume of his writings, which is incredible, has to do with him trying to respond to what people wanted him to do or what he thought needed to be said when asked to address people in specific historical situations. Some of his most informative writings on Christian ethics are produced as he writes a letter to so-and-so who had asked some concrete question of him, like what it means to be an evangelical prince.

SH: He probably discovered stuff he didn't know he knew, or needed to know, by having to respond to people's requests. That certainly happens to me all the time.

BB: I think that brings something very interesting into view, that there might be a lot more theological explication we could give of your refrain, "I just did what people asked me to do."

SH: Yeah, I think that's right.

BB: Have you ever done that?

SH: No. I don't know how much it involves, but that's how John Yoder worked. John primarily wrote in relationship to what people asked him to do. Notice how many of his essays will start, "The assignment I've been given . . ."⁵⁷ He tries to meet the assignment as it has been given, unless he tells you that he will not be able to do that. I try to do that. It's also the case that I try to do, like I'm sure

John did too, like Peggy Lee: She was faithful to her lovers in her own way! I was faithful to the assignments I've been given in my own way. But that is the only way I can do it.

BB: There's work to be done to explicate what's going on here, and I only note it as an observation of my own, which was crystallized also when Hans Ulrich told me at one point in passing that he had never submitted a paper to a peer-reviewed journal in his whole career!

SH: I did, early on. But I haven't done it in years.

BB: Obviously seniority plays a major part in that. But it might be useful for us to try to articulate for younger theologians what it means to be focused first and primarily on saying something as theologians. In practical terms, I'm assuming that American students feel they need to worry about being cited, to raise their citation statistics.

SH: Oh they do.

BB: Thank God in Britain we've so far avoided that. But when that game starts, the logic of management has firmly taken a seat in the mind of the author.

SH: One of the secrets about those citation games is that some people in some disciplines get very good at citing themselves. Then that's taken as a citing. So, sociologists will cite article after article they have written in an article, and that becomes a way of establishing their importance. When they come up for tenure people say, "Gee, look at this, they've been cited 120 times!" Sixty of those may be them citing themselves!

BB: But how to teach contemporary theologians to learn what they need to learn to be a functioning member of a guild but not to be determined by those parameters? It's important to try to articulate out loud what it means when we agree that it is theologically important to "write because people asked" and that "theological writing should be about something." We have to distinguish the essential task of writing theology as different in kind from all sorts of external constraints that are put on it in the academy.

SH: That's true. There's no question!

One of the things I have intentionally not done is drop footnotes that say, "You need to read *this* that I wrote in the past, in relationship to *that*." I hate footnotes that tell readers they have to read X or Y if they are going to understand me. No doubt that is sometimes true, but I have always thought what you write should be intelligible without people having to read everything.

BB: But you have still done that on occasion?

SH: A little bit, but not very much.

BB: That's part of what got me thinking about the commentary because you do say, "For a more developed version of this argument . . ."

SH: Yes, it's probably more in the commentary than anywhere else, because the commentary is so different. You had to keep going.

BB: And there is a draconian word limit on that series. That would be almost inevitable.

SH: I have thought that one of the reasons that I seem to be misunderstood, oftentimes, is that people don't see the connections that I could have made in the footnotes. But I just found that a kind of arrogance that I wanted to avoid.

BB: You just mentioned Yoder and in the Preface to the commentary you say, "I hope I have avoided making the political character of Matthew 'what Matthew is all about.'"[58] Is this a qualified distancing from Yoder's Gospel commentary, *The Politics of Jesus*? And alongside that question, what do you think was at stake in your dispute with him about his belief that "The *Politics of Jesus* was nothing more than a report on where the [historical critical] scholarship had taken us."[59]

SH: I don't think I'm right to say I hope to have avoided making the political character of Matthew what Matthew is all about. I mean, it is all about the political! So why should I not want to make the political character what Matthew is all about? I should. I do want to do that. It just depends on what you mean by politics, obviously. So that sentence is just wrong!

In terms of John's claim that he's just reporting on critical scholarship and then in the second edition where he updates it, there is no question that much of modern scholarship supports his views about the politics of Luke. But what I worried about was his assumption that he was just reporting on what the scholarly consensus now is. I think the work of people like E.P. Sanders and W.D. Davies in particular before E.P. Sanders, about the rediscovery of how the Gospels have deep continuities with much of the developments within first-century Judaism, is one of the great achievements that historical scholarship has given us. John's reading is certainly consistent with that, but I don't think it comes from that.

BB: But he did?

SH: He did.

BB: Why do you think he thought that?

SH: Well he was a European *Wissenschaft* kind of guy. I'm not. He had a big stake in the development of "scholarship," and I thought if he hadn't been a Mennonite, he surely wouldn't have come up with this reading of *The Politics of Jesus*. Therefore, to say he's just reporting on scholarship is just wrong.

BB: Avoiding making the political character of Matthew what Matthew is all about is a useful way of distinguishing what you've done in the *Matthew* Commentary from Yoder's *Politics of Jesus* in the sense that *The Politics of Jesus* is decidedly shaped by his aim to refute Reinhold Niebuhr's account of Jesus as apolitical. In my view this lends the book a certain narrowness of interest that is not true of your commentary. That's my reading. You simply are not engaged in refuting anybody's political theology. You're interested, as you have just articulated, interested in God. God is political. That means you don't have to focus your treatment of Matthew on disproving anybody in the contemporary academic landscape.

SH: That's right.

BB: The reason why I have been drawn to your *Matthew* commentary from my first reading is perhaps not the one you would expect—I've always considered it a brave endeavor to "test"[60] your well-rehearsed emphases and slogans by setting them alongside particular biblical passages. I might even be so bold as to say that if there is an opponent whose theology is being challenged in *Matthew*, it is the "character Stanley Hauerwas." This is to read it as a vulnerable and intentional, open submission to having your cherished ideas challenged. Just so it is also a dangerous act because in bringing your own points of greatest conceptual clarity to the text you can be tempted to overwhelm or run roughshod over the text. This is why it seems right that you note from the outset that "Some may find disconcerting that some of the readings of Matthew that I offer confirm positions that I have taken in previous work."[61]

For me that discomfort is most acute in your treatment of the Sermon on the Mount, in which you attempt in various ways to mesh the book's overall apocalyptic and Christological account of the Christian life with your familiar espousal of virtue. The criticism here is stated even more strongly by Darren Sarisky: "The problem that afflicts Hauerwas's experiment in theological commentary is that it does not establish an organic connection between the historical text and the doctrinal material that he brings to bear upon it."[62] I can see his point, but I think I'd be tempted to put the point precisely the other way around: because you have allowed the apocalyptic Christocentricism of Matthew's Gospel genuinely to shape your reading of the book as a whole from the outset—in addition to your reliance on Bonhoeffer's reading of the Sermon which is similarly positioned—this makes your talk about virtue in your treatment of the Sermon on the Mount seem relatively distant from some of the ways you present it in your more academic works. Do you have a horn of that dilemma on which you are most comfortable?

SH: What two horns do you see? The horn of the apocalyptic and the horn of the virtues?

BB: That's right.

SH: What I'm not sure I understand is why the apocalyptic in principle makes virtue talk problematic.

BB: I don't think it makes it problematic in principle. Perhaps these examples make the point more clearly: "Virtue may be its own reward, but for Christians the virtues, the kind of virtues suggested by the Beatitudes, are names for the shared life made possible through Christ."[63]

Also:

> There seem, therefore, to be some similarities between Jesus's admonition that we are not to act righteously in order to call attention to ourselves and what some understand to be the meaning of virtuous. Yet Christians are not called to be virtuous. We are called to be disciples. Such a calling may be analogous to the need for a master to acquire the virtues, but the kind of master that Jesus is makes all the difference. Those who are called to follow Jesus are able to do so because Jesus has no master to imitate. We are able to follow him only because he was able to do what we cannot do, that is, he alone was capable of freeing us from the grip of sin through his cross.[64]

SH: Did I write this?

BB: Straight out of the commentary, page 75.

SH: Amazing.

BB: "That is why Christians believe, in contrast to Aristotle, that we are capable of becoming his disciples even if we acquired destructive habits early or late in our lives."[65]

SH: So we can be converted!

BB: I'm certainly not suggesting that this disproves the possibility of putting apocalyptic and virtue together, but the inflection is noticeable.

SH: And the stress is more on the apocalyptic than the virtue.

BB: That would be my reading.

SH: Well, that's right.
    But the ability to have our lives turned around from destructive habits is a possibility that has been given by the fact that God doesn't leave us alone. And that's another way of saying apocalyptic: God doesn't leave us alone. That means the whole language of virtue is put in a different register.

BB: It by no means evacuates the force of the many things you've said about habit or virtue, but it does, for instance, help us to make better sense of the discussion we had earlier about the relationship between habit and repentance.[66] This apocalyptic overarching account is always positioning your understanding of virtue, and so situating it is sometimes going to do some pretty weird things to that language.

SH: Think about Augustine's *Confessions*. Augustine took up and read.[67] He took on a whole new way of life, but in some ways, this new life displayed the same kind of intensity that his life had always exhibited. The habits were transformed, but there was also a kind of temperamental continuity that's there that I think is a kind of sign that it does make a lot of difference: the kind of people we've been to the kind of people we'll be through God's good grace. I don't think that's always true, I think sometimes a person is just a completely different person. The only way to display that is to have accounts of lives like Augustine's.

BB: That example again usefully connects us back to our earlier discussion about the relationship between Aristotle and Socrates,[68] because you just gave a Socratic account of how the Sermon on the Mount is an interruption, a wisdom that comes from outside of us that must substantively shape our picture of habit in a way that Aristotle was trying to repress.

SH: One of the things that no one has picked up from the *Matthew* commentary is that I'm really doing Christological reflections throughout, because I want to try to show that you can't separate the life from the crucifixion and resurrection. One of the problems with "very God, very man" is that it can be a shorthand that stops the reader from seeing the relationship between the life and the death and the resurrection. I didn't want to call attention to that endeavor in a way that would distract from what I was trying to do, but my own understanding of the *Matthew* commentary was as a follow up to the development of the kind of Christological reflection I was about in *The Peaceable Kingdom*.

BB: That makes a lot of sense of what I found to be extremely educational about the text, even as a close reader of Barth—your unbroken insistence on every word of the Gospel being read Christologically. The Sermon on the Mount is helping us recognize Jesus, it's a self-referential sermon. This is a long way from Jesus who is "propounding a doctrine for his disciples to live by." If we start that way, when we say that recognizing Jesus as he teaches about the Beatitudes is what virtue means, well, some potent material has just been set up to inform how we use the language of virtue that is not running in Aristotle or any other contemporary virtue thinkers I can think of.

SH: Right. The argument—and I think this argument is developed in the *Matthew* commentary—that the Gospels themselves must be read Christologically is a very important argument that, on the whole, is not widely recognized today. People say, "Oh you've got to read the Old Testament Christologically." But you need to read the New Testament Christologically too.

BB: We're all still trapped by the Jesus of history, who was a good teacher, whose teachings we ought to follow?

SH: Right.

BB: Another remarkable hermeneutical axiom from your commentary also struck me. The commentary is, to my knowledge, the only example I've run across in which the Shoah is explicitly noted as a constituent of the author's hermeneutical horizon. You have explained why you decided not to enter the hermeneutics surrounding the synoptic problem, and you bracket investigating any impact on the received text of the tumultuous contemporary events surrounding the destruction of the Temple. All this serves your stated aim of reading our lives into the story Matthew tells. "Nor do I make any apology for assuming that the challenge of reading Matthew after the Shoah is not to be avoided."[69] That's a really interesting explication of what you take to be the situation in which we read Matthew today. Could you help us get further into your reasons for that decision?

SH: Well, let me begin with Sarisky's point.[70] I was explicit I was not going to let the synoptic problem determine how I read Matthew. By that, I meant I wasn't going to speculate about "Matthew must have meant this because he's clearly now disagreeing with Mark and he knew Mark." I wasn't going to do that because I wanted to show that Matthew is rightly read as Matthew, without the presumption there is something called "the synoptic problem" that had to be settled before we could read Matthew. Let me say, I think historical criticism was given us by God to resist the Gnosticism of Protestantism that wanted to turn justification by faith through grace into everything that the gospel was about. So, I'm somewhat sympathetic with Sarisky's point that I should have dealt with the synoptic problem exactly to the extent that it was a given by God to help us to avoid turning the gospel into an ahistorical possibility.

Given that set of issues, the question of the Shoah might be understood this way, namely, that the historical method could have helped us recover the relationship between Christianity and Judaism that might have helped Protestants resist the Shoah. I think that is a real stretch of possibilities. The recovery of the significance of Judaism for Christianity was largely the result of the Shoah, not the other way around.

BB: Is your core point that the witness of Israel, or God's witness to the church through Israel, must not be ignored? More precisely, I'm attracted to Scott Bader-Saye's suggestion that your insistence that we not forget the Jews is an attempt to preserve the Christian vulnerability and openness that we saw to be essential to your thought in our previous conversation. Because the Jews are neither simply the church nor the world, we who confess ourselves to be followers of a first-century Jew are a "haunted church that remains vulnerably open to the voices of strangers (both inside and outside) precisely because it recognizes that the voice of Jesus is the voice of a Jew who exceeds and complicates our categories of church and world."[71]

SH: That's right. And to the extent that wrestling with the synoptic problem helps you not ignore those issues, Sarisky is probably right, and I should have dealt more with it.

BB: All right. Now to a long question. It would be tedious to ask why you didn't comment on this or that verse, so I am only going to ask one question of that type. The theological move that gives the whole commentary its shape is made right up front when you state that you understand the story of Matthew to be about the in-breaking of God's time and what it reveals about all creation. In the most determinative sense, creation is founded in the apocalypse of the Messiah.[72] I've already noted my surprise at how early you developed this position, as early as the sermon in *Christian Existence Today*, and we've already discussed what it means that this largest apocalyptic frame is holding the whole narrative together and situating all the terms used within it. Given all this, here is the question I'm left with.

Why then make so little of the various annunciations in the first four chapters of Matthew?[73] Why skip over the places in the narrative where people or angels speak, but the faithful "hear God" or "see God's time"?[74] For instance, your comment on 4:4 ("Man does not live on bread alone, but on every word that comes from the mouth of God") does not introduce the primary biblical resonance of such language, that hearing God's word means to listen and obey but moves immediately to the Eucharistic sense of "eating the Word": "Satan would have us believe that food and the word of God can be separated. Christians believe that Jesus is the word that we now eat in his very body and blood in the Eucharist."[75]

This movement seems overly hasty because we can live from the Eucharist only if we first hear and embrace the words of Christian worship articulated over it by a human: "This is my body, given for you." A few lines later you negatively acknowledge this distinction between the enscripturated word, Jesus, and Eucharist in the statement, "Again, Jesus teaches us how to read Scripture by refusing to 'go behind the text' to discover what God must have 'really meant.' When you are in a struggle with the devil, it is unwise to look for 'the meaning' of the text."[76] Clearly to look for the "meaning" of "this is my body" beyond simply eating it would be a problem.

A similar set of observations could be made about how you interpret Matthew 25:35–45, "If you have done it unto the least of these, you have done it unto *me*."[77] I think a sympathetic reader could construct an account of the important distinctions between *the* Word, the word of God, and the "word we now eat," but some themes that seem important in the text seem obscured in the commentary.

Here is where things get interesting for me. Your explicit accounts of preaching often deploy precisely these same distinctions to emphasize how God speaks through creatures. In a prayer for preachers in *Disrupting Time* you say, "[L]et us revel in the wonder that you would speak through us,"[78] you enjoin preachers to have steadfast confidence that God is "really present" in the sermon,[79] and insist that the enemy of truthful preaching is the lack of trust that "God will show up in the words we use."[80] How would you like us to read the ambivalence in your different writings about "hearing God" in creaturely utterances?

SH: How does that question relate to the commentary?

BB: I think it is generally true that, for reasons we've already discussed at length, you avoid saying, "God said . . ." or speaking directly about revelation. Your skipping over the various annunciations in Matthew displays your general tendency not to speak about revelation directly. But this results in your passing over moments in the texts that are pretty central to the tale, especially in its first acts.

SH: I guess I think that's a point well-made and I take it as a criticism that I should have paid attention to the annunciations. It does indicate my hesitation of speaking about revelation as if it were an epistemological means of having God present in our lives that is like you being present in my life right now. My allergy to those kinds of moves may mean that I'm too reticent about annunciation. That I could say this in the prayers shows that I am freer to do that there than in the commentary, and I'm not sure why.

BB: I was pretty struck by those last comments from *Cross-Shattered Church* where you flat-out say that you can't preach truthfully if you don't trust that God is going to show up.

SH: And I really mean that too. I think that one of the problems of contemporary preaching, and why it so oftentimes becomes bad entertainment, is preachers don't trust in God showing up. I take seriously Luther's sense of the Word creating, which I think is not that different from the Spirit transforming the wine and the bread into the body and blood. So, I think preaching creates reality. It's not just making clear reality that already exists. It makes a reality exist. God does that through the Spirit. Preachers have to have confidence in that and be frightened of it.

BB: I think it was Luther who alerted me to this presence not being emphasized in your commentary. For him it was pastoral actions that were paradigmatic for understanding how human and divine actions relate to one another. When in the Bible, it says, "God said . . ." Luther in almost every case glosses it, "We know God didn't speak directly, so what is meant here is that one of the saints was speaking." When God pronounces punishment on Cain, for instance, Luther thinks it was just obvious that this judgment came through Adam's rebuke of Cain.[81] That's just the way God talks. God always talks through people. He sends you a Korean student to say, "It's about discipleship, dummy."

SH: Through inadequate secondary causes, in Aquinas's language.

BB: Exactly! Barth also gives you a high awareness that there are all kinds of dynamics immanently describable going on in human action but that God is not reducible to those immanent dynamics. Given that, you have to learn to respond to the right things when they are happening in and among immanent dynamics or you'll be ignoring God's address to you. That's what annunciation and advent are about.

SH: Indeed. That's a point well-made. And some of my favorite paintings are those depicting the annunciation.

BB: As we wind down our discussion of *Matthew* I can't resist asking about your passing comment right at the end of the introduction, that writing the commentary was "hard work." I'm wondering, given our previous discussions

8. Preaching, Praying, and Primary Christian Language

about work, and even some of your descriptions of discipleship in this book,[82] might you be tempted to call it, in retrospect, "good work"?

SH: Yes. It's a simple answer! I taught Matthew twice in seminars, and I had the students choose a commentary on Matthew, on which they would then report, each time, from the text we were looking at. So I did a lot of reading of one commentary after the other. Ulrich Luz is of course *the* Matthew commentator. He's too Bultmannian for me, but I admire his work. I also did a lot of what I would regard as hard work in the writing of the commentary. I wrote it over a summer. I would just go in every day and I had, from teaching, notes I had made about what I wanted to do. It kind of flowed. There was a certain sense it wasn't that hard, but I guess I was referring to the hard preparation I had done to be able to write it.

Praying with God and in front of people

BB: Let's talk about prayer.

SH: *Prayers Plainly Spoken* came about because Paula asked me, "Do you pray before class?" And I said no. And she said, "Well you ought to." So I started. I'm not a spontaneous pray-er, so I started taking time before each lecture to write a prayer. It would take me an hour or more. I found it a good discipline for myself to focus what I was doing with the students.

BB: How did it reshape what you did at the lectern or in preparation?

SH: It was always a reminder to me that the subject of what we were about was how God is calling these students in this class to service in God's ministry and that this was not, therefore, just a theoretical exercise.

BB: What is your sense about how it reframed the student experience?

SH: I think probably the prayers were much more influential on them than my lectures. They would constantly ask for copies, and that's why I finally put the little book together. The problem is the students were shaped by prayers that are so pious that you can't hear them. You just go dead. So my writing prayers in plain language made them think, "Oh, so this is possible?" I think that is what was really influential.

BB: It raised some fascinating insights for me, about the status quo in the university. To back up one step, I have lived through the British academy's extirpation of prayer before lecturing, primarily because people were becoming more aware of being in a secular university context.

SH: I could do it before the core class in Christian Ethics, and I don't do it in seminars, because it is at least my presumption that people in that course are people preparing for the ministry. They should be people for whom saying a prayer before a lecture is not coercive.

BB: And I suspect it's no less important for us. We've stopped asking what it means for those of us in the guild to become uncomfortable uttering first order Christian speech. Sometimes I point out that it is just a historical accident that we teach what is essentially catechesis in secular institutions. My colleague Don Wood has occasionally warned me about the self-deception that can be involved in that stance of critical distance. For instance, we do make assumptions about who is going to be in our classes, so we have to temper acts of worship in the classroom. It's not actually just the church catechizing its own. At the same time, I think it's probably accurate to say that many, especially of the graduate students that I teach, have come to a secular university looking for intense study of the things of the church and of God that is simply not accessible to them at this moment in time in many theological institutions in the US, probably because the piety has overridden the critical thought in the ways you've just indicated with your comment about the prayers in evangelicalism being worn toothlessly smooth. To feed their hunger for further theological instruction they do a PhD, which for many seems not quite the right solution. And to do it in a secular university is kind of absurd! Nevertheless, that is the location in which we find ourselves doing theology today.

Given these problems, I'd like to delve into what I would tentatively call the external context of Christian prayer today. By external, I mean before the world. In the essay "A Christian Critique of Christian America,"[83] for instance, you vigorously argue against prayer in schools, yet in the first line of *Prayers Plainly Spoken* you thank the students at Duke Divinity School, "for allowing me to pray before my classes in Christian ethics."[84] Explain how these two positions fit together. You've already alluded to what I assume is a main component of your answer, that it was the willingness of the students that allowed your prayers not to be a violence of speech imposed upon them.

SH: That's certainly right. The essay you're referring to begins with a dialogue between myself and "The Philosopher."[85] That was with Peter Ochs. It was the first time we'd ever met. I don't want prayer legitimating what's happening in "public education." I say in America today, "public education" ought to be called "nationalistic education." Certainly I don't want Christian prayers identified with nationalistic education, exactly for Constantinian reasons.

BB: Is your point that the war about "prayer in schools" in America is of a piece with the war over having the 10 Commandments in courthouses? Is it a Constantinian debate because everyone is assuming that when we no longer have these Christian actions ensconced in the institutions of the state then we no longer have a Christian nation?

SH: That's why my praying in the core course in Christian Ethics in the Divinity School could assume students are here because they are studying for the ministry. That seems to me to be a completely different context.

BB: I can't resist asking about a prayer that clearly has an interesting backstory, "Addressing the God who is not the ultimate vagueness."[86] You hint that you

8. Preaching, Praying, and Primary Christian Language 275

wrote this prayer in a rare attempt to perform with what integrity you could muster, under a certain amount of duress, an act of civil religion of the prayer-in-school type. Readers who have stayed with us this far in our conversations will not be surprised that you effectively exploded the event by offering a prayer that drew attention to the corrosive implications of precisely such prayers.

SH: While still trying to be a prayer.

BB: That's the trick! How to say, "I can't pray the way I think I should pray, nor can I do the violence by praying as people normally do in this context, so I am going to try to do what kind of prayer I can." I presume that you consider it a victory that your performance meant that the protocol now calls at that moment for a "moment of silence." In what sense should Christians today be happy or satisfied even with rituals like "moments of silence" in the twilight of Christendom?

SH: That prayer was at one of the lunches for distinguished professors that the president sponsored. It was for Reynolds Price. President [Nannerl] Kohane's secretary called me about two hours before the lunch and said, "Nan would like you to say the prayer today" and I said, "No" and hung up. Then I thought, "Well, that's cowardly." So I called her up and I said, "OK, I'll do it, but I've got to think about it." So I wrote the prayer and said it and immediately Nan said, "Well, if we have prayers like that, maybe we should continue to have prayers!" But that was the last prayer ever said before the distinguished professors. It ended it. I thought that was a good result!

I'm even against moments of silence. In the debate about prayers in public schools, in Congress, after they defeated proposals to legitimate prayers, then there was a proposal to have moments of silence. Lowell Weicker, the senator from Connecticut, said, "I'm sorry I cannot vote for that; it's against my religion." And they said, "What do you mean?" He said, "I'm an Episcopalian. We don't believe in silent prayers!"

BB: That's a great line.

SH: So I honor Reynolds in that way.

BB: How did he like it?

SH: He absolutely loved it. Reynolds was a deeply committed Christian who was gay. He never went to church, but he was very knowledgeable. He was a good friend. He liked the prayer. I think it was a good prayer. I thought the sentence, "You have, of course, tried to scare the hell out of some of us through the creation of your people Israel and through the life, death and resurrection of Jesus," made it Christological. And the sentence, "So we thank you for giving us common gifts such as food, friendship and good works that remind us our lives are gifts made possible by sacrifice," invited identification that was not coercive.

BB: Given the Constantinian settlement of which you've made us all so aware, those of us from the South cannot but experience the problems associated with what

I'm calling the external context of prayer as still a very live one. My skin crawls every time at all the praying at American sporting events.

SH: Oh it's awful. High school football games? It's just *there*. Still there.

BB: And all these steroid-pumped NFL guys who are going to end up in old folk's homes at forty years old with crushed knees and brains totally destroyed by impact are praying on the field, heads down, crossing themselves and pointing to heaven when they score.

SH: It's against the law now, but they still do it.[87]

BB: It is?

SH: Oh yeah. There are court cases that have now said you can't do that before games.

BB: How do they know it's not a moment of silence?

SH: I don't know.

BB: All right, that was a joke appropriate for a relatively light subject, but I find some of what I'd now tentatively call the internal questions of contemporary Christian prayer anything but light. I want to discuss this internal context of Christian prayer today, where we get a very different set of questions about the relation between the public and private aspects of prayer.

SH: I wouldn't use the language of private.

BB: What language would you use?

SH: Personal.

BB: OK, good. Let's use that language. You've noted that one of your difficulties in conceiving how to approach prayer in public concerned maintaining the integrity of your "normal" persona as you prayed while avoiding a falsely pious tone.[88] I think it is no accident that Jesus's prayer in Gethsemane is kept between him and the Father. Sometimes our hates are too particular and our pains too overwhelming to be coherently brought to public speech. You do manage to bring things to speech that I am not sure I could pray out loud without weeping.[89] It is hard for me to imagine there not being some prayers that we could never pray, and should never pray, if overheard by anyone other than God—and note that I'm not suggesting that such prayer be "in our head." My point is that there's no reason to sanitize our thoughts for God, and being really honest is often raw, agonizing, meandering, and platitudinous—and if overheard by others could be hurtful.

You must have seen Flannery O'Connor's recently published prayer journal.[90] It's a nice illustration of this dynamic. She's essentially struggling in an extended way with God about her own ambition. It just seems obvious that that sort of depth and type of prayer could never be articulated in public. All this suggests that there is always a reconfiguration of prayer when we pray "before" other Christians. You do express the worry in the preface to *Prayers Plainly Spoken* that your praying not be co-opted as a performance by being written for performance at the beginning of class[91] or by thoughts of publication.[92] As one who has both thought about and negotiated this boundary for many years, what words would you offer to the Christian who wants to pray, and how would you explain the relation of personal to public prayer?

SH: Let me address the latter. I think we always pray in the communion of the saints, so we don't pray alone. But you are also quite right that we don't pray certain prayers before everyone exactly because of the other people that are implicated in the prayer. I have some conflicts in my life with certain people that I find it very hard to pray that we be reconciled. All I can pray is that God will create in me, and possibly in them, the conditions for the possibility of praying for reconciliation! I wouldn't trust reconciliation with them because I don't think they have souls sufficient for being reconciled or recognizing why reconciliation is so difficult! So, I think that that would be using prayer to get at somebody, and that would be wrong. But there is a relation. If personal prayer is prayer in the communion of the saints, so is public prayer. There's got to be some connection between them.

BB: What about the other aspect highlighted by Flannery's prayer journal? I mean, you and I write when we pray, and I find that I distrust my personal prayers, for all sorts of reasons, if I don't commit them to the page. It's really interesting that Flannery wrote that journal, presumably never intending it to be published, because that's what she needed to do in order properly to pray. And there are people mentioned by name there. But the whole exercise and the type of discipline on display there is taking place in an interiority which you typically shy away from. It's a discipline of interiority, but it is not wholly interior—by no means. But the most intimate works of this discipline seem to be pretty personal.

SH: And it's not, exactly in terms of your own description—which I take is a description of me—namely, that you need something on the page means that the internal has externality as testament. I say it would take me an hour, usually, to write one of those prayers, if not more. I think I may have prayed when I was in the business of trying to write it. I am not sure when I prayed it in class that I was praying! I hope I was.

BB: Is that because the horizontal referent of the performance is so distracting?

SH: Right. You are very conscious of it. It's true that I was getting so many requests for the prayers over four or five years that I finally published them. Of course, I have a lot more than I put in the book, but I just thought to keep it short. It was a wonderful exercise for me, because I did learn to pray more because I was having to do it.

BB: What's fascinating to me is how difficult it is to negotiate these questions in life without slipping into the sorts of descriptions to which your Wittgensteinian sensibilities tend to be pretty strongly resistant. We're talking about struggling to come to terms with our internal monologue, to discipline it and turn it from its natural self-absorption into an address to God. To do that I need to write, submitting as I attempt to do so to the voices of the communion of saints. All that happens in solitude in the sense of not being heard by my living neighbors, and to that extent, it looks primarily like an inner discipline aided by a physical practice of externalizing my thoughts through writing so that I can examine them. In the end, though, I can't imagine the Christian life without that discipline going on.

SH: Yes. That's good. I do say, and you'll recognize this is true, that our lives are largely lived in solitude, if you take the reading of books and the writing as solitude. I certainly think they are.

BB: This is fascinating, because at the end of the day, I want to say it's not real solitude, because it's a conversation.

SH: It is, but there is a certain sense that you are by yourself?

BB: I think if we take our own theological descriptions seriously, what we in fact are doing when we read and pray is aiming at an intensity of uninterrupted conversation. That's what we crave because it's the condition of being extricated from our self-absorption and superficiality. We're back to your point about friendship taking time, Aristotle's old truth. I in fact know and love Paul because I spent ten years reading one of his letters with a friend, and that was anything but solitude. They never leave me now. You and I are having this conversation because I could not bear just talking about "what you're working on" or talking to you about the logistics of your visits to Aberdeen. Depth of conversation is the point. The quest for conversation with depth ultimately means interacting with an alternative set of people than I might have interacted with over a given span of time. I might have used those hours to get to know Seinfeld![93]

SH: God save us! Once I was asked by some kids in one of the dorms at Duke, they were supposed to make contact with a faculty member, and they said, "Would you come over and talk to us about friends?" And I said, "Well, yes. I've thought quite a bit about friendship." And he said, "No, no. The show; *Friends*!"[94] And I said, "I'm sorry, I have no idea what you're talking about. I've never seen it." They could not believe it, that here is a human being who had never heard or seen *Friends*. They said, "We want to watch an episode of *Friends* and have you talk about it with us." So I went over and I watched an episode of *Friends*, and of course I was stunned. When it was over I said, "Who would want to be friends with any of those people?" End of conversation.

BB: We've begun to get into some of the reasons why, for me, prayer seems to be one of the great question marks, the crucible at the heart of Christian existence precisely, as you note, because "all theology must begin in prayer."[95] I was directed into the depths of this heart of the Christian life by Barth's book *The Christian Life*,[96] which I found dissatisfying in some respects, but which stunned me with the clarity on display about the connections between prayer and Christian living. I wrote *Singing the Ethos of God* in an attempt to press toward this dark center, this Holy of Holies where we dare the unbelievably presumptuous act of approaching a holy God. In *Prayers Plainly Spoken* you write:

> Theology is the never-finished discipline of learning to speak with, to and about God. Prayer, accordingly, is our most determinative speech. Any theology, therefore, that is finally not about helping us to pray cannot be Christian.[97]

Could you say more about how you understand the relationship of these three terms, "with, to and about" and whether or not they have an order of priority?

SH: Enda McDonagh once told me that prayer is letting God loose in the world. I think that's a lovely way to put it. It means you pray *with* God, it seems, first and foremost, rather than to God. Though, since our prayers are inadequate we pray *to* God to make them adequate for the *with*. *About* is clearly secondary. That we pray with God means we always pray that we conform to God's will prior to our will, and that's not easy. I find prayer frightening. If you are letting God loose in the world you ought to be frightened.

BB: I pair it with the Holy of Holies because Israel was held together because there was a Holy of Holies and the Shekinah dwelled there. It was an extremely dangerous place to venture into.

SH: You can't touch it!

BB: Exactly, and it seems to me that your attack on the platitudinousness of Christian prayer is a helpful *askesis* heading toward what has to sustain the Christian life, ultimately because—and this is tied in with some discussions we've also had— the saints cannot displace that Holy of Holies.

SH: Take the good people who do this: "Good Lord, we just want to ask you . . ." You hate to be critical but that language of "just" is so ugly. What does that language of "just" do? It says, "God, we know you are a powerful sonofabitch and you do what you damn well want, but we need this so we 'just' ask you . . ." How can you turn on such a good people? But I *just* think it's ugly.

BB: It's that ugliness that I find the discipline of writing personal prayer useful to expose, because of course, that ugliness *is us*. Trying not to say, "Could you please wave the magic wand?" to God is very difficult. Extremely. It puts a big dampener on the obvious things we want to say and if, furthermore, we say we are actually addressing a God who is also our judge, when we say, "I really do hate this person," we make ourselves the prime witness against ourselves in the heavenly court.

SH: The idea in prayer, oftentimes, is that we can pull one over on God! Boy, I mean, you talk about how deep our commitment to deceiving ourselves is? It's really deep.

BB: I wasn't sure how you would approach that, but I am very taken with how you have explained the relationships between "with, to, and about" by proposing that they have a hierarchical ordering. Bonhoeffer and Barth famously talked about worship and theology as the Fall. Before the Fall, we spoke *with* God, and to speak *to* God is already a sign of problems, and to speak *about* God is an extremely dangerous business. And that is what theology is.[98] After the Fall we can't avoid it, but you're playing with fire. Our most important aspiration is to speak with God, in the pneumatological sense that you've just situated it, which I would say is the way I'd like to think about it.

You make a comment in your foreword to *Disrupting Time* that also indicates another aspect of this hierarchy of different types of Christian speech. "I did not want to dedicate one of my more 'academic' books to [my grandson] Kendall. . . . I like my more 'academic' books, but often the analysis and arguments in those books have only an indirect relation to that about which I most care."[99] So, let's go a little bit further into what's at stake in the more or less direct forms of Christian language. The phrase I'm keying on is, "only an indirect relation to that about which I most care."

SH: It has to do with what we were talking about earlier, about theology assembling reminders of why it is we say something this way rather than that way. What we say is first and foremost what is found in the prayers of the church that it has taken hundreds of years to write. I listen very closely to the collects because the collects give an intensified form to the liturgy of the day. I think they are really important because they are direct addresses to God. You wouldn't want to fool around with them. That's the kind of thing that I mean by the direct form.

BB: How then do prayer and preaching relate to one another? Are both first order languages? You deploy some subtle linguistic distinctions to describe their importance to soon-to-be ministers in 2010.

> The sermon is not your reflections on how to negotiate life. The sermon rather is our fundamental speech act as Christians through which we learn the grammar of the faith. . . . Prayer is the heart of Christian speech. . . . you are called to a life of prayer.[100]

It looks like you're suggesting a distinction between sermonic speech acts as "fundamental" and prayer as the "heart" of that action. As you continue addressing them you explain that, as ministers, they are "called to help those like me learn to pray."[101] What's the precise distinction you're making here between preaching and praying?

It sounds like you are suggesting that both are primarily pedagogical activities, at least for ministers. You even present your own praying as a sort of self-formation. In *Learning to Speak Christian* you present the sermons and prayers in that book as "examples of my writing, my work, and, in particular, my attempt to work on myself so that I might be a more adequate Christian speaker."[102] Do you court a solipsistic account of prayer and preaching with this strong pedagogical emphasis?

SH: I hope not. What I hope defeats the solipsism is the very content of the prayer itself. But then, the content has to be made up of significant words that you are taught.

As far as the sermon goes? I'm not very good at it, but sermons often are prayerful, before the majesty of God, and that makes them like prayers.

BB: OK, if you put it that way, designating prayer as the most basic first order language for Christians, can we ever escape it? Can our speaking ever disavow its location within the economy of God's works or declare by fiat that it is not an address to God, and God should therefore butt out? My suspicion is that we can't, and some of your prayers could be read in this direction as well: "All I can do is ask you, Creator and Redeemer of all that is, to take this jumble of words and transform them, this class, and me into prayer."[103]

What's at stake here for me is a question about whether we should narrate the church-world distinction as "two cities" or as "two churches." In other words, your prayer seems to me to raise a fundamental question: What happens if God does not answer this prayer? How are we to understand not being rescued from the community of "jumbled words"? Will our speaking and that of the group to which we belong *not* be prayer then, or will it just not be prayer to *the Trinitarian God*? Even in your recent work you can sometimes approach such questions from natural theological starting points.

> Learning to say "God" requires that I learn to acknowledge that I am a "dependent rational animal." It may be possible to acknowledge that we are rational dependent animals without learning to say "God," but to learn to say I am dependent without regret at least creates the space the practice of prayer can occupy. To be human is to be an animal that has learned to pray. Prayer often comes only when we have no alternatives left, but prayer may also be the joy that comes from the acknowledgment of the sheer beauty, the absolute contingency of existence.[104]

This is a description articulated from outside first order and even second order Christian language. And it seems to work very well without invoking the activity of the Holy Spirit, the "praying with" that you have just spoken about, and also makes no reference to the collective reality of Christian prayer that you have emphasized today and elsewhere.[105] Perhaps the question here is best crystallized by asking whether we are in the position to say that we are human because we have (already) learned to pray as this passage seems to suggest. Is being "in the world" being a *non*-prayer, or a *misguided* prayer?

SH: I haven't thought this through, but I do want to say, the claim that we are animals that pray can be understood as a form of natural theology. I don't have any reason to resist that. And I would want to say we are more fully human just to the extent that we know how to pray.

There is also the point that Jeff Stout goes after me for saying we are first and foremost beggars.[106] But I think I am going to continue to maintain that as the truth. We are beggars before God, because we live by being gifted. We are created by God to beg so that we know how to pray. Prayer is a form of begging. It's a begging that doesn't destroy the beggar. I want to be careful. I don't want to make prayer, as you put it, an abstraction from the activity of the Holy Spirit, because we pray through the Spirit.

BB: Part of what I'm after here is a better view of the Western tradition of evil understood as deprivation. Take our current obsession with technological and biomedical enhancement. The debates we constantly have in public about whether we should clone babies or pharmaceutically enhance our brain functioning seem to me transparently to be energized by the Western secular world's understanding of what it means to be human. If our starting position for thinking about our present is the first order performances of our prayer, we get a fresh angle on what you've just called natural theology: we cannot help but beg the gods for power.

Theologically speaking, to say that the church exposes the world as world is saying nothing more than that people are already deeply enmeshed in praying to the wrong powers. The nothingness on which the Western account of evil insists is an affirmation that those powers don't "really exist" as genuine rivals to God's power. But as we say that we have to be careful not to let that theological confession of evil's nonexistence obscure the fact that we human beings are fully engaged in beseeching powers *as* gods.

SH: Absolutely! That's wonderfully put.

BB: All that's a lateral step, an internal critique of the common Augustinian description of the church and world as two cities aiming to move that discussion toward an insistence that we're always talking about the two churches. The upshot is that if we want to show the world that it is the world we need to reveal its praying to it *as prayer*; that it really is a begging from the gods. It's not as secular as it thinks it is.

SH: And nothing is worse than a false church.

BB: That's right. I take that to be the implication of learning to pray as a Christian, a learning that must reconfigure our understanding of what is going on amid the noisy activity of those who understand themselves not to be praying—which of course is going on in us as well.

You often remark that the Psalms taught you to pray,[107] and because they are " 'first order' religious convictions . . . I take a lot of comfort from the Psalms."[108] But, you continue, most Christians today are so wedded to sentimental platitudes that they "cannot imagine what kind of people would write and sing the Psalms."[109] This sounds a lot like your remark that Christians today could never manage to write a biography like Augustine's *Confessions*.

Does this also imply that Christians today are not capable of writing psalms? When you say in your *Matthew* commentary that "Jesus is God's Psalm for the world,"[110] do you mean to suggest that Jesus closes the era of Psalm writing as he closes the era of sacrifice?

SH: And prophecy.

BB: So you think the Psalter is now closed?

SH: Yes.

BB: How does taking that position situate your own prayers, your published prayers?

SH: What I learned from the Psalter is that there is nothing worse than the presumption that you need to protect God in order to pray. God is God, and God does not need protection. I think there is a constant temptation in modernity to protect God. Since we have so much trouble believing in God we think, "Well I have to make sure that God is always on the right side." We're basically atheists who think that we need to make sure that God is OK. It's perfectly fine in prayer to bring to God our desire that God be more obvious. But God refuses, and that's part of what it means to undergo the training to be a Christian and to learn to pray.

BB: Your comment that Jesus ends the writing of new Psalms is an elucidation, then, of the irreducibility of the biblical canon?

SH: Yes, absolutely.

BB: Just as we shouldn't aspire to write new biblical books but we write commentaries on the biblical books, so too our prayers are always commentaries on the biblical prayers?

SH: Right, I certainly think that's right.

The fearful joy of being Christian

BB: My last few questions jump off from observations about themes that seem to me to be more potently presented in your sermons, prayers, and sundries. If we return to where we began this conversation, it seems like we might at least be able to say that your academic writings are more cool and distant in tone, more second order when placed beside your published prayers and sermons. "I am sure that prayer rightly forces us to discover speech otherwise undiscoverable," as you note in the introduction to *Prayers Plainly Spoken*.[111] The different performative demands of sermons and prayers, as well as the different capacities of Christian first order language, allow you to connect older thoughts from your academic writings in obviously new ways, lending them a fresh starkness and urgency. It may turn out that if we adjust to the very different pace and style of these writings, they may in fact be more persuasive in important ways than your academic writing, and almost certainly extend the range and penetration of positions you have developed in second order discourse. This is how I'm reading the comment to which I referred earlier, about how Will Willimon's sermons spurred you to consider sermons to be a more potent form of argument than academic prose.[112]

I'd like to end with a few observations about themes that do seem to stand out more starkly in these texts. In my view, none of them are absent from your academic texts, but it seems obvious that they do carry a very different balance of gravity and reticence when you articulate them in first order language. I use the language of reticence here because I don't think you are ever hesitant, as you report someone saying to you in *The Work of Theology*.[113] In my view your own characterization of these writings as foregrounding the ways in which the "cross shatters" our views of God is both accurate and illuminating.[114]

Again I will just list my observations to which I'll just let you respond as you wish.

a) First, throughout your career you have been focused on the importance of the Jews for reminding Christians that their God is not some ephemeral spirit, but this theme is regularly unfolded in your sermons in a more powerful way than it is in your academic work. To take one example, "if Christian envy of the Jews is ever so effective that we are able to destroy the last Jew from the face of the earth, then God will destroy the earth. Our God is not some generalized spirit, but a fleshy God whose body is the Jews."[115] You often make such points in order to introduce much more earthy depictions of God's touch.[116]

b) The frightening God who "scares the hell out of us"[117] is much more present in your sermons and prayers than in your ethical theory with its regular recourse to the language of friendship and even friendship with God. The implicit judgment that cannot be extracted from God's holiness remains palpable in this literature.[118]

c) On a related note, there is a strong tradition in the West—from Augustine to Nietzsche—in which love of Jesus manifests as anger at a decadent church.[119] An incredible prayer in *Prayers Plainly Spoken* displays just that intertwining of love and anger[120] while another just as clearly displays a healthy self-suspicion about that anger.[121] That's obviously your exemplification of the point you've just made about how the Psalms teach us to pray without pretension. There are good theological reasons for anger and good theological reasons to be suspicious of the duplicity of our anger, and none of that should be hidden from God. Your prayers, I think, nicely show how that works.

SH: How odd of God to choose the Jews! That's a theme that's been strong. I am not sure where I got it, but I think it was from Mr. Frei. I do think the physical presence of the Jews is absolutely essential for making the gospel coherent. If you don't believe that, you are going to have great difficulty believing that God is present in Jesus Christ. That's a set of convictions that I think has been there from the beginning.

Whether the frightening God is more present in my prayers, I think the expression of it is more present in my prayers. I think the lack of presence

8. Preaching, Praying, and Primary Christian Language 285

in some of my more academic writings is hopefully an expression of my fear of God.

BB: And that's related then to your self-suspicion about your anger?

SH: One of my graduate students, a lovely guy, once told me, "Stanley, you just have to understand, I don't have a fire burning in my belly the way you do."

BB: That was honest of him.

SH: It was. I hadn't really thought about it, but I do have fire in my belly. I'm an angry sonofabitch. You don't try to be angry. It just happens to you. I get angry primarily at Christians, myself included. I think, "How in the world have we screwed this up so much, when we have been given such a great gift?" Anger is the other side of love and it helps us locate what we love. I'm not apologetic about being angry. Although, I think there are perverse forms of anger that probably seize me at times.

BB: The anecdote about your student immediately raised the question for me: How do you get through the day as a scholar and a theologian if you have no fire? There needs to be a fire, even if it's not anger. I get very nervous about there being no fire in the belly. Now that may not be what your student was saying.

SH: I don't think it was what he was saying. He is a student who really cares about preaching and now teaches in a very good seminary, but I would find it hard for any student of mine not to care. This student cares, but it doesn't translate into anger.

BB: Two personal anecdotes. First, when I went to Oxford, I discovered to my great surprise that most undergraduates in theology plan to do something else for their "real job," primarily law at that time. Why? Because theology is interesting, and I'm going to have to go dig through case law for the rest of my career, so why shouldn't I do something now that I want to do? That is to lack the fire in the belly entirely, or at least for it to be nothing more than an expression of intellectual curiosity.

When I was studying in Germany I had a different kind of shock. When I asked why the number of theological students in German universities was dropping so precipitously, I got the explanation, "Well, because there are no jobs." And I thought, "How odd!" Like most English speakers, it hadn't occurred to me that it was a condition of studying theology that there be some guaranteed job at the end of it! Maybe Socrates really was right—serving a god is a compulsion that may or may not bring you financial stability! I think those are very important considerations to keep in mind when studying theology.

SH: Absolutely!

BB: There's really only one appropriate place to end our conversation, on a theme that I've only discovered through these conversations to be shot through your work, and which is especially evident in this literature, the sundries: God's eschatological presence as indicated by joy and with it laughter. In *The Work of Theology* you emphasize that you learned from Barth that irony is intrinsic to the Christian condition because we are constantly realizing how absurd our time looks from God's eternity. If this apocalyptic time is taken into account, you say, you "regard most of what I have written as ironic,"[122] which is important because "irony is a more inclusive category than either jokes or what is funny."[123]

Joy as a mark of the new kingdom inaugurated at Pentecost is front and center in that first sermon you introduce into your academic writing. Emphasizing that the descent of the Spirit at Pentecost is a healing of the punishment of Babel, you continue that:

> the joy of that healing surely must have made them ecstatic. It is literally a joy not possible except by God's creation. It is a joy that comes from recognizing that we have been freed from our endless cycle of injury and revenge. It is the joy of unity that we experience all too briefly in moments of self-forgetfulness.[124]

The formulation seems remarkably close to the theology of joy and laughter that Luther reinvigorated for the Christian tradition in his decisive break with the tenor and sensibility of the patristic era. Luther understood this joy and laughter as the fore-presence of our redeemed state in Jesus Christ. Listen, for instance, how he speculatively fills out what was going on when Abraham laughed at the announcement that Sarah will bear a child. He first "wept for joy, until he finally regained his composure, as it were, and laughed when at last he felt this joy with a calm heart, a feeling which is a part of eternal life."[125] How would you trace the source of your theological account of joy and laughter, and what are the basic theological claims we need to keep its different valences supple and mobile?

SH: Well, you know how to answer that as quickly as I do: Barth. I learned joy is central from Barth. Joy isn't something you try to have. It's an overwhelming that you suddenly find yourself taken up in an activity that just offers satisfaction that you could not have imagined as possible. Yesterday when I came in and you and I looked at each other it was joy, wasn't it? I find it when I'm at worship, over and over, the joy of having been made part of this wonderful world that otherwise could not be imagined. I find it in the joy of the work we have been given as theologians. Funny as it is! How silly to think you could know how to talk about God? But that's what we've been given to do. I just find it a constant surprise.

To speak in another key, I wonder what it means that I'll be 76 in July. I don't have more than five—or a little more—years to live. I thought I would be afraid of death, and I may be, but I haven't experienced it that way yet. Probably because I still don't know I'm going to die. I think, one, I have had such a wonderful life and, two, whatever heaven may be, it will be joy. I don't know what it means to be part of that, but I am sure it is there, because I think that all that is is surrounded by joy.

I think the attraction of my work has everything to do with the fact that it is an enthusiasm that invites joy. To take me seriously is an invitation to do it better, and people respond to that with joy, because it gives you something to do. I really think one of the most determinative things that the gospel does to save us is to give us something to do. So many people don't have anything to do. How can you account for a Donald Trump? He didn't have anything to do. So, he's running for president. Ugh! Save us from that! He doesn't see how having children, being kind to your neighbor, gives you something to do and it gives your life joy.

BB: What a stunning formulation: "all that is is surrounded by joy." It helps me articulate something I've sensed for a while without yet being able to find the words. I'm not a naturally funny guy like you, and I never can manage to warm up a crowd with jokes. I've spoken already about this, but it has been a real satisfaction to me that our theological ethics research seminar in Aberdeen—in which a group of extremely interesting people have slowly come together to do the sort of theology that you and I care about—has become a place that regularly erupts with laughter. That to me is one of the most reassuring signs that something right has got to be going on. It probably also has to do with what you have observed about the infectiousness of enthusiasm. The analysis of joy you've just outlined gives me a nicer way to articulate why we should expect studying theology to be a joyous thing. I feel like it must have been like that for you at Yale, with Mr. Holmer and Mr. Frei, and you just never recovered from that joyous experience.

SH: Yesterday, in the research seminar, when I told that funny story I felt like there needed to be some lightening up, and I thought it kind of worked.

BB: I think the will for joy was there which you have a nose for and met with that well-timed story. Barth really got this. He discusses humor in III/4 under the overarching heading of the will for joy, which, like for the will for health, we are beholden to seek even though it can only come unbidden. Precisely because it is about God, he insists, theology should foster in us a will for joy. If we are really doing theology, joy should be in attendance.

SH: The difficulty of course is the will for joy makes you so liable to disappointment. That's why you also need to see how the will for joy invites you to, for example, have the virtue of courage to sustain it.

BB: And with that the cruciformity of the Christian life reappears. Again, Barth is very precise on this: discouragement and patience are the enduring conditions of genuine joy because we do not inhabit the final joy, and therefore we will only experience an anticipatory joy in part and at times. That's a real joy even if it is also not the fullness for which we wait.

We've been having a nice chat about what we both learned from Barth, but as we've done so I've also been trying to figure out why I feel a little discomfort at your assertion a while back that we are in the same tradition. I've only gotten as far as thinking it must have something to do with how long you've spent in a given discursive community. I've just been out of the live American Christian ethics conversation ever since the first few years of my training.

I think one of the ways this sensation crystallizes a bit for me comes by noting how Barth's treatment of joy is very brief in III/4, but extremely sophisticated and theologically literate in a historically deep sense. If you were seriously studying what is, remarkably, only a ten page discussion, you'd be led backward into a rich continental tradition of philosophy and biblical studies. He's in constant dialogue with that continental tradition, right? Nietzsche famously foregrounded joy as he wrestled with the dour affective flatness of secularity in comparison with his reading of the ancient Greeks,[126] the pessimism of his precursor Schopenhauer,[127] and the dark clouds of glowering disapproval in Christianity that he found corroborated in passages throughout the patristic tradition.[128] Barth is responding to all those discussions and more.

I bring that up because I feel like the modern traditions that continue to resource me are largely continental. You have long read analytical and modern American philosophy. It's now becoming much clearer to me, given that reading habit, how remarkable it is that you, on this topic and many others, are often reinventing the wheel in a North American context. Now you could say that all of *Christian Existence Today* is a reinvention of the wheel. You are saying, "OK, I've got to talk to pastors in this context and I'm in a tradition that doesn't really work very seriously with it and what they do I can't abide, so I'm just going to think about what's going on in a church as it decides whether to move out of a poor area or not." The continental tradition would have had a practical theology corpus dealing with many of the questions that might arise in such a discussion, all presented very *Wissenschaftlich*.

SH: Which would be unfortunate as far as I'm concerned.

BB: Exactly! But to extricate yourself from a tradition that has covered all the bases already is different from the position you were in where all that had just fallen away. You were left thinking that you needed to develop fresh ways of talking about all sorts of things. *The Blackwell Companion* is a *de novo* entity. It really is. It's a marker of the ways in which you often were forced by what you experienced as the poverty of your tradition to develop new thoughts. What continually impresses me is how fertile you were in finding ways to pull that off. Most of us are just too superficial to manage it, which is why these older and thicker traditions seem to offer us a fully stocked toolshed we can just rummage around in to find ideas that will be useful.

SH: It wasn't anything I was trying to do, it's just what I did.

BB: It simply has to be pointed out here, though, that it is remarkable enough to see that something no one else is thinking or doing needs to be done and is an order of magnitude more impressive to point to what is missing in a way that tempts people actually to try to live it. And you did that.

SH: I remember once, Oliver [O'Donovan] and I were at a meeting in Germany for a seminar of German theologians, and someone said something about my presentation. Oliver was very sympathetic with what I had done. He said, "Well, he's doing the best he can in a church in freefall self-destruction." I thought that was insightful. I think that is consistent with the observations you were just making.

BB: It's certainly the case that the incredible weight of the continental tradition can crush the plain speaking out of anyone, and even stunt any capacity to come to terms with life-events that you need to come to terms with, because you can find yourself believing that it will simply take too long to get the background study done if you are going to say something.

Two last questions about joy.

How do you understand joy playing in the Christian life? Sometimes you pray about joy as something you do not have, but desire, comparing this longing to what Augustine meant when he said that our hearts are restless until they rest in God.[129] In *Cross-Shattered Christ* you strike a note of the older tradition by saying that you could not see your way to introduce your trademark humor into your sermons on Christ's seven last words.[130] At the same time, in your prayers you speak of joy as the believer's assurance of God's care,[131] something that is discovered in prayer, and when found, makes prayer "effortless work."[132] That was the only time I'd seen you using that particular language, though you just used it to describe writing the commentary. It's a nice theologically loaded way of naming that activity. You even write a "humor prayer" in which you ask God to "make us laugh, and in the laughter may the world be so enthralled by your entertaining presence that we lose the fear that fuels our violence."[133]

When you get down to discussing the Christian ministry the ambiguity evaporates: the minister must be constant and have faith. Only this combination will yield joy in the ministry. "[W]e must ask of those in the ministry whether they are capable of joy, if they are not they lack a character sufficient to their calling. For a person incapable of joy will lack the humor necessary for the self-knowledge that character requires."[134]

SH: I love those sentences.

BB: They are good. In them one senses why you understand freedom and joy to be essential constituents of sermon preparation, and why you hope this joy is contagious and makes people laugh, because "humor is correlative to an apocalyptic perspective."[135] Is joy for you a synonym for "lived eschatology"?

SH: Well, the easy answer to that is yes! Right! I think it is. It refers back to your earlier comment about what it means to live in the light of God's eternity. Yes, I think humor is so important. Humor is not taking yourself seriously. Humor is taking yourself as a creature before God in a manner that the alternative of seriousness or non-seriousness is not determinative of our lives.

BB: As we draw our conversations to a close, I want to make an observation about one of your most recent books, *The Work of Theology*. There are only two chapters that end with prayers from *Prayers Plainly Spoken*, "How to Be Theologically Ironic," and "How to be Theologically Funny." I do not know if this was intentional or not, but it seems noteworthy to me that in the end you can't articulate a description of two of your most well-known modes of speech without invoking three terms: worship,[136] prayer,[137] and joy[138]—and then proceed to perform this invocation in first order Christian speech. What seems to be going on here is stated more descriptively at the end of *Matthew*:

> The world is not what it appears to be, because sin has scarred the world's appearance. The world has been redeemed—but to see the world's redemption, to see Jesus, requires that we be caught up in the joy that comes from serving him. That is what it means to live apocalyptically.[139]

These are the passages that I see as having come to anchor the grammar of your mature work, or at least it would be these linguistic performances to which I would point if I was asked why it is that you find these "sundries" your most important work.

SH: "Apocalyptic is the disruption of time by God's time so that time might be redeemed. Apocalyptic means that there is another world, another time than the one in which we live; but it turns out to be the same world in which we live. As Rainer Maria Rilke puts it: 'There is another world, the same as this one.'"[140]

That's what I think. I think that's what it means to live in apocalyptic time. The refusal to let the old world overwhelm the world that we have been given in Christ is the great adventure.

BB: I could not agree more, neither could I have hoped for a better thought on which to conclude.

AFTERWORD

THE END WAS THERE IN THE BEGINNING

Brian Brock and Kevin Hargaden

Ours is not the first attempt to offer guidance to readers wishing to dip their toes in the ocean of text produced by an uncommonly prolific writer over a forty year writing career. The most well known readers' guide is the insightful treatment of Michael Cartwright appended to *The Hauerwas Reader*.[1] This afterword will offer neither a map of Hauerwas's main ideas[2] nor an account of their chronological development.[3] Our more modest aim is to suggest that Hauerwas is best understood by readers who have become alert to certain theological threads that arise at sensitive points throughout his writings. Put as precisely as we can, our interest is in resourcing future readers who wish to discover a genuinely theological Hauerwas beyond those versions supposedly reducible to an obsession with America, pacifism, virtue theory, and so on. Because it has not been sufficiently recognized how deeply woven and enduring the theological threads in Hauerwas's thinking are, debates about the balance or coherence of Hauerwas's theology have proliferated and have by now become rather stale. Given the regularity with which he has deployed indirect modes of theological communication, it is not surprising that these debates have arisen. Our modest aim in entering this fray is to display what we think are the most important senses in which his apparently nontheological arguments are funded by robustly theological commitments. Our hope then, is to have achieved a twofold goal: to have revealed the enduring theological wellsprings of Hauerwas's work, and to have done so in a manner that will allow these insights to be taken forward by a new generation.

As is by now well known, Stanley Hauerwas has arrived at his office every weekday at 6 a.m. to work long days. This is just the sort of disciplined habit that makes one a successful and productive scholar. But has the habit made "Stanley"? While it is clear that only a negative reply will do here, it seems just as clear that somehow this practice was an important condition for Stanley to become "Stanley." The question remains, however, what attending to this habit could tell us about the features of Stanley's writings that really sparkle, are incisive to the point of forcing the reader to pay attention. Were stubborn discipline all that was needed to write like he does, there would be a lot more Stanleys in the academy. How then might we take Stanley's long-standing emphasis on habit and virtue seriously without simply reducing him to being an epiphenomenon of those habits?

One might think that a figure as influential as Hauerwas would have been appreciated for his own distinctive merits, but this has often not been the case—if it is ever true of first generation receptions. In this volume Brock has attempted to tease out specific ways in which Hauerwas transcends several types of reductionist reading. To do so has meant holding Hauerwas's own self-descriptions at a critical distance as was on display in their discussions of his 1980 AAR speech as well as the thought that went into "constructing Stanley" in the writing of *Hannah's Child*.[4]

One of the more widespread tendencies among contemporary interpreters has been to read Hauerwas as philosophically indistinguishable from Alasdair MacIntyre, a line made plausible by Hauerwas's own self-descriptions and the duration of his intellectual engagement with MacIntyre. In *Three Rival Versions of Moral Enquiry* MacIntyre famously suggested that every late modern thinker cannot escape taking up one of three all-determining starting points: that of the encyclopaedist, the genealogist, or the Aristotelian/Thomist.[5] MacIntyre himself clearly opts for the Aristotelian/Thomist approach, though one much more deeply informed by the genealogist's sensitivities than is often appreciated by many of the new Thomists. The regularity with which Hauerwas uses virtue langue as well as his emphasis on the importance of habit in Christian ethics has led many readers to see him as teaming up with MacIntyre to breathe new life into a Thomist virtue theory shorn of its more embarrassing aspects.

This is a reading that we think underplays the role Christology and the critique of religion have played in Hauerwas's thought, which position him closer to the pure genealogical approach of which MacIntyre is so critical.[6] Hauerwas often proceeds by way of genealogical forms of argument that shake the reader's sense of certainty about their commonsense notions of ethically potent but historically specific ideas such as family, childhood, or old age. Hauerwas and MacIntyre do both affirm the Aristotelian insistence that our moral beliefs are always embedded in everyday language and the forms of life that sustain them in our respective communities.[7] Hauerwas is fond of reminding readers of the fluidity this introduces into Christian ethics by quoting Gerard Manley Hopkins: "the just man, justices."[8] What we call justice is always configured by frameworks of intelligibility we inherit from some community. But the way that justice is born among human beings cannot but receive subtle but substantively different explanations from the two thinkers since Hauerwas ultimately sees the existence of such communities as an artifact of God's gracious refusal to leave humans alone.

In the course of the conversations in this book it has become clearer how deeply and early Hauerwas drank from the wells of Barth with his complex relation to natural knowledge. Barth is highly suspicious of Christian moral reasoning beginning with the assumption that our common sense can be equated with Christian faithfulness, as if the morality that it decrees could be taken as mediating the divine claim. The issue is ultimately an epistemic one: How and to what extent is the common sense by which our moral landscape is made intelligible *true* in relation to the story of the Christian gospel? Hauerwas, MacIntyre, and Barth all agree that our common sense is true in some sense and also misguided or self-destructive in some sense. Setting Stanley between MacIntyre and Barth allows us to begin to see that, though all three assume that common sense must be criticized, Barth and Hauerwas assume that criticism and reorientation of our common sense toward a theological rationality takes place in our being inducted into the practice of first-order Christian speech that is primarily learned in the apocalyptic space that is Christian worship.[9] In our view one of the more important contributions of this volume is to display how routinely Hauerwas points to this theological affirmation as decisively orienting his creative and critical forays into a range of different linguistic and practical domains.

Similar questions can be raised about Hauerwas's relation to John Howard Yoder, with all its tragic complications. Again we need to distinguish Yoder's actual influence on Hauerwas from Hauerwas's own various accounts of his relation to a man whom he considered a friend and admired for his intellect and theological work. The importance of avoiding conflating the two is revealed by the subtle but importantly different methodological starting points of their two Gospel commentaries. Yoder, aiming to be *Wissenschaftlich*, considered his commentary nothing more than a summary of the best and most interesting historical critical work on the Gospel of Luke. Hauerwas, in contrast, insists that the secular history assumed by the historical critics never really existed because time, space, and reason are not entities knowable by natural reason alone. They are not, Hauerwas asserts, because we can only know that "there was a beginning, because we have seen the end in the life, death, and resurrection of Jesus Christ."[10]

That Hauerwas's distinctive emphasis on the particularity and everydayness of Christian faith grows directly from Christological affirmations is made clear in a chapter we take to be indispensable for any genuinely theological understanding of his body of work, the essay in *Community of Character* entitled "Jesus: The Story of the Kingdom."[11] Extending the Social Gospelers's emphasis on the Kingdom of God as the central term in Christian ethics, Hauerwas's decisive move is to insist that we only properly understand it by way of a high Christology. This insistence is immediately linked with an equally robust account of an eschatology with significant revelatory force. He concludes, quoting Warren Groff, that

> The person-event of Christ precedes particular responses of faith. Yet it is precisely by means of such responses—those of the original witnesses no less than their successors—that revelation has its on-going content and power. So completely is the truth of faith tied in with what is transmitted historically. Christological language is meaningful in relation to the actual life and impact of the man Jesus.[12]

To protect this prioritization of the eschatological rule of Jesus Christ, Hauerwas firmly resists all attempts to distill the teaching or example of Jesus into moral principles or programs. He likewise repudiates all attempts to collate some list of biblical passages in order to lay out "the" Christian social ethic. "[T]his strategy is doomed to fail because such norms fail to do justice to the eschatological character of the kingdom."[13]

In short, we cannot have Jesus without being claimed by and co-opted into his sphere of rule, and it is the cross that most clearly displays the form of his rule. It is this cruciform grammar that establishes the demand that Christians "rethink our everyday sense of the 'political.'"[14] The domain of Christ's rule brings into the world service to and love of others as expressions of the presumption that Christians have in themselves no power to secure outcomes. Jesus's kingdom is therefore one that will only be received by those content to live in reliance on God's intervention. Having thickened and reinforced the Christological and eschatological themes in the Social Gospel tradition in this manner Hauerwas is positioned to conclude with an appreciative citation from Walter Rauschenbusch:

> Christ's kingdom needs not the spears of the Roman legionnaires to prop it, not even the clubs of Galilean Peasants. Whenever Christianity shows an inclination to use constraint in its own defense or support, it thereby furnishes presumptive evidence that it has become a thing of this world, for it finds the minds of this world adapted to its end.[15]

Here Hauerwas is both owning his continuity with the Social Gospel tradition and signaling why he resisted the deflated Christologies that came to dominate it. It was the Christological atrophying of this tradition, he believed, that rendered it incapable of sustaining the critique of the Constantinian co-option of the church that had become so important to him. His diagnosis of the malaise of this tradition of Christian ethics made Yoder attractive to him, whose ringing apocalyptic notes could be used to resource Hauerwas's interest in disengaging the church from national interests.

We would make the further and more contentious claim that a full appreciation of "Jesus: The Story of the Kingdom" is best served by noticing how fundamentally Hauerwas's theological instincts are shaped by Barth.[16] Yoder is at least sometimes tempted to look to methodologically secular historians to tell us about Jesus. Following Barth, however, Hauerwas never wavers in his insistence that only being claimed by Jesus can disclose what history is.[17] This divergence is important because of the ways it positions the role played by God's self-revelation. And though it has not yet made a significant impact in the voluminous secondary literature, Hauerwas does indeed supply such an account. If it is only in being co-opted by the rule of Jesus Christ that we come to know what history truly is, it follows that revelation cannot be a past-tense event, something that happened in a certain place any number of centuries ago. It must still be happening. Jesus's death and resurrection must be present through his Lordly ruling of world history, in the way suggested by the prophet Isaiah (and echoing our chapter title): I am God, and there is no one like me, declaring the end from the beginning and from ancient times things not yet done, saying, "My purpose shall stand, and I will fulfill my intention."

Whatever his reasons for hesitating to speak directly about it, it is equally clear that revelation—including manifestation, annunciation, the ruling of the Spirit—is indispensable to Hauerwas's entire theological project. As he emphasized several times in these conversations, to be a Christian is to have been faced with the total claim of Jesus Christ: "Apocalyptic is the disruption of time by God's time so that time might be redeemed. Apocalyptic means that there is another world, another time, than the one in which we live; but it turns out to be the same world in which we live."[18] Such a claim is foreign to MacIntyre and differently enough comported in Yoder that he must explain why he diverges from Barth.[19] In the conversations gathered in this volume we repeatedly see Brock bringing Hauerwas to articulate more clearly and in much more detail how this apocalyptic horizon of the Lordship of Jesus Christ inflects a range of Hauerwas's typical formulations and theological moves.

Hauerwas's emphasis on the rule of Christ is also characterized by another long-standing emphasis: a staunch refusal of the individualism so characteristic of modern liberal thought and post-reformation accounts of the church. The conversations in this volume flesh out Hauerwas's reasons for insisting on the irreducibility of the church. One of the more important reasons for his reticence to speak directly of God's ruling and self-revelation is his desire not to draw attention away from the worshipping community as the indispensable space given to human beings in which to encounter the apocalypse of Christ.[20]

The persistent emphasis Hauerwas has laid on the role played by the church in God's economy allows him great freedom to point to the working of the Trinitarian God and the wholly free activity of the Holy Spirit in many domains of human life. This complex of thoughts also situates the central terms in Hauerwas's ethics—friendship and virtue—as we see in this typical formulation from *Christians among the Virtues*.

> For the church, no description holds more authority than that reiterated so often in the Epistles, namely that the church is a body with many parts, each with its own beauty and difference. As gifts of the Spirit, these differences are less learned in a virtue friendship, more supplied directly from God, who is building the kingdom through the church. Yet they do not exist separate from the friendship—indeed, they inhere in it, for as Paul sees them, they include gifts such as exhortation, wisdom, diligence, and even cheerfulness.[21]

It is true that at times Hauerwas seems to be presenting the church *itself* as the horizon for intelligible Christian action as in comments like; "Christian beliefs about God, Jesus, sin, the nature of human existence, and salvation are intelligible only if they are seen against the background of the church—that is, a body of people who stand apart from the 'world' because of the peculiar task of worshiping a God whom the world knows not."[22] While such claims have led many to accuse

Hauerwas of leaving the church to do all the work in his theology, we believe that the conversations in this book establish that the claim that central Christian affirmations are only intelligible "against the background of the church" is itself only theologically intelligible as an expression of the more basic affirmation that the church is neither intelligible nor actual if God is not establishing and sustaining it as the kingdom of Jesus Christ.

Our reading is not imposed on Hauerwas's texts. Nor did he develop it simply in response to criticisms of his supposed "ecclesiocentricity." This is already evident in the early 1980s:

> It is not as if we [Christians] are the kingdom, or that the Church is even the beginning of the kingdom but that as a people Christians can begin to point to the fact that the kingdom has been and is present in our midst.... That the fruit of the Spirit is such is not an accident as we can risk being peaceful in a violent world, risk being kind in a competitive society, risk being faithful in an age of cynicism, risk being gentle among those who admire the tough, risk love when it may not be returned, because we have the confidence that in Christ we have been reborn into a new reality.[23]

Insofar as this theme could be said to have come more obviously to the surface of Hauerwas's writings in the past decade, it is not because he has changed his position, but because he has wrestled in more sustained ways with its practical and metaphysical entailments. The essay "Bearing Reality," to which he referred several times in the conversations in this volume, is an important example of Hauerwas's thickening account of the entailments of this basic affirmation. And this richer account helps him clarify for his critics that "there is indeed something the church cannot do. The church cannot make the difficulty of reality less difficult. What I hope the church can do, a hope that I think is the heart of Yoder's work, is help us bear the difficulty without engaging in false hopes."[24]

Hauerwas's enduring interest in Yoder's apocalypticism lay in its power to catalyze his thinking about how an ethics of Christian witness must result in a doxological vision of the whole of creation and history. Since it is God's revelatory, and behind that creative, work that begins everything, only worship can be the appropriate end of creatures. The role of Christian ethics in the contemporary world is in this way dramatically resituated. The community that can only be imagined if Christ has in fact been raised from the dead is one that has been raised to see history doxologically. This means that "we do not bear reality alone, but rather we share the load by being called to participate in the body of Christ."[25]

By the early 1990s Hauerwas had explicitly laid out why this resituating of Christian ethics within an apocalyptic account of divine activity should be understood as a fundamental component of his Constantinian critique. Constantinianism names the assumption by Christians that they have a stake in the power of the state since causal relations are cyclical and therefore predictable. The self-evidence of such causal relationships leads to the embrace of the responsibility to describe and reshape them toward good outcomes. Remarkably, it is at just this point that Hauerwas finds the connection between apocalyptic and Wittgenstein, in his claim that "The truly apocalyptic view of the world is that things do *not* repeat themselves."[26] Only if the Crucified one is in fact ruling human history are Christians warranted in refusing to make pragmatic compromises with the normal order of power and force. The active ruling of Jesus Christ again appears as the condition for any Christian capacity to "risk being peaceful in a violent world, risk being kind in a competitive society, risk being faithful in an age of cynicism, risk being gentle among those who admire the tough, risk love when it may not be returned."[27] Thus, again, "It is the Eucharistic community that is the epistemological prerequisite for understanding 'how things are.' Only as we stand in the reality of the Eucharist can we see that 'the causal point of view' is not the final truth of our lives."[28]

Nowhere is the intense practicality of this theoretical insistence more penetratingly deployed than in his response to the attack on the Twin Towers, written during a time of acute distress for the American polity. "So we find ourselves in the midst of two apocalyptic events," he begins, by which he means the in-breaking of Jesus Christ and political terror. "These events produce two people with two quite different stories. The one fears and worships death as their only lord; the other fears and worships the Lord of death."[29] The point is reiterated by entitling a subsequent collection of sermons *Disrupting Time*. In introducing that book he affirms that Christians do indeed "believe we live in a disrupted time," but the crucial question is *which* disruption is determinative of our self-narration? Because all such narratives so deeply shape what will count for us as right and wrong action, we need constantly to be reminded of the disruption of causality that really matters: the one that happened in 33 AD.[30]

Returning to the question of the extent to which it is his habits that have made "Stanley," we are now in a better position to indicate the substantive point we think has sustained Hauerwas's enduring emphasis on virtue and habit. What becomes clear on close reading is that he does not deploy these terms in a manner that fits easily with the conventions of contemporary virtue theory, including MacIntyre's. We understand his continual refusal to offer a definition or even a list of the attributes of justice in preference for phrases like "the just man justices" as a resistance to any displacement of initiative from moral agents. The subject-centered account of Christian ethics developed in Hauerwas's earliest works endures. Christian sanctification demands that agents take responsibility for their lives and also that any attempt at the complete specification of the good act by ethicists is prone to overturning the centrality of agent-centered ethical deliberation. Setting this emphasis beside Hauerwas's increasing insistence on attending to the central role played by contingency in the moral life, we begin to see how an agent capable of genuinely good acts in a local context is responding to many layers of contingent considerations that in principle could never be specified beforehand.

At the same time Hauerwas's use of the language of narrative and virtue can obscure the reality that in his writing he is not just trying to offer us a comprehensive theory (like Milbank, for instance) nor a logically coherent and so ultimately closed narrative with all loose ends tied up as demanded, for instance, by the logic of the novel. His lifelong deployment of the essayistic style can be read as effecting a long string of offers to modern Christians of snippets of advice and tips for living, practical shortcuts about how we might "get the job done" of being Christians in our time and place. The potency of this approach rests on timing and perspicuity. It is at this point that we discover the inner link between Hauerwas's emphasis on practical reason, everyday Christian life, and apocalyptic. The "radical ordinary" is politically fertile precisely because it is here that we must step out into life lived in the embrace of Jesus's cruciform rule.

In order to embrace this rule, however, we must perceive it, and in recent efforts Hauerwas has been at pains to fill out how Christian ethics is centrally concerned with pointing to the words by which God has chosen to reveal the ongoing rule of Jesus Christ. This perception can never transcend the eschatological tension that also shaped the lives of the disciples and Christ-followers whose stories are recounted in the New Testament. As a result—and here we should recall our opening discussion of the unsettling of common sense bequeathed by the critique of religion on Hauerwas's approach—"Christians are a people who may never quite know who and where they are. That means descriptions are never settled."[31] This affirmation also explains why the church is irreducible, because "any Christianity abstracted from flesh-and-blood manifestations of the lordship of Christ embodied in concrete communities of witness would, in fact, no longer be recognizable to those whose lives [the Gospel writers] sought to narrate—that is, to Christians."[32] This is what Hauerwas means in claiming that the church is the world that has been turned upside down in acquiring another politics and habit of seeing.

Having set out this tightly interweaved set of insights we are emboldened to take one step further and to propose that the term "radical ordinary" is a more revealing descriptor of the central focus of Hauerwas's analytical eye than the language of virtue, tied as it most often is to generic interpretative frameworks. This is, of course, to take up a critical stance to the claim he uttered often in these conversations, "Why do we have to choose?" We think that a choice about how different strands of his thought are to be weighted in relation to one another materially affects how we read the ethical entailments of his thought. For instance, we think that what is most important about Hauerwas's use of bricklaying as a paradigm example of Christian ethics is the ways it focuses our attention on the infinite number of constant adjustments to local, contingent variations that are going on when the bricklayer is producing outcomes that look like they should—straight and true—like saints. As Hauerwas put it in the sermon he preached at his father's funeral, "To lay rock well you must see each rock individually yet in relation to what may be the next rock to be laid. To see each rock requires a humility founded on the love of the particular that so characterized my father's life."[33]

To read Hauerwas in this way allows us to see the stories told by Vanier, for instance, as displaying the importance of this art of particular judgment. His capacity to tell just the right story about a specific person to a particular audience with their particular questions and confusions is what makes his speech memorable. We have seen throughout these conversations that Hauerwas's theology is also positioned by constant judgments about context and audience. Vanier's telling of *this* story in *this* context thus performs a different type of judgment than the ones authors of the novels on which Hauerwas so often draws must make, marked as they are by a drive to narrative coherence that the aphoristic story resists in speech, and the essay in writing. Could we even follow this logic to its conclusion and say that Hauerwas has all along been *displaying* the form Christian life takes when lived in eschatological expectation? In light of the rule of Jesus Christ, Christians are freed from playing the strategists' long game of ensuring the future into the rebel's search for the best tactics for attending to the wounds of their neighbors, knowing they are themselves wounded, vulnerable, and even at times self-deceived. If this reading is true to the most important impulses of Hauerwas's work, it can only be sustained alongside the admission that, like all of us, he has enacted such a life at times better than he has been able to explain it.

In short, the self-evidence of the insights that Hauerwas has been able to provoke with his arguments and jokes could be said to constitute their revelatory or apocalyptic character. His writings and especially their oral performances have often powerfully exposed the common sense of Christians as worldly and distorting of our perception. This has often been accomplished by way of pithy comparisons with commonsense views of previous Christians in all their dissimilarity to ours. His constant enjoinder to Christians to become more creative by refusing to resort to the easy answer of force can likewise be read as an expression of messianic expectation for the arrival of the Kingdom of God. This also suggests that, like the detective novels that he so thoroughly enjoys, Hauerwas's writing aims neither to "capture" the everyday ordinary in a comprehensive description nor to "tell a good story" that entertains and intellectually distracts us. It is better understood as configured to direct our attention in a theologically informed way to our own utterly particular lives by pointing us to the cracks in the routines that govern them. These pointers are invitations to enter the unlived alternatives that will be discovered by those who seek the peace and truth that Jesus Christ through the Spirit is already holding out to us—but which we habitually overlook and resist in our preference for the results that can undoubtedly be gained by relying on power and violence.

If this reconstruction of Hauerwas's emphasis on habit formation and virtue is on the right track, it suggests that the force of his enduring stress on habit formation might be glossed in this way: "Look and pray to be given exemplars both near you and in the stories of the saints who make Christ's rule tangible and so can serve as a template for your own efforts to orient your action and intelligibly narrate your own story." In *Resident Aliens* this line of thinking is explored and the assumption that it rests upon—that it requires first Jesus's revelatory disruption to be perceived—is stated explicitly. "There is no substitute for 'saints'—palpable, personal examples of the Christian faith—because, as Jesus knew that day he set a child in the midst of his disciples, we cannot know the Kingdom unless our eyes are opened to see it."[34] The church serves this quest not only by preserving and handing on the stories of saintly exemplars but also in training us to speak the first-order speech through which Christians learn to speak of themselves and how to speak to God. With this vocabulary a new, unified, coherent account of their own lives can emerge. Exemplars in the use of Christian first-order language also serve as moral exemplars for Hauerwas, and it was this aspect of Hauerwas's account that Brock probed several times when asking how Hauerwas would conceive virtuous action when virtuous exemplars were apparently unavailable. Hauerwas has occasionally answered such questions by saying that having good exemplars requires a bit of good luck, and here Brock was able to evoke several important clarifications about how this might be narrated in terms of advent, revelation, or the work of the Holy Spirit.

For readers intrigued by this presentation of the animating center of Hauerwas's work, we offer a few hints in conclusion to guide readers toward the thread we have just suggested holds the whole corpus together.

At the center of his memoir Hauerwas arrays in usefully terse compass the main theological themes that have oriented his thinking over the years.[35] His life with Anne, he begins, should not be understood as an "experience" that inflected his theology, which would be to grant his subjectivity far too defining a role in his account of God and reality. But through that marriage he did learn how to live without believing himself to be in control of events—which, he explains, is one of the entailments of his affirmation of human creaturely status as well as the importance of narrative in shaping our concrete responses to the lives we have been given. This is a metaphysical claim learned from Barth, he continues. Yoder is then invoked to emphasize the eschatological horizon that the gospel constantly forces on Christians, given its insistence that the Kingdom of Heaven is more real than the time and history of unbelievers and governing powers. These introductory points lead to this central statement:

> My claim, so offensive to some, that the first task of the church is to make the world the world, not to make the world more just, is a correlative of this theological metaphysics. The world simply cannot be narrated—the world cannot have a story—unless a people exist who make the world the world. That is an eschatological claim that presupposes we know there was a beginning only because we have seen the end. That something had to start it all is not what Christians mean by creation. Creation is not "back there," though there is a "back there" character to creation. Rather, creation names God's continuing action, God's unrelenting desire for us to want to be loved by that love manifest in Christ's life, death and resurrection.[36]

Narrative is necessary for Christian ethics because Christian reality descriptions are irreducibly eschatological. This same narrative punctures our sinful, self-justifying, and so self-deceptive desire to tell our story independently of the gospel story, to "talk Christian" without having to admit where and how we live our lives by the laws of force and strategy by which the world achieves its objectives. In short, Hauerwas's persistent resistance to the Constantinian co-option of the church has been designed to emphasize the qualitative difference between the ways of worldly power and the ways of the Prince of Peace. "Stated differently," he concludes, "my early concerns about the truth of Christian convictions were political—not epistemological."[37]

The whole thrust of Hauerwas's dissertation, *Character in the Christian Life*, is very easily read as an attempt to repair and supplement Barth, an impression that becomes clearest if we begin with its fourth chapter. "Barth's exposition of the Christian life," he says, "is not so much wrong for what he says, but for what he does not say."[38] Here his main criticism is that Barth does not take the language of character seriously enough because he thinks of the Christian life as a series of atomistic acts and has strong reservations about agents claiming a unified past. As we have seen in the course of the conversations in this book, both sides of this equation remain in play right into Hauerwas's late wrestling with the theme of repentance.

It is also illuminating to attend to the first line of the fifth chapter of the programmatic work *The Peaceable Kingdom*: "Everything I have done in this book has been preparation for this chapter."[39] Though earlier chapters have emphasized habits and virtues, and though this chapter begins with talk about imitating Jesus, at the heart of the chapter is the eschatological picture of the Kingdom of God that we have seen Hauerwas later calling apocalyptic.

> [T]he proclamation of the coming kingdom of God, its presence, and its future coming is a claim about *how* God rules and the establishment of that rule through the life, death, and resurrection of Jesus. Thus the Gospels portray Jesus not only offering the possibility of achieving what were heretofore thought to be impossible ethical ideals. He actually proclaims and embodies a way of life that God has made possible here and now. . . . he proclaims that the kingdom is *present* insofar as his life reveals the effective power of God to create a transformed people capable of living peaceably in a violent world.[40]

What is also clear is that this life is a cruciform one that demands a continual renunciation of the certainties of the believer.

In the course of these conversations the origins of these emphases have become clearer and none is more surprising than Paul Holmer's influence at Yale. Despite the fact that he has rarely written on Holmer, it is equally striking that this Kierkegaard scholar shaped Hauerwas's reception of the Danish philosopher while pointing him toward Wittgenstein and Barth, displaying the role novels play in thinking about ethics and theology, and even demonstrating a humorous and ironic stance within the academy remarkably close to the persona taken up by the young Hauerwas. Excavation of his work will no doubt indicate in much more obvious ways how the apocalyptic thread in Hauerwas's work is intrinsically tied to his constant and central critique of Constantinianism—despite the fact that Hauerwas himself has usually attributed his anti-Constantinianism to the influence of Yoder.

The apocalyptic framing of the whole *Matthew* commentary appears most visibly in the first chapter, though it is a constant refrain throughout the book. The methodological import of this framing becomes most obvious in the way it inflects the categories of virtue ethics in his treatment of the Beatitudes in the Sermon on the Mount of *Matthew* (chapter 5). This framing of his commentary is by no means new, but we find it here in a polished and nuanced form.

In his late work the apocalyptic and eschatological edge of Hauerwas's work becomes much more pronounced, especially in his sermons and commentaries. When teamed with an appreciation of the full scope of his Constantinian critique it becomes clear how throughout his work he has been constantly "queering" the idea of natural theology as well as common-sense usages of familiar terms like casuistry and virtue.

The claim that "Karl Barth is the great 'natural theologian' of the Gifford Lectures"[41] in *With the Grain of the Universe* is as good an example of Hauerwas's queering of terms of art as one could hope to find. These lectures offer an extended explication of Hauerwas's previously stated emphasis on the importance of a visible church populated by Christians engaged in determinative practices. The claim that "Christian orthodoxy cannot be Christian truth without living Christians"[42] again springs from an apocalyptic sensibility, and here Hauerwas explicitly signals its source in Barth. Christians cannot engage with the world "on the basis of a general or human responsibility interpreted as the responsibility to conscience or to supposed or real orders and forces of the cosmos. Rather, every person is to be addressed as one who exists and stands in the light of Jesus Christ."[43] Christian witness is the event by which the revelation of God is unveiled.

This thread is taken up again in *Approaching the End* where the rupturing force of an encounter with Jesus is contrasted with what appears to be the straightforward ways of the world. Christian witnessing to Jesus is not like the witness in a law court who is called "to testify dispassionately to events they may have seen or head, like bits of facts that have no bearing on their own lives and that they pass over to judge or jury to do with as they please."[44] It is a disruption that "lives with them daily, shaping the contours of their lives henceforth."[45] This is so, he continues, because Jesus's disciples:

> are called to be witnesses to the reality of a new age, a new time, constituted by his life, death, and resurrection. Apocalypse is the name given to describe the inauguration of this new beginning. The story of Jesus is the story of a new creation, the telling of which cannot but challenge the reigning stories that legitimate the practices of the old age.[46]

The essay "How to Tell Time Theologically" in *The Work of Theology* clarifies the centrality of the apocalyptic horizon in Hauerwas's thinking. Following on the work of Oscar Cullmann, Hauerwas notes that it is its account of time "that makes Christianity so offensive in modernity."[47] That Christians gather for worship on the Eighth day testifies to the "conviction that the resurrection of Jesus was a new creation," and that "entails the belief that the eternal can be present in time."[48] Put slightly differently later on, "Christians believe they exist in the time God enacted in the Son. Accordingly Christians tell time on the basis of that enactment."[49] It is the liturgical calendar, not the Gregorian calendar, the International Fixed calendar,[50] or even the quarterly reports of multinational firms, which shapes the sacramental worship of the people of God. This time "is made possible by forgiveness" and is encountered in worship where "the Lord can remind us we have been given all the time we need to be reconciled to one another and thus to God."[51] The Christian so reminded must "submit to an extended exercise and training" that helps them come to terms with being temporal creatures.[52] Hauerwas's emphases on habits and virtues, his alleged ecclesiocentrism, his preoccupation with peaceableness—so many of the classic themes commonly associated with his work are brought together here. They are brought together under the shadow of God's breaking-in on the time of this world, which gives us "a way to go on in which hope overwhelms despair."[53] The apocalypse of God is the revelation of a hope we could not hope to imagine.

In Hauerwas's most recent work, *The Holy Spirit*, cowritten with Will Willimon, the apocalyptic is never far from the surface. Both authors were raised in the Methodist Holiness tradition, and when it comes to explaining the day-by-day reality of Christian sanctification, they declare that "the Holy Spirit is 'from another world' because the Holy Spirit is God. Yet through the work of the Holy Spirit that 'other world' turns out to be the same world in which we live and move and have our being."[54] They expand the point to argue that "the proper task of truly *Christian* ethics is to display how the Holy Spirit makes a difference for Christian living."[55] Our suggestion that this theme is present throughout Hauerwas's career is especially clearly supported by the final pages of *The Holy Spirit*. There Willimon and Hauerwas propose that the work is a sort of appendix to *Resident Aliens*, correcting one thing that "looking back we wish we had more strongly asserted," which is that courageous Christian witness is only ever conceivable when it is sourced from the bold prayer, "Come, Holy Spirit!"[56]

An ethics of reliance on "one who comes and rules" generates a peculiar understanding of human agency. Human willing remains important for the moral integrity and responsibility of agents, but it does not thereby establish itself as the *source* of the faithful witness of Christians. It can always only enact a "hastening that waits," to use Barth's famous phrase. Hauerwas has most often gestured to this refiguring of human agency using the language of "learning the patience required when we refuse violence." It is now clear enough that this setting of human agency within the agency of Jesus Christ's active ruling is fundamental both to Hauerwas's Christology and in his ethics. One possible weakness of our reading is the frequency with which Hauerwas can lapse into modern-sounding depictions of human agency that appear to have lost their conditioning as responses to prior divine working. If this is taken as springing from his interest in protecting the integrity of human moral agency and not a contradiction of the reading we have just outlined, we believe our reading has a range of important knock-on effects not only on methodological debates in Christian ethics, but more importantly, on how we understand living the Christian life in the twilight of Christendom.

Stanley Hauerwas arrived at his office every weekday at 6 a.m. Retirement might mean little more for him than this is no longer *always* the case. He will continue doing what he has always done. He will get up, read, and write.[57] He will continue to affirm that "Christians could not conceive how their lives could make sense if they did not assume they had particular responsibilities and obligations as they grew old in Christ."[58] It is these responsibilities and obligations of the Christian life that we think have most mattered to Stanley. They matter because they involve living and dying as a witness of Jesus Christ. And this witness only matters because of its source: the call of Jesus. Finding the words and the actions to respond to the inescapable call of Jesus has been the work of Stanley's theology. It has been "one long thought experiment in trying to imagine what it would mean for Christians to be possessed by what we say or, at least, should say."[59] This is hard work. This is good work. This is work that will continue.

NOTES

Foreword

1. Stanley Hauerwas and Jean Vanier, *Living Gently in a Violent World* (Downer's Grove, IL: InterVarsity Press, 2008).
2. Stanley Hauerwas, *The Peaceable Kingdom* (Notre Dame, IN: Notre Dame University Press, 1984); and Stanley Hauerwas and William H. Willimon, *Resident Aliens* (Nashville, TN: Abingdon Press, 1989).
3. *Resident Aliens*, 19.
4. Stanley Hauerwas, *The Work of Theology* (Grand Rapids, MI: Eerdmans, 2015), 22.
5. Stanley Hauerwas and Charles Pinches, *Christians among the Virtues* (Notre Dame, IN: University of Notre Dame Press, 1997), 39.
6. Stanley Hauerwas, *Disrupting Time* (Eugene, OR: Cascade, 2004), 12.
7. Brian Brock, *Christian Ethics in a Technological Age* (Grand Rapids, MI: Eerdmans, 2010).
8. Brian Brock, *Singing the Ethos of God* (Grand Rapids, MI: Eerdmans, 2007).
9. Brock, *Christian Ethics in a Technological Age*, 181.
10. Brian Brock, *Captive to Christ, Open to the World* (Eugene, OR: Cascade, 2014), 31.
11. Karl Barth, *The Theology of John Calvin* (Grand Rapids, MI: Eerdmans, 1995), 4.
12. Stanley Hauerwas, *Unleashing the Scriptures* (Nashville, TN: Abingdon Press, 1993), 85.
13. Hauerwas and Vanier, *Living Gently in a Violent World*, 15.
14. Ibid., 16.

Chapter 1

1. Hans Reinders, "The Virtue of Writing Appropriately. Or: Is Stanley Hauerwas Right in Thinking He Should Not Write Anymore on the Mentally Handicapped?" in L. Gregory Jones, Reinhard Hütter, and C. Rosalee Velloso Ewell (eds.), *God, Truth, and Witness: Engaging Stanley Hauerwas* (Grand Rapids, MI: Brazos, 2005), 53–70; Hans Reinders, *Receiving the Gift of Friendship* (Grand Rapids, MI: Eerdmans, 2008), 197–206.
2. The American Academy of Religion holds an annual conference that serves as the major meeting of theologians, Biblical scholars and researchers in Religious Studies.
3. Chad C. Pecknold, "Beyond Our Intentions: An Augustinian Reading of Hannah's Child," *Pro Ecclesia* XX, no. 3 (2011): 298–309.
4. "Stuart was a Calvinist. The world was dark. But poor Stuart was condemned to live with Methodists, who seemed to think there was no darkness at all." Stanley Hauerwas, *Hannah's Child* (Norwich: SCM, 2013), 182.

5. Stanley Hauerwas, *Vision and Virtue* (Notre Dame, IN: Fides Publishers, 1974).
6. *Hannah's Child*, 300-301.
7. M*A*S*H was an American comedy television show which aired from 1972 to 1983. It was an adaptation of the novel *M*A*S*H: A Novel about Three Army Doctors* (New York, NY: William Morrow, 1968) by Richard Hooker. It took a darkly comedic look at the lives of medical staff stationed at a US base during the Korean War. Alan Alda played the role of the surgeon Hawkeye Pierce, who is not slow to bend or break army regulation or protocol in the care of his patients.
8. *Hannah's Child*, xii.
9. Stanley Hauerwas, "Bearing Reality: A Christian Meditation," *Journal of the Society of Christian Ethics* 33, no. 1 (2013): 3-20.
10. Stanley Hauerwas, *Naming the Silences* (Grand Rapids, MI: Eerdmans, 1990).
11. J.M. Coetzee, "Thematizing," in *The Return of Thematic Criticism*, ed. Werner Sollers (Cambridge, MA: Harvard University Press, 1993), 289.
12. *Hannah's Child*, 300.
13. Ibid., 136.
14. Ibid., xi.
15. Ibid., xii.
16. Ibid., 290.
17. Ibid., 294.
18. Ibid., 299.
19. Ibid., xi.
20. Jonathan Tran, "Anne and the Difficult Gift of Stanley Hauerwas's Church," in *The Difference Christ Makes: Celebrating the Life, Work, and Friendship of Stanley Hauerwas*, ed. Charles M. Collier (Eugene, OR: Cascade Books, 2015), 51-70.
21. Stanley Hauerwas, *The Work of Theology* (Grand Rapids, MI: Eerdmans, 2013), 167.
22. Eberhard Bethge, *Dietrich Bonhoeffer: A Biography* (Minneapolis, MN: Fortress Press, 2000).
23. Eberhard Busch, *Karl Barth: His Life from Letters and Autobiographical Texts* (Eugene, OR: Wipf & Stock, 2005).
24. Cameron Jorgenson and Barry A. Jones (eds.), *Review and Expositor*, February 2015, 112 (1).
25. Stanley Hauerwas, *Matthew (Brazos Theological Commentary on the Bible)* (Grand Rapids, MI: Brazos, 2007).
26. In the opening of Book I Rousseau declares, "Let the trumpet of the last judgment sound when it will; I shall come with this book in my hands to present myself before the Sovereign Judge. I shall say loudly, 'Behold what I have done, what I have thought, what I have been. I have told the good and the evil with the same frankness; I have been silent about nothing bad, added nothing good and if I have happened to use some inconsequential ornament, this has never happened except to fill up a gap occasioned by my lack of memory.'" Jean Jacques Rousseau, *The Confessions and Correspondence, including Letters to Malesherbes*, translated by Christopher Kelly, edited by Christopher Kelly, Roger D. Masters, and Peter G. Stillman (Hanover, NH: University Press of New England, 1995), 5.
27. Ann Hartle, *The Modern Self in Rousseau's "Confessions": A Reply to St. Augustine* (Notre Dame, IN: Notre Dame University Press, 1984).
28. The reference is to *The Idiot*, Part III, chapters 5-7.
29. Jason David BeDuhn, *Augustine's Manichaean Dilemma, Volume 1: Conversion and Apostasy* (Philadelphia, PA: University of Pennsylvania Press, 2009) and *Augustine's*

Manichaean Dilemma, Volume 2: Making a "Catholic" Self (Philadelphia, PA: University of Pennsylvania Press, 2013).
30. *Hannah's Child*, 300.
31. Coetzee's autobiography was published in three volumes entitled, *Boyhood: Scenes from a Provincial Life* (1997), *Youth* (2002), and *Summertime* (2009). He reflects on the methodological and ethical quandaries of autobiographical writing in "Confession and Double Thoughts: Tolstoy, Rousseau, Dostoyevsky (1985)," in *Doubling the Point*, ed. David Atwell (Cambridge MA: Harvard University Press, 1992), 251–293 an; J.M. Coetzee and Arabella Kurtz, *The Good Story: Exchanges on Truth, Fiction and Psychotherapy* (London: Harvill Secker, 2015).
32. The building in question is called simply the "Rothko Chapel."
33. *Hannah's Child*, 115.
34. Ibid., 86.
35. Ibid., 114.
36. Ibid., 159. See also p. 246.
37. Ibid., 74–75.
38. *The Manns—Novel of a Century*, directed by Heinrich Breloer (2001; Paris: Arte, 2002), DVD.
39. *Hannah's Child*, 203.
40. Ibid., 45.
41. Stanley Hauerwas, *Prayers Plainly Spoken* (Eugene, OR: Wipf & Stock, 2003), 43.
42. *Hannah's Child*, 18.
43. Ibid., 180.
44. Ibid., 261.
45. Ibid., 294.
46. Ibid., 234.
47. Ibid., 212.
48. Ibid., 222.
49. Ibid., 36.
50. Ibid., 31.
51. Ibid., 29–30.
52. Ibid., 42.
53. In Stanley Hauerwas, *Christian Existence Today* (Durham, NC: Labyrinth Press, 1988), 25–45.
54. Ibid., 36.
55. Ibid., 37.
56. Ibid., 39.
57. Ferguson is a suburb of St. Louis, Missouri. On August 9, 2014, an unarmed black teenager named Michael Brown was shot dead by a white police officer, Darren Wilson. His body was left in the street for over four hours before being taken to a local morgue. In the immediate aftermath, demonstrations were held that both marked Brown's death and protested the use of violence by police forces against African American people. The protests informed a wider debate in the United States, often organized around the slogan #blacklivesmatter, about the systemic nature of white privilege, the persistence of racist policies in American public life, and the militarization of policing.
58. Jennifer Harvey, *Dear White Christians: For Those Still Longing for Racial Reconciliation* (Grand Rapids, MI: Eerdmans, 2014).

59. The interview was conducted months prior to the shootings at the AME church in Charleston, South Carolina, on June 17, 2015.
60. Quoted on p. 122 of *Naming the Silences*. (MacIntyre, quoted by Thomas A. Long, "Narrative Unity and Clinical Judgment," *Theoretical Medicine and Bioethics* 7, no. 1 (1986): 75-92, 84.)
61. Stanley Hauerwas and William H. Willimon, *The Holy Spirit* (Nashville, TN: Abingdon Press, 2015).
62. *The Work of Theology*, 262.
63. Ibid., 264.
64. Ibid.

Chapter 2

1. Stanley Hauerwas, *Sanctify Them in the Truth* (Nashville, TN: Abingdon, 1991).
2. Stanley Hauerwas, "Chapter 5: How to Tell Time Theologically," in *The Work of Theology* (Grand Rapids, MI: Eerdmans, 2013), 90-102.
3. The theme of joy as an alternative to post-Cartesian certainty is strong from Nietzsche's early work, especially from the period of *Fröliche Wissenschaft*, *The Joyful Science* (which has now become known under the much less evocative translation *The Gay Science*), to his late *Thus Spake Zarathustra*.
4. "All the terms used in the science books—'law,' 'necessity,' 'order,' 'tendency,' and so on—are really unintellectual, because they assume an inner synthesis, which we do not possess. The only words that ever satisfied me as describing Nature are the terms used in the fairy books, 'charm,' 'spell,' 'enchantment.' They express the arbitrariness of the fact and its mystery. A tree grows fruit because it is a *magic* tree. Water runs downhill because it is bewitched. The sun shines because it is bewitched." G.K. Chesterton, *Orthodoxy* (Peabody, MA: Hendrickson, 2006), 48; emphasis in the original.
5. Alasdair MacIntyre, *A Short History of Ethics* (London: Routledge, 2002), 87.
6. *Nicomachean Ethics* 1139a 6-9.
7. The Treatise on Law is found in questions 90-108 of the *Prima Secundae* of the *Summa Theologica*. Thomas Aquinas, *Summa Theologica* II-I, Q. 90-108.
8. The Treatise on Habit is found in questions 49-54 of the *Prima Secundae* of the *Summa Theologica*. Thomas Aquinas, *Summa Theologica* II-I, Q. 49-54.
9. MacIntyre, *A Short History of Ethics*, 58, 80.
10. Ibid., 79, 93, 96.
11. Ibid., 95.
12. Ibid., 77.
13. Ibid., 63.
14. Amélie O. Rorty, "The Place of Contemplation in Aristotle's *Nicomachean Ethics*," in *Essays on Aristotle's Ethics*, ed. Amélie Oksenberg Rorty (Los Angeles, CA: University of California Press, 1980), 377-394.
15. MacIntyre, *A Short History of Ethics*, 73.
16. Ibid., 81.
17. Stephen C. Barton, "1 Corinthians," in *Eerdmans Commentary on the Bible*, ed. James D.G. Dunn and John W. Rogerson (Grand Rapids, MI: Eerdmans, 2003), 1318.
18. Augustine, *Confessions* (Oxford: Oxford University Press, 2005), translated by Henry Chadwick, Book VII, 130.

19. Carlo Natali, *Aristotle: His Life and School* (Princeton, NJ: Princeton University Press, 2013), 66.
20. 1 Kings 22:21–23.
21. Samuel Wells, *God's Companions* (Malden, MA: Blackwell, 2006), 62.
22. Sarah Coakley, *God, Sexuality and the Self: An Essay "On the Trinity"* (Cambridge: Cambridge University Press, 2013). This is the first of a projected four-volume endeavor.
23. Stanley Hauerwas and Charles Pinches, *Christians among the Virtues* (Notre Dame, IN: University of Notre Dame Press, 1997), 118.
24. Ibid., 181 n. 13.
25. "There is a picture by Klee . . . [that] shows an angel who seems about to move away from something he stares at. . . . This is how the angel of history must look. His face is turned toward the past. Where a chain of events appears before *us*, *he* sees one single catastrophe, which keeps piling wreckage upon wreckage and hurls it at his feet. The angel would like to stay, awaken the dead, and make whole what has been smashed. But a storm is blowing from Paradise and has got caught in his wings . . . This storm drives him irresistibly into the future to which his back is turned, while the pile of debris before him grows toward the sky. What we call progress is *this* storm." Walter Benjamin, "On the Concept of History," in *Walter Benjamin: Selected Writings, Volume 4, 1938–1940*, ed. Howard Eiland and Michael W. Jennings (Cambridge, MA: Harvard University Press, 2003), Thesis IX, 392; emphases in the original.
26. Hauerwas and Pinches, *Christians among the Virtues*, 128.
27. Ibid., 143.
28. Stanley Hauerwas, *Hannah's Child* (Norwich: SCM, 2013), 28, 120.
29. Mark Oppenheimer, "For God, Not Country: The Un-American Theology of Stanley Hauerwas," *Lingua Franca* Volume 11, No. 6, September 2001.
30. The reference here is to mortar being demanded by a bricklayer on a building site.

Chapter 3

1. Stanley Hauerwas, *Character and the Christian Life* (South Bend, IN: University of Notre Dame Press, 1994).
2. Ibid., xvii.
3. Ibid., xxviii.
4. This essay was published under the subtitle "Where We Went Is What We Do: A Nostalgic Interlude Or, Not Much Has Changed Over the Last Fifteen or So Years," in Stanley Hauerwas, *A Better Hope: Resources for a Church Confronting Capitalism, Democracy and Postmodernity* (Grand Rapids, MI: Baker, 2000), 57–64.
5. "It can please the Holy Spirit—and it continually pleases Him—that not merely ethical advice and direction but the very command of God should be given in a very concrete form immediately from one man to another or to many others. To this extent there is a practical casuistry, an active casuistry, the casuistry of the prophetic *ethos*. It consists of the unavoidable venture—in the final judgment this venture rests with God—of understanding God's concrete specific command here and now in this particular way, of making a corresponding decision in this particular way, and of summoning others to such a concrete and specific decision." Karl Barth, *Church Dogmatics III.4* (Edinburgh: T&T Clark, 2009), 9.

6. *A Better Hope*, 64.
7. The show was actually called "Have Gun—Will Travel," and it aired on CBS from 1957 through to 1963.
8. Stanley Hauerwas, *The Peaceable Kingdom* (Notre Dame, IN: University of Notre Dame Press, 1984), 165 n. 2.
9. Stanley Hauerwas and Charles Pinches, *Christians among the Virtues* (Notre Dame, IN: University of Notre Dame Press, 1997), 206.
10. "This irony is not meant to be corrective; unlike simple or stable irony, its meaning cannot be reconstructed by appeals to the context of the utterance and the author's real intention. In general or unstable irony, life is at odds with itself, revealing fundamental and irremediable contradictions. Perhaps the most interesting feature of this irony is that the ironist is both the detached observer and the fellow victim." Stephen Webb, *Re-figuring Theology* (Albany, NY: SUNY Press, 1991), 120.
11. Barth's actual comment is that Kierkegaard is "a teacher whose school every theologian must enter once. Woe to him who misses it—provided only he does not remain in or return to it." "A Thank You and a Bow—Kierkegaard's Reveille," in *Fragments Grave and Gay*, ed. Martin Rumscheidt, trans. Eric Mosbacher (London: Colllins, 1971), 100-101. Not unlike Kierkegaard before and Hauerwas after him, Barth is overstating his case. See Philip P. Zeigler, "Barth's Criticisms of Kierkegaard—A Striking out at Phantoms?" *International Journal of Systematic Theology* 9, no. 4 (October 2007): 434-451.
12. Stanley Hauerwas, *The Work of Theology* (Grand Rapids, MI: Eerdmans, 2013), 147-169.
13. Paul L. Holmer, *Communicating the Faith Indirectly: The Paul L. Holmer Papers Volume Three*, ed. David J. Gouwens and Lee C. Barrett III (Cambridge: James Clarke & Co., 2013), 165; italics are in the original.
14. Paul L. Holmer, *The Grammar of Faith* (San Francisco, CA: Harper & Row, 1978), 14.
15. David Burrell and Stanley Hauerwas, "Self-Deception and Autobiography: Theological and Ethical Reflections on Speer's 'Inside the Third Reich,'" *The Journal of Religious Ethics* 2, no. 1 (Spring 1974): 99-117; also in Stanley Hauerwas, *Hauerwas Reader* (Durham, NC: Duke University Press, 2001), 200-220.
16. This familiar Hauerwasian claim deserves one clarification: the claim here is not that at some point Hauerwas soured on Kierkegaard's insights, but is expressing a resistance to any characterization of his theology as organized by Kierkegaard's familiar theological emphases. It is easily overlooked, for instance, that Hauerwas's often criticized denial of the Bible to individual Christians comes directly and explicitly from Kierkegaard's journals, which are quoted approvingly and at length in the 1993 book *Unleashing the Scriptures* (Nashville, TN: Abingdon Press, 1993), 16-17.
17. Holmer, *The Grammar of Faith*, 5.
18. Stanley Hauerwas and Samuel Wells, "Why Christian Ethics Was Invented," in *The Blackwell Companion to Christian Ethics*, 2nd ed., ed. Stanley Hauerwas and Samuel Wells (Oxford: Wiley Blackwell, 2011 [1st ed. 2004]), 28-38.
19. "Some moral philosophers assume that an analysis of the truth functions of moral propositions is sufficient to account for how moral agents should decide how they ought to act. Because of this assumption they fail to see that the 'typical moral problem is not a spectator's problem or a problem of classifying or describing

conduct, but a problem of practical choice and decision.'" *Character and the Christian Life*, 32. "The primary question should be what is the right thing to do, not how what I do will contribute to my character." Ibid., 168.
20. "The Case for the Virtues," in Paul L. Holmer, *Thinking the Faith With Passion: The Paul L. Holmer Papers Volume Two*, ed. David J. Gouwens and Lee C. Barrett III (Eugene, OR: Cascade, 2012), 304–320.
21. Stanley Hauerwas, *Wilderness Wanderings* (Boulder, CO: Westview Press, 1997), 148.
22. Holmer, "The Case for the Virtues," 313.
23. *Wilderness Wanderings*, 144–145.
24. In Holmer, *Thinking the Faith with Passion*, 286–303.
25. *The Work of Theology*, 229–249.
26. Holmer, "Something about What Makes It Funny," Chapter 17 in *Thinking the Faith with Passion*, 286–303, 298.
27. Ibid., 295.
28. Ibid., 294.
29. Ibid., 296.
30. *The Work of Theology*, 147–169.
31. Holmer, "Something about What Makes It Funny," 303.
32. Ted Cohen, *Jokes: Philosophical Thoughts on Joking Matters* (Chicago, IL: University of Chicago Press, 1999).
33. Holmer, *Communicating the Faith Indirectly*, 3–19.
34. Ibid., 6.
35. Ibid., 7–8.
36. *The Work of Theology*, 1–2.
37. Holmer, *Communicating the Faith Indirectly*, 10.
38. Stanley Hauerwas, "Why Jean Vanier Matters: An Exemplary Exploration," in *Knowing, Being Known, and the Mystery of God; Essays in Honor of Professor Hans Reinders: Teacher, Friend, Disciple*, ed. Bill Gaventa and Erik de Jongh (Amsterdam: VU University Press, 2016), 229–239.
39. Stanley Hauerwas, *With the Grain of the Universe* (Grand Rapids, MI: Brazos, 2001).
40. "Ever since historians and other research scholars have begun to look for religious 'foundations' in the fact, skepticism has also grown. With research in every field, the facts don't become plainer, as a superficial use of fact might suggest, but become more difficult to get at, more technical to state and plainly upset the realm of facts with which one starts. The facts about Jesus get harder and harder to translate, the more they are translated into a function of historical and critical studies." Holmer, *The Grammar of Faith*, 104.
41. Ibid., 134.
42. Ibid.
43. *The Work of Theology*, 11–31.
44. Eugene Garver, *For the Sake of the Argument* (Chicago, IL: University of Chicago Press, 2004).
45. Stanley Hauerwas, "How to Go On When You Are Going To Be Misunderstood, or how Paul Holmer Ruined My Life, or Making Sense of Paul Holmer," in *Wilderness Wanderings* (Boulder, CO: Westview Press, 1997), 143–152.
46. *The Grammar of Faith*, 53.
47. J.L. Austin, *How to Do Things with Words* (Oxford: Clarendon Press, 1962).
48. Stanley Hauerwas, *Hannah's Child* (Norwich: SCM, 2013), 88.

Chapter 4

1. Stanley Hauerwas, "Peacemaking, the Virtue of the Church" (1985) in *The Hauerwas Reader*, ed. John Berkman and Michael Cartwright (Durham, NC: Duke University Press, 2001), 318–326, 321.
2. Ibid., 325.
3. John Howard Yoder, *Karl Barth and the Problem of War* (Eugene, OR: Cascade, 2003).
4. John Howard Yoder, *The Politics of Jesus* (Grand Rapids, MI: Eerdmans, 1996).
5. John Howard Yoder, *The Original Revolution* (Scottsdale, PA: Herald Press, 1971).
6. Stanley Hauerwas, "Christians in the So-Called State (We Are In): A Meditation on Loyalty after September 11, 2001," in Stanley Hauerwas, *The State of the University* (Oxford: Blackwell, 2007), 137–146, 145.
7. Stanley Hauerwas, *After Christendom* (Nashville, TN: Abingdon Press, 2001), 17–18.
8. "Although it does not require it, baptism prepares Christians for the death of the martyr. . . . As sacrament, baptism gathers the individual body into the corporate body of the church, a community whose politics is rooted in another way than that which predominates in the world. If this other way is lived clearly and plainly it will stand as a witness; and as such it can and sometimes will provoke a response among the nations that attempt to annihilate it as a rival." Stanley Hauerwas, *Approaching the End* (Grand Rapids, MI: Eerdmans, 2013), 61–62.
9. American Association of Retired Persons.
10. Stanley Hauerwas, *The Work of Theology* (Grand Rapids, MI: Eerdmans, 2013), 253.
11. Oliver O'Donovan, *The Desire of the Nations* (Cambridge: Cambridge University Press, 1996).
12. "In 1671, the full extent of the Quaker challenge to civic and religious unity became apparent. Friends that year purchased their first property in Aberdeen, a kale yard on the east side of the Gallowgate where they intended to bury their dead. Behind 'great dycks of stone and morter' they dug their first grave for a child of the shoemaker Thomas Milne. Everyone except suicides and executed criminals was expected to be interred in a churchyard, but Quakers rejected the idea of consecrated ground and knew there was no law requiring churchyard burial. Legal or not, their new burial yard was seen as an affront to decency and good order. Three days after the burial, Provost Robert Forbes and two bailies supervised the exhumation and removal of the corpse to the burial ground of the Futty kirk. The magistrates ordered the walls of the Quaker graveyard pulled down, and Thomas Milne was fined and made to pay the gravediggers' wages and the kirk's standard burial fee. Over the next five years, however, the walls were rebuilt and torn down six times as one adult and five more children (including another of Milne's) were buried and exhumed." Michael Lunch, Gordon DesBrisay, and Murray G.H. Pittock, "The Faith of the People," in *Aberdeen Before 1800: A New History*, ed. E. Patricia Dennison, David Ditchburn, and Michael Lynch (East Linton: Tuckwell, 2002), 305.
13. Subsequent to this conversation, the Scottish government published a national investigation into cremation services, focusing in a large part on the Aberdeen crematorium. The conclusion begins with the claim that the "evidence discloses unethical and abhorrent practices at Aberdeen Crematorium over years, including the cremation of foetuses and babies along with unrelated and unknown adults." "Expedient" techniques were given priority over care for human remains and

the well-being of the families involved. The Rt. Hon. Dame Elish Angiolini DBE QC, *Report of the National Cremation Investigation* (Edinburgh: Government of Scotland, 2016), 40, 109.
14. Augustine, *The City of God*, I.13.
15. "[T]hough the Mennonites are perhaps most widely identified by their commitment to pacifism, that commitment is but part of their practice of reconciliation based on Matthew 18. So 'pacifism' does not simply name their refusal to go to war, but rather is an aspect of their practice of resolving disputes and conflicts through confrontation, forgiveness and reconciliation. . . . rightly understood, the ban is an act of love by the community to help erring members discover that they in fact are not living in unity with the body." Stanley Hauerwas, *Dispatches from the Front* (Durham, NC: Duke University Press, 1994), 212.
16. Stanley Hauerwas and Romand Coles, *Christianity, Democracy and the Radical Ordinary: Conversations between a Radical Democrat and a Christian* (Eugene, OR: Cascade, 2008).
17. Ibid., 128, 136, 138.
18. Stanley Hauerwas, *Hannah's Child* (Norwich: SCM Press, 2013), 73, 84.
19. James C. Scott, *Two Cheers for Anarchism* (Princeton, NJ: Princeton University Press, 2012).
20. "How to (Not) Be a Political Theologian," in *The Work of Theology*, 170–190.
21. Vaclav Havel, *Living in Truth* (London: Faber & Faber, 1989).
22. *After Christendom*, 165, note 5.
23. *Christianity, Democracy and the Radical Ordinary*, 2.
24. Ibid., 197.
25. Ibid., 311.
26. See Stanley Hauerwas, *Performing the Faith* (London: SPCK, 2004), 217.
27. "I am bold to suggest that the gentle character of the practices constituting the work of L'Arche are not peculiar to L'Arche, but rather necessary for any polity that would be about the goods held in common." Stanley Hauerwas and Jean Vanier, *Living Gently in a Violent World* (Downer's Grove, IL: IVP, 2008), 92.
28. "[T]he politics of gentleness cannot be a triumphalistic politics. . . . It is not for us as Christians to regret the loss of Christendom. But the loss of Christian structures and institutions makes it all the more important that the gentle care exemplified by Jesus in washing his disciples' feet—that gentleness exemplified in L'Arche—be unapologetically a witness to the One who would save us through the cross. Otherwise how would the world know that our loneliness has been overwhelmed and it is possible for us to trust one another?" Ibid., 98–99.
29. *Christianity, Democracy and the Radical Ordinary*, 312. The question of violence being raised includes a reference to the endemic problem of gender violence discussed in the "Gender Troubles" section of chapter 6. Père Thomas Phillipe (died 1993) was the priest with whom Jean Vanier founded L'Arche and who, it was just emerging at the time of this interview, had been under investigation by Mgr Pierre d'Ornellas, the archbishop of Rennes and accompanying bishop for L'Arche International. The investigation concluded that Phillipe had abused his position by engaging in inappropriate sexual behaviour toward adult women.
30. Ibid., 218.
31. Stanley Hauerwas, "Seeing Peace: L'Arche as a Peace Movement," in *The Paradox of Disability: Responses to Jean Vanier and L'Arche Communities from Theology and the Sciences*, ed. Hans Reinders (Grand Rapids, MI: Eerdmans, 2010), 113–126. In

both his Introduction and Conclusion to *Living Gently in a Violent World* (17, 102), John Swinton draws explicitly on this article to frame Hauerwas's contribution to that volume.

32. Stanley Hauerwas, "Seeing Peace: L'Arche as a Peace Movement," in *Christianity, Democracy and the Radical Ordinary*, 309–321.
33. See the discussion of Duke University's lemur colony in "Taking Time for Peace: The Ethical Significance of the Trivial," *Christian Existence Today*, 252–263, 259.
34. Brian Brock, *Singing the Ethos of God* (Grand Rapids, MI: Eerdmans, 2007), 32.
35. J. Alexander Sider, "Friendship, Alienation, Love: Stanley Hauerwas and John Howard Yoder," in *Unsettling Arguments: A Festschrift on the Occasion of Stanley Hauerwas's 70th Birthday*, ed. Charles R. Pinches, Kelly S. Johnson, and Charles M. Collier (Eugene, OR: Cascade, 2010), 61–86.
36. *Christianity, Democracy and the Radical Ordinary*, 34, 46.
37. Ibid., 41–42.
38. Ibid., 48–49.
39. Ibid., 67.
40. Ibid., 81.
41. Ibid., 63.
42. "That I go to church does not mean I think that Jesus is only to be found there. It just means that he has promised to show up there in a manner than can help us discern how he shows up in other places." Ibid., 105.
43. "I should like to think that vulnerability is at the heart of what it means to be Christians, because through worship we are trained to have our lives disrupted by that strangest of strangers—God." Ibid., 112.
44. Ibid., 105.
45. "One phrase Wolin uses to evoke this quality of our political and social world (and my favorite) is 'emergent regularities,' which are so at odds with the methodological expectation of and insistence upon regularity. Emergent irregularities are more likely to be witnessed and engendered in the world, when our mode of being and sensibility become not only 'mindful of logic, but more so of the incoherence and contradictoriness of experience' that is beyond all formulation; when we 'believe that because facts are richer than theories it is the task of theoretical imagination to restate new possibilities.'" Ibid., 127, citing Sheldon Wolin's article "Political Theory as Vocation," *The American Political Science Review* 63, no. 4 (1969), 1062–1082.
46. Ibid., 315, n. 14.
47. Ibid., 316, n. 19.
48. Brian Goldstone and Stanley Hauerwas, "Disciplined Seeing: Forms of Christianity and Forms of Life," *South Atlantic Quarterly* 109 (2010): 765–790, 790, n. 51.
49. *Performing the Faith*, 22. "A familiarity with the grammatical criteria of Christianity presupposes both a training in the exercises that comprise it *and* an awakening to the limits place on our ability to know certain things in anything like the way we might otherwise have sought to know them." In "Disciplined Seeing," 790, n. 51.
50. Ibid., 97.
51. Ibid., 108–109.
52. Stanley Hauerwas and Charles Pinches, *Christians among the Virtues* (Notre Dame, IN: University of Notre Dame Press, 1997), 119.
53. Ibid., 146.
54. Ibid., 176.
55. Ibid., 217 n. 32.

56. The verses in question here are Genesis 2:24 and Matthew 19:4–5.
57. *Approaching the End*, 72–73.
58. *Performing the Faith*, 26.
59. Ibid., 97–98.
60. Ibid., 137.
61. Ibid., 100.
62. Ibid., 103.
63. Ibid., 133.
64. Ibid., 144.
65. Ibid., 156.
66. Ibid., 164.
67. "According to Aristotle, characteristics (*hexis*, which I think is best translated as skilled, or complex, habits) develop from corresponding activities. That is the reason 'we must see to it that our activities are of a certain kind, since any variations in them will be reflected in our characteristics. Hence it is no small matter whether one habit or another is inculcated in us from early childhood; on the contrary, it makes a considerable difference, or rather, all the difference.'" Ibid., 157. The Aristotle quotation comes from *Nicomachean Ethics* (Martin Oswald trans.) 1103b20–25.
68. Ibid., 164.
69. Ibid.
70. Ibid., 157.
71. *The State of the University*, 120–121.
72. Kelly S. Johnson has explored this criticism in some detail in "Worshipping in Spirit and Truth," in *Unsettling Arguments: A Festschrift on the Occasion of Stanley Hauerwas's 70th Birthday*, ed. Charles R. Pinches, Kelly S. Johnson, and Charles M. Collier (Eugene, OR: Cascade, 2010), 300–314.
73. *Christianity, Democracy and the Radical Ordinary*, 210–211.
74. Brian Brock, "Praise: The Prophetic Public Presence of the Mentally Disabled," in *Blackwell Companion to Christian Ethics*, 2nd edn, ed. Stanley Hauerwas and Sam Wells (Oxford: Wiley-Blackwell, 2011), 139–151.
75. Brock has for years taken students to St. Andrews Cathedral in Aberdeen to investigate the grammar of traditional Western liturgical forms. Hauerwas had recently attended this lecture.

Chapter 5

1. Stanley Hauerwas, *Christians among the Virtues* (Notre Dame, IN: University of Notre Dame Press, 1997), 38–51.
2. William K. Frankena, *Ethics* (Englewood, NJ: Prentice-Hall, 1980).
3. See "Obligation and Virtue Once More," in *Truthfulness and Tragedy* (Notre Dame, IN: University of Notre Dame Press, 1977), 40–56.
4. Tom L. Beauchamp and James F. Childress, *Principles of Biomedical Ethics* (New York, NY: Oxford University Press, 1979). 6th Edition published 2009.
5. Stanley Hauerwas, "Casuistry in Context: The Need for Tradition (1995)," in *The Hauerwas Reader*, ed. John Berkman and Michael Cartwright (Durham, NC: Duke University Press, 2001), 267–284, 276.

6. Ibid., 277.
7. Ibid., 278
8. Stanley Hauerwas, *The Peaceable Kingdom* (Notre Dame, IN: University of Notre Dame Press, 1984), 131. See also Stanley Hauerwas, *Performing the Faith* (London: SPCK, 2004), 159.
9. "Casuistry in Context: The Need for Tradition," 271.
10. *The Peaceable Kingdom*, 116–117.
11. "Casuistry in Context: The Need for Tradition," 276.
12. *The Peaceable Kingdom*, 117.
13. Stanley Hauerwas, *Christian Existence Today* (Durham, NC: Labyrinth Press, 1988), 67–88.
14. Ibid., 82.
15. Oliver O'Donovan presents the basic position for Anglo-American Protestant ethicists: "What we recognize when we recognize a *moral* claim is the claim of certain generic categories of relation that can be grasped as transhistorical realities." "What Can Ethics Know About God?" in *The Doctrine of God and Theological Ethics*, ed. Alan Torrance and Michael Banner (London: T&T Clark, 2006), 38; emphasis in the original. Given this starting point, "[i]n moral deliberation we attempt to fit our action to the conditions in which we have to act. This is what traditionally has been called 'casuistry.' The general moral rules which we have learnt or formulated must be adapted to recognize the specificities which define the moral field more precisely... Thus we may speak, in a secondary sense, of having to 'compromise' between the ideal and the actual." Oliver O'Donovan, *Resurrection and the Moral Order* (Leicester: Apollos, 1994), 96. In essential agreement with this position ("The role of theological ethics is to derive basic ethical principles from dogmatics." Nigel Biggar, *Behaving in Public: How to Do Christian Ethics* (Grand Rapids, MI: Eerdmans, 2011), 20.) Nigel Biggar modifies it by replacing the language of compromise with the language of vocation. This account draws on Barth's notion of the divine command and how he understands it to have "the advantage of being compatible with the casuistic exercise of the full analytical powers of moral reason... on two conditions... first... that the command be reckoned in principle intelligible in generic terms... second... casuistic deliberation about right action must be conceived as involving more than generic reason. It must be understood to comprise, within the terms set by generic reason, the discernment of a particular, personal vocation to do something particular here and now." Nigel Biggar, *The Hastening That Waits* (Oxford: Oxford University Press, 1993), 44–45. That this discussion rests on Kantian premises is evident in the preface to Kant's essay, "On the common saying: That may be correct in theory, but it is of no use in practice."
16. *The Peaceable Kingdom*, 119.
17. Germain Grisez has a four-volume moral theology entitled *The Way of the Lord Jesus*. The first three volumes are available from St. Paul's publisher. Volume 1 is subtitled "Christian Moral Principles," Volume 2 is subtitled "Difficult Moral Questions," and Volume 3 is subtitled "Living a Christian Life." The fourth volume, subtitled "Fulfillment in Christ," was published by the University of Notre Dame Press in 1991.
18. *The Peaceable Kingdom*, 120.
19. Ibid., 120.
20. Ibid., 130–131.
21. David Clough, *Ethics in Crisis* (Aldershot: Ashgate, 2005), 89–103.
22. Biggar, *The Hastening That Waits*, 40–45.

23. Karl Barth, *Church Dogmatics III/4* (Edinburgh: T&T Clark, 2009), 203.
24. *The Peaceable Kingdom*, 134.
25. Ibid., 122.
26. This story is told in chapter 5, "Rational Suicide and Reasons for Living" of *Suffering Presence* (Notre Dame: IN, Notre Dame University Press, 1986), 100–103.
27. "Casuistry in Context: The Need for Tradition," 277.
28. *The Peacable Kingdom,* 63.
29. Ibid ., 69.
30. Ibid., 102–103.
31. "Irony has been essential for my attempt to expose the sentimentalities I associate with the Christian attempt to make our faith compatible with the reigning presumptions of our time." Stanley Hauerwas, *Work of Theology* (Grand Rapids, MI: Eerdmans, 2013), 166.
32. "[I]nternal to the gospel is an ironic grammar that is necessary in order to grasp what it means to be a disciple of Christ. . . . The use of irony in the Gospel of Mark as a means to indicate the training the disciples had to undergo that they might recognize who it is they follow I take not only to be a literary device but an indication of what is required by every Christian." Ibid., 167.
33. Patrick M. Clark, *Perfection in Death* (Washington, DC: Catholic University of America Press, 2015).
34. *The Peaceable Kingdom*, 67, 76–81.
35. *Christians among the Virtues*, 16.
36. Ibid., 122, 124–5.
37. Ibid., 46.
38. John Smith's invitation to his congregation to hand over their guns is discussed in the section "Radically ordinary" in Chapter 4.
39. *Christians among the Virtues*, 116.
40. The reference here is to the discussion in the subsection "On MacIntyre and becoming holy."
41. "Davos" is shorthand for the annual meeting held in Davos, Switzerland, of the World Economic Forum. This foundation is devoted to bringing together the global elite of business, government, and journalistic professions. Informal agreements are often hashed out at these meetings about the directions that will be pursued through business and governmental policy in the year to come.
42. "Few Europeans see the exercise of force outside of immediate self-defense as imaginable, and Europe is 'turning inward,' changed from NATO-centered to EU-centered; it is absenting itself from the world stage as it focuses upon the project of creating the EU. At the same time, extremist views—nativist extremists, anti-American extremists, and immigrant extremists—are on the rise, while moderates seem unable to muster much energy. In Europe the best lack all conviction, while the worst are full of passionate intensity." Charles Matthewes, *The Republic of Grace: Augustinian Thoughts for Dark Times* (Grand Rapids, MI: Eerdmans, 2010), 100.
43. "I think the greatest immorality of the contemporary ministry is its willingness to substitute socialization for belief in God . . . Pastors fail to challenge the congregation to trust that God creates and sustains the church." Stanley Hauerwas, *Christian Existence Today* (Durham, NC: Labyrinth Press, 1988), 147 n. 21.
44. "Often in the Psalms the psalmist pours out despair, asking God to help. . . . Why are you cast down, O my soul, and why are you disquieted within me? Hope in God, for

I shall again praise him, my help and my God. (Ps 42:11)." Stanley Hauerwas, *Cross-Shattered Christ* (Grand Rapids, MI: Brazos, 2011), 42–43.
45. *Christians among the Virtues*, 55.
46. Ibid., 82.
47. Ibid., 59.
48. Ibid., 102–104.

Chapter 6

1. Stanley Hauerwas, *The Work of Theology* (Grand Rapids, MI: Eerdmans, 2013), 256.
2. Stanley Hauerwas, *Against the Nations* (Notre Dame, IN: University of Notre Dame Press, 1992), 16.
3. John Howard Yoder, *Christian Attitudes towards War, Peace and Revolution* (Grand Rapids, MI: Brazos, 2009).
4. Roland Bainton, *Christian Attitudes toward War and Peace* (Nashville, TN: Abingdon, 1960).
5. Stanley Hauerwas, *Disrupting Time* (Eugene, OR: Cascade, 2004), 48–49.
6. Stanley Hauerwas, "On Being a Church Capable of Addressing a World at War: A Pacifist Response to the United Methodist Bishops' Pastoral *In Defense of Creation* (1988)," in *The Hauerwas Reader*, ed. John Berkman and Michael Cartwright (Durham, NC: Duke University Press, 2001), 426–458, 429.
7. Stanley Hauerwas, "September 11, 2001: A Pacifist Response," in *Dissent from the Homeland*, ed. Stanley Hauerwas and Frank Letricchia (Durham, NC: Duke University Press, 2003), 181–194, 187.
8. Drawing on an argument made by Yoder, Hauerwas and Wells characterize Christian ethics in America after H. Richard Niebuhr's *Christ and Culture* as having "become—indeed, for the 200 years of its life has, perhaps always been—the story of how the Church has set aside its practice and adopted a Kantian epistemology in an effort to secure relevance and consensus." Stanley Hauerwas and Sam Wells, "Why Christian Ethics Was Invented," in *The Blackwell Companion to Christian Ethics*, ed. Stanley Hauerwas and Sam Wells (Oxford: Wiley Blackwell, 2011), 28–38, 33.
9. Paul Ramsey, *The Patient as Person* (New Haven, CT: Yale University Press, 1974).
10. Stanley Hauerwas, *Dispatches from the Front* (Durham, NC: Duke University Press, 1994), 140.
11. *Against the Nations*, 24.
12. Tertullian, *The Chaplet, or De Corona*, see especially Chapter X.
13. Stanley Hauerwas, *War and the American Difference* (Grand Rapids, MI: Baker Academic, 2011), 19.
14. Charles Pinches, *A Gathering of Memories* (Grand Rapids, MI: Brazos, 2006).
15. Acts 22:28.
16. John Howard Yoder, "Quakerism in Early America: The Holy Experiment," in *Christian Attitudes to War and Peace*, ed. Theodore J. Koontz and Andy Alexis-Baker (Grand Rapids, MI: Brazos Press, 2009), 240–252.
17. "Whose 'Just' War, Which Peace?" in *Dispatches from the Front*, 130.
18. Ibid., 136–152.
19. Ibid., 133.
20. Stanley Hauerwas, *The State of the University* (Oxford: Blackwell, 2007), 142.

21. *Dispatches from the Front*, 128.
22. Stanley Hauerwas and Romand Coles, *Christianity, Democracy and the Radical Ordinary* (Cambridge: The Lutterworth Press, 2008), 22 n.5.
23. Paul Ramsey, *Christian Ethics and the Sit-In* (New York, NY: Association Press, 1961).
24. Quoted in *Against the Nations*, 189–190.
25. *Against the Nations*, 154.
26. *Christianity, Democracy and the Radical Ordinary*, 26.
27. *Against the Nations*, 195.
28. Ibid., 195.
29. Jana Bennett, *Water Is Thicker Than Blood: An Augustinian Theology of Marriage and Singleness* (Oxford: Oxford University Press, 2008).
30. *War and the American Difference*, 61.
31. Quoted in Seymour Hersh, "The Killing of Osama bin Laden," *London Review of Books* 37, no. 10 (2015): 3–12, 7.
32. *War and the American Difference*, 62–67.
33. Stanley Hauerwas, *The Peaceable Kingdom* (Notre Dame, IN: University of Notre Dame Press, 1984), 169 n.19.
34. *Against the Nations*, 208, n. 45.
35. Stan Goff, *Borderline: Reflections on War, Sex, and Church* (Eugene, OR: Cascade, 2015).
36. Ibid., 102.
37. Mohamedou Ould Slahi, *Guantanamo Diary*, ed. Larry Siems (Edinburgh: Cannongate, 2015).
38. "On Honor: By Way of Comparison of Karl Barth and Trollope," in *Dispatches from the Front*, 58–79.
39. *Dispatches from the Front*, 121–122.
40. Tommy Givens, *We the People: Israel and the Catholicity of Jesus* (Minneapolis, MN: Fortress, 2014), 97–98. Chapter 2 engages this question in detail.
41. John Howard Yoder, "Tertium Datur: Refocusing the Jewish–Christian Schism," unpublished manuscript, October 13 1977. Box 133, "Tertium Datur 1977." John H. Yoder Papers, 1947–1997. HM1-48. Mennonite Church USA Archives—Goshen. Goshen, Indiana. An online copy can be retrieved from: http://brandon.multics.org/library/John%20Howard%20Yoder/tertium_datur.html.
42. Francesca Aran Murphy, *I Samuel Brazos Theological Commentary* (Grand Rapids, MI: Brazos, 2010), 209–214.
43. 1 Chronicles 22:8 and 28:3.
44. Robert Alter, *The David Story: A Translation of 1 and 2 Samuel* (New York, NY: W. W. Norton, 2000).
45. Robert Alter, *The Book of Psalms: A Translation with Commentary* (New York, NY: W. W. Norton, 2007).
46. Goff, *Borderline*, 396.
47. Paul Martens and David Cramer, "By What Criteria Does a 'Grand, Noble Experiment' Fail? What the Case of John Howard Yoder Reveals about the Mennonite Church," *Mennonite Quarterly Review* 89, no. 1 (2015): 171–193.
48. *The Mennonite Quarterly Review*, 84, no. 3 (July 2010).
49. David Cramer, Jenny Howell, Jonathan Tran, and Paul Martens, "Scandalizing John Howard Yoder," *The Other Journal* http://theotherjournal.com/2014/07/07/scandalizing-john-howard-yoder/ (accessed April 19, 2016).

50. "MacKinnon notes how many issues that seem sexual from the male standpoint have not properly been seen as the defining of a politics.... I think she is right that the ethics of sex is from the beginning to tend a question of power, dominance, and thus, politics." Stanley Hauerwas, *After Christendom* (Nashville, TN: Abingdon Press, 2001), 116–117.
51. Margaret Mead, *Coming of Age in Samoa: A Psychological Study of Primitive Youth for Western Civilization* (New York: W. Morrow & Company, 1928).
52. Mathew Guest, Sonya Sharma, and Robert Song, *Gender and Career Progression in Theology and Religious Studies* (Durham, UK: Durham University, 2013).
53. Stanley Hauerwas, *Hannah's Child* (Norwich: SCM Press, 2013), 27. Hauerwas also says, "Paternalistic scripts die hard in the souls of Southern males." Ibid., 15.
54. Sarah Morice Brubaker, "*The Work of Theology*, by Stanley Hauerwas Review," *The Christian Century*, October 14, 2015, 48–50.
55. The transition in question is recounted in Didier Eribon, *Insult and the Making of the Gay Self* (Durham, NC: Duke University Press, 2004), 300–305.
56. The US Supreme Court decision in question is *Obergefell v. Hodges* (576 U.S. ___(2015)).
57. An influential American television sitcom, which aired from 1957 to 1963, that presented an idealized version of the life experience of a middle-class, suburban American family of the era.
58. *Dispatches from the Front*, 152.
59. "I am aware that I have done more talking about such performance than I have actually performed." *Against the Nations*, 1.
60. *War and the American Difference*, xiii.
61. "War and Peace," in Stanley Hauerwas, *Approaching the End* (Grand Rapids, MI: Eerdmans, 2013), 124–136.
62. Stanley Hauerwas, "War and Peace," in *The Oxford Handbook of Theology and Modern European Thought*, ed. Nicholas Adams, George Pattison, and Graham Ward (Oxford: Oxford University Press, 2013), 361–374.
63. *Against the Nations*, 117.
64. From the Foreword to *The Just War*. Paul Ramsey, *The Just War* (Lanham, MD: Rowman & Littlefield, 2002), ix.

Chapter 7

1. John H. Evans, *Playing God? Human Genetic Engineering and the Rationalization of Public Bioethical Debate* (Chicago: University of Chicago Press, 2002).
2. Brian Brock, "Christian Ethics," in *Mapping Modern Theology: A Thematic and Historical Introduction*, ed. Kelly M. Kapic and Bruce L. McCormack (Grand Rapids, MI: Baker, 2012), 293–317.
3. Stanley Hauerwas, *Suffering Presence* (Notre Dame, IN: Notre Dame University Press, 1986), 1–2.
4. Joel Shuman, *Heal Thyself: Spirituality, Medicine, and the Distortion of Christianity* (Oxford: Oxford University Press, 2002).
5. *Suffering Presence*, 4–5, 11–12, 71–72.
6. Ibid., 173–179.
7. The book was John Swinton, ed., *Critical Reflections on Stanley Hauerwas's Theology of Disability: Disabling Society, Enabling Theology* (Binghamton, NY: Hayworth Pastoral Press, 2004).

8. *Suffering Presence*, 186.
9. "I tried to remember that she was in pain. It was often hard to remember her pain because I was the subject of her anger. She was unbelievably cruel. That cruelty is what finally exhausted me." Stanley Hauerwas, *Hannah's Child* (Norwich: SCM, 2013), 128.
10. Alasdair MacIntyre, *After Virtue* (London: Gerald Duckworth, 2007), 79–87.
11. Stanley Hauerwas, Samuel Wells, and friends, *Living out Loud*, ed. Luke Bretherton and Russell Rook (Milton Keynes: Paternoster, 2010), 8.
12. *Suffering Presence*, 13.
13. Paul Ramsey, *The Patient as Person* (New Haven, CT: Yale University Press, 1974).
14. "In Defense of Cultural Christianity: Reflections on Going to Church," in Stanley Hauerwas, *Sanctify Them in the Truth* (Nashville, TN: Abingdon, 1991).
15. Jeffrey Stout, *Democracy and Tradition* (Princeton, NJ: Princeton University Press, 2004).
16. *Suffering Presence*, 171.
17. Ibid., 184–185.
18. Ibid., 128.
19. Ibid., 208.
20. "What I hope I have at least suggested is that the struggle, the pain, the suffering, and the joy of the 'insiders' is not insignificant for those of us on the outside. For without you and your children, our communities would be less rich in the diversity of folk that we need in order to be good communities." Ibid., 217.
21. Neo-neo-Constantinianism is the "continuing moral identification" of Christians with their home nations, "despite mutual ideological disavowal." Yoder cites the examples of the Eastern European socialist states as expressions of this phenomenon. John Howard Yoder, "Constantinian Sources of Western Social Ethics" in *The Priestly Kingdom* (Notre Dame, IN: University of Notre Dame Press, 2001), 135–147, 142.
22. Ibid., 169.
23. "That is why in the face of the retarded we are offered an opportunity to see God, for like God they offer us an opportunity of recognizing the character of our neediness . . . they can serve for us all as a prophetic sign of our true nature as creatures destined to need God and, thus, one another." Ibid., 179.
24. "While we preachers sit before you and recommend what will do you good, the one who sits before the doors of the church addresses you no less than we do, by his mere appearance, without saying a word." The sermon preached by the poor, Chrysostom continues, is that "[m]an's life is a shifting and precarious thing . . . Our condition is like a swift river that never wants to stand still but always rushes downhill." John Chrysostom, *Homily*, 29, cited in Judith Kovacs, trans. and ed., *1 Corinthians: Interpreted by Early Christian Commentators* (Grand Rapids, MI: Eerdmans, 2005), 208.
25. Alasdair MacIntyre, *Dependent Rational Animals: Why Human Beings Need the Virtues* (Chicago: Open Court, 1999).
26. *Suffering Presence*, 6–7.
27. Ibid., 48.
28. Ibid., 80–81.
29. "Then very early one Sunday morning I received a phone call from Bob requesting that I come to see him immediately. He was sobbing intensely but through his crying he was able to tell me that they had just found his mother dead. She had committed suicide by placing a shotgun in her mouth. I knew immediately I did not want to go

to see him or confront a reality like that. I had not yet learned the desperation hidden under our everyday routines and I did not want to learn of it. Moreover, I did not want to go because I knew there was nothing I could do or say to make things even appear better than they were. Finally, I did not want to go because I did not want to be close to anyone who had been touched by such a tragedy." "Salvation and Health: Why Medicine Needs the Church (1985)," in *The Hauerwas Reader*, 539–555, 540.
30. *Suffering Presence*, 63, 205.
31. Hauerwas's Rule is "you always marry the wrong person." Stanley Hauerwas, "Christianity: It's Not a Religion, It's an Adventure," in *The Hauerwas Reader* (Durham, NC: Duke University Press, 2001), 522–535, 524.
32. Luther's exegesis of Genesis 2:2 appears in *Luther's Works Vol. 1: Lectures on Genesis Chapters 1–5*, 134. One contemporary Lutheran formulary situates the pastor as the representative of the church responsible to ask each spouse whether they consent to this marriage as a task given by God, to be worked out through the active and grateful receipt of a spouse whom they confess to be given by God. "Obwohl die geläufige Form der Traufrage Ähnlichkeit mit der Konsensfrage des Standesbeamten hat, ist sie im Kontext unseres Traugottesdienstes mehr als nur eine Wiederholung dessen, was zuerst unter vier Augen und dann auf dem Standesamt geschah. Die Verkündigung im Traugottesdienst zielt auf das Ja der Eheleute zur göttlichen Ordnung und zu einer christlich gelebten Ehe. Die *Traufrage* ist insofern eine *Bekenntnisfrage*, als die Antwort eine Antwort des Glaubens ist: *Ein Ja zum ehegatten als Gottesgabe, ein Ja zur Ehe als Gottes Aufgabe, ein Ja zum lebenslangen Beieinanderbleiben und ein Ja zur immerwährenden Angewiesenheit auf Gott: Ja, und Gott helfe mir* [. . .] Dabei ist wichtig: *Beide* Ehegatten werden vor Gott das gleiche gefragt, sie geben auch die *gleiche* Antwort." http://www.evkirche-oberholzheim.de/fileadmin/mediapool/gemeinden/KG_oberholzheim/pdf/a-z_traugottesdienst.pdf (emphasis added).
33. The discussion in question occurs at the end of Chapter 3.
34. Stanley Hauerwas, *Naming the Silences* (Grand Rapids, MI: Eerdmans, 1990), 46.
35. Ibid., 1–29.
36. Ibid., 89–95.
37. Ibid., 126–151.
38. Ibid., 138–139.
39. Ibid., 139.
40. Elaine Scarry, *The Body in Pain* (New York, NY: Oxford University Press, 1985).
41. *Naming the Silences*, 143.
42. Brian Brock and Stephanie Brock, "Being Disabled in the New World of Genetic Testing: A Snapshot of Shifting Landscapes," in *Theology, Disability and the New Genetics: Why Science Needs the Church*, ed. John Swinton and Brian Brock (London: T&T Clark, 2007), 29–43.
43. *Suffering Presence*, 121.
44. Oliver O'Donovan, *Ways of Judgement* (Grand Rapids, MI: Eerdmans, 2005), 59–66.
45. *Naming the Silences*, 127.
46. Ibid., 127.
47. Trosly is the village in northern France where the first L'Arche community was opened in 1964. Hauerwas and Brock were participating in the symposium that yielded the book edited by Hans Reinders, *The Paradox of Disability: Responses to Jean Vanier and L'Arche Communities from Theology and the Sciences* (Grand Rapids, MI: Eerdmans, 2010).
48. Jean Vanier, *Man and Woman God Made Them* (London: Darton, Longman & Todd, 2007), 29.

49. Jean Vanier, *Made for Happiness* (Toronto, ON: Anansi, 2001).
50. The experiential-expressivist understanding of religion is described in George A. Lindbeck, *The Nature of Doctrine: Religion and Theology in a Postliberal Age* (Philadelphia: Westminster Press, 1984). See especially chapter 2.
51. Vanier, *Made for Happiness*, 66, 67, 73.
52. Miguel J. Romero, "Aquinas on the *corporis infirmitas*: Broken Flesh and the Grammar of Grace," in *Disability in the Christian Tradition: A Reader*, ed. Brian Brock and John Swinton (Grand Rapids, MI: Eerdmans, 2012), 101-151.
53. Vanier, *Made for Happiness*, 18-19.
54. Ibid., 30-31.
55. Stanley Hauerwas and William H. Willimon, *The Holy Spirit* (Nashville, TN: Abingdon Press, 2015), 81.
56. "Then one of the seraphs flew to me, holding a live coal that had been taken from the altar with a pair of tongs. The seraph touched my mouth with it and said: 'Now that this has touched your lips, your guilt has departed and your sin is blotted out.'" Isaiah 6:6-7.
57. Emmanuel Célestin Suhard (1874-1949) was the archbishop of Reims from 1930. He was elevated to cardinal in 1935. In 1940 he was appointed to the Archbishopric of Paris, where he served until his death. Under the Vichy regime, he spent a period of time under house arrest for his public protests against the deportation of French Jews.
58. Herman Paul, "Stanley Hauerwas: Against Secularization in the Church," *Zeitschrift für Dialektische Theologie* 59, no. 2 (2013): 12-33.
59. Stanley Hauerwas, *Prayers Plainly Spoken* (Eugene, OR: Wipf & Stock, 2003), 76.
60. Joseph Fletcher, *Situation Ethics: The New Morality*, James F. Childress intro. (Louisville, KT: Westminster John Knox Press, 1966), 78-81.
61. This question is the premise of his famous work, *Meditations on First Philosophy*.
62. John Dewey, *The Later Works of John Dewey, Volume 4, 1925-1953*, ed. Jo Ann Boydston (Carbondale: Southern Illinois University Press, 2008).
63. Charles M. Collier, ed., *The Difference Christ Makes: Celebrating the Life, Work, and Friendship of Stanley Hauerwas* (Eugene, OR: Cascade Books, 2015), 90.
64. Jonathan Tran, "Anne and the Difficult Gift of Stanley Hauerwas's Church," in *The Difference Christ Makes: Celebrating the Life, Work, and Friendship of Stanley Hauerwas* (Eugene, OR: Cascade Books, 2015), 51-70.
65. Ibid., 68.
66. Ibid., 69.
67. Peter Dula, "The Limits of Theology: A Response to Jonathan Tran," in *The Difference Christ Makes: Celebrating the Life, Work, and Friendship of Stanley Hauerwas* (Eugene, OR: Cascade Books, 2015), 71-76.
68. Ibid., 74.
69. "Bearing Reality," in *Approaching the End* (Grand Rapids, MI: Eerdmans, 2013), 139-157.

Chapter 8

1. Stanley Hauerwas, *A Cross-Shattered Church* (Grand Rapids, MI: Brazos, 2009), 9.
2. Stanley Hauerwas, *The Work of Theology* (Grand Rapids, MI: Eerdmans, 2013), 274.
3. Nicholas M. Healy, *Hauerwas: A (Very) Critical Introduction* (Grand Rapids, MI: Eerdmans, 2012), 12.

4. *The Work of the Theology*, 276.
5. See the chapters, "How Christian Universities Contribute to the Corruption of Youth" and "Truth and Honor: The University and the Church in a Democratic Age" in Stanley Hauerwas, *Christian Existence Today* (Grand Rapids, MI: Brazos Press, 2001).
6. Discussed in Chapter 3.
7. This course is described in "The Liturgical Shape of the Christian Life: Teaching Christian Ethics as Worship," in *In Good Company* (Notre Dame, IN: University of Notre Dame Press, 1995), 153–168.
8. "How I became a member at Broadway is a tale in itself, but I was at least initially attracted by being challenged by the pastor. After he had given a talk at a continuing education seminar for [clergy] . . . he had the nerve to ask me (in the bathroom) where I went to church. After I reported that I tended to bounce around, he suggested that I certainly did not live out the theological claims I professed. I figured that anyone who would challenge me that way could not be all bad." Stanley Hauerwas, *Christian Existence Today* (Durham, NC: Labyrinth Press, 1988), 129.
9. That accusation was leveled in James Gustafson, "The Sectarian Temptation: Reflections on Theology, the Church and the University," in *Proceedings of the Catholic Theological Society* 40 (1985): 83–94. One of Hauerwas's most direct responses to these criticisms are found in *Christian Existence Today*, 2–19.
10. *Christian Existence Today*, 237–252.
11. "The emphasis on narrative, therefore, is not first a claim about the narrative quality of experience from some unspecified standpoint, but rather is an attempt to draw our attention to where the story is told, namely, in the church; how the story is told, namely, in faithfulness to Scripture; and who tells the story, namely, the whole church through the office of the preacher." Ibid., 61.
12. Ibid., 47.
13. Hans Frei, *The Eclipse of Biblical Narrative: Study in Eighteenth and Nineteenth Century Hermeneutics* (New Haven, CT: Yale University Press, 1980).
14. "What is 'the Public'? Theological Variations on Babel and Pentecost," in *The Authority of the Gospel: Explorations in Moral and Political Theology in Honor of Oliver O'Donovan*, ed. Robert J. Song and Brent Waters (Grand Rapids, MI: Eerdmans, 2014), 160–178.
15. "I did try to write the sermon drawing on what I have learned about the narrative character of theological convictions from Professor Frei, as well as others such as David Kelsey, George Lindbeck, Ron Thiemann, James McClendon, and many others." *Christian Existence Today*, 54.
16. Ibid., 61.
17. Ibid., 135.
18. "The Ministry of the Congregation: Rethinking Christian Ethics for a Church-Centered Seminary," in ibid., 111–131.
19. "In Defense of Cultural Christianity: Reflections on Going to Church", in *Sanctify Them in the Truth* (Nashville, TN: Abingdon, 1991), 157–173.
20. This discussion appears in the section "Caring, curing, and cracks in the social order" of Chapter 7.
21. Stanley Hauerwas, "Bearing Reality: A Christian Meditation," *Journal of the Society of Christian Ethics* 33, no. 1 (2013): 3–20.
22. Stanley Hauerwas, *Learning to Speak Christian* (Norwich: SCM, 2011), 143–144.
23. Ibid., 7; emphasis in the original.

24. Stanley Hauerwas, *Disrupting Time* (Eugene, OR: Cascade, 2004), 30–32, 85
25. Ibid., 46.
26. Stanley Hauerwas, *Matthew Brazos Theological Commentary on the Bible* (Grand Rapids, MI: Brazos, 2007), 41.
27. Muller's forthcoming work will be entitled *Donald M. MacKinnon, 1913–94: An Intellectual Biography*.
28. The papers from this conference were published as *Christ, Ethics and Tragedy: Essays in Honour of Donald MacKinnon* (Cambridge: Cambridge University Press, 1989), edited by Kenneth Surin.
29. *Cross-Shattered Church*, 21.
30. "What I find so wonderful is that you have found a way to elicit that through the images provided in the sermon without getting into theoretical discussion. All of which is to say that it gives me pause about the relation between theory and sermonic form. I think that the sermonic form may well be the better argument." William H. Willimon and Stanley Hauerwas, *Preaching to Strangers* (Louisville, KY: Westminster John Knox Press, 1992), 28.
31. *Cross-Shattered Church*, 21.
32. *Preaching to Strangers*, 11.
33. Ibid., 1.
34. Ibid., 2.
35. John Howard Yoder, *He Came Preaching Peace* (Kitchener, ON: Herald Press, 1986).
36. *Preaching to Strangers*, 11.
37. Ronald Boyd-Macmillan, "The transforming sermon: a study of the preaching of St. Augustine, with special reference to the *Sermones ad populum*, and the transformation theory of James Loder," Doctoral Thesis, Aberdeen University, 2009.
38. *Learning to Speak Christian*, ix.
39. Ibid., 86. To this claim Hauerwas immediately adds, "[T]here is an essential relation between reading and speaking; because it is through reading that we learn how to discipline our speech so that we say no more than needs to be said" (87).
40. Ibid., 87.
41. *The Work of Theology*, 165.
42. Brock is referring to the practice of the Bible Memory Association (BMA).
43. The reference here is to the argument of *Unleashing the Scriptures*.
44. *Matthew*, 18.
45. *Learning to Speak Christian*, 101.
46. Ibid., 102.
47. Ibid., 112.
48. *Matthew*, 19.
49. "[T]he Christian reading of the Bible is a delicate task, as complex and beautiful as a spider's web. But spiders' webs are fragile, requiring constant repair, which means that in the process of repair connections are revealed that had not been anticipated. There is an order to orthodoxy that is beautiful and fragile—beautiful because of its fragility." *Cross-Shattered Church*, 159. Also, "the work of preaching and theology is finding the connections between stories. The Bible is an anthology of wildly different stories, and it is not immediately apparent how they interrelate. Preaching, and the theology that serves preaching, is the ongoing exploration of the church to discover the connections Christian doctrine is the hints the church has discovered that help us see the connections." *Disrupting Time*, 232.
50. *Matthew*, 19.

51. *Preaching to Strangers*, 2.
52. Hans Frei, *The Identity of Jesus Christ* (Eugene, OR: Wipf and Stock, 1997).
53. The earlier sermon was published as "Citizens of Heaven," in *The Freedom of a Christian Ethicist: The Future of a Reformation Legacy*, ed. Brian Brock and Michael Mawson (London: Continuum, 2015), 11–15.
54. *Matthew*, 243.
55. Ibid., 20.
56. These lectures are contained in the first eight volumes of *Luther's Works, American Edition*.
57. As a representative example, "Firstfruits: The Paradigmatic Public Role of God's People" begins with a note stating, "This paper was presented on 4 October 1992, at Christian Theological Seminary, Indianapolis, as part of an event inaugurating the work of the seminary's Insitute for the Study of the Public Good, an instrument for continuing education and community service. The title was dictated by the event." John Howard Yoder, "Firstfruits: The Paradigmatic Public Role of God's People," in *For the Nations*, ed. John Howard Yoder (Grand Rapids, MI: Eerdmans, 2007), 15.
58. *Matthew*, 20.
59. *Learning to Speak Christian*, 101.
60. *Matthew*, 20–21.
61. Ibid., 21.
62. Darren Sarisky, "A Prolegomenon to an Account of Theological Interpretation of Scripture," in *Theological Theology: Essays in Honour of John Webster*, ed. R. David Nelson, Darren Sarisky and Justin Stratis (London: Bloomsbury T&T Clark, 2015), 264. This criticism is not different in kind from Richard Hays's much earlier formulation of this worry in *The Moral Vision of the New Testament* (Edinburgh: T&T Clark, 1997), 263.
63. *Matthew*, 65.
64. Ibid., 75.
65. Ibid.
66. The discussion in question is in Chapter 3.
67. *Confessions*, Book XII, 152.
68. The discussion in question is in Chapter 2.
69. *Matthew*, 21.
70. Darren Sarisky argued, in the essay cited earlier, that such a reading undermines the claim that this book can legitimately be called a theological commentary. Sarisky, "A Prolegomenon," 262–265.
71. Scott Bader-Saye, "Haunted by the Jews: Hauerwas, Milbank, and the Decentered Diaspora Church," in *Unsettling Arguments: A Festschrift on the Occasion of Stanley Hauerwas's 70th Birthday*, ed. Charles Pinches, Kelly Johnson, and Charles Collier (Eugene, OR: Cascade, 2010), 208.
72. *Matthew*, 23–25, 244.
73. There is an acknowledgment that "Joseph still required a revelation so that he would know the character of Mary's pregnancy" and a strong affirmation of the centrality of Mary's virginity in the logic of the incarnation, which turns on how Matthew "uses the formula 'all this took place to fulfil what had been spoken by the Lord.'" Ibid., 36.
74. Martin Luther, *Luther's Works Vol. 3: Lectures on Genesis Chapters 15–20*, ed. Jaroslav Pelikan (St. Louis, MO: Concordia, 1961), 220.
75. *Matthew*, 52.

76. Ibid., 53–54. Hauerwas then continues to argue that Jesus, in this use of scripture, is simultaneously prophet, priest, and king because, "[t]o be king of Israel . . . requires the knowledge of the law acquired by having the law read every day of the king's life (Deut. 17:19)." Ibid., 54.
77. The bulk of the treatment presents Jesus's example as commending seriousness about charitable works. "Day and Maurin knew that attempts to create a 'better world' without being a people capable of the works of mercy could not help but betray Jesus's response to his disciples' question of what sign will there be of Jesus's coming and the end of the age. The sign is that they have time to feed the hungry, clothe the naked, give drink to the thirsty, welcome the stranger, care for the sick and those in prison." Hauerwas complicates this reading, however, with the concluding line of the chapter, in which Christ's presence is much more tangibly explicated: "Jesus has given us all the time in the world to visit him in the prisons of this world." Ibid., 212.
78. *Disrupting Time*, 35.
79. *Cross-Shattered Church*, 19.
80. Ibid., 18.
81. Luther, *Luther's Works Vol. 1*, 276.
82. *Matthew*, 207.
83. *Christian Existence Today*, 171–190.
84. Stanley Hauerwas, *Prayers Plainly Spoken* (Eugene, OR: Wipf & Stock, 2003), 9.
85. *Christian Existence Today*, 172.
86. That prayer begins, "God, you alone know how we are to pray to you on occasions like this. We do not fear you, since we prefer to fear one another. Accordingly, our prayers are not to you but to some 'ultimate vagueness.' You have, of course, tried to scare the hell out of some of us through the creation of your people Israel and through the life, death and resurrection of Jesus. But we are a subtle, crafty and stiff-necked people who prefer to be dammned into vagueness." *Prayers Plainly Spoken*, 47–48.
87. Prayer at school sporting events is a contentious issue as a result of restrictions on prayer in schools generally. While it has not actually been made illegal, prayer at school sporting events is regularly a topic of dispute in the American court systems. The First Amendment Center at Vanderbilt University maintains a database of such cases which can be accessed at http://www.firstamendmentcenter.org/tag/game-prayer.
88. "God does not want us to come to the altar different from how we live the rest of our lives. Therefore I do not try to be pious or to use pious language in my prayers. I try to speak plainly, yet I hope with some eloquence, since nothing is more eloquent than simplicity." *Prayers Plainly Spoken*, 14.
89. Such as: ibid., 117.
90. Flannery O'Connor, *A Prayer Journal* (New York, NY: Farrar, Straus and Giroux, 2013).
91. "That most of these prayers were written to be prayed before a class, moreover, does not mean they are 'academic.' It is true that they open a class in Christian ethics and that I did often write the prayers in relation to what we were studying in the class. But since the class is shaped by the liturgy of the church, I do not think the prayers are in any particular way limited to the interest of students and teachers." *Prayers Plainly Spoken*, 15–16.
92. "I continue to worry about publishing prayers, but I do so because my students and friends ask me to include my prayers in what I write. I worry about publishing

prayers because I think we ought to pray in a way disciplined by the prayers the church has honed through the centuries." *Disrupting Time*, 9.
93. *Seinfeld* is an American sitcom that ran for the majority of the 1990s.
94. *Friends* is an American sitcom that ran for a decade from 1994.
95. *Matthew*, 76.
96. Karl Barth, *The Christian Life: Church Dogmatics Volume IV, Part 4: Lecture Fragments* (London: Bloomsbury Continuum, 2004).
97. *Prayers Plainly Spoken*, 15.
98. On Barth, see Matthew Meyer Boulton, *God against Religion: Rethinking Christian Theology Through Worship* (Grand Rapids, MI: Eerdmans, 2008), chapters 1–3. On Bonhoeffer, see Tom Greggs, *Theology against Religion: Constructive Dialogues with Bonhoeffer and Barth* (London: T&T Clark, 2011), chapters 2–3.
99. *Disrupting Time*, 3.
100. *Learning to Speak Christian*, 93. Compare *Cross-Shattered Church*, 12: "I have, however, increasingly come to the recognition that one of the most satisfying contexts for doing the world of theology is in sermons. That should not be surprising because throughout Christian history, at least until recently, the sermon was one of the primary places in which the work of theology was done. For the work of theology is first and foremost to exposit Scripture. That modern theology has become less and less scriptural, that modern theology has often tried to appear as a form of philosophy, is but an indication of its alienation from its proper work."
101. Ibid., 93.
102. Ibid., xiii.
103. *Disrupting Time*, 90. "Make all our thinking, jumbled as it is, prayer, so that we may be brought back to the quiet love, the eloquent silence, of your creation." *Prayers Plainly*, 98.
104. *Learning to Speak Christian*, xiii.
105. "[W]hen we pray we pray with the whole communion of saints who surround the Father in heaven. . . . To pray to the Father in heaven means that our voice is joined with the "angels surrounding the throne and the living creatures and the elders; they numbered myriads of myriads and thousands of thousands, singing with full voice, Worthy is the Lamb that was slaughtered (Rev 5:11–12)." *Matthew*, 77.
106. Jeffrey Stout, *Democracy and Tradition* (Princeton: Princeton University Press, 2004), 205.
107. "The psalms are the great prayerbook of the church because they teach us to pray without pretension." *Matthew*, 71.
108. *Disrupting Time*, 178.
109. *Learning to Speak Christian*, xiii.
110. *Matthew*, 237.
111. *Prayers Plainly Spoken*, 17.
112. *Preaching to Strangers*, 28.
113. "A friend recently observed that my prayers have a very different tone, a tentativeness or hesitancy, than the lectures I gave in the course meant to introduce students to Christian ethics. I think that is a very astute observation, to which I can only respond that if you are to understand me, it is the prayers that make the lectures possible." *The Work of Theology*, 148.
114. *Cross-Shattered Christ*, 64–65.

115. *Disrupting Time*, 42. See also 44 and 30–32, 39–43. "Part of my work has been a re-Judiazation of Christianity, even though I want to be—and I hope that I am—a thoroughly orthodox Christian." Ibid., 191.
116. *Prayers Plainly Spoken*, 75.
117. "I think it would be terrific if on entering a church people would think, 'This is very frightening.' God, after all, is frightening." *Disrupting Time*, 81.
118. This prayer presents the salient issues: ibid., 46.
119. "Who among us would be a freethinker if it were not for the Church? We loathe the Church, *not* its poison [Jesus] . . . Apart from the Church, we too love the poison." Friedrich Nietzsche, *On the Genealogy of Morality*, ed. Keith Ansell-Pearson, trans. Carol Diethe (Cambridge: Cambridge University Press, 1994), I.9, 21. "[T]here is even then no lack within the Church of those who by their abandoned morals torture the hearts of those who live piously. Indeed, there are many such, who blaspheme the name of 'Christian' and 'Catholic.' And the dearer this name is to those who 'will live piously in Christ,' the more deeply are they grieved when evildoers within cause it to be less beloved than the minds of the pious desire." Augustine, *The City of God against the Pagans*, ed. And trans. R. W. Dyson (Cambridge: Cambridge University Press, 1998), 18:51, 899.
120. "Furious, Spirit of Pentecost, I am furious. Suddenly, your creation, your church looks so damned ugly. Where in the world are you in this mess? Christians in America suddenly celebrate the 'we' of being Americans." *Disrupting Time*, 55.
121. "I fear that my anger comes not from charity, but pretensions and pride. I say that I want to love you and yours, but I despise those smooth lives that claim the name Christian. So, I pray, dear God, that you shake my anger, our anger, by your harsh and dreadful love." Ibid., 79. More succinctly, "So, I must pray that you destroy my pride and anger." Ibid., 82.
122. *The Work of Theology*, 165.
123. Ibid., 235.
124. *Christian Existence Today*, 50.
125. Luther, *Luther's Works Vol. 3*, 156.
126. See *The Birth of Tragedy* "Foreword to Richard Wagner," part 1.
127. See *On the Genealogy of Morality*, Third Essay, sections 6–8.
128. See *On the Genealogy of Morality*, First Essay, section 15.
129. *Disrupting Time*, 151.
130. *Cross-Shattered Christ*, 11.
131. "We pray, therefore, not for certainty but for joy at the discernment that you have discovered us and given us a way to go on in the midst of confusion." *Prayers Plainly Spoken*, 76.
132. Ibid., 17.
133. Ibid., 99–101.
134. *Christian Existence Today*, 143.
135. *Disrupting Time*, 7.
136. "Truth and humility . . . require one another, but their most intimate relationship is to be found in worship." *The Work of Theology*, 168.
137. "I took one of my tasks as a teacher of theology to be giving students renewed confidence in the vocabulary of the faith. Yet how can that be done without acknowledgement of my inadequate ability to live what I say? My only recourse

is to pray that those I teach recognize the irony that constitutes the life of such a teacher." Ibid.
138. "How silly we must look to you, building anthills to no purpose. Help us to take joy and rest in your time, Eucharistic time, a time redeemed through Jesus's resurrection, that we can rest easy in our dying." Ibid., 169.
139. *Matthew*, 247.
140. Ibid., 24.

Afterword

1. Michael G. Cartwright, "Stanley Hauerwas's Essays in Theological Ethics: A Reader's Guide," in *The Hauerwas Reader*, ed. John Berkman and Michael Cartwright (Durham, NC: Duke University Press, 2001), 623–671.
2. Alongside Cartwright's chapter, one might consider consulting chapter 2 of Nicholas Healy's *Hauerwas: A (Very) Critical Introduction* (Grand Rapids, MI: Eerdmans, 2012), 17–38.
3. Samuel Wells, *Transforming Fate Into Destiny* (Carlisle: Paternoster, 1998).
4. See Chapters 1 and 4 of this volume. In this Brock joins the authors of several fine volumes of appraisal and critical celebration of Hauerwas's lifetime of work: Charles R. Pinches, Kelly S. Johnson, and Charles M. Collier, eds., *Unsettling Arguments: A Festschrift on the Occasion of Stanley Hauerwas's 70th Birthday* (Eugene, OR: Cascade, 2010); L. Gregory Jones, Reinhard Hütter, and C. Rosalee Velloso Ewell, eds., *God, Truth, and Witness: Engaging Stanley Hauerwas* (Grand Rapids, MI: Brazos, 2005); Mark Thiessen Nation and Samuel Wells, eds., *Faithfulness and Fortitude: In Conversation with the Theological Ethics of Stanley Hauerwas* (Edinburgh: T&T Clark, 2000).
5. Alasdair MacIntyre, *Three Rival Versions of Moral Enquiry* (Notre Dame, IN: University of Notre Dame Press, 1990).
6. MacIntyre's criticisms are in *Three Rival Versions of Moral Enquiry* (Notre Dame, IN: University of Notre Dame Press, 1990), 54–55. These criticisms are criticized in turn by Geoffrey Rees, who deploys the apparatus of the critique of religion to raise questions about MacIntyre's account that we think are consonant with our reading of Hauerwas. *The Romance of Innocent Sexuality* (Eugene, OR: Cascade, 2011), 140–144.
7. "The Church's One Foundation Is Jesus Christ Her Lord; or, in a World without Foundations: All We Have Is the Church," in *Theology without Foundations: Religious Practice and the Future of Theological Truth*, ed. Stanley Hauerwas, Nancey Murphy, and Mark Nation (Nashville, TN: Abingdon Press, 1994), 143–162.
8. These connections are made explicitly in Stanley Hauerwas, *Cross-Shattered Church* (Grand Rapids, MI: Brazos, 2009), 45:

> If we are to avoid fantasy and pretense, however, much will depend on how we have learned to allow the Word, Jesus Christ, to shape our words. So much will depend on our being made into Christ's body by the words that speak us. So much will depend on those who have patiently attended to the hard work of word care that we might see the bright beauty of God's kingdom in the blood washed white of the martyr's robes. And so much will depend on our seeing in and with one another that:
>
> "the just man justices;
> Keeps grace, that keeps all his goings graces;

>   Acts in God's eye what in God's eye he is—
>   Christ. For Christ plays in ten thousand places,
>   Lovely in limbs, and lovely in eyes not his,
>   To the Father through the features of men's faces."

9. Hauerwas has criticized what he considers MacIntyre's overly rigid separation of nature and grace. Stanley Hauerwas, "The Virtues of Alasdair MacIntyre," *First Things* 176 (October 2007): 35–40.
10. Stanley Hauerwas, *Matthew Brazos Theological Commentary on the Bible* (Grand Rapids, MI: Brazos, 2007), 23.
11. In Hauerwas, *A Community of Character: Toward a Constructive Christian Social Ethic* (Notre Dame: University of Notre Dame Press, 1981), 36–52.
12. Ibid., 44.
13. Ibid.
14. Ibid., 46.
15. Ibid.
16. This claim has been defended in admirable detail by Robert J. Dean in *For the Life of the World: Jesus Christ and the Church in the Theologies of Dietrich Bonhoeffer and Stanley Hauerwas* (Eugene, OR: Cascade, 2016), esp. chapters 1–2.
17. It might be read as a partial admission of this point that in recent work Hauerwas has begun explicitly to emphasize the role of apocalyptic in Yoder's work. "The End of Sacrifice: An Apocalyptic Politics," in *Approaching the End* (Grand Rapids, MI: Eerdmans, 2013), 22–36.
18. *Matthew*, 24.
19. Hauerwas notes this comment by Yoder in *Approaching the End*, 55.
20. The reasons for Hauerwas's reticence on this point are summarized in D. Stephen Long's "Capitalism and Fetishizing the Particular: Is Hauerwas a Nominalist," in *Unsettling Arguments: A Festschrift on the Occasion of Stanley Hauerwas's 70th Birthday*, ed. Charles R. Pinches, Kelly S. Johnson, and Charles M. Collier (Eugene, OR: Cascade, 2010), esp. 54–55.
21. Stanley Hauerwas and Charles Pinches, *Christians among the Virtues* (Notre Dame, IN: University of Notre Dame Press, 1997), 50–51.
22. Stanley Hauerwas, "On Keeping Theological Ethics Theological (1983)," *The Hauerwas Reader*, 72.
23. Stanley Hauerwas, "The Reality of the Kingdom: An Ecclesial Space for Peace," in *Against the Nations* (Notre Dame, IN: University of Notre Dame Press, 1992), 117–118.
24. Stanley Hauerwas, "Bearing Reality," in *Approaching the End*, 157.
25. *Approaching the End*, 157.
26. Quoting Wittgenstein, *Culture and Value*, in "Creation as Apocalyptic: A Tribute to William Stringfellow," with Jeff Powell, in *Dispatches from the Front* (Durham, NC: Duke University Press, 1994), 109; emphasis in the original.
27. *Against the Nations*, 210–211.
28. "Creation as Apocalyptic," 112–113. As discussed in Chapter 8, an early example of Hauerwas's understanding of role of the church as the formative space and time of apocalyptic appears in "The Church as God's New Language," in *Christian Existence Today* (Durham, NC: Labyrinth Press, 1988). His mature account can be found in, "Suffering Beauty: The Liturgical Formation of Christ's Body," in *Performing the Faith* (London: SPCK, 2004).

29. "September 11, 2001: A Pacifist Response," in *Dissent from the Homeland*, ed. Stanley Hauerwas and Frank Letricchia (Durham, NC: Duke University Press, 2003), 192.
30. Stanley Hauerwas, *Disrupting Time* (Eugene, OR: Cascade, 2004), 5.
31. Brian Goldstone and Stanley Hauerwas, "Disciplined Seeing: Forms of Christianity and Forms of Life," *South Atlantic Quarterly* 109 (2010): 785.
32. Ibid.
33. Stanley Hauerwas, *Theology without Foundations: Religious Practice and the Future of Theological Truth*, ed. Stanley Hauerwas, Nancey Murphy, and Mark Nation (Nashville, TN: Abingdon Press, 1994), 159.
34. Stanley Hauerwas and William H. Willimon, *Resident Aliens* (Nashville, TN: Abingdon Press, 1989), 103.
35. Stanley Hauerwas, *Hannah's Child* (Norwich: SCM Press, 2013), 156–160.
36. Ibid., 158.
37. Ibid.
38. Stanley Hauerwas, *Character and the Christian Life* (South Bend, IN: University of Notre Dame Press, 1994), 176.
39. Stanley Hauerwas, *The Peaceable Kingdom* (Notre Dame, IN: University of Notre Dame Press, 1984), 72.
40. Ibid., 83; italics in original.
41. Stanley Hauerwas, *With the Grain of the Universe* (Grand Rapids, MI: Brazos, 2001), 9–10.
42. Ibid., 200.
43. Ibid., 200–201.
44. *Approaching the End*, 45.
45. Ibid.
46. Ibid.
47. Stanley Hauerwas, *The Work of Theology* (Grand Rapids, MI: Eerdmans, 2013), 90.
48. Ibid., 91.
49. Ibid., 100.
50. A thirteen month "rational" calendar famously adopted by the Kodak Corporation. Duncan Steel, *Marking Time: The Epic Quest to Invent the Perfect Calendar* (New York: John Wiley & Sons, 2000), 308–309.
51. *The Work of Theology*, 102.
52. Ibid.
53. Ibid.
54. Stanley Hauerwas and William H. Willimon, *The Holy Spirit* (Nashville, TN: Abingdon Press, 2015), 66.
55. Ibid., 67; emphasis in the original.
56. Ibid., 91.
57. *The Work of Theology*, 257.
58. Ibid., 255.
59. Ibid., 265.

BIBLIOGRAPHY

Alter, Robert. *The Book of Psalms: A Translation with Commentary*. New York, NY: W. W. Norton, 2007.

Alter, Robert. *The David Story: A Translation of 1 and 2 Samuel*. New York, NY: W. W. Norton, 2000.

Angiolini, The Rt. Hon. Dame Elish DBE QC. *Report of the National Cremation Investigation*. Edinburgh: Government of Scotland, 2016.

Aquinas, Thomas. *Summa Theologica*, translated by Fathers of the English Dominican Province. 5 vols. Westminster, MD: Christian Classics, 1948.

Augustine. *The City of God against the Pagans*, edited and translated by R. W. Dyson. Cambridge: Cambridge University Press, 1998.

Augustine. *Confessions*, translated by Henry Chadwick. Oxford: Oxford University Press, 2005.

Bainton, Roland. *Christian Attitudes toward War and Peace*. Nashville, TN: Abingdon, 1960.

Barth, Karl. *The Christian Life: Church Dogmatics Volume IV, Part 4: Lecture Fragments*. London: Bloomsbury Continuum, 2004.

Barth, Karl. *Church Dogmatics III.4*. Edinburgh: T&T Clark, 2009.

Barth, Karl. *The Theology of John Calvin*. Grand Rapids, MI: Eerdmans, 1995.

Barth, Karl. "A Thank You and a Bow–Kierkegaard's Reveille." In *Fragments Grave and Gay*, edited by Martin Rumscheidt, translated by Eric Mosbacher. London: Colllins, 1971.

Barton, Stephen C. "1 Corinthians." In *Eerdmans Commentary on the Bible*, edited by James D.G. Dunn and John W. Rogerson, 1314–1350. Grand Rapids, MI: Eerdmans, 2003.

Beauchamp, Tom L., and James F. Childress. *Principles of Biomedical Ethics*. New York, NY: Oxford University Press, 1979. 6th Edition published 2009.

Benjamin, Walter. *Walter Benjamin: Selected Writings, Volume 4, 1938-1940*, edited by Howard Eiland and Michael W. Jennings. Cambridge, MA: Harvard University Press, 2003.

Bethge, Eberhard. *Dietrich Bonhoeffer: A Biography*. Minneapolis, MN: Fortress Press, 2000.

Biggar, Nigel. *Behaving in Public: How to Do Christian Ethics*. Grand Rapids, MI: Eerdmans, 2011.

Biggar, Nigel. *The Hastening That Waits*. Oxford: Clarendon Press, 1993.

Boulton, Matthew Meyer. *God against Religion: Rethinking Christian Theology through Worship*. Grand Rapids, MI: Eerdmans, 2008.

Boyd-Macmillan, Ronald. "The Transforming Sermon: A Study of the Preaching of St. Augustine, with Special Reference to the Sermones ad populum, and the Transformation Theory of James Loder." PhD Diss., University of Aberdeen, 2009.

Brock, Brian. *Captive to Christ, Open to the World*. Eugene, OR: Cascade, 2014.

Brock, Brian. "Christian Ethics." In *Mapping Modern Theology: A Thematic and Historical Introduction*, edited by Kelly M. Kapic and Bruce L. McCormack, 293–317. Grand Rapids, MI: Baker, 2012.

Brock, Brian. *Christian Ethics in a Technological Age*. Grand Rapids, MI: Eerdmans, 2010.

Brock, Brian. *Singing the Ethos of God*. Grand Rapids, MI: Eerdmans, 2007.

Brock, Brian. "What Is 'the Public'? Theological Variations on Babel and Pentecost." In *The Authority of the Gospel: Explorations in Moral and Political Theology in Honor of Oliver O'Donovan*, edited by Robert J. Song and Brent Waters, 160–178. Grand Rapids, MI: Eerdmans, 2014.

Brock, Brian, and John Swinton (eds.). *Disability in the Christian Tradition: A Reader*. Grand Rapids, MI: Eerdmans, 2012.

Brock, Brian, and Stephanie Brock. "Being Disabled in the New World of Genetic Testing: A Snapshot of Shifting Landscapes." In *Theology, Disability and the New Genetics: Why Science Needs the Church*, edited by John Swinton and Brian Brock, 29–43. London: T&T Clark, 2007.

Busch, Eberhard. *Karl Barth: His Life from Letters and Autobiographical Texts*. Eugene, OR: Wipf & Stock, 2005.

Chesterton, G.K. *Orthodoxy*. Peabody, MA: Hendrickson, 2006.

Clark, Patrick M. *Perfection in Death*. Washington DC: Catholic University of America Press, 2015.

Clough, David. *Ethics in Crisis*. Aldershot: Ashgate, 2005.

Coakley, Sarah. *God, Sexuality and the Self: An Essay "On the Trinity."* Cambridge: Cambridge University Press, 2013.

Coetzee, J.M. *Boyhood: Scenes from a Provincial Life*. London: Vintage, 1998.

Coetzee, J.M. "Confession and Double Thoughts: Tolstoy, Rousseau, Dostoyevsky (1985)." In *Doubling the Point*, edited by David Atwell, 251–293. Cambridge, MA: Harvard University Press, 1992.

Coetzee, J.M. *Summertime*. London: Vintage, 2010.

Coetzee, J.M. *Youth*. London: Vintage, 2003.

Coetzee, J.M., and Arabella Kurtz. *The Good Story: Exchanges on Truth, Fiction and Psychotherapy*. London: Harvill Secker, 2015.

Cohen, Ted. *Jokes: Philosophical Thoughts on Joking Matters*. Chicago, IL: University of Chicago Press, 1999.

Cramer, David, Jenny Howell, Jonathan Tran, and Paul Martens, "Scandalizing John Howard Yoder," *The Other Journal*. http://theotherjournal.com/2014/07/07/scandalizing-john-howard-yoder/ (accessed June 5, 2016).

Dean, Robert J. *For the Life of the World: Jesus Christ and the Church in the Theologies of Dietrich Bonhoeffer and Stanley Hauerwas*. Eugene, OR: Cascade, 2016.

Dennison, E. Patricia, David Ditchburn, and Michael Lynch (eds.). *Aberdeen before 1800: A New History*. East Linton: Tuckwell, 2002.

Dula, Peter. "The Limits of Theology: A Response to Jonathan Tran." In *The Difference Christ Makes: Celebrating the Life, Work, and Friendship of Stanley Hauerwas*, edited by Charles M. Collier, 71–76. Eugene, OR: Cascade, 2015.

Eribon, Didier. *Insult and the Making of the Gay Self*. Durham, NC: Duke University Press, 2004.

Frankena, William K. *Ethics*. Englewood, NJ: Prentice-Hall, 1980.

Frei, Hans. *The Eclipse of Biblical Narrative: Study in Eighteenth and Nineteenth Century Hermeneutics*. New Haven, CT: Yale University Press, 1980.

Frei, Hans. *The Identity of Jesus Christ*. Eugene, OR: Wipf and Stock, 1997.

Garver, Eugene. *For the Sake of the Argument*. Chicago, IL: University of Chicago Press, 2004.
Givens, Tommy. *We the People: Israel and the Catholicity of Jesus*. Minneapolis, MN: Fortress, 2014.
Goff, Stan. *Borderline: Reflections on War, Sex, and Church*. Eugene, OR: Cascade, 2015.
Goldstone, Brian, and Stanley Hauerwas. "Disciplined Seeing: Forms of Christianity and Forms of Life." *South Atlantic Quarterly* 109 (2010): 765–790.
Greggs, Tom. *Theology against Religion: Constructive Dialogues with Bonhoeffer and Barth*. London: T&T Clark, 2011.
Guest, Mathew, Sonya Sharma, and Robert Song. *Gender and Career Progression in Theology and Religious Studies*. Durham, UK: Durham University, 2013.
Hartle, Ann. *The Modern Self in Rousseau's "Confessions": A Reply to St. Augustine*. Notre Dame, IN: Notre Dame University Press, 1984.
Hauerwas, Stanley. *After Christendom*. Nashville, TN: Abingdon Press, 2001.
Hauerwas, Stanley. *Against the Nations*. Notre Dame, IN: University of Notre Dame Press, 1992.
Hauerwas, Stanley. *Approaching the End*. Grand Rapids, MI: Eerdmans, 2013.
Hauerwas, Stanley. "Bearing Reality: A Christian Meditation." *Journal of the Society of Christian Ethics* 33, no. 1 (2013): 3–20.
Hauerwas, Stanley. *A Better Hope: Resources for a Church Confronting Capitalism, Democracy and Postmodernity*. Grand Rapids, MI: Baker, 2000.
Hauerwas, Stanley. *Character and the Christian Life*. South Bend, IN: University of Notre Dame Press, 1994.
Hauerwas, Stanley. *Christian Existence Today*. Durham, NC: Labyrinth Press, 1988.
Hauerwas, Stanley. "The Church's One Foundation Is Jesus Christ Her Lord; or, in a World without Foundations: All We Have Is the Church." In *Theology without Foundations: Religious Practice and the Future of Theological Truth*, edited by Stanley Hauerwas, Nancey Murphy, and Mark Nation, 143–162. Nashville, TN: Abingdon Press, 1994.
Hauerwas, Stanley. "Citizens of Heaven." In *The Freedom of a Christian Ethicist: The Future of a Reformation Legacy*, edited by Brian Brock and Michael Mawson, 11–15. London: Continuum, 2015.
Hauerwas, Stanley. *A Community of Character: Toward a Constructive Christian Social Ethic*. Notre Dame: University of Notre Dame Press, 1981.
Hauerwas, Stanley. *Cross-Shattered Christ*. Grand Rapids, MI: Brazos, 2011.
Hauerwas, Stanley. *A Cross-Shattered Church*. Grand Rapids, MI: Brazos, 2009.
Hauerwas, Stanley. *Dispatches from the Front*. Durham, NC: Duke University Press, 1994.
Hauerwas, Stanley. *Disrupting Time*. Eugene, OR: Cascade, 2004.
Hauerwas, Stanley. *Hannah's Child*. Norwich: SCM Press, 2013.
Hauerwas, Stanley. *The Hauerwas Reader*, edited by John Berkman and Michael Cartwright. Durham, NC: Duke University Press, 2001.
Hauerwas, Stanley. *In Good Company*. Notre Dame, IN: University of Notre Dame Press, 1995.
Hauerwas, Stanley. *Learning to Speak Christian*. Norwich: SCM, 2011.
Hauerwas, Stanley. *Matthew Brazos Theological Commentary on the Bible*. Grand Rapids, MI: Brazos, 2007.
Hauerwas, Stanley. *Naming the Silences*. Grand Rapids, MI: Eerdmans, 1990.
Hauerwas, Stanley. *The Peaceable Kingdom*. Notre Dame, IN: University of Notre Dame Press, 1984.

Hauerwas, Stanley. *Performing the Faith*. London: SPCK, 2004.
Hauerwas, Stanley. *Prayers Plainly Spoken*. Eugene, OR: Wipf & Stock, 2003.
Hauerwas, Stanley. *Sanctify Them in the Truth*. Nashville, TN: Abingdon, 1991.
Hauerwas, Stanley. "Seeing Peace: L'Arche as a Peace Movement." In *The Paradox of Disability: Responses to Jean Vanier and L'Arche Communities from Theology and the Sciences*, edited by Hans Reinders, 113–126. Grand Rapids, MI: Eerdmans, 2010.
Hauerwas, Stanley. *The State of the University*. Oxford: Blackwell, 2007.
Hauerwas, Stanley. *Suffering Presence*. Notre Dame, IN: Notre Dame University Press, 1986.
Hauerwas, Stanley. *Truthfulness and Tragedy*. Notre Dame, IN: University of Notre Dame Press, 1977.
Hauerwas, Stanley. *Unleashing the Scriptures*. Nashville, TN: Abingdon Press, 1993.
Hauerwas, Stanley. "The Virtues of Alasdair MacIntyre." *First Things* 176, October 2007, 35–40.
Hauerwas, Stanley. *Vision and Virtue*. Notre Dame, IN: Fides Publishers, 1974.
Hauerwas, Stanley. "War and Peace." In *The Oxford Handbook of Theology and Modern European Thought*, edited by Nicholas Adams, George Pattison, and Graham Ward, 361–374. Oxford: Oxford University Press, 2013.
Hauerwas, Stanley. *War and the American Difference*. Grand Rapids, MI: Baker Academic, 2011.
Hauerwas, Stanley. "Why Jean Vanier Matters: An Exemplary Exploration." In *Knowing, Being Known, and the Mystery of God; Essays in Honor of Professor Hans Reinders: Teacher, Friend, Disciple*, edited by Bill Gaventa and Erik de Jongh, 229–239. Amsterdam: VU University Press, 2016.
Hauerwas, Stanley. *Wilderness Wanderings*. Boulder, CO: Westview Press, 1997.
Hauerwas, Stanley. *With the Grain of the Universe*. Grand Rapids, MI: Brazos, 2001.
Hauerwas, Stanley. *The Work of Theology*. Grand Rapids, MI: Eerdmans, 2013.
Hauerwas, Stanley, and Charles Pinches. *Christians among the Virtues*. Notre Dame, IN: University of Notre Dame Press, 1997.
Hauerwas, Stanley, and Frank Letricchia (eds.). *Dissent from the Homeland*. Durham, NC: Duke University Press, 2003.
Hauerwas, Stanley, and Jean Vanier. *Living Gently in a Violent World*. Downer's Grove, IL: IVP, 2008.
Hauerwas, Stanley, and Romand Coles. *Christianity, Democracy and the Radical Ordinary*. Cambridge: The Lutterworth Press, 2008.
Hauerwas, Stanley, and Sam Wells (eds.). *The Blackwell Companion to Christian Ethics*. 2nd ed. Oxford: Wiley Blackwell, 2011.
Hauerwas, Stanley, Samuel Wells, and friends. *Living out Loud*, edited by Luke Bretherton and Russell Rook. Milton Keynes: Paternoster, 2010.
Hauerwas, Stanley, and William H. Willimon. *The Holy Spirit*. Nashville, TN: Abingdon Press, 2015.
Hauerwas, Stanley, and William H. Willimon. *Preaching to Strangers*. Louisville, KY: Westminster John Knox Press, 1992.
Hauerwas, Stanley, and William H. Willimon. *Resident Aliens*. Nashville, TN: Abingdon Press, 1989.
Havel, Vaclav. *Living in Truth*. London: Faber & Faber, 1989.
Hays, Richard. *The Moral Vision of the New Testament*. San Francisco, CA: Harper One, 1996.

Healy, Nicholas M. *Hauerwas: A (Very) Critical Introduction*. Grand Rapids, MI: Eerdmans, 2012.

Hersh, Seymour. "The Killing of Osama bin Laden." *London Review of Books* 37, no. 10 (2015): 3–12.

Holmer, Paul L. *Communicating the Faith Indirectly: The Paul L. Holmer Papers Volume Three*, edited by David J. Gouwens and Lee C. Barrett III. Cambridge: James Clarke & Co., 2013.

Holmer, Paul L. *The Grammar of Faith*. San Francisco, CA: Harper & Row, 1978.

Holmer, Paul L. *Thinking the Faith with Passion: The Paul L. Holmer Papers Volume Two*, edited by David J. Gouwens and Lee C. Barrett III. Eugene, OR: Cascade, 2012.

John Howard Yoder, "Tertium Datur: Refocusing the Jewish-Christian Schism," unpublished manuscript, October 13, 1977. Box 133, "Tertium Datur 1977." John H. Yoder Papers, 1947–1997. HM1-48. Mennonite Church USA Archives—Goshen. Goshen, Indiana. An online copy can be retrieved from: http://brandon.multics.org/library/John%20Howard%20Yoder/tertium_datur.html.

Jones, L. Gregory, Reinhard Hütter, and C. Rosalee Velloso Ewell (eds.). *God, Truth, and Witness: Engaging Stanley Hauerwas*. Grand Rapids, MI: Brazos, 2005.

Kovacs, Judith (trans. and ed.). *1 Corinthians: Interpreted by Early Christian Commentators*. Grand Rapids, MI: Eerdmans, 2005.

Lindbeck, George A. *The Nature of Doctrine: Religion and Theology in a Postliberal Age*. Philadelphia, PA: Westminster Press, 1984.

Luther, Martin. *Luther's Works Vol. 1: Lectures on Genesis Chapters 1–5*. St. Louis, MO: Concordia, 1958.

Luther, Martin. *Luther's Works Vol. 3: Lectures on Genesis Chapters 15–20*. St. Louis, MO: Concordia, 1961.

MacIntyre, Alasdair. *After Virtue*. London: Gerald Duckworth, 2007.

MacIntyre, Alasdair. *A Short History of Ethics*. London: Routledge, 2002.

MacIntyre, Alasdair. *Three Rival Versions of Moral Enquiry*. Notre Dame, IN: University of Notre Dame Press, 1990.

Martens, Paul, and David Cramer. "By What Criteria Does a 'Grand, Noble Experiment' Fail? What the Case of John Howard Yoder Reveals about the Mennonite Church." *Mennonite Quarterly Review* 89, no. 1 (2015): 171–193.

Matthewes, Charles. *The Republic of Grace: Augustinian Thoughts for Dark Times*. Grand Rapids, MI: Eerdmans, 2010.

Mead, Margaret. *Coming of Age in Samoa: A Psychological Study of Primitive Youth for Western Civilization*. New York, NY: W. Morrow & Company, 1928.

Morice Brubaker, Sarah. "The Work of Theology, by Stanley Hauerwas Review." In *The Christian Century*, October 14, 2015.

Murphy, Francesca Aran. *I Samuel Brazos Theological Commentary*. Grand Rapids, MI: Brazos, 2010.

Natali, Carlo. *Aristotle: His Life and School*. Princeton, NJ: Princeton University Press, 2013.

Nation, Mark Thiessen, and Samuel Wells (eds.). *Faithfulness and Fortitude: In Conversation with the Theological Ethics of Stanley Hauerwas*. Edinburgh: T&T Clark, 2000.

Nietzsche, Friedrich. *On the Genealogy of Morality Keith Ansell-Pearson*, edited and translated by Carol Diethe. Cambridge: Cambridge University Press, 1994.

O'Connor, Flannery. *A Prayer Journal*. New York, NY: Farrar, Straus and Giroux, 2013.

O'Donovan, Oliver. *The Desire of the Nations*. Cambridge: Cambridge University Press, 1996.
O'Donovan, Oliver. *Resurrection and the Moral Order*. Leicester: Apollos, 1994.
O'Donovan, Oliver. *Ways of Judgement*. Grand Rapids, MI: Eerdmans, 2005.
O'Donovan, Oliver. "What Can Ethics Know about God?" In *The Doctrine of God and Theological Ethics*, edited by Alan Torrance and Michael Banner, 33–46. London: T&T Clark, 2006.
Oppenheimer, Mark. "For God, Not Country: The Un-American Theology of Stanley Hauerwas." *Lingua Franca* 11, no. 6, (2001): http://linguafranca.mirror.theinfo.org/print/0109/feature.html.
Paul, Herman. "Stanley Hauerwas: Against Secularization in the Church." *Zeitschrift für Dialektische Theologie* 59, no. 2 (2013): 12–33.
Pecknold, Chad C. "Beyond our Intentions: An Augustinian Reading of Hannah's Child." *Pro Ecclesia* XX, no. 3, (2011): 298–309.
Pinches, Charles. *A Gathering of Memories*. Grand Rapids, MI: Brazos, 2006.
Pinches, Charles R., Kelly S. Johnson, and Charles M. Collier (eds.). *Unsettling Arguments: A Festschrift on the Occasion of Stanley Hauerwas's 70th Birthday*. Eugene, OR: Cascade, 2010.
Ramsey, Paul. *Christian Ethics and the Sit-In*. New York, NY: Association Press, 1961.
Ramsey, Paul. *The Just War*. Lanham, MD: Rowman & Littlefield, 2002.
Ramsey, Paul. *The Patient as Person*. New Haven, CT: Yale University Press, 1974.
Rees, Geoffrey. *The Romance of Innocent Sexuality*. Eugene, OR: Cascade, 2011.
Reinders, Hans. *Receiving the Gift of Friendship*. Grand Rapids, MI: Eerdmans, 2008.
Rorty, Amélie O. "The Place of Contemplation in Aristotle's Nicomachean Ethics." In *Essays on Aristotle's Ethics*, edited by Amélie Oksenberg Rorty, 377–394. Los Angeles, CA: University of California Press, 1980.
Rousseau, Jean Jacques. *The Confessions and Correspondence, Including Letters to Malesherbes* translated by Christopher Kelly, edited by Christopher Kelly, Roger D. Masters, and Peter G. Stillman. Hanover, NH: University Press of New England, 1995.
Sarisky, Darren. "A prolegomenon to an account of theological interpretation of Scripture." In *Theological Theology: Essays in Honour of John Webster*, edited by R. David Nelson, Darren Sarisky, and Justin Stratis, 247–266. London: Bloomsbury T&T Clark, 2015.
Scarry, Elaine. *The Body in Pain*. New York, NY: Oxford University Press, 1985.
Slahi, Mohamedou Ould. *Guantanamo Diary*, edited by Larry Siems. Edinburgh: Cannongate, 2015.
Steel, Duncan. *Marking Time: The Epic Quest to Invent the Perfect Calendar*. New York: John Wiley & Sons, 2000.
Stout, Jeffrey. *Democracy and Tradition*. Princeton, NJ: Princeton University Press, 2004.
Swinton John (ed.). *Critical Reflections on Stanley Hauerwas's Theology of Disability: Disabling Society, Enabling Theology*. Binghamton, NY: Hayworth Pastoral Press, 2004.
Tran, Jonathan. "Anne and the Difficult Gift of Stanley Hauerwas's Church." In *The Difference Christ Makes: Celebrating the Life, Work, and Friendship of Stanley Hauerwas*, edited by Charles M. Collier, 51–70. Eugene, OR: Cascade Books, 2015.
Webb, Stephen. *Re-figuring Theology*. Albany, NY: SUNY Press, 1991.
Wells, Samuel. *God's Companions*. Malden, MA: Blackwell, 2006.
Wells, Samuel. *Transforming Fate into Destiny*. Carlisle: Paternoster, 1998.
Willimon William H., and Stanley Hauerwas. *Preaching to Strangers*. Louisville, KY: Westminster John Knox Press, 1992.

Yoder, John Howard. *Christian Attitudes towards War, Peace and Revolution.* Grand Rapids, MI: Brazos, 2009.
Yoder, John Howard. *Discipleship as Political Responsibility.* Scottsdale, PA: Herald Press, 2003.
Yoder, John Howard. *For the Nations.* Grand Rapids, MI: Eerdmans, 2007.
Yoder, John Howard. *He Came Preaching Peace.* Kitchener, ON: Herald Press, 1986.
Yoder, John Howard. *Karl Barth and the Problem of War.* Eugene, OR: Cascade, 2003.
Yoder, John Howard. *The Original Revolution.* Scottsdale, PA: Herald Press, 1971.
Yoder, John Howard. *The Politics of Jesus.* Grand Rapids, MI: Eerdmans, 1996.
Zeigler Philip P. "Barth's Criticisms of Kierkegaard—A Striking out at Phantoms?" *International Journal of Systematic Theology* 9, no. 4 (2007): 434–451.

INDEX OF NAMES

Adams, James Luther 66
Alda, Alan 9, 306 n.6
Alter, Robert 183
Anscombe, Elizabeth ix, 187
Aquinas, Thomas ix, 43–6, 130, 137, 147, 227, 233, 272
Aristotle ix, x, 42–52, 53, 59–60, 66, 75, 86, 90, 110, 123, 129–32, 137, 146, 155, 160, 192, 207, 222–8, 233, 268–9, 278, 315 n.67
Armstrong, Lance 21
Augustine 8, 9, 13, 17–23, 42, 50, 92, 96, 100–1, 109, 171, 233, 254–7, 268–9, 282, 284, 289
Austen, Jane 47
Austin, J. L. 90
Ayers, David 5

Bader-Saye, Scott 270
Bainton, Roland 163
Barth, Karl ix, xi, xii, 16, 39, 50, 64, 65, 68, 76, 77, 86, 92, 96, 139–40, 143, 180, 183, 233, 241, 244, 269, 272, 280, 286–8, 292–5, 300–2
Barton, Stephen 50
Baxter, Mike 180
Beauchamp, Tom L. 131, 196
BeDuhn, Jason David 18
Bender, Harvey 199
Benjamin, Walter 59, 112, 309 n.25
Bennett, Jana 175
Berry, Wendell 197
Bethge, Eberhard 16
Biggar, Nigel 135, 139, 316 n.15
Bin Laden, Osama 163, 176, 258
Bluebond-Langner, Myra 214–15, 219
Bobbitt, Philip 45, 194
Bonhoeffer, Dietrich 16, 182, 267, 280
Bowes-Lyon, Elizabeth Angela Marguerite [Queen Mother] 98
Brock, Adam 27–8, 92, 100, 117, 120–1, 201–2, 209, 212, 216, 219–21, 231

Brock, Stephanie xiii, 72, 117, 121, 156, 202, 212, 216, 220
Brod, Max 181
Bruner, Frederick Dale 251
Burrell, David 46, 77
Busch, Eberhard 16
Bush, George Jr. 193

Cain, David 76
Calvin, John ix, 68, 264
Cameron, Andrew 87
Campbell, Dennis 20
Cartwright, Michael 291
Cavell, Stanley 117
Chesterton, G. K. 43, 308 n.4
Childress, James F. 131, 196
Chrysostom, John 208, 321 n.24
Clarke, Patrick, 147
Clough, David, 139, 160–1
Coakley, Sarah, 57
Coetzee, J. M. 12, 17–19, 22–3
Cohen, Ted 85
Coles, Romand 5, 102–4, 109, 112–15, 125
Cone, James 35

Davies, W. D. 266
Day, Dorothy 10, 87, 106, 326 n.77
Descartes, René 43, 233, 235
Dewey, John 234
De Vreis, Peter 214
Diamond, Cora 11
Dostoevsky, Fyodor 17, 83, 252
Dula, Peter 237

Edwards, Jonathan 68
Evans, John 196–7

Firestone, Shulamith 186
Fleming, Richard 87
Fletcher, Joseph 233
Foucault, Michel 4, 118, 188

Frankena, William K. 130–1, 134
Freeman, Curtis 16
Frei, Hans 88–9, 245, 262, 284, 287, 324 n.15
French, Clark 55, 101

Gandhi, Mahatma 184, 185
Garver, Eugene 89
Gibson, Mel 109
Gilbert, Paula 7, 32, 55, 101, 165, 170, 221–2, 244, 273
Givens, Tommy 181
Goff, Stanley 179, 184–5
Gregory, Eric 5, 146, 173
Grisez, Germain 137
Groff, Warren 293
Guest, Mathew 186
Gunton, Colin 91
Gustafson, James 20, 66, 85

Hammett, Dashiell 39
Harper, George 32, 34
Hartle, Ann 17
Harvey, Jennifer, 37
Havel, Vaclev, 104–5
Hauerwas, Adam 26, 68, 214, 236, 240, 243–4
Hauerwas, Anne 2, 5, 8, 13–14, 25–8, 201–2, 212–14, 235–8, 300
Hauerwas, Johnny 27–8
Healy, Nicholas 240–1
Heidegger, Martin 217
Hemingway, Ernest 39
Henry, Stuart 6
Herdt, Jennifer 146
Hesburgh, Theodore 103
Hitler, Adolf 168, 174, 182
Hollenbach, David 173, 175–6
Holmer, Paul x, 76–81, 83–5, 87–90, 287, 301, 311 n.40
Hopkins, Gerard Manley 43, 292

James, William ix, 69, 72
Jenson, Robert and Blanch 178
Johnson, Kelly 5
Johnson, Samuel 75
Jones, Greg 5, 32
Jonsen, Albert 133

Kafka, Franz 20, 181
Kant, Immanuel 134
Keen, Craig 24

Keohane, Nannerl 275
Kennedy, John F. 141
Kennedy, Robert F. 84, 141
Khrushchev, Nikita 83
Kierkegaard, Soren xi, 75–6, 78, 81, 84–6, 88, 181, 189, 301, 310 n.11, 310 n.16
Kimbrough, Timothy 7, 55
King, Martin Luther 37, 84, 161–2, 184–5
Kroeker, Travis 5

Lewis, C. S., 165–6
Lindbeck, George 79, 162, 168, 224, 253–4
Linzey, Andrew 217
Luther, Martin 92–3, 144, 213, 263–4, 272, 286, 321 n.32
Luz, Ulrich 273
Lysaught, Tracy 5

Machiavelli, Niccolò 45
MacIntyre, Alasdair ix, x, xii, 6, 17, 38, 44–8, 51, 57, 59, 109, 112, 128, 169, 179, 202, 208, 292–3, 295, 297
Mann, Thomas 26
Martens, Paul 184
Marx, Karl 45
Mathewes, Charles 173
Mattson, Stanley 165
McBrien, Richard 20
McDonagh, Enda 279
McDonald, Alonzo 5
McFague-TeSelle, Sally 187
McFarland, David 257
McKenny, Gerald 5, 11, 75, 79, 139
MacKinnon, Catherine 185–6, 320–50
MacKinnon, Donald 252
MacMillan, Ronald Boyd 254
Mead, Margaret 185
Meeks, Wayne 88
Meilaender, Gilbert 151
Meyer, Paul 88
Milbank, John 107, 113, 252, 297
Moore, George Edward 90
Muller, Andre 252
Murdoch, Iris ix, 6, 45, 96, 187
Murphy, Francesca 182
Myer, Ray and Mary-Ellen 184

Natali, Carlo 51
Nation, Mark 184
Neuhaus, Richard 16, 68

Index of Names

Newman, Joseph 202
Niebuhr, Reinhold ix, 66, 73, 75, 96, 163, 167, 266
Niebuhr, H. Richard 66, 318 n.8
Nietzsche, Friedrich 43, 45, 284, 288, 308 n.3
Noyce, Gay 83
Nussbaum, Martha 243

Ochs, Peter 274
O'Connor, Flannery 276–7
O'Donovan, Oliver 99, 135, 218, 288, 316 n.15
Oppenheimer, Helen 187
Ould Slahi, Mohamedou 179

Paul, Herman 232
Pecknold, Chad 5
Pelikan, Jaroslav 264
Penn, William 171, 176, 179
Pinches, Charles 169–70
Plato 51, 227
Plutarch 17
Poobalon, Isaac 231
Price, Reynolds 275

Rainey, Bonnie 199
Ramsey, Paul ix, 68, 73, 160, 162, 166, 168–9, 172–3, 185, 193–4, 203–4, 218
Rauschenbusch, Walter 20, 75, 294
Reinders, Hans 2, 38
Rilke, Rainer Maria 290
Romero, Miguel 227
Rorty, Amélie 48
Rorty, Richard ix
Rothko, Mark 19
Rousseau, Jean Jacques 16–18, 306 n.25

Sacks, Jonathan 183
Sanders, E. P. 266
Sarisky, Darren 267, 270, 326 nn.62, 70
Scarry, Ellen 215
Schopenhauer, Arthur 288
Score, John 6, 69
Scotus, John Duns 43
Sider, Alex 111
Siggins, Ian 264
Smith, Adam 198
Smith, John 105, 243–4
Sharma, Sonya 186

Shuman, Joel 197
Socrates, 51–2, 72, 243, 269, 285
Sonderegger, Katherine 15
Song, Robert 186
Speer, Albert 77
Stout, Jeffrey 260, 282
Swinton, John xii, 100, 313 n.31

Tertullian 168–9
Thomas, Pére 108, 313 n.29
Thurber, James 83
Tillich, Paul 66, 169
Tran, Jonathan 14, 44, 184, 236–7
Troeltsch, Ernst 57
Trollope, Anthony ix, 6, 8, 11, 47, 180
Trump, Donald 287
Twain, Mark 229

Ulrich, Hans 44, 92, 152, 265

Vanier, Jean xi, xii, 9, 87, 105–12, 115, 151, 188, 200, 220, 222–38, 298, 299
Vazeille, Molly 2

Wainwright, Geoffrey 244
Ward, Graham 194
Webb, Stephen 73, 310 n.10
Webster, John 121
Weicker, Lowell 275
Wells, Sam, 36–7, 56, 113, 125, 127, 204, 318 n.8
Wesley, John 2, 68–9, 75
West, Cornel 113–14
Wetzel, James 5
Williams, Rowan 250, 252
Willimon, Will viii, 253, 255, 283, 303
Wittgenstein, Ludwig ix, 77, 80, 81, 86, 88, 117–18, 297, 301
Wolfensberger, Wolf 207
Wolin, Sheldon 103, 115–16, 314 n.45
Wood, Don ix, xiii, 15, 274

Yoder, John Howard ix, xi, 25, 96, 106–7, 112, 131, 162–3, 167, 171–4, 176, 179, 180–3, 184–5, 208, 243, 246, 253, 264, 266, 293–6, 300–1, 331 n.17

Ziegler, Philip xiii, 76

Index of Bible References

Genesis 2:2, 322 n.32
Genesis 2:24, 315 n.56
Exodus 29:3, 258
1 Chronicles 22:8, 183, 319 n.43
1 Chronicles 28:3, 183, 319 n.43
1 Kings 22:1–28, 54, 309 n.20
Psalm 103:15–16, 43
Matthew 4:4, 271

Matthew 18, 23, 96, 101–2, 108, 313 n.15
Matthew 19:4–5, 119, 315 n.56
Matthew 25:35–45, 271
Acts 22:28, 170, 318 n.15
1 Corinthians 11:30, 248
2 Corinthians 11–12, 7
Ephesians 5:21–33, 140
Colossians 3:18–19, 140

INDEX OF SUBJECTS

1980 AAR address 2, 23, 63, 65–8, 72–3, 75–6, 80, 83–4, 88, 148, 198, 214–15, 242, 292
1960s as a context for theology 2, 21, 24–5, 35, 92, 102–4, 188

Aberdeen, University of xii, xiii, 139, 160, 235, 278, 287
abortion 49, 98, 104, 132, 136–7, 142, 152
adultery 132, 139, 154
apocalyptic theology x–xii, 20, 76–8, 81, 146, 267–8, 271, 286, 289–90, 291–304
Augustana University 13, 25, 36, 37, 93, 103

Babel 245–6, 257, 286
Babette's Feast 85
Baptism vii, 66, 68–9, 97, 121, 143, 210, 312 n.8
Barth
  as teacher 92
  in an apocalyptic key 75–7, 81, 292–5, 300–3
  on biography 16
  on casuistry 139–44
  on ethics 63–5
  on Grenzfall cases 96
  on irony and joy 286–8
  on retirement 39
  on revelation 50, 182, 272
  on prayer 280
  on preaching 241
bricklaying x, 3–4, 24, 31–5, 55, 141, 148, 298

Camp Hill 152
casuistry 129–44, 302, 309 n.5, 316 n.15
celibacy 154, 175
Chicago, University of 64, 142–3
Christendom 56, 100, 181, 204, 260–1, 275, 303, 313 n.28

Church vii–viii, xi–xii, 3, 4, 10, 19, 33–40, 68, 82, 140–1, 155, 168, 190–1, 207, 239–40, 263–4, 274–5, 284, 294–6, 298–302, 314 n.42, 318 n.8, 321 n.24, 328 n.107, 328 n.117, 328 n.119, 331 n.28
  and disability 120–1, 197–9, 201–4, 209, 211–15, 222–4, 229–31, 237
  and its distinctive politics 103–6, 110, 113, 115, 121–2, 145–6, 161–2, 164, 171, 173–5, 194, 280–2, 312 n.8
  as a Sunday wasted 92–3, 127, 254, 317 n.43, 329 n.120
  as center of moral formation 64, 71–2, 95–102, 123–5, 199, 242–4, 288–9, 324 n.8, 327 n.92
  as the location for theology 79–80, 87–8, 126, 244, 246–9, 251–60, 325 n. 49, 327 n.91
  considered along with Scripture and authority 7, 10, 23, 46, 50, 55–6, 111, 182, 230, 270, 324 n.11
Cliché 6–7
Constantinianism 53–4, 77–8, 80, 107, 114, 146, 165, 168, 173, 196, 204, 208, 248, 261, 274–5, 296, 300–2
  anti-constantinianism 77, 80, 100, 248, 301
contingency x, xii, 1, 41–51, 79, 91–2, 113, 119, 123–5, 134–5, 145–87, 199, 210, 246, 281, 297–8
creation 39, 42, 64, 117–19, 123, 145, 245, 256, 270–1, 275, 286, 296, 300, 302, 327 n.86, 328 n.103
Christian traditions
  Amish 135, 180
  Anabaptists 96, 101, 170, 264
  Baptists 16

Episcopalians 101–2, 124, 127, 217, 275
Evangelicalism 92, 103, 203, 214, 254, 274
Lutherans 68, 78, 85, 92–3, 322 n.32
Mennonites 102, 134–5, 184, 243, 266, 313 n.15
Methodists 6, 60, 242–3, 303, 305 n.3
Orthodox Christianity 19
Quakers 100, 171, 312 n.12
Roman Catholics 73, 134–5, 182, 225, 243, 264
Communio sanctorum 59, 112–13, 125, 229–30, 251, 277–8, 328 n.105

Dallas Theological Seminary 262
death 17, 28, 38, 49, 95–101, 105–6, 110, 118, 121, 166, 204, 208, 215, 217, 219–20, 222, 245, 248, 250, 260, 263, 269, 275, 286, 293–4, 297, 300–2, 304, 307 n.56, 312 n.8, 327 n.86, 329 n.138
Churchyard cemeteries 100, 312 n.12
definitions 15, 58, 109, 128
democracy 25, 95–6, 102–3, 115, 168, 172–3, 206
disability x–xi, 2, 4, 27–8, 106, 110, 116–17, 126, 187–9, 194, 195–238, 248
Church hospitable to 202–3
on its subtle instrumentalisation 208–11
discipleship x–xi, 85, 109, 113, 147, 162, 184, 272–3
Duke Divinity School 8, 16, 36–7, 47, 79, 91, 102–4, 164, 204, 238, 242, 244–5, 247, 253, 274, 278

elitism 10, 48, 50, 167
embodiment xi, 110, 116–22, 181, 215, 298
eschatology 15, 59, 84–5, 95–128, 144, 162, 173, 181–2, 230, 286, 289, 293–4, 298–302
Eucharist 79, 93, 97, 112, 120–1, 192, 231, 242–4, 271, 297, 329 n.138

Facebook 156–7
Flourishing (Eudaimonia) 49, 228
forgiveness 66, 95, 109, 153, 194, 303, 313 n.15
friendship viii–ix, xii, 2, 25, 27, 35, 40, 82, 90, 97, 148–9, 164, 202, 211, 229, 234, 236–7, 293, 327 n.92, 328 n.113

Aristotle on friendship 48, 129, 225–6, 278
as factor in theological work 87, 88, 148, 162, 167, 181, 255, 260, 275
contemporary difficulties 155–7
expanding boundaries of marriage and family 190–1, 207
Hannah's Child and friendship 5–18
with God 12, 157, 275, 284, 295

gentleness xii, 11, 34, 72, 105–8, 114, 229–30, 296–97, 313 n.27, 313 n.28
grace 17, 19, 42, 59, 64, 118, 138, 145, 269–70, 330 n.8, 330 n.9
guns 101, 105, 108, 116, 150, 163–4, 172, 178–9, 185, 317 n.38

habit x, xii, 98, 100, 110, 112, 187, 193, 206, 257–8, 291–2, 297–9, 301, 303, 308 n.8
habit and discipleship 51, 61, 124
habit and virtues 46, 160, 179, 226
habits and repentance 147–54, 268–9
habits and work 24, 26, 30, 34, 288
temperament and habit 65–93, (63–72), 315 n.67
the body's habits 121, 148, 228
Harvard Divinity School 64, 66
Herods of this world 251, 258, 261
heroism, danger of 7, 14, 109, 170, 237, 243
Hexis 123–8, 315 n.67
Holy Spirit xi, 38, 56–7, 59, 113, 115, 124, 152, 161, 209, 229–38, 245, 249, 260, 272, 281–2, 286, 295–6, 299, 300, 303, 309 n.5, 329 n.120
holiness 60–1, 118, 143–4, 229, 247, 284

IVF and IVD 124, 190, 216

Jesus Christ 39, 113, 115, 120, 125, 146–7, 194, 229, 231, 248, 262, 284, 286, 291–304
Christology 44–5, 56, 64, 76, 79, 116, 118, 129, 146–7, 183, 194–5, 208, 225, 237, 263, 267, 269, 275, 292–4, 303
crucified and resurrected 12, 245, 260, 262–3, 269, 275, 293–4, 300–2, 327 n.86, 329 n.138

L'Arche xi, 105, 108, 110, 115, 116, 151–2, 222–8, 229, 234, 313 n.27, 313 n.28, 313 n.29, 322 n.47
local churches
  Broadway United Methodist in South Bend, Indiana 105, 242–5, 247, 324 n.8
  Christ Church in Nashville, Tennessee 263
  Holy Family Episcopal in Chapel Hill, North Carolina 77, 97–8, 101, 108
  Sacred Heart Basilica in Notre Dame, Indiana 243
  St. Andrew's Cathedral in Aberdeen 126, 315 n.75
  St. John's Episcopal in Aberdeen 97, 231
  Saint Thomas Church in New York 259
Logan Center 199–200, 202
Love of God 12

marriage 2, 14, 27, 140, 154, 175, 189–92, 202, 212–14, 231, 234, 300, 322 n.32
  being known in 108–9
  egalitarianism 10, 187–8
  gay marriage 188–9, 192
Martial virtue 164, 179–80
Medicine and war 166
memoir x, 1–12, 12–25, 25–9, 30, 36–7, 60, 201, 300
memory 6, 8, 14, 17, 24, 59, 66, 76, 80–1, 99–100, 112–13, 132, 148, 151, 153, 174, 232, 306 n.25
moral exemplars vii, 111, 150–1, 192–3, 299–300
Mull, the Inner Hebredian island 205–6

narrative x–xi, 6, 15, 17–18, 20–2, 24, 30, 34–5, 58, 61, 68–9, 79–81, 109, 119–20, 122, 125, 139, 141–4, 145–7, 148, 182–3, 192, 211–12, 219, 231, 236, 242–6, 251, 262, 271
  narratives of self 4, 13, 18, 66, 69, 73, 112, 184, 229
  nation-state narratives 114, 159–70
  theology and narrative 13, 42–4, 64, 130–6, 297–300, 324 nn.11, 15
nationalism 169–70
nation-states 168, 174–5, 194, 218
  memory of 153, 163–4
National Health Service (NHS) 204

natural law xi, 45–6, 129–59 (144–7), 167, 175, 177, 197
natural theology 42, 117, 138, 146, 223–5, 281–2, 302
Notre Dame University 8, 13, 68, 73, 79, 96, 103–4, 154, 199, 243, 247
#notallmen style arguments 58

peacemaking xi, 21, 24, 95–6, 98, 106, 108–9, 122, 159–94
platonism 50–1, 227
polygamy 139–40, 143, 189
postliberal theology 81, 95, 115, 122, 162, 167
prayer vii–viii, xi, 13, 30, 43, 64, 82–3, 88, 122, 124, 150, 193, 210–11, 217, 233, 236, 299, 303, 321 n.24, 91, 92, 328 nn.103, 105, 107, 113, 329 nn.137, 138
  as the primary Christian speech 9, 40, 79, 239–90 (273–83)
  prayers 30, 233, 327 nn.86, 88, 91, 328 nn.103, 118, 329 nn.120, 121, 131
preaching vii–viii, xi, 39, 69, 85, 97, 101, 105, 114, 150, 185, 208, 231, 238, 239–90, 297–98, 302, 321 n.24, 324 n.11, 324 n.15, 324 n.30, 325 n.49, 328 n.100
privilege 10, 30, 33, 35–7, 47, 210, 307 n.56

racism x, 32, 33–40, 150, 162, 172, 307 n.56
rationality and Capacities 226–8, 231–2
reading vii, ix, xii, 4, 6, 12, 14, 25, 65, 80, 232, 250–3, 256–73, 278, 288, 325 n.39, 325 n.49
repentance 21, 35, 59, 61, 108–9, 120, 147–55, 183, 268, 301

sanctification 59–61, 144, 151
seagulls 88–9
self-deception 9, 23–4, 58, 66, 77, 82, 111, 140, 152, 180–4, 185, 238, 274
September 11th 2001 96, 98, 193
shame 18, 21–2
shuffleboard 99
suicide 17, 26, 100, 132, 142–3, 235, 312 n.12
swearing 60

television shows
  friends 278
  Have Gun, Will Travel 68

Leave it to Beaver 190
M*A*S*H 9, 306 n.6
Seinfeld 278
temperament x, 63–94 (63–72), 212, 268
Texas 33, 36, 69, 92, 135, 148–9, 154, 257, 262
theocracy 172
torture, 179, 215, 220–1
   victim

United States Air Force Academy 179–80

victimhood 17–18
virtue x–xii, 2, 4, 6, 31, 41–62, 64–6, 69, 71–2, 72–80, 80–1, 95, 108, 117, 122, 129–58, 179, 212, 214, 224–8, 233, 243, 267–9, 287, 291–2, 295, 297–9, 301–3

war, 52, 75, 92, 159–94, 252, 306 n.6
   just war thinking 25, 95, 103, 110, 170–80
   King David and war 182–3
   World Slaughter I & II 160

   the role of the Christian in the military 175–7
wealth, the problem of 3–4
Wittgensteinian thinking 77, 80–1, 83, 85–8, 117, 120, 277, 297, 301
writing 77, 166, 188, 278–80, 289, 291–2, 297, 299, 307 n.30
   complexities of writing the self 1–12, 12–25, 25–9
   writing approaches 135–6, 193–4, 223, 232, 242–8, 251–4, 257–65, 271, 272–3, 282–6
   writing and privilege 37–8
   writing and thinking 87, 257, 278
   writing well 39, 206
women, influence of 186
work, hard and good 3, 13, 29–33, 33–40, 187, 207, 244, 272–3, 304 n.8

Yale, University of 23–4, 61, 64, 66–8, 73, 79, 82, 85, 115, 162, 244–5, 287, 301
Yoder and accusations of Marcionism 180–2
Yoder and his sexual assaults xi, 180–4, 184–5, 243, 293

Lightning Source UK Ltd.
Milton Keynes UK
UKHW020559130319
339042UK00003B/97/P